The
Dublin
Lockout, 1913

This book is dedicated to the memory of the late
Fr Walter Forde, Castlebridge, County Wexford,
chairman of the Byrne-Perry Summer School
held annually in Gorey, for which these
papers were initially produced.

Conor McNamara is the 1916 Scholar in Residence at
Moore Institute, NUI Galway, for 2015/17. His books include
The Easter Rebellion 1916: A New Illustrated History (2015) and
The West of Ireland in the Nineteenth Century: New Perspectives (2011).

Pádraig Yeates is a member of the 1913 Committee. He is
a journalist, trade union activist and author whose books
include *Lockout: Dublin 1913* (2010), *A City in Wartime:
Dublin 1914–1918* (2011), *A City in Turmoil: Dublin 1919–1921*
(2012) and *A City in Civil War: Dublin 1921–1924* (2015).
He previously edited the *Irish People* and worked for
The Irish Times as Community Affairs and as Industry
and Employment Correspondent.

The Dublin Lockout, 1913

New Perspectives on Class War & its Legacy

Conor McNamara
& Pádraig Yeates

IRISH ACADEMIC PRESS

First published in 2017 by
Irish Academic Press
10 George's Street
Newbridge
Co. Kildare
Ireland
www.iap.ie

9781911024781 (paper)
9781911024798 (cloth)
9781911024811 (Kindle)
9781911024828 (epub)
9781911024804 (PDF)

British Library Cataloguing in Publication Data
An entry can be found on request

Library of Congress Cataloging in Publication Data
An entry can be found on request

Interior design by www.jminfotechindia.com
Typeset in Adobe Caslon Pro 11/14 pt

Cover design by www.phoenix-graphicdesign.com
Cover/jacket front/back:
'Murphy Must Go!' (Image Courtesy of the National Library of Ireland)

Contents

Acknowledgements   vii

Foreword by Joe O'Flynn, General Secretary, SIPTU   viii

Foreword by Denis Brennan, Bishop of Ferns   x

Introduction   xii

1.   Chronology of the Great Dublin Lockout, 1913–1914   1
   Pádraig Yeates

2.   A Tale of Two Cities: The 1913 Lockout,
   The View from Belfast   30
   Peter Collins

3.   'Quick-Witted Urchins': Dublin's Newsboys in
   Challenging Times, 1900–1922   47
   Donal Fallon

4.   American Social Reform and the Irish Question:
   An Irish-American Perspective on the 1913 Lockout   62
   Meredith Meagher

5.   Insult and the Locked-Out Workers of 1913   85
   John White

6.   'Into the Sun': Helena Molony's Lost Revolution   101
   Fearghal McGarry

7.   Glorious Forever? The Political Evolution of the
   Irish Citizen Army, 1913–1921   124
   Conor McNamara

8.   'The Layers of an Onion': Reflections on 1913,
   Class and the Memory of the Irish Revolution   144
   Brian Hanley

9. 1913: The Cinderella Centenary   161
    Pádraig Yeates

10. The Legacy of the Lockout: Lessons from Oral History   185
    Mary Muldowney

11. An Introduction to Manuscript Sources on the
    Irish Citizen Army   205
    Conor McNamara

Contributors   236
Select Bibliography   239
Index   244

Acknowledgements

The authors would like to thank the organisers of the Byrne-Perry Summer School, particularly Patrick Brown and Eileen O'Loughlin, for their steadfast endeavours. Sheila Fitzpatrick, Seán Mythen and Hazel Percival were central to the running of the conference.

This publication would not have been possible without the generous support of the Diocese of Ferns and SIPTU. We are grateful to Bishop Brennan for providing a fitting preface in memory of the late Fr Forde and to SIPTU General Secretary Joe O'Flynn for his introduction on the continuing relevance of the Lockout legacy.

We would like to thanks all of the team at Irish Academic Press whose professionalism has been most appreciated, in particular, Conor Graham and Fiona Dunne.

We would also like to acknowledge the support of Mary Harris and John Cunningham at the History Department and Dan Carey, Moore Institute, NUI Galway; Maire Kennedy and Enda Leaney for putting the invaluable resources of the Dublin City Library and Archive at our disposal; and Eibhlin Colgan for access to the Guinness Archive, Diageo Archives magnificent photographic section.

We are deeply grateful to the contributors for their professionalism, enthusiasm and perseverance.

Foreword

by Joe O'Flynn, General Secretary, SIPTU

The 1913 Lockout continues to resonate with everyone interested in Irish history and with the development of modern Ireland. The strike by Dublin tramway workers for better pay that began on 26 August that year quickly escalated into a major political crisis after Bloody Sunday, when hundreds of people were batoned by the Dublin Metropolitan Police and Royal Irish Constabulary five days later. It developed into a much broader struggle that embraced not just the right of workers to collectively bargain with their employer and seek union recognition, but battles over the rights to freedom of assembly, free speech, gender equality, access to decent and affordable housing, and even the right of parents to decide how their children were educated. It also raised questions about what it meant to be Irish and who could be included, and excluded, from society. Over one hundred years on these issues are still of vital concern today. They go to the very essence of what it is to be a citizen, or a denizen on this island, north and south.

Then as now there were powerful vested interests that defended the status quo and questioned the legitimacy of those who challenged it, such as Jim Larkin and James Connolly, children of the Irish diaspora who came in their very different ways to epitomise the hopes of those who sought social justice, and radical political and economic change. Many of those who aligned with them in that fight, people as diverse as Dr Kathleen Lynn, Sean O'Casey, Francis and Hanna Sheehy-Skeffington, Tom Clarke and Countess Markievicz, either did not survive the Irish revolution or were marginalised in its counter revolutionary aftermath.

And yet some of the revolutionary ideas that emerged during the 1913 Lockout survived in the 1916 Proclamation and the Democratic Programme of the First Dáil, ensuring the survival of these subversive principles at the very heart of the modern state's constitution; even though the Free State that emerged in 1922 was much closer to the claustrophobically parochial vision of the Home Rule movement, mirrored by its Unionist counterpart in Northern Ireland. The course of the 1913 Lockout is therefore of concern to everyone, not just trade unionists. The fact that many of the rights sought then are still denied affects us all. Notwithstanding recent legislation, the right to full collective bargaining, which is the most effective means of redistributing wealth after taxation in a capitalist society, remains an objective we must constantly strive to achieve, particularly on behalf of vulnerable workers in low-paid and precarious employment. When this right is eroded, or denied, the certainty of inequality increases. Erosion of incomes, in turn, affects long-term life choices, such as the possibility of further education and career development for our children, and limit the aspirations of the general working population, as well as causing immediate falls in living standards.

The richer those at the top of society become the greater their capacity to manipulate the world to suit their agendas. The individualisation and commercialisation of people's rights are not just imperatives of the market. They pose fundamental challenges to the social solidarity values that manifested themselves when the trade union movement emerged as a force to be reckoned with in 1913. If the dominance of unfettered market forces is not constantly challenged they will continue to promote the agendas of a wealthy elite, who pose a serious threat to democracy itself as they find it easier to manipulate a fragmented society than one underpinned by mass democratic movements acting collectively to defend people's rights. Without such movements society falls easy prey to fear and the manipulation of its purveyors, whatever guise they assume, to stoke hate and division in pursuit of their agendas.

That is why the legacy of the 1913 Lockout remains relevant today, and that is the meaning of Larkin's famous declaration: 'The great appear great because we are on our knees. Let us arise.'

Joe O'Flynn,
General Secretary, SIPTU

Foreword

by Denis Brennan, Bishop of Ferns

Fr Walter Forde (1943–2015): An Appreciation

The invitation to pen a short article on the late Walter Forde was one I was most glad to receive. Over forty years of service to the Diocese of Ferns, the people of Gorey and Castlebridge, local and national organisations dedicated to the common good, Walter's life was a full one, a life fully poured out in the service of people and causes, enterprises and initiatives.

In my own life, I knew Walter as a fellow student and as a co-worker. A true son of the Second Vatican Council, Walter combined the Gospels with social reports, the mission of the Church with the betterment of society and people.

Three words stand out for me in Walter's life:

Service – an absolute dedication to the needs of Church, society, local and national groups, individual people – with no distinction. A lively mind and a generous heart combined easily in a soul that dedicated itself to assistance – a word of absolution or counsel, a call to a social worker or a politician, a word of encouragement or humour – all people being treated as equally deserving of care.

Respect – prince or pauper and all in between – Walter could engage with friend or foe with equal courtesy and kindness. Nobody was made to feel less as Walter did his daily tasks, the gifts of others were applauded and the shortcomings more often than not brought out a smile. Clearly a very aware type of man, his was never the need to make less of another that he might be judged better himself.

Graciousness – Walter didn't exaggerate the small stuff, but neither did he minimise the larger issues. A disarming inner strength and graciousness saw him always invited early into dilemmas or difficulties. Patience, insight, an ability to put shape on solutions, these were his natural gifts. And when a matter was solved, it was time to move on. A new start, the capacity to let issues go, fresh beginnings – many benefitted from Walter's kindly style and his eager welcome for the new day.

In conclusion, this tribute book, drawn from the many years of the Byrne Perry Summer School, is a wonderful tribute to the man, the family member, the priest and Christian, the animateur, the innovator, the lifelong ecumenism, the problem-solver, the politician and friend – who was Fr Walter Forde.

Denis Brennan,
Bishop of Ferns, June 2017

Introduction

You'll see it clearer, dear, when busy Time in space has set another scene of summer's glory, and new-born spring's loud voice of hope hushes to silence th' intolerant dead.

Inspector Finglas, *Red Roses For Me*, Act IV (Sean O'Casey, 1943)

The essays in this collection originated from the Byrne-Perry Summer School, Gorey, Co. Wexford, held in June 2013. The conference was entitled 'Men and Masters – The Great Lockout of 1913' and was one of the many hundreds of public events that commemorated and debated the impact and legacy of the 1913 Lockout. The 'decade of centenaries' was originally approached with pronounced caution by academia, the state and the political establishment. By the end of the 2016 centenary year, however, it was abundantly clear that an unprecedented popular interest and engagement with Irish history was taking place. As the initial fears concerning the possibility of the political manipulation of commemorative events receded – for the moment at least – the remarkable role of community groups, and in particular, youth groups and schools, in exploring contemporary political issues demonstrated the inherent value of public history.

The role of social class as a formative factor in the exploration of the revolution should be encompassed into any study of the revolutionary period. Ireland in the decade before Independence cannot be understood without reference to the awkward place of the urban poor within the paradigm of an emerging nationalism that idealised rural life and the peasants' inherent connection with the soil. As several authors argue in this collection, the urban poor and, in particular, the unfortunate tenement dwellers, became a peculiar sort of 'other' within an emerging Irishness that regarded the poor of the towns as merely 'the garrison and its hangers on', outside the bounds of respectability and thoroughly un-Irish. The absence of the very poor among the revolutionary cadre in 1920–21 is unsurprising given the universal tendency of the poorest to belong to the local rather than the national, and be positioned furthest from the levers of power; powerlessness and poverty have always been faithful companions.

For the benefit of newer readers to the period, the collection commences with a concise chronology of events during the Lockout by Pádraig Yeates. This should serve as an accessible starting point to the turmoil of the period for students and the reading public. Likewise, the collection concludes with an introduction to manuscript sources pertaining to the Irish Citizen Army by Conor McNamara – many of which are fully accessible online. The way history is read has changed and the publication online of a growing number of sources by bodies such as the National Archives has revolutionised how people can access their past. The inclusion of this chapter reflects the increasing democratisation of archives pertaining to Irish history through digitisation and online publication and the greater appetite for research among the reading public.

Peter Collins' chapter, 'A Tale of Two Cities: The 1913 Lockout, The View from Belfast', examines the conflicting experience of the Lockout from Belfast and Dublin, Ireland's two industrial hubs. Belfast was a relative industrial and commercial giant at its zenith with a diversity of industries during this period, while Dublin had experienced a century of decline. Belfast had linen, shipbuilding and engineering, tobacco and distilling. It had the biggest spinning mill and rope-works in the world. With the multiplicity and diversity of industrial enterprises in the city, workers could move easily from one to the other. Seventy thousand workers, mainly women, were employed in the linen industry, mostly in and around Belfast.

This was in stark contrast to Dublin which had been in economic decline since the proroguing of the Irish parliament, under the Act of Union of 1800. The consequent exodus of Irish parliamentarians to London contributed to the devastation of those native industries and services that depended on them. No major industrialisation, on the Belfast scale, followed during the long nineteenth century and, by the 1900s, there were few large industrial concerns. The biggest, such as the Guinness brewery and Jacob's biscuits, though highly profitable, employed less than three thousand workers each. In Dublin, for the great mass of unskilled men, casual and seasonal labour in the building trade and the docks, and in transport, was all that was available.

The Lockout was an economic catastrophe for Dublin, especially for the locked-out workers and their families. Belfast, in contrast, had done well commercially, as an alternative port to Dublin. James Connolly's involvement in both the Dublin Lockout and Easter Week imprinted negatively on the minds of many northern unionists. To take the long view, the Dublin Lockout may be seen as part of the litany of events from the Home Rule crisis to the Great War, the Easter Rising, the Battle of the Somme, the 1918 General Election, the War of Independence and the setting up of parliaments in both cities. Each in its own way contributed to the coming of partition. A growing sense of apartness has since been engendered through living apart in, at times, hostile, separate states. This has resulted in an even greater lack of symbiosis between the two cities than existed in 1913.

Newsboys were a prominent feature of urban working-class life in the first half of the twentieth century, a constant presence on the streets of towns and cities. Donal Fallon's essay, 'Quick-Witted Urchins': Dublin's Newsboys in Challenging Times, 1900–22', examines the young street sellers who were the backbone of newspaper distribution, and in many cases provided a vital source of income to their families in cities where labour was precarious and irregular. Newsboys were an unavoidable presence on the streets of the capital, in particular, and a visitor to Dublin bemoaned the 'brazen-throated newsboys' in a letter to the *Irish Times* in 1907, noting that 'the rudeness of these journal vendors amazes a stranger. They push themselves in your path, push their papers in your face, and deliberately shout in your ears til your head aches.'

Fallon examines newsboys in Dublin in the early twentieth century, looking at how the young workers were viewed and treated by different strands of society, and the complex relationships that existed between this large working-class body and others, ranging from those in authority to the radical political movements of the day. Fallon discusses the manner in which these youngsters were seen by charities and philanthropists, who identified the boys as being amongst the most impoverished workers in the city. Key events, such as the 1911 newsboy strike in the capital and the Lockout of 1913 are discussed in detail, to examine evidence of radicalism among a section of the boys.

Modern labour laws ensure that the barefooted newsboy are a thing of the past, yet, for a group which once comprised a sizeable body in Dublin and other cities, newsboys have gone largely unstudied. Some oral histories have survived, through the work of inner-city history societies; and that of charitable organisations such as the Belvedere Newsboys' Club is well documented. This chapter shows that newsboys were a significant ally to Larkin and the labour movement in Dublin during a period of heightened class tensions in the capital. That newsboys in Dublin and Derry modelled their own 'strikes' on those of their elders shows the influence of trade unionism on the popular consciousness of young workers in early twentieth-century Ireland. The lives of these children were incredibly difficult, both in terms of their working conditions and their living standards, with many hailing from the slums of the city. The historiography of the Lockout has primarily focused on children and the deprivation occasioned during the dispute; this chapter demonstrates that many adolescents were workers in their own right, capable of organising and taking militant action.

Meredith Meagher brings an international dimension to the collection in her contribution, 'American Social Reform and the Irish Question: An Irish-American Perspective on the 1913 Lockout'. The plight of the locked-out Dublin workers challenged Irish-Americans to reconcile their traditional narrative on the Irish right to self-determination with more divisive issues concerning workers' rights and social progress. For those of Irish descent in the United States, class warfare in Dublin in 1913 threatened to contradict their traditional narrative that emphasised the historic struggle for self-determination of a united Catholic community. As Irish-Americans historically framed 'the national question' within a paradigm that emphasised British subjugation, the plight of the Dublin workers illuminated a less familiar and ideologically more problematic dimension to Irish political culture. The 1913 crisis unequivocally pitted Irish workers against their Irish masters, and for the first time, many of the Irish in the United States could relate to the industrial unrest in the nation they left behind through the prism of working conditions in America.

Meagher focuses on Irish-American perceptions of the Lockout, immigration to the US and the Home Rule question published in leading Irish-American nationalist newspapers, including Patrick Ford's constitutional nationalist newspaper, the *Irish World and American Industrial Liberator*, and its separatist, Fenian counterpart, the *Gaelic American*, edited by John Devoy; along with the writings of James Connolly in the period preceding the crisis, published in *The Harp*, the newspaper of the Irish Socialist Federation. Meagher argues that while Ford and Devoy represented the constitutional and physical force traditions respectively, the rhetoric of their newspapers shared many common assumptions regarding the Irish-American community and the Home Rule movement in Ireland. Both papers emphasised the need for civic reform in Ireland throughout and saw their role as promoting their own particular brands of Irish nationalism on the international stage. *The Harp*, on the other hand, was published in New York and Dublin between January 1908 and June 1910 and reflected James Connolly's characteristic blend of socialism and republicanism.

With Home Rule pending, nationalist politicians were greatly concerned with cultivating an image of national respectability, an image that the grievances of the Dublin poor threatened to undermine. John White's essay, 'Insult and the Locked Out Workers of 1913', argues that prejudice based on social class dominated depictions of the striking workers and the urban poor during the 1913 Lockout. Workers and their families were continually portrayed within a framework of moral degeneracy, representative of the deep social chasm that existed between 'respectable' Ireland and the urban poor of Dublin's slums. The antagonism shown towards the workers' plight within contemporary political discourse was illustrative of the wider contempt for the urban poor based on their perceived moral inadequacies. The Lockout became a class battle that played itself out, not only on the streets of Dublin but within contemporary newspapers and publications. Leading journalists such as W.P. Ryan, writing some years after the Lockout noted how the press, the professions, clerics, and most politicians agreed that Larkin and his kind 'should be treated as outlaws'. Throughout the dispute the striking workers were labelled by 'respectable' Catholic opinion as 'scum', 'roughs', 'parasites', 'corner-boys' and 'thugs' from among 'the lowest sinks of humanity'. By placing the urban poor outside of the common culture of respectable Catholic Ireland, the dominant discourse of the period facilitated opponents of the workers to label the dispute a product of a degenerate Anglo-centric and materialistic culture, incubated by the city's slums.

Focusing on the life of Helena Molony, a largely-forgotten trade-unionist and rebel, Fearghal McGarry highlights more problematic aspects of the role of labour during the revolutionary decade than those foregrounded by the centenary. In McGarry's essay, 'Into the sun': Helena Molony's Lost Revolution', he argues that commemoration can be an unpredictable business. Heralding the centenary of the Lockout, one historian predicted that it would be 'passed over for the most part by the mainstream media and political establishment', an omission that would demonstrate how the working class are 'written out of history'. It was in fact marked by a remarkably comprehensive programme of conferences, documentaries, talks, exhibitions, publications, press supplements and arts and community initiatives, and by a formal state commemoration one hundred years to the day after 'Bloody Friday' (featuring a mass re-enactment of the DMP's infamous baton-charge).

As always when collective memory collides with history, there were disconcerting facets of this commemorative binge. Strikingly, one of the most divisive events of early twentieth-century Ireland was recalled almost entirely without controversy. With the commemorative programme dominated by historians of (and from) the left, public attention – and sympathy –

was focused on one side of the dispute; in contrast, the preceding year's centenaries of the Home Rule Bill and Ulster Covenant witnessed a more vigorous contestation of the motives and actions of those on both sides of the conflict. While Jim Larkin's significance as the embodiment of dignity for an oppressed people was emphasised, there was little awareness of the destructive legacy of the most divisive figure in Irish labour history. Such was the tone of the commemorative programme, McGarry notes, it would have been easy to miss the fact that many Irish people – including the bulk of middle-class opinion and many advanced nationalists and republicans – had not supported the workers in 1913.

Despite the prominence of accomplished historians such as Emmet O'Connor, Pádraig Yeates and Brian Hanley, aspects of the commemorative programme had the potential to mislead. The idea that the losing side had remained hidden from history was frequently asserted, prompting a characteristically acerbic intervention from Kevin Myers, one of the few media voices to rain on the commemorative parade: 'Statues are not erected to the central figures of "hidden histories", nor are bridges named after them.' Reflecting its function as a foundation myth for the modern labour movement, the Lockout was depicted as a 'moral victory' or 'great turning-point' that had laid the foundations for the future success of the trade union movement rather than a devastating defeat. In this latter respect, the significance of class was overlooked in 2013, but this occurred as a result of how the Lockout was remembered. Rather than highlighting the consequences of organised labour's defeat in a conflict that foreshadowed its marginalisation in an independent Ireland dominated by reactionary figures such as William Martin Murphy, the tone of much of the commemoration – harshly described by Myers as 'witless triumphalism' – did little to prompt consideration of the revolutionary decade's conservative legacy.

The Irish Citizen Army was founded at the height of the Lockout in November 1913 as a means of raising striking workers' morale and to provide protection at pickets and political meetings. Conor McNamara's essay, 'Glorious Forever? The Political Evolution of the Irish Citizen Army, 1913–21' offers an overview of the evolution of the movement. The ICA went through several re-incarnations during the Irish revolution, from a loosely organised workers' protection force, to a socialist republican militia committed to violent revolution, and finally, a militant micro-group on the margins of the republican movement. The Lockout generated sustained violence with street fighting and riots erupting across the city throughout the period. Street violence between semi-organised gangs had long been a feature of working-class culture and the absence of an organised militia in the early phase of the Lockout did not mean the workers were helpless in the face of the violent excesses of the DMP. The Citizen Army, however, represented a new development in working-class culture as the organisation was conceived as a conventional and disciplined force whose presence was designed to act as a deterrent to the DMP, ensuring the safety of workers while intimidating their perceived persecutors. The movement played a minor role in the Lockout and James Larkin took little interest in the day-to-day running of the organisation.

With the collapse of the Lockout in January 1914, the Irish Citizen Army ceased to have an obvious role in the trade union movement. From late 1914 until the Rising, it reinvented itself as Connolly's private militia with an ambiguous relationship with the ITGWU. The men and women of the ICA performed valiantly in Easter Week and were involved in some of the most intense fighting of the Rebellion. Following Connolly's execution, however, the movement lacked any clear political direction and charismatic leadership, as thousands of trade unionists, including ITGWU members, rushed to join the Irish Volunteers. The movement failed to play a central role in the War of Independence due to the apathy of its membership and the elitism of its leadership. Without a clear political strategy, its members drifted away or joined their rivals in the Volunteers, and their inability to organise a Connolly memorial concert in May 1920 was a painful reflection of their limitations. That the movement existed was a tribute to the charisma of James Connolly, Seán Connolly, William Partridge and other early leaders, and their ability to engender personal loyalty from their small band of followers. Ultimately, McNamara argues, the mistrust of the trade union movement inhibited the Citizen Army from developing beyond the fringes of the revolution, exacerbated by the limitations of its post rebellion leadership. With the unprecedented rise of the Volunteers, a movement replete with charismatic leaders, the support for a separate revolutionary force simply did not exist.

One of the most positive results of the centenary has been a new interest in the importance of class division in Ireland. Brian Hanley's contribution, 'The Layers of an Onion': Reflections on 1913, Class and the Memory of the Irish Revolution' examines the awkward challenges that the Lockout presented to contemporary Ireland in terms of the contemporary saliency of class divisions and class prejudice. There has been a prevalent view that while class certainly mattered under British rule, it ceased to be as important after independence. Class was everywhere during the centenary of 1913. Not so much through the efforts of the trade unions or the left but because it informed everyday attitudes to a whole range of issues. The plight of the so-called 'squeezed middle' caused much angst throughout the recession. Cabinet minister Leo Varadkar asserted the need 'to protect the middle-class' and lamented that many of our 'best and brightest', defined as doctors, lawyers, entrepreneurs and artists, were emigrating. The suggestion in much of the coverage of emigration was that the tragedy lay in the exodus of the educated. Implicitly, the departure of 500,000 people during the 1950s did not represent either a 'brain drain' or as much of a calamity. This narrative goes mostly unchallenged because the working class is largely absent from modern Irish popular culture, except in caricature. The trade unions may still organise almost 700,000 people on this island, many of them professionals such as doctors and teachers, but they are invisible in cultural terms.

While many tend to see the Lockout as naturally foreshadowing the Easter Rising, there were fundamental differences between the two events. The Lockout involved over 20,000 workers and their families. In contrast around 1,800 people were 'out' in 1916. Most ordinary Dubliners, large numbers of whom participated in the Lockout, were observers in 1916 and could not have been otherwise. It is almost certain that some of those who had fought the police in 1913 were among the 'rabble' who turned on the rebels during and after Easter Week. How republicans compared themselves to their enemies also tells us something about perceptions about class. British soldiers were the 'pale, puny anaemic products of English factory towns' while the Volunteers were 'the pick of Irish manhood, the product of our Irish soil, clean-limbed, strong and wholesome'.

Hanley concludes that until recently most historians have agreed with Kevin O'Higgins' self-serving claim that the Irish republicans of his generation were the 'most conservative minded revolutionaries that ever put through a successful revolution'. Tom Garvin has suggested that since the Irish working class 'scarcely exists, or ever has existed, outside Belfast, as a classic industrial working class' there is little point in seeking evidence of the potential for radical social change. Yet it is quite obvious that the revolutionary period saw intense class struggle and that the labour movement was acknowledged to be an important force.

In his contribution, '1913: The Cinderella Centenary', Pádraig Yeates argues that in the context of the revolutionary decade, the legacy of the Lockout was residual. Nevertheless, it was the nearest thing we ever had in this country to a debate on the type of society we wanted in the twentieth century. The values that triumphed then have shed their religious foliage and blossomed into an unabashed brand of possessive individualism not very different from that of contemporary Britain – in the process neo-Redmondism has given way to neo-liberalism. This provocative essay examines the role of class divisions in the modern Irish state and the challenges this poses for communal memory and 'official' interpretation of the Lockout. 1913 was a harbinger of what the future held in store for the Irish proletariat, for the working poor, for the marginalised generally and for emigrants, who were the most marginalised of all. If we cannot ask the question over a century later whether 1916 and all that followed was worth it, when can we ask it? For all these groups the Lockout, the Cinderella of Centenaries, is their 1916.

The basic issues at stake in the Lockout, those of collective bargaining and the right to union representation in the workplace remain unresolved. They are important because, apart from taxation, collective bargaining is the most effective means of redistributing wealth within a capitalist economy. The more the right to collective bargaining is restricted, the more imperfect its influence and the greater the risks of social inequality and political instability. By 1924 the Irish political superstructure may have changed dramatically but Dublin's slums remained intact. The only major housing project in the city was at Killester, where the British War Office was building homes for ex-servicemen. We had more children incarcerated in institutions than the United Kingdom we had just left.

It looks at the vital role that support from the British TUC played in sustaining the struggle which, paradoxically, fuelled separatist tendencies within the Irish labour movement. This is not to deny that some form of self-government for the southern part of Ireland was well-nigh inevitable by 1912 and that southern labour leaders shared the nationalist consensus that Home Rule or some form of greater independence from Britain was perceived as an innately 'good thing'. This included, of course, many Irish women who chose to disregard the warnings by veteran Unionist suffrage campaigner Anna Haslam that their interests would be better served by remaining part of a liberal, urban democracy, than being left to the mercies of a predominantly church dominated, peasant society.

In 'The Legacy of the Lockout: Lessons From Oral History' Mary Muldowney argues that oral history can give voice to unsung heroes and can thereby play a valuable part in restoring the role of the working class to its rightful place in the contemporary historical record. Muldowney examines the folk memory of the Lockout passed down through oral history for generations of Dubliners. The 1913 Lockout occupies an important place in the collective memory in many Dublin communities, as well as in the consciousness of the trade union movement. It was not just the members of the Irish Transport and General Workers Union and the unions who supported them who felt the impact of the Lockout. In families who have relatives who participated in the Lockout, oral history has been passed down through generations, providing sometimes surprising insights. Many families have been silent on the subject, often because of the trauma they suffered during the period and because they did not feel they could celebrate the role played by their relatives; it is also probable that family stories have simply been forgotten. The latter is one of the problematic elements of researching events that predominantly affected so-called, 'ordinary people', mainly because accounts that survived did so because they fitted particular agendas. The scarcity of written records about those experiences is one reason why oral history is so valuable in challenging 'the condescension of posterity', facilitating the restoration of neglected accounts to the historical record.

The struggle in 1913 was essentially about the right of all workers to belong to the trade union of their choice and for employers to be obliged to recognise and negotiate with that union. It is not a battle that had been won when the strikers were forced to return to work in the spring of 1914 but neither was it a war that was lost. The employers, even with the full force of the State at their beck and call, abjectly failed to destroy the trade union movement, although full recognition rights have not been secured one hundred years later. The many improvements in workers' employment rights that have been achieved during the 100 years since the Lockout owe much to the agency of 'ordinary' trade union members.

CHAPTER ONE

Chronology of the Great Dublin Lockout, 1913–1914

Pádraig Yeates

The Great Dublin Lockout was the first major urban-based conflict in modern Ireland to dominate the political agenda. For a time, it overshadowed the Home Rule crisis and in the second half of 1913 proved an unwelcome distraction to the leadership of the Irish Party. The dispute aroused intense emotions on all sides and constituted a major challenge to the conservative middle-class Catholic consensus that dominated nationalist politics.

The conflict did not emerge from a vacuum. Several attempts had been made since the 1880s to introduce the 'new unionism' to Ireland, aimed at organising unskilled and semi-skilled workers who had traditionally been excluded from the predominantly British-based craft unions. It was 1907 when Jim Larkin arrived in Ireland as an organiser for the National Union of Dock Labourers (NUDL), whose general secretary, James Sexton, was himself a former Fenian. The Liverpool-Irishman's fiery brand of trade unionism, characterised by militant industrial action combined with a syndicalist political outlook, proved more than the NUDL could tolerate. After spectacular initial success in Belfast, where he succeeded briefly in uniting workers across the sectarian divide in a campaign for better pay and conditions, Larkin proceeded to organise NUDL branches in most of Ireland's ports. It was his handling of a Cork docks strike in 1908 that provided an opening for his dismissal. Sexton accused him of unauthorised use of union funds by issuing strike pay before the NUDL executive had sanctioned it. Larkin was imprisoned for embezzlement following a court case in which Sexton was the main witness for the prosecution.

Far from destroying Larkin's reputation, however, his imprisonment made him a hero for a generation of young Irish socialists who campaigned successfully for his release. Even before he was sentenced, Larkin set up the Irish Transport and General Workers Union (ITGWU). Dublin became the centre of gravity for the new union, which rapidly became the largest in the country, displacing the NUDL in most locations. In the first half of 1913, an aggressive campaign of industrial action in Dublin resulted in wage increases of between 20 and 25 per cent for groups ranging from dockers in the port to agricultural labourers in the county. So successful was the campaign that the Lord Mayor, Lorcan Sherlock, prompted by Dr William Walsh, the Catholic Archbishop of Dublin, proposed a conciliation board for the city. The Chamber of Commerce had nominated its members and Dublin Trades Council was about to nominate its representatives when the Lockout began. If it had gone ahead Dublin would have been the first city in the United Kingdom with a geographically-based industrial relations mediation body covering all manual occupations.

The prime mover in preventing this system from being established was Ireland's leading Catholic nationalist businessman and former anti-Parnellite MP, William Martin Murphy. He had been ill in early 1913, but when he discovered that Larkin had been recruiting members in the Dublin United Tramway Company (DUTC), of which he was chairman, Murphy began to root them out systematically. He began by summoning the workers to a midnight meeting in the Antient Concert Hall in July 1913, and gave due warning that any man who stayed in the ITGWU would be sacked. The late hour was to ensure the tramcar operators and conductors could all attend after services stopped running for the night. They could reflect on Murphy's warning on the long walk home.

Murphy subsequently began dismissing employees suspected of ITGWU membership in the DUTC and in another of his major businesses, Independent Newspapers. Larkin advised his members in the DUTC against going on strike, but when the handful still employed said they would leave the union if he did not sanction industrial action, and he was told that workers in the company's power station would come out in sympathy, he allowed a ballot to be held on 25 August 1913 in the ITGWU headquarters at Liberty Hall. They struck the next day, 26 August. He told them to stop the trams at 9.40 a.m. when most of the vehicles with ITGWU crews would be in the vicinity of Nelson's Pillar on Sackville (later O'Connell) Street, the nexus of the system because he had far too few members left for mass pickets at the tram depots. However, the power workers failed to strike after being threatened with instant dismissal and Murphy had the trams up and running within the hour by using 'scabs', or strike-breakers.

The following days saw numerous rallies in support of the strikers, the stoning of the trams, the arrest of strike leaders for making seditious speeches and the proclamation of a meeting Larkin called for 1 p.m. in Sackville Street on Sunday 31 August. Other trade union leaders tried to defuse the situation in the city, where widespread rioting had broken out, by organising a march from Liberty Hall to the union's recreational centre, Croydon Park in Fairview.

Larkin had other ideas, however. He had himself smuggled into William Martin Murphy's Imperial Hotel on Sackville Street and he managed to speak briefly from the balcony on the first floor before being arrested. Dublin Metropolitan Police (DMP) and Royal Irish Constabulary (RIC) constables baton-charged the crowd, leaving 400 to 600 seriously injured, many of them respectable, middle-class mass-goers. These events became known as Bloody Sunday.

The next morning the British Trade Union Congress (TUC) conference began in Manchester. Delegates were appalled at newspaper reports of police brutality. These were confirmed by William Partridge, a Labour councillor, ITGWU organiser and member of Dublin Trades Council, who travelled over to describe in graphic detail what had happened. The TUC pledged total support for the Dublin workers. During the Lockout over £93,000 was sent in cash, food and fuel by the labour movement in Britain. This support enabled strikers to hold out until January 1914, but it could not win their dispute for them in the face of Murphy's intransigence and support from other employers.

1913

July

19 July: William Martin Murphy, President of the Dublin Chamber of Commerce and Chairman of the Dublin United Tramway Company (DUTC) calls his workers to a midnight meeting in the Antient Concert Hall in Great Brunswick (now Pearse) Street. He warns them that he will sack anyone who is a member of the Irish Transport and General Workers Union (ITGWU). Over the next six weeks he dismisses hundreds of employees.

21 July: Management issues dismissal notices to employees in the parcels department of the DUTC and tells them only to re-apply for their jobs if they are not in the ITGWU.

August

15 August: Murphy sacks forty men and boys in the despatch and delivery office of the *Irish Independent*. Newsboys refuse to sell Independent newspapers and delivery vans are attacked. The newspaper carries notices offering £10 rewards for anyone with information leading to the arrest and conviction of those involved.

17 August: The Dublin Farmers' Association agrees to increase weekly wages for agricultural labourers from 14s to between 17s and 20s for a sixty-six hour week and to use ITGWU members to cart produce to city markets.

22 August: Murphy visits the headquarters of the British government in Ireland, Dublin Castle, and is promised support from the Dublin Metropolitan Police (DMP), Royal Irish Constabulary (RIC) and the military, if he goes ahead with his plan to force a showdown with Larkin and his union.

26 August: The first day of Royal Dublin Horse Show sees all trams on Sackville Street stop and the strike begin. Workers seek pay rises ranging from 1s to 2s a week. Murphy brings in 'scab' crews to operate buses with DMP escorts to provide protection. Trams are stoned and the company has to stop services after dark. A mass meeting is held in Beresford Place outside Liberty Hall. Thousands attend and Larkin tells followers it is not a strike but a Lockout.

28 August: DMP detectives raid the homes of Larkin and other trade unionists who addressed the previous evening's rally outside Liberty Hall. They are charged with incitement before Police Magistrate E.G. Swifte, who is a substantial shareholder in the DUTC. Dozens of trade unionists are charged in the courts with intimidation, obstruction and for stoning trams. Another rally is held outside Liberty Hall that evening where Larkin calls for a mass demonstration on Sackville Street on Sunday 31 August.

29 August: Swifte proclaims the meeting on Sackville Street and Larkin burns a copy of the proclamation at yet another rally outside Liberty Hall. He promises to speak on Sackville Street on Sunday, 'dead or alive'. The police baton charge the crowd.

30 August: James Connolly, who has come from Belfast to help run the strike, is arrested and charged with incitement. He tells Swifte, 'I do not recognise the English government in Ireland at all.' Swifte tells him he is talking treason and sentences him to three months. Riots break out in Ringsend and spread to Great Brunswick (now Pearse) Street, then to the north inner city around Liberty Hall. Fifty-year-old labourer John Byrne is beaten senseless by police on Butt Bridge and 33-year-old labourer James Nolan is attacked by police on Eden Quay. They are taken to Jervis Street hospital where both men die of their injuries.

31 August: Dublin Trades Council and senior DMP officers agree that the unions can hold a rally at Croydon Park in Fairview without breaching the Proclamation on a meeting in Sackville Street. Larkin ignores the rally and goes to the Imperial Hotel, where he attempts to address the crowd on Sackville Street. He is arrested and police baton charges inflict between 400 and 600 casualties. Trade unionists returning from Croydon Park attack the police and rioting breaks out across the city. Cavalry are deployed in Sackville Street and infantry in Inchicore to help contain the rioting.

September

1 September: The TUC conference in Manchester is appalled at 'Bloody Sunday' reports in newspapers and in an eye witness account by William Partridge, delegates pledge support for ITGWU men locked out in Dublin. Meanwhile, more employers lock out ITGWU members.

Dublin Corporation discusses the crisis. It is dominated by shopkeepers and small businessmen who support John Redmond and Home Rule. While the mercantile community resents the rise of Larkin, many are appalled by the behaviour of the police. The Lord Mayor, Lorcan Sherlock, calls for a public inquiry. Dr James McWalter, whose surgery 'was crowded with absolutely harmless, inoffensive citizens returning from devotions, who had all been batoned', proposes that the DMP and RIC be withdrawn from the city.

The Coroner's inquest into the death of James Nolan takes place. He was a member of the ITGWU, which paid for his family to be legally represented. Several witnesses give the numbers of the policemen who attacked Nolan, but the hearing is adjourned and no charges follow. There are disturbances outside George Jacob's biscuit factory as ITGWU members on the afternoon shift are turned away at the gate. Rioting resumes on both sides of the Liffey.

2 September: Seven people, including three children, die when two tenements at 66 and 67 Church Street collapse. Seventeen-year-old Eugene Salmon, an ITGWU member locked out by Jacob's is killed when he tries to rescue his 4-year-old sister, Elizabeth, from the collapsing buildings.

3 September: The funeral of James Nolan takes place. Thousands follow the coffin to Glasnevin cemetery. A guard of honour is provided by 200 striking tramway workers in uniform and Keir Hardie, Britain's first Labour MP, attends.

William Martin Murphy unveils his strategy to smash the ITGWU at a meeting of the Dublin Chamber of Commerce. Over 400 employers agree not to employ members of the ITGWU. Over the next few days thousands of workers are told to sign forms resigning from the union or disassociating from it if members of another union. One thousand five hundred men are laid off in the coal trade alone. Larkin is released from prison on bail facing charges of riot, unlawful assembly and sedition.

Keir Hardie, addresses a mass meeting in Beresford Place and warns Dublin Castle that the Labour movement in Britain will back Larkin and the strikers against any move to crush them.

5 September: The funerals of the Church Street victims are held. William Martin Murphy is given police protection as effigies of him are burnt in the city by angry crowds.

6 September: The female suffrage paper, the *Irish Citizen,* expresses concern at the plight of women workers locked out at Jacob's. It says, 'A conflict which suddenly throws out of employment over 600 girls cannot fail to be of deep concern to all who are interested in women's conditions of work.' It reminds readers that Larkin has always promoted women's rights, and contrasts his position with that of John Redmond, who refuses to seek votes for women in the promised Home Rule parliament.

7 September: British TUC and Labour Party leaders join speakers from the Dublin Trades Council at a mass rally on Sackville Street to assert freedom of assembly. It is one of the largest demonstrations ever seen in Dublin. The leaders later meet with employers in an unsuccessful bid to end the Lockout.

8 September: The poem 'September 1913' by W.B. Yeats appears in the *Irish Times* denouncing the philistinism and greed of Murphy and his allies.

9 September: James Connolly goes on hunger strike in Mountjoy prison and Larkin takes the ferry for England on his first fundraising tour.

13 September: Connolly is released from prison after escalating his protest to a hunger and thirst strike in which he is joined by another ITGWU, prisoner, Kingstown branch secretary, James Byrne. A rally is held outside Liberty Hall to celebrate his release but Connolly is too weak to attend.

Industrial unrest spreads to County Dublin where agricultural labourers riot in Finglas, walk off the St Lawrence estate in Howth, and place pickets on farms across the county. Farmers in several districts seek police protection.

14 September: Larkin tells a mass open-air meeting in Manchester: 'I have got a divine mission, I believe, to make men and women discontented ... Hell has no terrors for me. I have lived there. Thirty-six years of hunger and poverty have been my portion ... Better to be in hell with Dante and Davitt than be in Heaven with Carson and Murphy ... I am out for revolution, or nothing.'

15 September: Ten thousand railwaymen in the English west midlands, and three thousand workers on Merseyside, black goods from Dublin in spontaneous unofficial strikes. Among the ships stranded is the *SS Hare* with a consignment of Guinness for London. British union leaders order the men back to work while another TUC delegation travels to Dublin to renew negotiations with the employers. The strike suffers a further setback when Dublin railway workers reject a call by the Trades Council to join the strike. They are still recovering from a lockout in 1911 organised by William Martin Murphy and Sir William Goulding, the chairman of the Great Southern and Western Railway. With the railways running, goods can be transported through other Irish ports.

The Coal Merchants' Association buys a motorised lorry and finds it can deliver forty tons a day – as much as nine horses and carts. More lorries are imported and Murphy sets up a fund to help smaller employers buy motor vehicles.

18 September: The Irish Women's Franchise League transfers its weekly open-air meetings from Foster Place, beside the Bank of Ireland, to Beresford Place, beside Liberty Hall, as a mark of solidarity with the strikers.

21 September: James Connolly, who is deputising for Larkin, tells the press. 'We are willing – anxious, in fact – to have a Conciliation Board.'

22 September: The employers formally reject Lord Mayor Lorcan Sherlock's proposal to set up a conciliation board. Only three of the city's six Irish Party MPs are willing to support his initiative. The army begins regular strike-breaking duties, taking over escorts for deliveries to state bodies and publicly funded institutions.

In Liverpool, TUC leaders negotiate the release of the strike bound, *SS Hare*. Dockers agree to unload the Guinness cargo and the ship is re-stocked with food. The TUC orders 12,500 loaves from the Co-Op bakeries in Belfast and Dublin for delivery at the City of Dublin Steam Packet Company's old Manchester shed on the South Wall.

27 September: The *SS Hare* docks with £5,000 worth of food supplies. James Seddon, Chairman of the Parliamentary Committee of the TUC, and Harry Gosling, President of the National Transport Workers' Federation (NTWF), accompany the ship. It sails into Dublin flying the NTWF colours.

The Lord Mayor convenes a meeting in the Mansion House to collect funds. Initially only £106 is raised, growing to £6,482 by the end of the dispute. The money is distributed through parish committees that vet applicants and generally ensure no help goes to strikers' families. Applicants can also be disqualified if they refuse an offer of work as a strike-breaker.

The British TUC raises over £93,000 to help the strikers and their families. Another £13,000 comes from other sources, mainly British Labour and Socialist Party branches, Irish unions and trades councils.

29 September: A Board of Trade inquiry opens in Dublin Castle, chaired by Sir George Askwith, a civil servant and industrial arbitrator. The tribunal also consists of Sir Thomas Ratcliffe Ellis, secretary of the British Mine Owners Association and J.R. Clynes, chairman of the Gas Workers and General Labourers' Union. At the hearings Larkin engages in sharp exchanges with William Martin Murphy, George Jacob and the employers' legal counsel, T.M. Healy MP. Larkin tells the tribunal that accommodation in Mountjoy prison is better than in the tenements. In his attack on the employers he declares: 'We are determined that Christ will not be crucified in Dublin by these men.'

While the tribunal sits many workers appear in the Dublin Petty Sessions for intimidation, obstruction or failing to pay rent. The bench is dominated by employers and landlords, who impose fines, prison sentences and evictions.

Farmers lock out ITGWU members and bring in the harvest themselves in parts of County Dublin. The ITGWU is prevented from holding a protest march through the village of Swords. Arson attacks on crops and farm buildings begin.

October

4 October: A second food ship, *SS Fraternity*, arrives from Britain.

5 October: The Parliamentary Committee of the TUC decides it will stop sending cash to Dublin, but will continue to send ships with food and fuel. This marks the beginning of a policy to distance itself from Larkin, who is refusing to cede leadership of the dispute to the TUC.

Askwith's tribunal recommends that workers abandon the sympathetic strike weapon and the employers end their lockout. It proposes a conciliation and arbitration system to resolve disputes. After a brief adjournment the unions accept the findings 'as a basis for negotiation', but the employers reject them.

6 October: The Miners Federation national conference in Scarborough calls for a general strike in Britain to support the Dublin workers. A Northumbrian delegate says he favours 'syndicalism, anarchism or even nihilism, if by those means we can combat Murphyism'. The motion is passed with one dissenting vote.

7 October: There is widespread criticism of the employers' decision to reject the Askwith recommendations, most famously in an open letter by the artist and writer, George Russell (Æ) in the *Irish Times* addressed to 'The Masters of Dublin'. In the letter, Russell issues a warning to 'the aristocracy of industry in this city, because like all aristocracies, you tend to grow blind in long authority ... You may succeed in your policy and ensure your damnation by your victory'.

Former Irish Party MP, Tom Kettle, now Professor of National Economics at University College Dublin, organises a meeting in the Mansion House to call for a 'truce' in Dublin's industrial war. His Industrial Peace Committee includes Oliver St John Gogarty, William Orpen and future 1916 Proclamation signatories, Joseph Plunkett and Thomas MacDonagh. The only employer representative is Edward Lee, a drapery chain store owner, who publicly challenges Murphy's lockout strategy. Kettle asks the audience: 'Does anyone think that hatred and uncharitableness are foundations on which we can build a great city... We cannot live an eternity in a state of war.'

Guinness boat crews refuse to handle 'tainted goods' in the port and are dismissed. Guinness chairman Lord Iveagh refuses to join Murphy in locking out workers, but the board donates £100 to the Dublin Employers' Federation contingency fund. Although a teetotaller, Larkin rejects calls to boycott Guinness products as unworkable.

10 October: Larkin is guest of honour at a rally in the Memorial Hall, London, where he tells the audience that British trade union leaders were 'about as useful as mummies in a museum' because they refuse to sanction sympathetic strikes in Britain. Dora Montefiore, a leading British socialist and feminist, proposes that strikers' children can be cared for by British families until the strike is over.

13 October: A delegation from the Industrial Peace Committee meets Dublin Trades Council, which agrees to a 'Truce', if the employers agree.

The *Toiler* appears. It replaces the *Liberator*, produced in August. Both claim, like the ITGWU's *Irish Worker*, to represent the trade unions' cause, but most of their stories attack Larkin. The *Liberator's* aim was 'to restore the esteem in which the Dublin Trades Council was held' before 'bogus socialists' took it over. The *Toiler* claims that Larkin is the illegitimate son of the notorious informer James Carey, who betrayed the Fenian group, the Invincibles in 1888.

14 October: Secretary of the Dublin Employers Federation, Charles Coghlan, issues a statement that it is impossible to deal with the workers, 'due to the domination of the legitimate trade unions by the Irish Transport Union'.

15 October: Police battle strikers in Bray harbour to protect coal imported by Heiton & Company.

18 October: Another food ship, the *SS New Pioneer*, arrives at Sir John Rogerson's Quay with 30,000 lbs of food stuffs.

Posses of strikers begin hunting down 'scabs'. In Luke Street strike-breakers flee their homes and workers riot in Denzille Street when the DMP rescue a strike-breaker at Wallace's coal yard.

Dora Montefiore arrives in Dublin to bring strikers' children to foster homes in Britain where 300 families have offered to take them. She has several helpers, including Lucille Rand, daughter of a former US Senator and Governor of California, Henry Gage and Grace Neal, a founder the Domestic Workers' Union in London. They talk to mothers in Liberty Hall where, Dora Montefiore recalled, 'The passage leading to our room was blocked from morning till evening with women and children.'

20 October: The first group of six children accompanied by their mothers take the mail boat to the country cottage of leading suffragist, Emmeline Pethwick Lawrence, in Surrey.

Tramway workers begin returning to work. Many are threatened with eviction from DUTC company cottages and car men (drivers) face having their licences revoked by the DMP. The DUTC only takes back 'men with a good record'.

21 October: Archbishop Walsh condemns Dora Montefiore's scheme and says that any women willing to part with their children, 'can be no longer held worthy of the name of Catholic mothers'.

22 October: Lucille Rand brings fifty children to Tara Street baths to be washed and 'clothed with English charity garments', as the *Evening Herald* describes them. A large mob led by five priests from St Andrew's church in Westland Row arrives and claim they are acting 'on the directions' of Archbishop Walsh. Most of the children are prevented from travelling to England and Rand is arrested on suspicion of kidnapping. The complaint has been lodged by Josephine Plunkett, the wife of Count Plunkett. One group of eighteen children successfully boards the *SS Carlow* at the North Wall with the support of ITGWU members chanting 'God save Jim Larkin' in defiance of the clerical-led pickets. At an evening rally in Beresford Place, Larkin declares the clergymen, 'a disgrace to their cloth'. He adds that the 'religion that cannot stand a fortnight's holiday in England does not have much bottom or very much support behind it'. Murphy's newspapers begin publishing the names of parents who consent to their children participating in the 'Dublin Kiddies Scheme'.

23 October: Lucille Rand is brought before the Police Magistrate in Kingstown and charged with 'receiving' 11-year-old George Burke, knowing him to be stolen. Dora Montefiore appears as a defence witness, but is herself charged with feloniously taking away George Burke with the intention of depriving his father of his custody. Both women are remanded on bail.

Members of the Ancient Order of Hibernians (AOH) organise patrols with priests at railway stations, Dublin port and Dun Laoghaire to prevent the 'deportation' of children. The shipping companies offer priests 'every facility in seeing that no children are being smuggled away'.

Eight thousand ITGWU members march through Dublin in protest at the employers' rejection of the Industrial Peace Committee's initiative. Women marchers head the parade with banners stating, 'Our men shall not give in' and 'Women workers locked out by the sweating employers of Dublin'. Increasing numbers of employers use their positions as Justices of the Peace to issue firearms licences and revolvers to strike-breakers.

24 October: On Larkin's advice, Dora Montefiore agrees that the next batch of seventeen children should be sent to Catholic homes in Belfast, but they are prevented from boarding the train at Amiens Street (now Connolly) station by, 'A compact, shouting, gesticulating, fighting crowd of Hibernians'. AOH leader, John Dillon Nugent, tells a rally, 'We are patient with poverty; we are patient with the violation of our rights; but ... we have no patience with them who would deprive the little ones of their faith.' There are clashes with ITGWU members outside Liberty Hall.

25 October: A last attempt to take children out of Dublin is made by Francis Sheehy-Skeffington and Mary Lawless, daughter of Lord Cloncurry, from Kingsbridge Station. An AOH mob led by Nugent and several priests seize a boy, and three younger children flee after their father is attacked. Sheehy-Skeffington is so badly beaten that the DMP intervene and arrest the assailants, including Nugent and two priests.

26 October: Larkin tells a mass rally in the Phoenix Park held on the eve of his trial for sedition that, 'The priest who says I dared to allow a child to be proselytised is a liar in his heart.' Robert Williams, secretary of the National Transport Workers' Federation, promises £2,000 to relieve immediate distress in the city. He is part of a TUC delegation in Dublin to discuss a new peace initiative by Archbishop Walsh.

27 October: The DMP raids Liberty Hall and seizes union records. Large crowds gather outside Green Street courthouse where mounted police maintain order as Larkin's trial begins. The handpicked jury only takes thirty minutes to find him guilty of sedition. He is sentenced to seven months. Two thousand workers gather outside Liberty Hall in driving rain to protest at his imprisonment. A procession of priests and Hibernians march past singing, 'Faith of Our Fathers' to drown out the speakers. The DMP keeps the two sides apart.

Former Parnellite MP, Pierse O'Mahony (The O'Mahony) tells a meeting of the Industrial Peace Committee in the Mansion House that, 'even if a victory were ultimately won by the employers it would not lead to permanent peace in this city', warning that 'organised labour is always more moderate than disorganised labour'.

Dr Walsh tells a meeting of the Society of St Vincent de Paul that three city parishes are providing 2,450 breakfasts daily in their schools, double the usual number and 2,045 children had been clothed in four other parishes. He says the most fundamental objection to the Dublin Kiddies Scheme is that sending children to England 'will but make them discontented with the poor homes to which they will return sooner or later'.

28 October: James Connolly takes over leadership of the ITGWU while Larkin is in prison. He announces the end of the Kiddies Scheme, saying the money spent on boat and train fares would be better spent on food in Dublin.

T.D. Rudmose Brown, Professor of Romance Languages at Trinity College, writes to the *Irish Times* protesting at the attacks he witnessed on Dora Montefiore and her helpers. He suggests that, 'All this seems to provide an interesting foretaste of the joys of unfettered Rome Rule to which we are hastening.'

29 October: A large group of strike-breakers from Britain arrives at the North Wall to work for T & C Martin timber merchants. Rumours spread that the TUC plans to reduce aid to Dublin.

Dora Montefiore and Lucille Rand appear in the Northern Police Court and the Attorney General agrees to hold over the kidnapping charges after the women give undertakings to leave Ireland. Lucille Rand subsequently appears to have suffered a breakdown while Grace Neal remains in Dublin to help run food kitchens in Liberty Hall. AOH members join with the clergy in celebrating the end of child 'exports' to England. The Order declares it will set up a union to replace the ITGWU.

At a meeting outside Liberty Hall, Connolly says that if Larkin is not released the labour movement in Dublin will send men to Britain to campaign against the Liberal government in a series of forthcoming by-elections. He warns employers that if they bring any more strike-breakers into the port, 'the streets of Dublin will run red with blood'.

A Liberal meeting in Poplar Town Hall, London, is broken up by protestors demanding Larkin's release and Edward Carson's arrest. Dublin Castle drops sedition charges against Dublin trade union leaders, P.T. Daly, William O'Brien, Tom Lawlor and William Partridge. So far, 158 workers have received prison sentences and/or fines for rioting, and there have been 114 convictions for intimidation in the Dublin courts. The average sentence is six months.

Major G.B. O'Connor, a former Unionist parliamentary candidate in Dublin, condemns the 'cowardly' refusal of the six sitting nationalist MPs to repudiate the behaviour of the priests and their supporters.

November

1 November: A prison letter from Larkin is published in the *Irish Worker*. He writes, 'This great fight of ours is not simply a question of shorter hours or better wages. It is a great fight for human dignity. For liberty of action, liberty to live as human beings should live.' He advises workers only to heed the advice of ITGWU officials, James Connolly, P.T. Daly, Michael McKeown and William Partridge while he is in prison.

George Bernard Shaw tells a meeting in the Royal Albert Hall, London, that he is there 'as a Dublin man to apologise for the priests of Dublin'. These are 'very simple and ignorant men in the affairs of the country' allowing themselves to be made 'the cat's paw of a gentleman like Mr Murphy'. At the same meeting, James Connolly calls once more on British workers to vote at every by-election 'against the Liberal jailers' until Larkin is released.

3 November: A group of women recruited in Crumlin to pick potatoes in north County Dublin march from Portmarnock railway station to Kinsealy under RIC protection while chanting 'Down with Larkin'.

Sixteen-year-old Mary Ellen Murphy from York Street is arrested after giving 'a box in the face' to another girl and calling her a 'scab' for passing the Jacob's picket. As there is no room in Mountjoy women's prison, she is sent to the Sisters of Charity at High Park, Drumcondra, where they run a Magdalen laundry. Connolly denounces the move as jeopardising the girl's virtue by making her associate with 'fallen women'.

4 November: The ITGWU buries James Byrne, union branch secretary in Dun Laoghaire (Kingstown) after he dies of pneumonia. He became ill after undertaking a hunger and thirst strike in custody to protest at allegations of alleged intimidation of a labourer at Heiton's coal depot. He claimed he had been framed. Over 3,000 workers march to Deans Grange cemetery for his funeral.

Fr Patrick Flavin of the Sodality of the Sacred Heart in Dun Laoghaire criticises the doctrine of the sympathetic strike and recruits men to his own Workers' Union. Several men appear in the Police Court charged with assaulting Francis Sheehy-Skeffington at Kingsbridge station, but as charges against the AOH leader, John Dillon Nugent, and several priests had already been dropped. Sheehy-Skeffington refuses to testify; 'If more astute persons ... cannot be put in the dock, I don't want to press for punishment against these men,' he tells the court.

5 November: A delegation from the Dublin branch of the Shipping Federation visits Colonel Renny-Tailyour, senior manager at Guinness's. The Federation is the biggest employer body in Britain and tells him it plans to bring more strike-breakers into the Alexandra Basin the next day. Dublin employers demand the Admiralty put 'a Gun Boat or a Destroyer in the Liffey for protection against violence' when the Shipping Federation brings 'free labourers' into the port. The Chief Secretary for Ireland, Augustine Birrell, rules out any naval involvement.

6 November: The Shipping Federation vessel, *SS Ella*, arrives in the Alexandra Basin with the first consignment of strike-breakers on board. The port is heavily guarded by the DMP and RIC while the military remain on standby. The *SS Ella* is joined by the *Lady Jocelyn* and the *Paris*. By the following Monday, 10 November, there are 600 strike-breakers operating in the port. Many sleep on board the depot ships for safety.

Birrell announces the establishment of a government inquiry into the housing conditions of the working classes that was promised after the collapse of the Church Street tenements two months earlier.

7 November: Murphy calls to Guinness's and asks for financial aid, as otherwise, 'it would be impossible to keep together the employers' interest in Dublin'. No commitment is given, but before the end of the year, Lord Iveagh privately donates £5,000 to the employers' fund.

11 November: The Cabinet discusses the Lockout and its adverse effect on by-election results in Britain. Birrell is told Larkin's seven-month sentence is 'excessive'.

The Industrial Peace Committee formally winds up its activities. Its final statement says, 'The employers feel their duty to themselves makes it impossible for them to pay any attention to the claims of Irish workers, or to public opinion in Ireland.'

12 November: Connolly pulls all of the ITGWU dockers out of Dublin Port. He says there have been 'a dozen messages today from various firms asking for permission to unload their goods, and saying that if it was refused they would have to dismiss their men. All the better; if it were fifty firms involved it would serve their [the union's] purpose just as well'.

13 November: Larkin is released from Mountjoy and is furious to find Connolly has called out the dockers in his absence as he was holding them in reserve as a final bargaining card. At a meeting outside Liberty Hall that night Connolly tells the crowd: 'The next time we go out for a march I want to be accompanied by four battalions of our own men ... Why should we not drill men in Dublin as well as in Belfast?'

14 November: The Shipping Federation holds a general meeting to review the Dublin situation. Several firms are unhappy at the stance of the Dublin employers, but £5,000 had already been spent supporting the Lockout and it was felt to be too late to draw back. £9,967 would be given to Dublin employers before the dispute ends. Like Lord Iveagh's donation to the employers, the details are kept secret.

Sympathetic action resumes in some British ports. Dockers refuse to load coal on the *Ella* when she returns to Liverpool to collect more strike-breakers. Railway workers in Wales refuse to handle 'tainted goods' from Dublin but the action does not spread. Other workers await the outcome of a meeting between Larkin and the Parliamentary Committee of the TUC in London on Tuesday, 18 November.

16 November: Larkin launches a propaganda campaign in Britain ahead of meeting the TUC Parliamentary Committee. He tells a crowd in Manchester that, 'Jails are nothing to the horrors of the slums and the degradation going on in Dublin day by day.'

17 November: Two leading members of the Dublin Employers' Federation, builders, John Good and Henry McLaughlin, travel to London to address the United Kingdom Employers' Defence Union (UKEDU), set up to create a £50 million fighting fund to smash sympathetic strikes. McLaughlin tells them, 'The union we are against is the union of Syndicalism and terrorism, and the whole secret of the Dublin strike is written in the one word, "Terror".'

In Dublin Lady Arnott tells the newly formed Women's Unionist Club that the present troubles in the city were but 'a prelude to the riot and strife and, perhaps, horrors unthinkable' that would follow Home Rule.

18 November: Larkin, accompanied by William O'Brien and Tom McPartlin from the Dublin Trades Council strike committee, meets the TUC Parliamentary Committee. They want the TUC to agree to hold a special delegate conference. They hope the conference will support sympathetic action. The TUC agrees to hold a conference, but only delegates from unions affiliated to the TUC can vote. This excludes most Irish-based unions, including the ITGWU.

Larkin continues his tour of Britain attacking the TUC leadership, while Connolly urges ITGWU members in Dublin to attend a meeting of the Civic League being established by former members of Tom Kettle's Industrial Peace Committee to discuss the establishment of a 'Citizens' Army'. The idea is that of Captain Jack White DSO, who wants 'to keep unemployed men fit and self-respecting'. White agrees to a proposal from Connolly that he train ITGWU members.

19 November: A protest meeting is held in the Metropolitan Hall, Dublin, over the dismissal of G.H. Walton, an employee of publishers M.H. Gill and Son, for proselytising. A member of the Church of Ireland, Walton had been assisting at the Dublin Free Breakfasts for the Poor on Sunday mornings at the Metropolitan Church Buildings. The Society of St Vincent de Paul and other Catholic lay groups threaten a boycott of the company if it continues to employ Walton.

Connolly tells a meeting in Beresford Place that, 'any man who means in future to become a member of the Transport Workers Union must be prepared to enrol himself in the Citizen Army, 'we want our men to be trained and drilled, so that when it comes to the pinch they will be able to handle a rifle; and when King Carson comes along here we will be able to line our own ditches'.

20 November: Baskin farm in Raheny is attacked and crops harvested by strike-breakers are destroyed. The owner, Miss Sarah Carey, is awarded £700, one of many claims for malicious damage made by farmers during the dispute.

22 November: There are now 900 strike-breakers in Dublin Port and the depot ships are no longer capable of accommodating all of them. A house in Sheriff Street near the Port entrance and two more houses on Beresford Place at the opposite end to Liberty Hall are taken over. They are placed under permanent police guard. Many of the strike-breakers have come from other parts of Ireland, as well as from Britain. When Lord Talbot de Malahide's estate workers strike, he has no problem acquiring replacements from Balbriggan.

23 November: Larkin publishes an attack on the TUC leadership in the *Daily Herald* in his opening salvo to win the vote at the special delegate conference. He calls on *Herald* readers to tell their union leaders, 'they are not apologists for the capitalist system'. The TUC paper, the *Daily Citizen*, responds by telling readers that Larkin, 'does no service to his cause, or to the cause of Labour, by sowing distrust between leaders and followers'.

Over 12,000 march in Dublin's annual Manchester Martyrs commemoration, including large trade union delegations invited to participate by the chairman, veteran Fenian, Tom Clarke. The Ancient Order of Hibernians and United Irish League boycott the event.

24 November: The Local Government Board begins its inquiry into the Housing Conditions of the Working Classes in the City of Dublin. There is widespread outrage as shocking statistics show that the number of people in bad housing has reached 118,461 and 13,800 people were living nine or more to a room. It subsequently emerges that seventeen city councillors are leading slum landlords, seven of whom are running for re-election in January.

The Citizen Army begins drilling at the ITGWU recreational centre in Croydon Park.

25 November: The Irish Volunteers are formed at the Rotunda Rink. Some Citizen Army men disrupt proceedings by heckling Lawrence Kettle. Besides being secretary of the Volunteers organising committee, he is Dublin City Treasurer and a son of Andrew Kettle, who had been one of the first farmers to bring in strike-breakers. Detonators are thrown and blows exchanged before the Citizen Army men are expelled from the meeting as the crowd sing, 'God Save Ireland'.

27 November: One hundred and fifty leading Unionist businessmen in the 'three Southern Provinces of Ireland' issue a joint statement warning of the commercial dangers of Home Rule. The largest group comprises Dublin employers.

The Citizen Army, which has enrolled 1,200 members, holds its first march through the city. The marchers block trams but there are no incidents.

28 November: Southern Unionists hold a mass rally in the Theatre Royal, Dublin, in opposition to Home Rule. Over two thousand attend and are addressed by Edward Carson, MP for Trinity College, and the Conservative Party leader, Bonar Law. The other MP for Trinity College, James Campbell, says, 'I would rather suffer under the whips of Larkin than under the scorpions of Joe Devlin [Irish Party MP and leader of the AOH]. I honestly believe that I would have a greater chance of liberty, of personal judgement and of conscience under Jim Larkin and the Irish Transport Union, than I would under Joe Devlin and the Molly Maguires [nickname of the AOH].'

Bread shortages loom in Dublin when ITGWU labourers refuse to deliver flour to bakeries using 'free labourers'. Connolly tries to negotiate a return to work for dockers on condition that they would not handle 'tainted goods' from companies such as Jacob's. His offer is rejected as all the employers have now recruited 'free labourers'.

Connolly is criticised at a meeting of dockers in Liberty Hall for calling them out. Some permanent men had been earning up to £3 a week because of work diverted from strike-bound companies. They were now trying to survive on 10s-a-week strike pay. They demand Larkin's return from his anti-TUC campaign in England to run the strike.

Havelock Wilson of the National Seamen's and Firemen's Union negotiates a return to work by members in Dublin over the head of local branch secretary George Burke, who supports Larkin. The union offices are moved from Liberty Hall to Commons Street.

28 November: Two strike-breakers with Tedcastle McCormick coal importers fire shots after being attacked by a crowd at Burgh Quay around 6.30 p.m. At least eight rounds are fired and 50-year-old Bridget Rowe of Waterford Street is shot in the face while watching the disturbance from the steps of the Tivoli Theatre. At 11.30 p.m. more shots are fired by strike-breakers and an off-duty DUTC conductor from the top of a tram in Sackville Street after a crowd of 500 surround the vehicle and try to immobilise it. Fittings are wrecked and the crew threatened. All charges against the strike-breakers who fired the shots are subsequently struck out by the Police Magistrates, who fine and imprison prosecution witnesses on the basis of their own evidence.

30 November: The *Sunday Independent* carries a cartoon of a worker pointing a gun at a barrel of gunpowder marked, 'English Trade Unions', and ending up heavily bandaged in bed under the slogan, 'To hell with contracts', after it explodes. The latter phrase had been attributed to Larkin.

December

1 December: At the quarterly meeting of the Dublin Chamber of Commerce, Edward Lee tries to force a debate on the Lockout by proposing a motion that 'while determinedly opposed to the principle of sympathetic strikes', the Chamber, 'in the interests of peace and good will, ought to withdraw the agreement they asked workers to enter into in respect of the ITGWU, which the workers consider infringed their personal liberty'. The Chamber decides not to put the motion to a vote.

2 December: Seventy ITGWU dockers return to work and unload the *Antiope*, which had been strike-bound for ten weeks. It contains grain for Shackleton's mill in Lucan, the first company to lock out its workers.

Larkin and William O'Brien are called to a meeting in London of the Joint Labour Board, consisting of the TUC Parliamentary Committee, the Labour Party Executive and the General Federation of Trade Unions. They reluctantly agree to one last attempt to find a settlement before the special delegate conference on 9 December.

4 December: New talks begin between the TUC, employers and the Dublin strike committee, but the employers insist on meeting with the TUC separately from local union leaders. The employers refuse to give any guarantees that all workers will be re-hired but want guarantees from the TUC that it will not assist unions that misbehave.

6 December: The TUC team brings Dublin unions and employers together for one last attempt to resolve the dispute. The TUC publishes figures demonstrating how much help has been given to the ITGWU. This is to counter Larkin's accusations of lack of support. They show that at the end of November 14,968 workers in Dublin were being supported by TUC funds, of whom 12,829 are ITGWU members.

7 December: Dublin union leaders offer to guarantee that 'no form of sympathetic strike or other strike will be entered upon until the matter in dispute has been the subject of investigation by a local conference of employers and workers representatives'. But the employers will not guarantee strikers their jobs back. They say they will make 'a bona fide effort to find employment for as many as possible and as soon as they can'. The talks collapse at 6 a.m.

More strike-breakers arrive in Dublin port and the *Irish Times* announces that Dublin stores will be well-stocked for Christmas as goods are being brought in by rail via Belfast, Newry, Dundalk, Drogheda, Rosslare and Cork. Despite support from National Union of Railwaymen (NUR) members in Britain, Dublin railwaymen still refuse to join the dispute.

8 December: TUC negotiators, as well as the Dublin Trades Council representatives, Connolly, O'Brien and McPartlin, have to sail on a boat crewed by strike-breakers to make the TUC conference in London on time.

9 December: The special delegate conference of the TUC opens in London. Nearly 600 delegates representing 350 TUC-affiliated unions with 2.5 million members gather for the debate on the Dublin Lockout. It quickly becomes a personalised clash between Larkin and his opponents in the TUC. The key debate revolves around a motion from the TUC leadership calling on the Joint Labour Board to convene a special conference in Dublin of all unions involved in the dispute to, 'consider the entire position, with a view to a united policy by which the dispute might be brought to a successful conclusion without the sacrifice of any trade union principle'. Jack Jones of the Gasworkers and General Labourers' Union proposes a more militant motion calling upon, 'all unions having members engaged in transport work, either on land or on sea, to notify the employers … that on a given date they will refuse to handle blackleg cargo or merchandise going to, or coming from firms which have locked out the workers of Dublin'. Delegates representing 203,000 workers vote for Jones's proposal, while the vote against imposing a blockade on Dublin is 2,280,000. Motions are passed calling for the release of strikers from prison and an end to the importation of strike-breakers, but the conference's outcome represents a repudiation of the sympathetic strike strategy.

10 December: When Connolly announces the outcome of the TUC conference at a rally of transport workers in Dublin next day, he tells them that 'Irishmen have been smashed up by Englishmen before, but they have always come up smiling.' They agree to stay out a little longer, but in Swords, farm labourers attend a meeting of a new Independent Labour Union sponsored by local farmers.

Connolly pens a furious article for the socialist magazine, *Forward*. He says the help of the British workers over the previous four months represented the Labour movement's 'highest point of moral grandeur ... But sectionalism, intrigues and old-time jealousies damned us in the hour of victory and officialdom was the first to fall to the tempter. And so we Irish workers must go down into Hell, bow our backs to the lash of the slave driver, let our hearts be seared by the iron of his hatred, and instead of the sacramental wafer of brotherhood and common sacrifice, eat the dust of defeat and betrayal. Dublin is isolated.'

By contrast, Connolly and Larkin's erstwhile ally, Robert Williams, writes of the TUC conference in the NTWF's *Weekly Record* that, 'We have now to regret that an epoch making movement has been temporarily stultified by Larkin's want of good judgement, foresight, and tact.' Bob Smillie of the Miners Federation, angry at Connolly's reference to aid from Britain as 'fetters' on the revolutionary potential of the Dublin working class, reminds him of the £1,000 a week in 'fetters' that miners supplied to keep Dublin's revolutionaries going.

12 December: Connolly phones Ernest Guinness and asks if he will take back boatmen dismissed in October for refusing to handle 'tainted' goods. Guinness refers the case to his father, Lord Iveagh, and says the situation is 'very hard on the [dismissed] men'; but Lord Iveagh decides against reinstatement, believing they must serve as an example. The biscuit manufacturer, George Jacob also rejects pleas by Connolly to take back strikers. Hundreds of women remain blacklisted.

Renewed violence erupts in the city as strikers react angrily to developments and strike-breakers open fire when confronted by hostile crowds.

16 December: Some 5,000 men march from Liberty Hall by various routes to Croydon Park and about 1,000 are drilled by Captain Jack White before marching in review past Larkin and Connolly. In Beresford Place Larkin says 'scabs' were not the only ones who could carry revolvers through the streets. He adds to cheers, 'When we have our brigades organised we will control ... all the means of wealth, so that the workers and the producers shall share equally in the wealth of the world.'

17 December: A Joint Labour Board delegation arrives for a last attempt to resolve the dispute. It meets with all the unions at the Dublin Trades Council Hall in Capel Street. The delegates demand full reinstatement of their members.

18 December: The meeting resumes and drafts four key points:

1. Withdrawal of the employers' demand for workers to renounce the ITGWU.
2. Consent to a commitment by the unions to refrain from any sympathetic strike action if a Board of Wages and Conditions of Employment is established by 17 March 1914.
3. No union member will be refused employment and no 'stranger' will be employed until all the 'old workers are re-engaged'.
4. The plight of any worker not re-employed by 1 February 1914 will be considered at a special conference on 15 February 1914.

This represents considerable movement by the unions from their demand for immediate reinstatement of all union members and a refusal to give an unconditional no-strike guarantee when talks had broken down on Sunday, 7 December.

Talks resume with employers in the Shelbourne Hotel while a few streets away serious shooting incidents occur. Leading ship broker, John Hollwey, vice-chairman of the Dublin Port and Docks Board, is shot accidentally by a strike-breaker as he passes an affray on Poolbeg Street but is not seriously injured. In another incident, a strike-breaker fires his revolver into the roadway in front of a crowd of women as a warning and a ricochet hits 16-year-old, Alicia Brady, in the hand. She is a member of the Irish Women Workers' Union.

At the talks William Martin Murphy, Charles Eason, master builder John Good and George Jacob dominate proceedings and insist on their right to retain 'free labourers' recruited during the Lockout. They will give no commitments on the number of union members who can expect re-employment. Their only concession is that no former employee will be refused work on the basis of membership of a 'particular union', in-other-words, the ITGWU.

19 December: The *Daily Herald* publishes an appeal from Larkin calling on 'rank-and-file' trade unionists to repudiate 'a black and foul conspiracy' by the TUC to betray Dublin. Direct contributions to the Dublin Trades Council strike fund rise from £1,125 for the whole of November to £1,700 in the next two weeks, but it is no substitute for the £10,000 a week that had been coming from the official Labour movement.

20 December: Talks between the TUC and employers collapse. Two strike-breakers are arrested after firing into a crowd on Sheriff Street.

The *Irish Worker* attacks 'free labourers' in terms that prefigure those used a few years later to characterise the Black and Tans. Free labourers represent, 'some of the lowest elements from the lowest depths of the criminal population of Great Britain and Ireland: this scum of the underworld have come here excited by appeals to the lowest instincts of their natures'. The paper rejoices that one of those shot was the ship broker, John Hollwey.

Free labourers brought before the courts in shooting incidents continue to be treated leniently. One strike-breaker who fired on a crowd on Sheriff Street is fined £2 and another is ordered to pay a surety of £20. The same magistrate imprisons an ITGWU member for a month after he trips up a DUTC cleaner and another striker receives a month's hard labour for throwing a stone at a tram.

22 December: The TUC ships £9,009 8s 9d worth of food to Dublin for the Christmas holiday period. The shipment is accompanied by James Seddon, one of Larkin's principal targets in his attacks on the TUC. Seddon plans to spend Christmas in Dublin distributing food.

23 December: Bailiffs try to evict Larkin's family from their rented home at 27 Auburn Street. He is out on union business, but his wife Elizabeth barricades the doors and refuses to leave. Solicitors for the ITGWU obtain a stay of execution.

Most strikers' families are now living on 4s or 5s a week. Since September an estimated £400,000 has been lost to Dublin's working-class communities in wages. About £17,000 has been received in strike pay, £50,000 in provisions and another £10,000 in other contributions. Meanwhile, the city-centre shops bulge with luxury Christmas goods.

25 December: The Christian Union feeds 550 men and women, the Mendicity Institution 1,000 men and the ITGWU throws a giant Christmas party for 5,000 strikers' children at Croydon Park with the assistance of James Seddon.

Trams running on Christmas Day are stoned on the High Street and Sergeant Kiernan of the DMP is thrown into the Liffey after scuffles between strikers and the police on City Quay. Members of the congregation leaving Christmas mass at the parish church join in the fracas on the side of the strikers. An ITGWU member, Patrick Higgins, is sentenced to ten years for his part in throwing the DMP Sergeant in the river. He is released in 1918.

29 December: Two hundred workers at the Morgan Mooney fertiliser plant in the Alexandra Basin become the first large contingent of ITGWU manufacturing workers to abandon the strike. However, Larkin has managed to ensure they return on their old pay and conditions.

The Miners Federation, the biggest contributor to the Dublin fund, issues a circular to members asking if they wish to continue making contributions. Durham miners' MP, John Wilson, says Larkin has become, 'inflated with pride ... and ... threatened to stop the whole of our industries'. Wilson denounces the sympathetic strike tactic as 'a boomerang policy, in that the greatest suffering falls on workmen'.

1914

January

4 January: The ITGWU buries its latest martyr, Alicia Brady, the 16-year-old Jacob's factory worker had contracted tetanus from her gunshot wound on 18 December and died on New Year's Day. Thousands follow her funeral cortege from her home to Glasnevin cemetery, where Connolly says, 'Every scab and every employer of scab labour in Dublin is morally responsible for the death of the young girl we have just buried.'

5 January: Nominations close for the Dublin municipal elections. Ten Labour or Larkinite candidates are nominated along with Walter Carpenter as a Socialist Party of Ireland candidate. Only three candidates are well-known strike leaders: Thomas McPartlin of the Carpenters' Union; P.T. Daly, secretary of the Irish Trade Union Congress; and Tom Foran, general president of the ITGWU. Nevertheless, the Dublin Strike Committee pins its hopes on winning seats to achieve a breakthrough in the dispute. The revelation that many sitting councillors are slum landlords is a further boost to the Labour campaign.

The Commission into the Dublin Disturbances opens. Augustine Birrell reneges on a promise to appoint a working-class representative and Larkin tells trade unionists not to testify before what he predicts will be a whitewashing exercise. There are seventy-nine civilian witnesses, most of them middle-class, and 202 police witnesses. Most of the civilian witnesses' testimony is highly critical of the police.

7 January: The Parliamentary Committee of the TUC finds there is only £1,500 in hand for the Dublin strike fund and writes to William O'Brien, treasurer of the Dublin strike committee, informing him that, 'remittances for this week would be the only ones that could be forwarded to meet the strike pay of the Dublin workers unless the rank and file responded more generously than at the present time'. Food shipments continue until February.

10 January: The most prominent eyewitness at the Dublin Disturbances hearing, Liberal MP Handel Booth, withdraws in protest at the 'tainted atmosphere'.

The Lord Mayor, Lorcan Sherlock, who is running for re-election, warns citizens that, 'Socialism is gradually making its way in Dublin; there is a growing feeling to disrespect even religious institutions, and clever Socialists are prostituting the labour movement and dragging it along the road to perdition.'

13 January: Larkinites hold a torch-lit procession through the city.

14 January: Polling day in the municipal elections.

15 January: When the votes are counted, the Larkinites secure 12,026 votes to 16,627 for the Nationalists (Irish Party), but only win one seat. Among the reasons are: the property and residency qualifications mean a lot of workers do not have a vote; the Larkinite candidates spurn clientelist politics and fail to organise a door-to-door canvass, relying on the *Irish Worker* and mass meetings to get their message across; too many Larkinite candidates are put forward in some wards; the weight of a hostile press and clergy tells against them across the city and some Nationalists run on a 'Home Rule Labour' platform to confuse the electorate further.

Nevertheless, the Larkinites come within 150 votes of winning four seats. The one successful candidate was Henry Donnelly of the Coachbuilders' union, who won a seat in the Labour stronghold of New Kilmainham. But the high hopes entertained by the Larkinites during the election campaign means they feel their electoral failure all the more. One consolation was that P.J. McIntyre, editor of the anti-Larkin black propaganda paper, *The Toiler*, only secures eleven votes in the New Kilmainham ward.

16 January: A convoy of coal carts belonging to Heiton & Company is attacked by a mob on Abbey Street. Five free labourers are dragged from the vehicles and beaten 'unmercifully'. The attack only stops when a strike-breaker fires shots. One of the horses, a coal cart and a lorry, are hijacked by the mob.

17 January: Two free labourers, Thomas Harten and George Maguire, leave the safety of the Employers' Federation House at 2 Beresford Place to go for a drink and are attacked on the quays. Harten is kicked to death and Maguire badly beaten. The Dublin Employers' Federation offers £100 reward for information leading to apprehension of the culprits. Police charge Thomas Daly, an unemployed coal labourer and ITGWU member, with Harten's murder. He is already facing assault charges over attacks on two other 'scabs'. The murder case against him quickly collapses, but he is given two years on the assault charges. By contrast, Patrick Traynor, the strike breaker who fatally injured Alicia Brady is acquitted. James Lewis, the strike breaker who shot John Hollwey is found guilty of grievous bodily harm but released on his own recognisances and allowed to return home to Wales. The only death connected with the Lockout that was publicly condemned by the Lord Lieutenant, is that of strike-breaker, Thomas Harten.

18 January: Strikers gather at Croydon Park where Larkin advises them to go back to work on the best terms available. His one injunction to members is not to sign the form renouncing the ITGWU. The next day 1,000 dockers try to return to work, but only half are taken back.

19 January: The *SS Hare* brings the last large food consignment to Dublin. Huge queues gather outside Liberty Hall next morning for food tickets

21 January: The TUC Parliamentary Committee tells Larkin and fellow Dublin strike leaders that no further material aid would be forthcoming. There are violent clashes in the city. One of the worst occurs when a group of strike-breakers arriving as a body for work at Tedcastle & McCormick's is attacked on Tara Street. They are subjected to a shower of bricks, bottles and stones. Shots are fired on both sides and twelve strikers are arrested. Following the incident Tedcastle & McCormick reopen negotiations on a return to work, as do several other companies.

23 January: The collapse of the Lockout overshadows the mayoral election on Dublin Corporation. Labour Councillor, William Partridge, launches a ferocious attack on the re-elected Mayor, Lorcan Sherlock, for his betrayal of Dublin's workers; Sherlock responds: 'Who would believe that anything I could have done would move Mr William Murphy?'

27 January: The annual general meeting of the Dublin Chamber of Commerce gives a vote of thanks to William Martin Murphy on his Presidency and commissions William Orpen to paint his portrait. There are queues outside Liberty Hall for strike pay, but the only help available is some food parcels and one-way tickets to Glasgow, which about 100 ITGWU members avail of.

31 January: The United Building Labourers' Union members return to work and agree to sign pledges renouncing the ITGWU.

February

3 February: The DUTC annual returns for 1913 show a fall in profits of 16 per cent and dividends are reduced from 6 per cent to 5 per cent.

16 February: The report of the Commission on the Dublin Disturbances is published. It is a whitewashing exercise and praises the police for their 'conspicuous courage and patience'. Without 'their zeal and determination, the outburst of lawlessness which took place ... would have assumed more serious proportions and been attended by far more evil results'.

18 February: The Local Government Board of Inquiry into the Housing Conditions of Dublin's Working Class is published and is unsparing in its description of the social crisis in the capital. It names the slum landlords who are members of the Dublin corporation.

June

1 June: Larkin is elected President of the Irish Trade Union Congress. He tells delegates, 'The employers know no sectionalism. The employers gave us the title of "the working class". Let us be proud of the term. ... Let us be comrades in the true sense of the word and join with our brothers the world over to advance the cause of the class to which we belong.'

CHAPTER TWO

A Tale of Two Cities: The 1913 Lockout, The View From Belfast

Peter Collins

For the two main cities in Ireland, in 1913, in the opening words of Charles Dickens' *Tale of Two Cities*, 'It was the best of times, it was the worst of times …'. Belfast was an industrial and commercial giant at its zenith with a vast diversity of industries, while Dublin had experienced a century of decline. Belfast had linen, shipbuilding and engineering, tobacco and distilling. It had the biggest spinning mill and rope-works in the world. The sinking of the Titanic in 1912 was a disaster, but the technological knowhow, displayed in the construction of the ship, was a stark illustration that Belfast was light years ahead of Dublin, both industrially and economically. The population of Belfast had grown from 19,000 in 1801 to 386,947 in 1911, in the process catching up on Dublin.[1] Protestants were in a big majority among both skilled and unskilled workers in the city. With the multiplicity and diversity of industrial enterprises in the city, workers could move easily from one to the other. Seventy thousand, mainly women, were employed in the linen industry mostly in and around Belfast. Thus, many working-class families had two wages coming in on a regular basis.

This was in stark contrast to Dublin which had been in economic decline since the proroguing of the Irish parliament, under the Act of Union of 1800. The consequent exodus of Irish parliamentarians to London contributed to the devastation of those native industries and services that depended on them. No major industrialisation, on the Belfast scale, followed during the long nineteenth century and by the 1900s, there were few large industrial concerns. The biggest, Guinness brewery, though highly profitable, employed only around two thousand workers while Jameson's and Power's whiskey distillers also provided some large-scale employment on a regular basis. The workforce in food manufactories, such as Jacob's biscuit factory and Savoy Chocolates, was overwhelmingly female. None of the Dublin enterprises could compare in employment terms with the powerhouses of Belfast. In Dublin, for the great mass of unskilled men, casual and seasonal labour in the building trade and the docks, and in transport, was all that was available.

An element of schadenfreude towards Dublin during the unrest of 1913 permeated all classes in Protestant Belfast. The Belfast City Hall, completed in 1906, was a symbol of its civic and commercial pride. E.M. Forster described it as, 'a costly Renaissance pile, which shouts "Dublin can't beat me" from all its pediments and domes, but does not say anything else'.[2] This feeling of economic and technological superiority underpinned Ulster unionist opposition to Home Rule. The fear among unionist industrialists was that, in a Home Rule Ireland, a Dublin administration dominated by mainly agrarian interests would interfere with their prosperity. Furthermore, if the legislation were to be implemented the north-east might lose irreplaceable trading links with Britain and the Empire. The deep religious hostility underpinning the northern unionists' attitude to nationalism was encapsulated in the slogan, 'Home Rule is Rome Rule'. Religious antipathy was exacerbated by the Papal *Ne Temere Decree*, which came into force in 1908. Contrary to previous custom, this forced the parents of a mixed marriage to bring up their children as Catholics. Unlike other countries, the decree was rigidly enforced by the Irish hierarchy. This in turn resulted in the sensational McCann case in 1910.[3] Alexander McCann, a Catholic took his children to America, leaving his Presbyterian wife Agnes, who had refused to comply with the *Ne Temere Decree*. It was widely believed that he had been encouraged in this by Catholic clergy and a Presbyterian minister Revd William Corkey became embroiled in the controversy on the side of the wife. Tragically the mother never saw her children again. As a result, a fresh sectarian fissure opened up and a miasma of extreme intolerance hung over the city. The McCann case seemed to point to a Home Rule Ireland which would be a cold house for Protestants and the controversy certainly hardened attitudes against Home Rule.

William Walker was the leading trade unionist and labour politician in Belfast. From the late 1890s, he controlled the Belfast labour movement and largely gave it its character. Originally a joiner in Harland and Wolff, he was a well-read autodidact, and a member of the Rechabite Order.[4] Rechab was an Old Testament character whose followers led a nomadic, abstemious lifestyle. A temperance body and friendly society organised in the United Kingdom, the United States and Australia, it was associated with evangelical Protestantism. Following a year-long strike, by his union, the Amalgamated Carpenters and Joiners, writing as secretary of the Belfast Trades Council, Walker graphically portrayed the yawning chasm between the status of workers in Belfast and those in the south:

> Whilst every other city in Great Britain, of like size to Belfast, can obtain substantial reductions in hours with a corresponding increase of wages and generally improved conditions of labour, Belfast, simply because it happens to be in Ireland, is to be denied any advance or improvement, is to go on without daring to seek for change, and is to model itself on the provincial towns of Ireland both in wages and hours and not upon those cities with whom we are so proud to compare when speaking about our commercial prosperity.[5]

Walker's labour unionist perspective is generally referred to as 'Walkerism'. Walker wanted labour in Ireland to be an integral part of the British labour movement, industrially and politically. He was elected to the British Labour national executive and elected to Belfast Corporation and as President of the Irish Trade Union Congress in 1904. With the Trades Council paper, *Belfast Labour Chronicle*, behind him, he became a leading force in both the political and industrial wings of the labour movement.[6] In 1904 he stood in a by-election in North Belfast against the Conservative Sir Daniel Dixon, narrowly failing to become the first Labour MP in Ireland. His defeat was probably occasioned by his ill-judged avowal of an anti-Catholic pledge, sent to candidates by the Belfast Protestant Association (BPA). This lost him the vital support of the Catholic minority in the constituency. In the 1906 general election he again narrowly failed to be elected. As a Labour unionist, Walker mainly appealed to the Belfast Protestant working class. In the 1900s the Conservative and Orange elite in the north faced a challenge from sections of the Protestant working class. Tom Sloan,[7] shipyard worker and member of the BPA and the Independent Orange Order (IOO), was elected MP for South Belfast, on a platform similar to that of Walker.[8] Sloan, with Lindsay Crawford,[9] Grand Master of the Independent Orange Order was moving in a socially progressive direction, clearly outlined in the so-called Magheramorne Manifesto.[10] Crawford presented his manifesto at the Independent Order's 1905 'Twelfth' demonstration, in the Co. Antrim village of that name and members of the Independent Orange Order worked for Walker in his election campaigns. However, this tendency receded in importance with the return of a Liberal government in 1906, which once more awakened fears among unionists of the possibility of Home Rule.

Belfast experienced its own industrial turmoil in 1907. James Larkin came to Belfast from Liverpool to attend the only British Labour annual conference ever to be held in the city. He remained to reorganise the local branch of the National Union of Dock Labourers (NUDL). This had been defunct since 1892 due to the trade depression. Larkin's parents had emigrated from Armagh to Liverpool. In the city's Irish Catholic community Larkin grew up in a nationalist environment. He later combined separatist nationalism with socialism, honed while working in the docks as a foreman and union organiser. In Belfast, he was soon identified as a Catholic and nationalist. This was problematic for a labour leader in the city, given the ever-present sectarian tension. Nevertheless, in a short time he had organised 4,000 dockworkers across the sectarian divide. After winning a strike over recognition and wages, he was drawn into conflict with Belfast's leading capitalist, Thomas Gallaher.[11] In many respects Gallaher may be seen as the precursor of William Martin Murphy. Aside from his huge tobacco company, he was chairman of the Belfast Steamship Company, and like Murphy, he persuaded many other employers to band against Larkin's unionisation of the city's many unskilled workers.

In May 1907, a strike was occasioned by dockers in Belfast who attempted to impose a 'closed shop' on the Belfast Steamship Company. Larkin persuaded the men to abandon this and went to the company to apologise on their behalf. However, Gallaher had already called on the Shipping Federation to send 'blackleg' labour, and the men were locked out. Larkin was forced into defensive action which included sympathetic strikes, involving carters and other unskilled workers. The 1907 Belfast strike bore striking similarities to the Dublin lockout. The same conditions were imposed on the men; to either give up their union membership or lose their jobs. Belfast was brought to a standstill for four months and Larkin managed for a time to unite Protestant and Catholic workers. Even the Independent Orange Order allowed collections for the strikers and their families at Twelfth of July demonstrations and blacklegs had to have police protection. This additional pressure on the Royal Irish Constabulary, as well as their own deteriorating conditions of service, led to a police strike, in stark contrast to the approach of the Dublin Metropolitan Police in 1913.[12] The alarmed authorities, who were clearly on the side of the employers, brought in the military to aid the civil power, inevitably leading to clashes with the strikers and their supporters. The army was provocatively sent into the nationalist, Falls Road, and during an ensuing riot, two young Catholics, Maggie Lennon and Charles McMullan, both innocent bystanders, were shot dead.[13]

The unionist press, especially the *Belfast Evening Telegraph*, depicted Larkin as a rebel and a socialist and the paper cited the disturbances as evidence of underlying motives to harm the prosperity of unionist Belfast. They continued to foment sectarianism and this exposed cracks in the workers' unity. The employers were able to hold out longer than the strikers and their families, and worse still, the national leadership of the NUDL withdrew strike pay, which had been on course to bankrupt the union. English union leaders were brought in to settle over the heads of Larkin and his lieutenants while the strikers had to return to work, cap in hand, and not all were reinstated. Larkin headed for Dublin, leaving behind a dock labour force divided along sectarian lines. The mainly Catholic, deep-sea dockers, under Michael McKeown, later joined the Irish Transport and General Workers' Union (ITGWU), which Larkin formed in Dublin in December 1908. The mainly Protestant, cross-channel dockers, led by Alex Boyd, a Walkerite and Larkin lieutenant in 1907, remained in the NUDL. A year after the Belfast debacle, Larkin, without relying on the NUDL, led a successful docks strike in Dublin. The ferocious tirades which Larkin launched against the British union leadership during the Dublin Lockout clearly had their origin in his experiences in Belfast. Belfast, in turn, would remember the turmoil of 1907 when reports of the Lockout in Dublin began to emerge in 1913.

The figure who, along with Larkin, most influenced Belfast attitudes in relation to the 1913 Lockout, was James Connolly.[14] Like Larkin, Connolly had Irish parents, who emigrated from Scotstown in Co. Monaghan to Edinburgh. Growing up he came under the influence of a Fenian uncle. After a spell in the British army in Ireland, he returned to Scotland, where he became an avid reader of Marxist theory. He put his political theories into practice when called to organise the Irish Socialist Republican Party in Ireland at the turn of the century. In 1903 he emigrated with his family to America, where he was a union organiser and member of the International Workers of the World, a Syndicalist movement known as the 'Wobblies'. On his return to Ireland, he was sent by Larkin, in 1911, to organise the ITGWU in Belfast. He also was committed to organising the Socialist Party of Ireland (SPI) in the city. Connolly had some early trade union success in the Catholic dominated, deep-sea docks, but less so with the mainly Protestant, cross-channel dockers. Connolly affiliated his ITGWU branch to the Belfast Trades Council in order to play a part in the wider trade union movement in the city. He also aimed to wean socialists in the city from the Labour unionism of William Walker.

Connolly was asked by some female linen workers to organise a union for them. The women were being penalised by fines for minor infringements of workplace regulations. He told them to approach Mary Galway, secretary of the existing Irish Textile Operatives' Society. William Walker had been instrumental in setting up this union, under the auspices of the Trades Council. Those who had approached Connolly were mainly female relatives of ITGWU members. They were critical of Galway for not being active enough in their interests. Many were not previously unionised and Connolly reluctantly set up the Irish Textile Workers' Union to cater for them. In angry debates in the Trades Council, he was accused of poaching members contrary to trade union practice.[15] The Trades Council was deeply divided over the issue and Connolly was supported by the more radical members, such as Thomas Johnson and David Robb Campbell, while Galway had the support of the Walkerite 'old guard'.

The dispute spilled out into the wider community with Connolly gaining the reputation of being an outside agitator. As such, he was castigated in a hostile editorial in *The Belfast Newsletter*: 'Larkinism is trying to raise its head in Belfast … All that need be said is that if the Trades Unionism of Belfast does not purge itself of Larkinism it will end in its own undoing.'[16] Connolly had the dubious privilege of being denounced from both Catholic and Protestant pulpits. His daughter Nora recalled sitting in a local church with her father as the priest denounced his activities in the linen workers' strike.[17] In Larne, aluminium plant and dock workers, most of whom were Protestant, had joined the Transport Union and gone on strike in June 1913. Connolly was denounced by the town's Protestant clergy and the strike declared a Fenian and Papist plot and the workers went back at the behest of the clergy. Desmond Greaves quotes Connolly's rueful comment that, 'the confraternities of Wexford (which experienced its own lock-out that year) could not break a strike, but the Protestant parsons could. North-east Ulster, not the south-east was the priest-ridden part of Ireland'.[18] Connolly was soon to be sorely disabused of that opinion during the Dublin Lockout.

Connolly's time in Belfast coincided with intense political unrest. He soon gathered around him the most advanced political thinkers in the Belfast labour movement, including prominent Trades Council activists, D.R. Campbell, Thomas Johnson and Danny McDevitt. Campbell was a Belfast Protestant, insurance agent and city councillor. Thomas Johnson was a veterinary salesman, originally from Liverpool. Both became presidents of the Irish Trades Union Congress (ITUC), Campbell in 1911 and Johnson in 1916. Johnson eventually became the first leader of Irish Labour Party in Dáil Éireann.[19] Connolly combined his trade union work with political activism. His Socialist Party of Ireland (SPI) an advanced socialist republican group, had an active membership of just twenty-five in Belfast, including Johnson, Campbell and McDevitt. The group met in an upstairs room, in McDevitt's city-centre tailor shop, in Rosemary Street. Most advanced socialists, republicans and language revivalists passed through, at one time or another. It was known to opponents and in the press as the 'Bounders' College'. Labour politics in the city were dominated by Walker and his Labour unionist ideology through five branches of the Independent Labour Party (ILP).[20] Connolly set out to wean these away from Walker's influence and he engaged Walker in a less than comradely debate about socialism and nationalism, in the Glasgow Labour paper *Forward*. Joint education lectures were held, involving members of the SPI and ILP, in the 'Bounders' College' during the winter of 1911–12.[21] Eventually a 'unity' conference was held in Dublin, during the Easter break in 1912 which only Walker's North Belfast ILP branch failed to attend. Out of this Dublin meeting emerged the Independent Labour Party of Ireland (ILP (I)). Connolly seemed to be having an impact on the labour activists in the city.

In 1912 the third Home Rule Bill was progressing through parliament. In the resultant highly charged political atmosphere in Belfast, there was great opposition to the Bill by the vast majority of Protestant workers. The ILP (I) held a mass meeting in support of the Home Rule Bill in the Catholic, St Mary's Hall on 17 May.[22] The main speakers were Connolly and Johnson. Connolly and his adherents were perforce becoming increasingly identified with the Catholic community. But even in Catholic Belfast, where Joe Devlin MP for West Belfast held sway, they were still seen as interlopers. Devlin, with John Redmond and John Dillon, made up the Irish Parliamentary Party (IPP) leadership triumvirate. He came from a Catholic working-class background in the Lower Falls. Before going into politics, he worked in a pub in central Belfast. Small in stature, he had little formal education but through participation in debating societies he developed brilliant oratorical skills, earning him the epithet 'the pocket Demosthenes'. Connolly's political activities in Belfast were marking him out for the ire of Ulster Unionists and the Irish Parliamentary Party alike.

In July 1912 an attack was made on a Protestant Sunday school party in Castledawson by members of the Ancient Order of Hibernians (AOH). The incident was greatly exaggerated in the unionist press and, as a result, large numbers of Catholic and socialist workers were expelled from shipbuilding, engineering and other workplaces. Belfast Trades Council, protested at the workplace expulsions.[23] D.R. Campbell led a deputation to try to get the workers reinstated. This in turn led to the Trades Council becoming further alienated from the Protestant workforce. The isolation of the Trades Council was further exacerbated by identification with Connolly and his support for Home Rule. The Walkerites were against Home Rule, as were most Protestant workers in the city, the majority of whom signed the Ulster Covenant in September 1912 and many later joined the Ulster Volunteer Force which numbered around 22,000 in Belfast.[24]

A further point of rupture came with Connolly and Larkin's involvement during 1912 and 1913 in the setting up of an Irish Labour Party through the Irish Trades Union Congress. They intended that the new party would provide opposition to the Irish Parliamentary Party in the anticipated Dublin parliament. Outside of north-east Ulster a growing number of trade unionists were in favour of an Irish Labour Party. However, a significant number of Catholics were supporters of the Irish Parliamentary Party. Indeed, Joe Devlin claimed that his party already represented the workers so there was no need for a Labour Party. Devlin controlled the Ancient Order of Hibernians whose opponents, both nationalist and unionist, dubbed the 'Molly Maguires'. The nickname derived from violent secret societies in Ireland and among Irish-American coal miners in nineteenth-century Pennsylvania. The Belfast 'Mollies' earned a violent reputation after shouting down William O'Brien, a nationalist opponent of Devlin and Redmond, and intimidating his supporters in February 1909. This was at a meeting in the Mansion House Dublin, which became known as the 'Baton Convention'.[25] The Belfast 'Mollies' were subsequently utilised to break up meetings organised by Connolly on the Falls Road. Devlin was a populist, who presented himself as the friend of the worker. He was a leading light in the campaign against 'sweated labour' and for the extension of the 1909 Trades Boards Act to the Irish linen industry. The Labour movement challenged the Irish Parliamentary Party's claim to speak for the workers, citing the party's blocking of the extension to Ireland of the medical benefits of the 1911 National Insurance Act.[26]

Northern unionists and supporters of the Irish Parliamentary Party became 'strange bedfellows' in opposing the setting up of an Irish Labour Party. At the 1911 Irish Trades Union Congress (ITUC) Walkerites combined with Redmondites, led by William McCarron of Derry, to defeat it. Connolly declared that, 'the unborn Labour Party of Ireland was strangled in the womb by the ILPers'.[27] After several failed attempts, the Congress voted for an Irish Labour Party at Clonmel in 1912. A resolution proposed by Connolly passed by forty-nine to nineteen votes, although an organisational structure didn't emerge until the following year. This development was due to the growing representation of the ITGWU at the ITUC. The name adopted, Irish Trade Union Congress and Labour Party (ITUC&LP) reflected the strong integration of the industrial and political wings of the movement. The hostile reaction to this development from some northern delegates did not bode well for the unity of the Labour movement. The new party was anathema to the Walkerites and the vast majority of trade unionists in Belfast. In 1913 the political climate in Belfast grew even worse, provoking a backlash in Belfast Trades Council. Attendances were meagre, no doubt due to the Clonmel Congress decision. A motion was passed not to send Trades Council delegates to the next ITUC, 'on the grounds that the political resolution, passed at last year's Congress was not acceptable to members of that Council and was impracticable'.[28] Connolly, Campbell and Johnson were now a beleaguered minority within the Trades Council, which itself was unrepresentative of the organised Belfast workforce. Campbell and Johnson attended the Congress representing their individual unions and took their place on the Parliamentary Committee of the ITUC, alongside Larkin and William O'Brien of the Transport Union. They now had control of the Congress and were guiding it in a nationalist and radical direction.[29]

Connolly was now losing patience with the lack of progress in Belfast. His grand design of uniting the working class in Belfast behind his brand of republican socialism seemed to have run into the ground. With the Home Rule crisis ever more divisive, the timing was especially bad for Connolly's project, if indeed it ever stood a realistic chance of coming to fruition. While Campbell and Johnson agreed with Connolly's aims, they disagreed with his tactics. From a Protestant unionist Belfast background, Campbell knew the mettle of the loyalist workers. He was acutely aware of the sincerity and determination with which they would oppose any attempt to place them under any perceived Catholic, nationalist domination. Connolly was also guilty of displaying autocratic tendencies when dealing with his Belfast lieutenants. They were evolutionary socialists, who saw the need for moderating principle with praxis. Connolly was a revolutionary, a visionary, who had little truck with compromising principles. During his unsuccessful Corporation election campaign in the Dock Ward in December 1912, he gave no quarter to the Walkerites who had magnanimously agreed to support him. Greaves described the fall-out, 'He thinks nobody knew anything till he came, grumbled Sam Geddis, whose speech was "corrected", publicly from the platform, immediately he had made it.'[30] Many thought Connolly inflexible, even doctrinaire. The marginalisation of Connolly and his adherents in Belfast is graphically illustrated by Greaves, 'On May 1 (1913) the Textile and Transport Workers' Unions paraded the Falls Road to the Custom House Steps, a point it was now possible to touch upon only with overwhelming strength.'[31]

The political, social and economic history of Belfast in the previous two decades and beyond, explains much about the attitudes and actions of all classes in the city during the Lockout. To a great extent, hostility and apathy were shared by both unionists and nationalists in Belfast, if for largely different reasons. A lack of sympathy towards their fellow trade unionists was in evidence among the majority of Belfast workers who were much more concerned with the fall-out from Home Rule than with events in Dublin. Despite this, Connolly's leadership of the Lockout, under Larkin, did have reverberations and undoubtedly contributed to a chill factor in Belfast. On 28 August, with the arrest of Larkin, William Partridge, P.T. Daly and William O'Brien, Connolly was called to Dublin to take over the leadership of the union. Connolly himself was arrested on 30 August. Despite the misgivings of many members, the Belfast Trades Council was persuaded to support the locked-out workers by Keir Hardie, who had come directly from Dublin specifically for that purpose. Speaking at a rally in Dublin on 1 September, the day after 'Bloody Sunday', William Thompson, vice-president of Belfast Trades Council, sounded a militant note, which echoed what was happening in the north:

> Owing to the way in which the people were batoned on the streets of Dublin, I now recognise that disciplined forces are required in connection with trade unions – disciplined and armed forces to meet disciplined and armed forces on somewhat equal terms ... the example set ... by Sir Edward Carson and his followers is to be disciplined and practised in their arms before entering into their fight; and ... that will happen in the case of the workers if they are to win their fight and maintain their place in the times that are ahead of them.[32]

The call to arms was taken up by Captain Jack White, of 'Whitehall', Broughshane, near Ballymena.[33] The son of Field Marshal Sir George White, he served in the Boer War, from which his father emerged as a hero. When his father was appointed Governor of Gibraltar he became his aide de camp. Despite his background, he was now an advanced socialist and nationalist, who would later join the Anarchists in the Spanish Civil War. With Connolly and Larkin, he organised and trained the Irish Citizen Army (ICA). Raised initially to protect the workers against the police, it later played a key role in Easter Week 1916.[34]

Thomas Johnson and his wife Marie, secretary of Connolly's Textile Workers' Union, along with D.R. Campbell, came to Dublin at the beginning of September 1913 to participate in the Lockout.[35] The trio later toured the north of England, from Leeds to Newcastle-on-Tyne, addressing meetings and collecting funds for the Dublin families. There they met Dr William Temple, later Archbishop of Canterbury, who gave a subscription to the strike fund.[36] These funds were used to supply the ships, *Hare* and *Fraternity*, which brought relief to Dublin. The ships arrived at the North Wall on 27 September and 4 October respectively bringing cargoes vital for the workers and their families. Johnson became a member of the committee directing the strike and both he and Marie spoke at many meetings. Marie also worked alongside Countess Markievicz and Larkin's sister, Delia, at the food depot for the starving children.[37] However, moderates such as Johnson were appalled at Larkin's campaign of vilification against prominent members of the British Trade Union Congress for opposing sympathetic strikes. Johnson attempted to repair the rift and, in the Labour, *Daily Herald,* he tried to restore the focus on the core issues of the Lockout, its causes and the suffering of the workers and their families.[38] But the damage was done and the dwindling support from the British unions was a major contribution to the failure of the strike.

Connolly's exploits in Dublin increased his notoriety in Belfast. This was fuelled by hostile press coverage of his imprisonment and subsequent hunger strike.[39] After seven days, Connolly was weak and feverish, and was released following a deputation on his behalf to the Viceroy. He spent another week resting in Dublin before returning to Belfast to recuperate. On his arrival at the Great Northern Railway station in Great Victoria Street, Belfast, he was greeted by his mill girl and docker supporters and the Non-Sectarian Labour Band. A loyalist mob besieged the station, singing party songs and firing pistol shots and a clash between the two groups was only prevented by a heavy police presence.[40] A similar siege occurred when Connolly's Textile Workers' Union excursion to Portrush arrived back at York Street railway station in August 1913.[41] By now his union had lost the support of its Protestant members in the cross-channel docks. After he had recovered from the effects of the hunger strike, Connolly returned to Dublin to replace

Larkin who had begun touring Britain to enlist the help of the trade unions and rank-and-file workers.

Support for the Lockout was just as sparse in the Belfast Catholic community. This was largely due to the AOH/IPP opposition to the workers. A big factor in this was the campaign of deliberate misinformation about the so-called 'kiddies' scheme, the aim of which was to bring the children of locked-out workers to sympathetic labour homes in England. It didn't help that the scheme was proposed by Dora Montefiore, an English socialist and feminist. The Catholic Church was alarmed at the potential for proselytising, which it believed was inherent in the scheme. The AOH provided the muscle to physically prevent the scheme and it was stopped in its tracks at the North Wall by groups of Hibernians and other Catholic zealots. It was then decided to send children to Belfast by train but there was a repeat performance by the opponents of the scheme, as Montefiore described, in the *Daily Herald:*

> It was then decided by Mr. and Miss Larkin that, as the ostensible reason for the disgraceful scene which took place on Wednesday was that the children were going across the water, and possibly to Protestant homes, we would send a detachment of children ... to Roman Catholic homes in Belfast. At one end of the platform, in front of the compartment into which the parents were attempting to get their children, there was a compact, shouting, gesticulating, fighting crowd of Hibernians. In the centre of this crowd was the little party of children and parents, and scattered among them were the priests, who were talking, uttering threats against the parents, and forbidding them to send their children to Protestant homes.[42]

Though well meaning, those behind the 'kiddies' scheme presented a hostage to fortune to their opponents. As national President of the AOH, Joe Devlin was clearly privy to its strike-breaking activities during the Dublin Lockout. Devlin was also chairman of the Belfast Catholic *Irish News* and as the Lockout progressed the paper carried stories hostile to the Dublin workers and their leaders, including resolutions from Ulster branches of the Ancient Order of Hibernians. One such resolution came from the Portadown and Drumcree AOH districts, passed on 30 November 1913:

> We ... do hereby emphatically denounce the unwarranted and abusive attacks on our National President and Secretary, Messrs. Devlin and

Nugent, because of the timely intervention of the Ancient Order of Hibernians in preventing the deportation and proselytising of the Catholic children of Dublin at the hands of alien Socialists who in their ungodly campaign, which aims at the ruination of happy homes and the extinguishing of our industries, have brought down the working classes of Dublin to the lowest depths of poverty, misery and despair; also we call on all Irish Nationalists to take immediate steps to stamp out Larkinism wherever it shows its head, as the avowed enemy of faith and country.[43]

There were also attempts in the *Irish News* to associate Larkin with anti-clericalism. In a leader column it told readers, 'Larkinism in Dublin has become directly and shamelessly identified with attacks on the Catholic Church and its ministers modelled on the infamies of the Continental enemies of God and Religion.'[44] Connolly's daughter, Nora, recalled the struggle they had in Belfast in countering the misrepresentation of the Dublin workers' case:

busy attending meetings, explaining the true story of the lock-out; trying to refute the lying propaganda against the Dublin workers; and collecting money for their assistance. It was an uphill thankless task. The church, the clergy, the press, the Hibernian organisation were all against them. [45]

As 1913 drew to a close both unionist and nationalist papers in Belfast were reporting, with some satisfaction, the growing inability of the workers to carry on the struggle, and the gradual drift back to work. Some ITGWU members in the Belfast docks had taken sympathetic action against goods destined for Dublin. In the Belfast Harbour Board annual report for 1913, the harbour police superintendent, J.A. Johnston, stated:

The Irish Transport Union workers in the employment of the Ulster Steamship Company have been almost two months on strike out of sympathy with their fellows in Dublin. At the beginning violence and intimidation were resorted to by the men on strike, but on the harbour estate the matter was promptly dealt with by the harbour police and on the Corporation area at the same time it was dealt with by the Royal Irish Constabulary. The Head Line steamers are still working under the protection of the harbour police. The affected steamers were able to leave port much as usual, as plenty of free labour offered itself, wages being good. [46]

Around a thousand ITGWU dockers were locked out in Belfast by the Head Line in 1913. Connolly noted the use by the Shipping Federation of 'scabs', but he reserved his greatest vehemence for the Seamen and Firemens' Union, whose General Secretary Havelock Wilson instructed members to collaborate in widespread blacklegging in the ports of Dublin, Liverpool and Belfast.[47] The Head Line fleet in Belfast and Dublin was particularly prominent in strike-breaking activities. In a letter to Francis Sheehy-Skeffington, Connolly noted, 'The Head Line boats are being worked in Belfast by the lowest class of free labourer, and the seamen and firemen who desired to leave were ordered by the union delegate to remain at their posts.'[48]

The Lockout was an economic catastrophe for Dublin, especially for the locked-out workers and their families. Belfast, in contrast, had undoubtedly done well commercially, as an alternative port to Dublin. End of year reports in the northern papers, from enterprises such as the Great Northern Railway Company and the Harbour Commissioners, showed a significant boost to profits. A *Belfast Evening Telegraph* headline on 2 January, referencing the customs and excise returns for the port of Belfast, trumpeted, 'BELFAST TRADE BOOM, WONDERFUL FIGURES, UPWARD LEAP OF £811,000, AGGREGATE RECEIPTS £4,425,626.'[49]

There was no such good cheer for Connolly. Undoubtedly he was demoralised by the workers' defeat in the Lockout and by his failure to make inroads into the sectarianised working-class movement of Belfast. No doubt also he was disillusioned by the patent lack of sympathy in Belfast for the struggle in Dublin. This disillusion was compounded by the response by many workers to the call to arms on the outbreak of the First World War. Connolly railed against this in his writings and speeches. He was referring of course to workers both in Dublin and Belfast. In the latter, both Protestant and Catholic workers, supported the war effort. Connolly's close associates in Belfast, Johnson, Campbell and McDevitt, called on him to desist from anti-war speeches and editorials, which were bringing unwelcome attention from unionists. In a letter to William O'Brien, dated 22 August 1914, he expressed his deep frustration at the extent to which his mission in Belfast had failed:

Principally through the machinations of McDevitt, there has been a cabal against me holding meetings against the war ... Campbell and

Johnson and McDevitt have always been on that style. Ready to cheer every stand made in Dublin, but always against any similar attempt in Belfast … I have spent myself pushing forward the movement here for the past three years, and as the result of this my activity is labelled as a desire for cheap notoriety. I am sick, Bill, of this part of the Globe.[50]

Connolly was no doubt relieved to receive the call to come to Dublin, when Larkin left for America in 1914. He was being drawn in an atavistic direction, believing that only a national revolution in wartime could solve the problems of the Irish working class. For him these problems were cruelly highlighted in the Dublin Lockout and manifest in the sectarian ghettoes of Belfast. Connolly's involvement in both the Dublin Lockout and Easter Week imprinted negatively on the minds of many northern unionists. To take the long view, the Dublin Lockout may be seen as part of the litany of events from the Home Rule crisis to the First World War, the Easter Rising, the Battle of the Somme, the 1918 election, the War of Independence and the setting up of parliaments in both cities. Each in its own way contributed to the coming of partition. A growing sense of apartness has since been engendered through living apart in, at times, hostile, separate states. This has resulted in an even greater lack of symbiosis between the two cities than existed in 1913.

Endnotes

1   Jonathan Bardon, *Belfast: An Illustrated History* (Belfast: Blackstaff Press, 1982), pp. 66; 156.

2   E.M. Forster, *Abinger Harvest* (London: Andre Deutsch, 1936), quoted in 'Literary Belfast', a publication of Belfast City Council.

3   W.A. Maguire, *Belfast* (Keele: Carnegie, 1993), pp. 120–1.

4   Alan Axelrod, *International Encyclopedia of Secret Societies and Fraternal Orders* (New York: Checkmark Books, 1997), p. 206.

5   *Belfast Trades Council Annual Reports 1889–1900*, (Coll. E D327), British Library of Political and Economic Sciences, LSE.

6   It was published between Oct. 1904 and Jan. 1906.

7   He was MP for South Belfast as an independent unionist from 1902 to 1910.

8   The Independent Order was founded by Sloan in 1903 after he was expelled from the traditional Orange Order for criticising it as being out of touch with working-class and evangelical Protestantism.

9   Crawford was expelled from the IOO in 1908 for supporting Home Rule. He later became more overtly nationalist and in 1922 was appointed Free State Trade Envoy to New York.

10 Henry Patterson, *Class Conflict and Sectarianism: The Protestant Working Class and the Belfast Labour Movement, 1868–1920* (Belfast: Blackstaff Press, 1980), pp. 45–6.

11 A native of Templemoyle, Co. Derry, Gallaher started his business, in 1857, selling hand-rolled tobacco from a cart. By the 1900s, Gallahers had become one of the largest tobacco manufacturers in the world. He had diverse business interests including shipping.

12 John Gray, *City in Revolt: James Larkin and the Belfast Dock Strike of 1907* (Belfast: Blackstaff Press, 1985), pp. 111–36.

13 Ibid., pp. 158–9.

14 C. Desmond Greaves, *The Life and Times of James Connolly* (London: Lawrence & Wishart, 1961) provides the best biography of Connolly.

15 Peter Collins, *Belfast Trades Council 1881–1921* (unpublished PhD thesis, University of Ulster, 1988), pp. 199–203.

16 *Belfast Newsletter*, 22 Nov. 1911.

17 Nora Connolly O'Brien, *Portrait of a Rebel Father* (Dublin: The Talbot Press, 1935), pp. 134–5.

18 Greaves, *The Life and Times of James Connolly*, p. 302.

19 J. Anthony Gaughan, *Thomas Johnson: First Leader of the Labour Party in Dáil Éireann* (Dublin: Kingdom Books, 1980) provides the best biography of Johnson.

20 The party was founded in Bradford in 1893. Keir Hardie MP was its first chairman. It was established in Ireland the same year and Walker and his followers made up the bulk of its membership in Belfast.

21 Greaves, *Life and Times of James Connolly*, pp. 278–9.

22 Ibid., p. 281.

23 Ibid., pp. 290–2.

24 Austen Morgan, *Labour and Partition: the Belfast working class, 1905–23* (London: Pluto, 1991), p. 182.

25 A.C. Hepburn, *A Past Apart: Studies in the History of Catholic Belfast, 1850–1950* (Belfast: Ulster Historical Foundation, 1996) pp. 170–1.

26 Collins, *Belfast Trades Council 1881–1921*, pp. 147–8.

27 Greaves, *The Life and Times of James Connolly*, p. 259.

28 Belfast Trades Council Minutes, 3 April 1913.

29 Arthur Mitchell, *Labour in Irish Politics, 1890–1930: The Irish Labour Movement in an Age of Revolution* (Dublin: Irish University Press, 1974), pp. 36–8.

30 Greaves, pp. 295–6. Belfast crowds gathered at the Custom House steps to hear political and religious firebrand oratory.

31 Ibid., p. 298.

32 Pádraig Yeates, *Lockout: Dublin 1913* (Dublin: Gill & Macmillan, 2000), p. 63.

33 Leo Keohane, *Captain Jack White: Imperialism, Anarchism and the Irish Citizen Army* (Dublin: Irish Academic Press, 2014).

34 Ibid.

35 Gaughan, *Thomas Johnson*, pp. 25–7.

36 Ibid.

37 Ibid.
38 Ibid.
39 Greaves, *The Life and Times of James Connolly*, pp. 311–13.
40 Ibid., p. 312.
41 Collins, *Belfast Trades Council 1881–1921*, p. 192.
42 *Daily Herald*, 21 Oct. 1913.
43 *Irish News*, 1 Dec. 1913.
44 *Irish News*, 22 Dec. 1913.
45 Connolly O'Brien, *Portrait of a Rebel Father*, p. 142.
46 *Belfast Evening Telegraph*, 2 Jan. 1914.
47 Greaves, *Life and Times of James Connolly*, p. 334.
48 Letter from James Connolly to Francis Sheehy-Skeffington (Sheehy-Skeffington Papers, NLI, MS 33,624/2).
49 *Belfast Evening Telegraph*, 2 Jan. 1914.
50 Letter to William O'Brien from James Connolly (William O'Brien Papers, NLI, MS 15,698).

CHAPTER THREE

'Quick-Witted Urchins': Dublin's Newsboys in Challenging Times, 1900–1922

Donal Fallon

Newsboys were a feature of the Irish urban working class in the first half of the twentieth century, a constant presence on the streets of towns and cities. These young street sellers were the backbone of newspaper distribution, and in many cases provided a vital source of income to their families, in cities where labour was precarious and irregular. Newsboys were an unavoidable presence on the streets of the capital in particular, and a visitor to Dublin bemoaned the 'brazen-throated newsboys' in a letter to the *Irish Times* in 1907, noting that 'the rudeness of these journal venders amazes a stranger. They push themselves in your path, push their papers in your face, and deliberately shout in your ears til your head aches.'[1]

This chapter will examine newsboys in Dublin in the early twentieth century, looking at how the young workers were viewed and treated by different strands of society. It will examine the complex relationships that existed between this large working-class body and others, ranging from those in authority to the radical political movements of the day. It will also show the manner in which these youngsters were seen by charities and philanthropists, who identified the boys as being amongst the most impoverished workers in the city. Utilising a variety of primary sources, such as the witness statements of the Bureau of Military History, the radical media of the early twentieth century, including the *Irish Worker*, and the mainstream press, we can examine the role of this young body of workers in a period of great change in Irish life, and investigate if any sense of unity or camaraderie existed between the youths. Key events, such as the 1911 newsboy strike in the capital, and the Lockout of 1913, will be discussed in detail, to examine evidence of radicalism among a section of the boys.

The origins of the newsboy

The emergence of newsboys on the streets of British cities and towns coincided with the arrival of a cheap, daily press. With newspapers needing mass circulation to finance themselves, the focus of shifting units was well and truly on the streets. From 1855, 240 young boys were being hired by the *Daily Telegraph* in London to sell papers, and Alan J. Lee has noted that while the *Daily Telegraph* 'was, perhaps, the first to used uniformed boys', it became commonplace soon after, as 'by 1874 similar clad sellers were to be found everywhere'.[2] One British periodical described the typical newsboy in 1885 as being 'dirty and ragged' with 'the same kind of expressive hungry look that the wandering street dog had'.[3] The sheer volume of the youngsters appearing on the streets here was noted by one author in the *Dublin University Magazine*, who complained in 1872 that:

> Why, it is but a very few years since it was scarcely possible to find a copy of a daily paper on the day of publication in a country town; and, if you did find one, it was only by going from house to house to beg the loan of it. Now, you are constantly tripping and stumbling over little newsboys in the streets, with armfuls of journals of every political hue.[4]

As in Britain, the boys were typically presented as dirty and ragged when discussed in the pages of Irish publications. One letter writer to the *Irish Times* in 1882 insisted the boys were only trying to make an honest living, and that 'many of these little boys are orphans and have no home, and many more do not reside with their parents for different causes'.[5] The perception of newsboys internationally was similar in the late nineteenth century, and as Jon Bekken has noted, in American culture the boys tended to be viewed as 'either plucky entrepreneurs turning an easy buck or two before or after school or exploited child workers needing to be saved from the corrupting influence of the street'.[6]

Among those concerned with the conditions Dublin newsboys faced in the late nineteenth century was Michael Davitt, and Carla King has noted that Davitt 'supported a plan to set up a technical school for the city of Dublin, and participated in a scheme to provide low-cost meals and housing for newsboys, visiting the dosshouses where they stayed in order to gather information'.[7] Davitt's admiration and sympathy for the young workers may have owed much to his own youth; Davitt himself had been employed as a printer's devil (a term meaning an apprentice in a printing establishment) and a newsboy, giving him a familiarity with the trade. That Davitt lost an arm in an industrial accident at the age of eleven, prior to working in the newspaper industry, may have also motivated his interest in the welfare of young workers.[8]

Claims were made in some political publications that newsboys were victimised for selling publications critical of the establishment. In *The Nation*, for example, a claim appeared in December 1890 that newsboys were being arrested for selling copies of *The Nation* and *United Ireland*.[9] *The Nation* championed newsboys as 'sprightly and vociferous', and praised their refusal to bow to the pressure of authorities.[10] It is clear that the boys were being used in significant numbers by a wide variety of publications, as a means of distributing copies to a mass audience, from the 1870s onwards.

Newsboys in Dublin in the early years of the twentieth century

By the early twentieth century, a wide variety of charitable organisations and philanthropic bodies were taking an interest in newsboys. Newspaper reports of their efforts give an idea of the numbers working on the streets, in what was, in the opening years of the century, a totally unregulated field. In 1904, a Christmas dinner was hosted by the Shamrock Dining Rooms, for the newspaper boys of Sackville Street and Great George's Street. The dinner was attended by sixty-six boys and described as a 'most happy evening'.[11] The boys were also well served by the Dickens Fellowship, an institution which listed among its objectives, 'to take such measures as may be expedient to remedy or ameliorate those existing social evils which would have appealed to the heart of Charles Dickens, and to help in every possible direction the cause of the poor and the oppressed'.[12] This grouping organised annual dinners for the financial aid of the young boys, and its 1909 dinner, the third of its kind, was attended by 'several hundred' newspaper selling youths, who had to be accommodated in relays. It was noted that this dinner was attended by management figures from both the *Irish Times* and the *Irish Independent*.[13]

The Philanthropic Reform Association made repeated calls for the regulation of child street trading in the early twentieth century. This association was founded in 1896 and has been described as 'similar in purpose to the Charitable Organisation Society in England'.[14] The association was significant in the life of Dublin's poor, beyond solely working-class youth, securing a £500 grant for a relief fund during a desperate winter in 1905, an action, which it has been noted, shamed Dublin Corporation into the adoption of an Unemployed Workmen Act.[15] Maria Luddy has argued that the Philanthropic Reform Association, which sought 'changes in the law with regard to the safety of children and the protection of the destitute', must be seen as among the most progressive philanthropic societies of the nineteenth century in an Irish context, and its good work continued into the following century.[16]

The calls of this body for regulation of child street trading raised considerable debate at the time, something that was evident in the pages of the *Irish Times*, where one writer noted in 1903:

The children who trade see the matter from their own particular standpoint, namely, that of food. The Philanthropic Reform Association sees it from quite another point of view. It is an excellent thing to determine the conditions under which children shall be allowed to trade. But it would be judicious, or even 'what is best for the children', with one stroke of the pen to debar, let us say, hundreds of their number from earning an honest living, merely because instances have come to light in which certain street traders of tender years have strayed from the path of rectitude.[17]

In January 1906, a wide-ranging series of new regulations were introduced in Ireland, when the Employment of Children Act, 1903, finally came into being. Under this Act young street traders were obliged to wear prescribed badges in public, marking themselves as licensed to trade. The young street traders were, 'to deliver up their badges every night, to be restored to them every successive morning'.[18] Young street traders were barred from entering public houses or places of public entertainment, and there was to be 'no trading in streets where prostitutes or thieves reside'.[19] The Act also attempted to tackle the issue of poor school attendance among working-class youths, by stating that every license holder under 14 was to produce a certificate from their school headmaster, four times a year, proving they were in education.[20] The Act proved difficult to enforce, as Dublin youngsters found their own ways to manoeuvre around it and avoid the detection of the 'Badge Man', as inspectors became known. One former newsboy, speaking to the North Inner City Folklore Project about his experience of selling papers decades later in the 1940s, recalled how the sight of the dreaded 'Badge Man' would be met by a shout of warning, and then 'away we would go like the hammers of hell, through the streets and he after us on his big black bike pedaling like mad trying to catch us'.[21]

The 1911 census lists ninety-eight boys and girls as newspaper vendors in the capital, but there are problems with the census as a source for examining the numbers of youths working on the streets.[22] Firstly, a sizeable percentage of newsboys in the city would have been operating without the required license, and secondly, as Kate Cowan has noted, 'the 1911 census indicates that 883 children under the age of 15 were working, though it does not give the figures for those children working who fell into the age category of 15 to 17'.[23]

Militancy among newsboys

Evidence of political radicalism among newsboys can be found outside of the capital. In 1907 in Derry there was, what contemporary observers termed, a 'newsboys strike', with young street traders seeking better terms. This September strike received significant attention in newspapers, with the *Irish Times* proclaiming: 'The newsboys of Derry City, who have struck for better terms, continue to take themselves quite seriously, and are conducting their campaign with quite remarkable knowledge of up-to-date trade union tactics, including the device of "peaceful picketing".'[24]

On occasion this strike was quite radical in tactical approach, with the windows of a city magistrate's private residence attacked by the boys, as well as acts of violence against youths who continued to sell papers.[25] Within a week, however, the same newspaper was proclaiming the strike as 'short lived as it was unique', as 'very few of the boys could afford to do without the little money they were in the habit of earning each evening by selling papers'.[26] References were made by newsboys at street meetings to the then on-going Belfast dock strike.[27] In Belfast, the trade union organiser, James Larkin, from the National Union of Dock Labourers, had succeeded in revitalising the dockers' union in the city, which led to an increase in recruitment to the NUDL in Derry, and sympathy strike action and the refusal to handle blackened goods.[28] There was a heightened climate of class consciousness in the province, and the young newsboys appear to have modelled their dispute on what was occurring in other industries.

Militancy among the Dublin newsboys can be seen from the time of James Larkin's arrival in the city in 1908, in the aftermath of the Belfast dispute. Larkin, who had succeeded in uniting workers across sectarian divisions in Belfast, attempted to replicate his success in the south of Ireland, though as Pádraig Yeates has noted, 'his aggressive tactics, disregard for head office instructions and readiness to spend union funds on strike pay landed him in serious trouble', and Larkin established his own union in January 1909, the Irish Transport and General Workers' Union.[29] A very significant relationship between the Dublin newsboys and the Liverpool-born leader emerged over time, a relationship that proved beneficial to each. This relationship originated from the *Irish Worker* newspaper, the organ of Larkin's trade union, which enjoyed a large readership in the capital among the working class. Emmet Larkin, has noted that the newspaper could only be described as an 'immediate and fantastic success' and 'remains unique in the history of working class journalism'.[30] The paper was scathing in its attacks on employers and utilised black humour and biting illustrations to make political points. It succeeded in winning a mass appeal beyond anything a radical labour publication had succeeded in doing in the capital before or since. John Newsinger has written of the rapid rise of the newspaper's circulation, noting that while the first issue sold some 5,000 copies, within a month, 20,000 copies were being sold.[31] Central to distributing the paper were the newsboys of the capital. The newsboys also appealed to the ITGWU as a force to potentially unionise, and as Pádraig Yeates has noted, 'by organising the newsboys, Larkin also ensured that his own newspaper had an effective distribution network'.[32] The boys earned a higher commission on the trade union papers than mainstream publications such as the *Irish Independent*, and in 1911 the *Irish Worker* encouraged customers to leave their half-penny change with the youngsters, as it would make the 'world of difference' to them.[33]

As had previously occurred in Derry, a newsboys strike unfolded on the streets of the capital in August 1911. The Derry strike had likely been inspired by heightened class tensions amidst on-going labour disputes in Ulster, with the *Irish Times* proclaiming that the boys had 'quite remarkable knowledge of up-to-date trade union tactics',[34] but such scenes were replicated in the capital, with the strike occurring in the midst of a serious railway strike. Inspired by the outbreak of a railway strike in Britain, 18 August witnessed labourers at the London and North Western Railway facilities at the North Wall in Dublin leave their positions of employment demanding a pay increase, with men at the Harcourt Street station doing likewise.[35] Workers were actively encouraged by union leadership to take militant action coinciding with what was occurring in Britain. At a meeting of railway workers held at Beresford Place on the night before the strike began, the secretary of the Dublin branch of the Amalgamated Society of Railway Servants urged the men to strike, stating that 'by doing so they would be able to share in the fruits of the victory which would shortly be won in Great Britain'.[36]

The dispute in Britain was brought to an end after mere days, with the railwaymen gaining some wage increases; something Irish workers took confidence from. The authorities in Britain were eager to bring the dispute to a quick conclusion. Britain had witnessed the deployment of troops during a series of disputes beginning in 1910, and as Ian J. Cawood has noted, the deployment of troops in the 1911 national railway strike was the third such occasion when the state felt compelled to take drastic means.[37] Lives were lost during riots in Liverpool during the strike, and Winston Churchill condemned the 'paralysis of the railway service' in Westminster, going as far to state that 'a continuance of the railway strike would have produced a swift and certain degeneration of all the means, of all the structure, social and economic, on which the life of the people depends'.[38] While the dispute had been brief in Britain however, in Dublin it escalated into something much broader, becoming the catalyst for a range of labour disputes, including a strike by newsboys.

The newsboys strike began on 18 August 1911, the same day that railway workers took strike action, and the following day it was reported that:

> During the afternoon a crowd of boys gathered outside the offices of the paper in Middle Abbey Street [Independent House], and when an edition of the paper was published at half-past 4 o'clock they made a hostile demonstration. As several vans were about to drive off with papers for city newsagents' shops, the boys surrounded them, threw stones and other missiles at the drivers, and then swarmed up the sides and pulled down the papers, which were torn to shreds.[39]

Dublin was also to witness scenes of considerable violence, with the boys clashing with the Dublin Metropolitan Police on several occasions and attacks made upon property belonging to William Martin Murphy. As was the case in Derry, where boys were seeking improved terms from newspapers, the boys in Dublin were seeking better terms from the suppliers, in this case, the *Evening Herald*.[40]

Despite their militancy, the newsboys were still considered children, something best illustrated by mention in contemporary reports that the boys marched to the offices of the *Evening Herald* that night from Beresford Place, and 'at the head of their procession was an imposing squad of youngsters decked out after the manner of Red Indians as they appear in lurid pictures illustrating tales of the Wild West'.[41] That the boys staged their rally at Beresford Place, adjacent to Liberty Hall, indicated the influence of the trade union movement.

Violence on the streets was a feature of the dispute; instigated at varying times by the newsboys themselves and by the authorities. It was reported on 21 August that two men who had left the office of the *Evening Herald* with papers, 'had not gone far when they were surrounded by a crowd of infuriated boys, who howled such meaningless epithets as scab and blackleg'.[42] Blows were exchanged between the rival factions on that occasion and the newspapers seized. The response of the Dublin Metropolitan Police was heavy handed, something James O'Shea, who later joined the Irish Citizen Army, detailed in his statement to the Bureau of Military History:

> At this time there was a newsboys strike and for the excitement of it I was out in it all the time. It was the first time I knew what the police could do and what a small organisation of lads could do to the police. Very early on in the strike the police used all they had, fists, boots and batons, and the poor lads here smashed wherever the police could get them, but the lads retaliated with interest after a couple of days due to some big lads organising. I was present at the smashing of two *Herald* motor vans in Liffey Street and I must say it was a great job, paving stones going through windscreens.[43]

Michael Mallin, later executed for his role in the 1916 rebellion, supported the efforts of the young boys, despite owning a newsagents on Meath Street. According to O'Shea, Mallin's shop had many policemen among its customers:

> ... they discussed openly in his shop what they had done and what they were prepared to do, to smash the newsboys. One evening a sergeant, a brute would be a respectable term to use in his case, openly stated what was going to be the outcome in a day or two and Mike attacked him, the police and the government and there was a great showdown in his shop. The consequence was that Mike's name was discussed in Newmarket police barracks and police customers thereafter were few and far between.[44]

Violent clashes between police and newsboys were witnessed by Ernie O'Malley, who later described the 'quick-witted urchins' of Dublin confronting the police, writing that, 'mounted police were charging quick-witted urchins who scattered and lured the attackers into narrow by-lanes. There the boys used stones and pieces of brick with accuracy and rapidity. My sympathies were with the newsboys.'[45]

The *Irish Worker* backed the newsboys, praising their character and condemning the violence of the police. The paper told readers that if one took 'all the simple faith of Dickens' *Little Joe*, all the whimsical gaiety and optimism of Mark Twain's *Huckleberry Finn* and all the glorious heroism of Victor Hugo's *Gavroche*, what they would have standing before them was a typical Dublin newsboy'.[46] The paper also hoped that the boys would seek future retribution against those in uniform who had attacked them, stating:

> It is against these boys that the whole force of the authorities in Dublin has been hurled; it is these boys that the Dublin police have kicked and batoned, it is one of these boys (aged 9) who has been crippled by the blow of a baton; it is another (aged 8) who had his head cut open with a baton. And let us hope to Heaven that it is these boys, who ten years hence (or sooner) when the time comes, will remember to-day, and remind the brutes of the DMP and the RIC what vengeance and retribution is.[47]

Several newsboys were brought before the courts on charges of assault and theft during the dispute, with a number receiving fines for scattering copies of the *Evening Herald* which had been taken from boys not observing the strike. The *Irish Times* placed the blame for the violent clashes between newsboys and police with Larkin, noting that the boys 'acknowledged the leadership of James Larkin, whose name has become so familiar in connection with labour disturbances in Dublin that no one expected the present violence to pass without its popping up'.[48] Ultimately, nothing was won by the strike. By 25 August, they had returned to work on the same conditions as before. The links that had been forged between the boys and the union movement, however, would come to the fore two years later, and the eruption of the Great Lockout.

Newsboys and the 1913 Lockout

In popular memory, the Lockout began with a symbolic act of defiance, when tramway drivers walked away from their trams and pinned the famous red hand badge to their uniforms. In reality, the first blow was actually delivered over a week previously by William Martin Murphy; on 15 August, Murphy removed forty men and twenty boys from the dispatch and delivery offices of the *Irish Independent*. As Yeates notes, there was an almost immediate response to this from the workers, who 'placed pickets on the office, and that afternoon the city's newsboys refused to sell the Independent's sister publication, the *Evening Herald*'.[49]

Murphy's *Irish Independent* accused Larkin's union of 'attempting to bully the newsboys into refusing to sell the *Evening Herald*'.[50] John Farrell, a young Dublin newsboy, appeared in court on 30 August charged with intimidating another newsboy who was selling the *Irish Independent* allegedly informing him he would 'tear his papers and report him to Larkin'.[51] A fine of twenty shillings, or an alternative of fourteen days imprisonment, was a harsh punishment, but worse was to come. On 23 September, the *Freeman's Journal* reported that two Dublin newsboys, aged 13 and 18 respectively, were punished with five years in Glencree Reformatory, in one case, and a month's imprisonment with hard labour in the other, for intimidating and physically assaulting a newsboy selling the *Irish Independent*. The paper reported that one of the boys denied the assault at first, before claiming it was one of 'Larkin's men' who put him up to it.[52]

William Martin Murphy discussed the situation regarding newsboys and his publications during the Askwith Inquiry. The inquiry, which had been instigated by the government, sought to establish the origins of the dispute and to find a solution. In October, Murphy claimed before the inquiry that newsboys who remained loyal to his publications had been attacked, as were newsagents which supplied the papers. When asked if sellers and newsagents were willing to display placards advertising the papers, he noted, 'all along the south side of the city the placards are shown now, but at the north side the people are still intimidated there to a large extent'.[53] The continuing loyalty of many young street traders to Larkin was evident from the consistent boycott of Murphy's publications during the bitter dispute.

Newsboys and the nationalist movement

There is evidence of individual Dublin newsboys being involved in the nationalist movement during the revolutionary period. While the Lockout had been a struggle involving the working class directly, nationalist movements, such as the Irish Volunteers and Sinn Féin were comprised of people of all social classes. Ernie O'Malley recalled in his memoirs that within his own IRA company, 'on my right in the ranks was a newsboy, a guttee, on my left an out of work, covering me in the rear rank was a Master of Arts, since professor of Romance languages, next to him a final medical'.[54] For many boys whose families depended on the pittance derived from selling papers, the 'national question' may have been a much less important motivation than their families basic survival.

On one occasion Ernie O'Malley visited the home of the young newsboy in his IRA company, an experience that evidently made an impact upon him:

> He lived in a tenement behind Marlborough Street. One night he said 'come on up.' Smells of bacon fat spiralling up insistently, the lingering decay of cabbage and a steady stench of sewage. I caught my breath in short, greasy coughs. Dirty paint hiccupped off the wall, banisters were splintered or broken away; 'for fuel', he said. Gaps in the wooden stairs, broken windows patched with cardboard or open to the rain, doors swung dully on lopsided hinges.[55]

No statement was given to the Bureau of Military History by any newsboys who participated in the national movement. Charles Donnelly, a member of the GPO garrison during the 1916 Rebellion, recalled a young newsboy being tasked with distributing copies of the Easter proclamation: 'He took a large bundle of same, and in less than an hour, came back holding his cap by the peak and the back, full of silver coins … I refused the money, telling him he was told to give them out free.' Hearing of the poverty of the young boy, who lived with his widowed mother and her children, Donnelly told him to bring the money back to his tenement home – the newsboy returned and joined the garrison the following day.[56]

Newsboys were willing to sell papers of many political hues during the revolutionary period. Darrell Figgis, in October 1922, raised the issue of republican newspapers being confiscated from Dublin newsboys in the Dáil, noting that he wanted:

> to ask the President if his attention had been drawn to the fact that all copies of last night's issue of *The Republic* were seized from the newsboys and destroyed, and if in view of the fact that the Government has not hitherto interfered with the publication of this sheet, and has not issued any Proclamation notifying that its sale was illegal, whether it is the

intention of the Government to compensate these lads and to issue a Proclamation for the future?[57]

The Belvedere Newsboys' Club

The most significant charity in the history of Dublin's newsboys emerged during the revolutionary period, in the form of the Belvedere Newsboys' Club. Established in 1918, the club provided for working-class inner-city Dubliners. Ironically, one of the founding members of the club, who would shape its policy and direction for many years afterwards, was Dr William Lombard Murphy, son of William Martin Murphy, who had clashed with Dublin newsboys in 1911 and 1913. William Lombard Murphy assumed control of his father's media interests following his passing in 1919, taking control of Independent Newspapers. The club, which was affiliated to the private Jesuit school, Belvedere College, provided shelter, food and a shared communal space. The Reverend Lambert McKenna SJ, noted at a 1922 meeting of the club that the lives of the young newsboys 'were very demoralising and unfitted them for anything that offered a definite livelihood in the future. The experience of the members of the club was that they were very amenable if taken in the right way'.[58]

By 1928 the Belvedere Newsboys' Club was operating from an impressive premises on Pearse Street and William Lombard Murphy noted at the opening of the new premises that 'Everyone who knows the Dublin newsboy knows what good qualities are to be found in him. He might not possess the greater civic virtues such as thrift and order and regularity, but he has immense loyalty to parents and an innate and essential decency of mind.'[59] A reflection of the regard the boys held William Lombard Murphy in was evidenced by the practice that those who worked at the club came to be known as 'Docs'. One newsboy, who availed of the Pearse Street facilities offered by the club, remembered that 'the Docs were the heroes of the newsboys who sold papers around the city centre'.[60]

Conclusion

Modern labour laws ensure that the barefooted newsboy are a thing of the past, yet, for a group who were once a sizeable body in Dublin and elsewhere, newsboys have gone largely unstudied. Some oral histories have survived, through the work of inner-city history societies, and the work of charitable organisations such as the Belvedere Newsboys' Club is well documented in the collections of the North Inner-City Folklore Project, a community history scheme in the heart of the capital. This chapter has shown that newsboys were evidently a significant ally to Larkin and the labour movement in Dublin during a period of heightened class tensions in the capital. That newsboys in Dublin and Derry modelled their own 'strikes' on those of their elders shows the influence of trade unionism on the popular consciousness of young workers in early twentieth-century Ireland. The lives of these children were incredibly difficult, both in terms of their working conditions and their living standards, with many hailing from the slums of the city. The historiography of the Lockout has primarily focused on children and the deprivation occasioned during the dispute; this chapter demonstrates that many adolescents were workers in their own right, capable of organising and taking militant action.

Endnotes

1   *The Irish Times*, 7 Mar. 1907, p. 7.

2   Alan J. Lee, *The Origins of the Popular Press in England, 1855–1914* (London: Croom Helm, 1976), p. 65.

3   Comment in *Temple Bar* (1885) cited in E.M. Palmegiano, *Perceptions of the Press in Nineteenth Century British Periodicals* (London: Anthem Press, 2013), p. 581.

4   Myles O'Loughlin, 'The Lot for Thrupence', *Dublin University Magazine*, 79 (Jan.–Jun. 1872), pp. 510–18; p. 511.

5   *The Irish Times*, 11 Oct. 1882, p. 6.

6   Jon Bekken, 'Newsboy Strikes' in Aaron Brenner, Benjamin Day, Immanuel Ness (eds), *The Encyclopedia of Strikes in American History* (New York: M.E. Sharpe, 2009), pp. 609–19; p. 609.

7   Carla King, 'Michael Davitt, the *Evening Telegraph* and Dublin Corporation, 1885–6', *Dublin Historical Record*, 60:2 (Autumn, 2007), pp. 196–207; p. 202.

8   Laurence Marley, *Michael Davitt: Freelance Radical and Frondeur* (Dublin: Four Courts Press, 2007), p. 222.

9   *The Nation*, 13 Dec. 1890, p. 5.

10 *The Nation*, 24 Oct. 1896, p. 8.

11 *The Irish Times,* 30 Dec. 1904, p. 8.

12 *The Irish Times*, 27 Dec. 1909, p. 7.

13 Ibid.

14 Joseph V. O'Brien, *Dear Dirty Dublin: A City in Distress, 1899–1916* (Berkeley: California University Press, 1982), p. 11.

15 Ibid.

16 Maria Luddy, 'Women and Philanthropy in Nineteenth-Century Ireland' in Kathleen D. McCarthy (ed.), *Women, Philanthropy and Civil Society* (Bloomington: University of Indiana Press, 2001), pp. 9–28; p. 24.

17   *The Irish Times,* 4 June 1903, p. 4.
18   *Irish Independent,* 5 Jan. 1905, p. 3.
19   Ibid.
20   Ibid.
21   Terry Fagan, *Dublin Tenements: Memories of Life in Dublin's Notorious Tenements* (Dublin: North Inner City Folklore Project, 2013), p. 182.
22   Census of Ireland, 1911. Digitised at www.census.nationalarchives.ie/pages/1911/.
23   Kate Cowan, 'The children have such freedom, I might say, such possession of the streets.' 'The Children of Dublin 1913', in Francis Devine (ed.), *A Capital in Conflict: Dublin City and the 1913 Lockout* (Dublin: Four Courts Press, 2013), pp. 129–43; p. 131.
24   *The Irish Times,* 11 Sept. 1907, p. 8.
25   *The Irish Times,* 18 Sept. 1907, p. 5.
26   Ibid.
27   *Donegal News,* 21 Sept. 1907, p. 8.
28   For an account of Larkin's early organising in Ulster, see, John Gray, *City in Revolt: James Larkin and the Belfast Dock Strike of 1907* (Belfast: Blackstaff Press, 1985).
29   Padráig Yeates, *Lockout: Dublin 1913* (Dublin: Gill & Macmillan, 2000), p. xxvi.
30   Emmet Larkin quoted in Peter Berresford Ellis, *A History of the Irish Working Class* (London: Pluto Press, 1996), p. 186.
31   John Newsinger, 'Jim Larkin and The Irish Worker' in Devine (ed.) *A Capital in Conflict: Dublin City and the 1913 Lockout* (Dublin: Four Courts Press, 2013), pp. 193–214; p. 193.
32   Yeates, *Lockout,* p. 9.
33   *The Irish Worker,* 26 Aug. 1911, p. 2.
34   *The Irish Times,* 11 Sept. 1907, p. 8.
35   *The Irish Times,* 19 Aug. 1907, p. 7.
36   *The Irish Times,* 18 Aug. 1907, p. 7.
37   Ian J. Cawood, *Britain in the Twentieth Century* (London: Routledge, 2004), p. 41.
38   *House of Commons Debates,* Fifth Series, Vol. 29, Cols. 2323–34, 22 Aug. 1911.
39   *The Irish Times,* 19 Aug. 1911, p. 8.
40   *The Irish Times,* 18 Sept. 1907, p. 5.
41   *The Irish Times,* 19 Aug. 1911, p. 8.
42   *The Irish Times,* 21 Aug. 1911, p. 9.
43   BMH WS 733 (James O'Shea), p. 2.
44   Ibid.
45   Ernie O'Malley, *On Another Man's Wound* (Dublin: Anvil, 1979) p. 24.
46   *The Irish Worker,* 26 Aug. 1911, p. 2.
47   *The Irish Worker,* 26 Aug. 1911, p. 2.
48   *The Irish Times,* 21 Aug. 1911, p. 5.
49   Yeates, *Lockout,* p. 8.
50   *Irish Independent,* 23 Aug. 1913, p. 5.
51   *Freeman's Journal,* 23 Sept. 1913, p. 10.

52 Ibid.
53 *The Irish Times*, 3 Oct. 1913, p. 10.
54 O'Malley, *On Another Man's Wound*, p. 53.
55 Ibid., p. 58.
56 BMH WS 824 (Charles Donnelly), p. 9.
57 Question raised in Dáil Éireann by Darrell Figgis T.D during Questions, 4 Oct. 1922. See *Dáil Éireann Debate* (1:17).
58 *The Irish Times*, 18 Nov. 1922, p. 8.
59 *The Irish Times*, 27 Nov. 1928, p. 9.
60 Fagan, *Dublin Tenements*, p. 179.

CHAPTER FOUR

American Social Reform and the Irish Question: An Irish-American Perspective on the 1913 Lockout

Meredith Meagher

The plight of the locked-out Dublin workers in 1913 challenged Irish-Americans to reconcile their traditional narrative concerning the Irish right to self-determination with more divisive issues concerning workers' rights and social progress. For those of Irish descent in the United States, class warfare in Dublin in 1913 threatened to contradict their traditional narrative that emphasised the historic struggle for self-determination of a united and long-oppressed Catholic community. As Irish-Americans historically framed 'the national question' within a paradigm that emphasised British subjugation and social injustice, the plight of the Dublin workers illuminated a less familiar and ideologically more problematic dimension to Irish political culture. The 1913 crisis unequivocally pitted Irish workers against their Irish masters, and for the first time, many of the Irish in the United States could relate to the industrial unrest in the nation they left behind through the prism of working conditions in America.

This chapter focuses on perceptions of the Lockout, immigration and home rule published in leading Irish-American nationalist newspapers, including Patrick Ford's constitutional nationalist newspaper, the *Irish World and American Industrial Liberator*, and its separatist, Fenian counterpart, the *Gaelic American*, edited by John Devoy; as well as the writings of James Connolly in the period preceding the crisis published in *The Harp*, the newspaper of the Irish Socialist Federation. All three papers were published in New York City and were aimed at an Irish-American audience. While Ford and Devoy represented the constitutional and physical force traditions respectively, the rhetoric of their newspapers shared many common assumptions regarding the Irish-American community and the Home Rule movement in Ireland. The *Irish World* was published between 1878 and 1958 and acted as a platform and support network for the Redmondite, United Irish League of America. Devoy's *Gaelic American* was published between 1903 and 1951 and served as the mouthpiece for the Fenian movement in both the United States and Ireland and espoused the traditional core values of the physical force tradition. Both papers emphasised the need for civic reform in Ireland throughout the Lockout and saw their role as promoting their own particular brands of Irish nationalism on the international stage. *The Harp* was published in New York and Dublin between January 1908 and June 1910 and reflected James Connolly's characteristic blend of socialism and republicanism. The paper frequently attacked the conservatism of traditional Irish nationalists in the United States while simultaneously appealing to their sense of ethnic pride.

Coverage of the Lockout in the United States

In April 1913, the *Freeman's Journal* pointed out in an article entitled 'America's debt to Ireland' that in terms of sheer numbers, the world's largest Irish cities were New York and Boston.[1] The Lockout gained significant attention in the United States with extensive coverage in the *New York Times*, the *San Francisco Tribune* and the *Detroit Free Press*, in particular.[2] *The Christian Science Monitor* undertook some of the most extensive coverage and published daily articles on the situation in Dublin that were largely sympathetic to the Irish workers.[3] In October 1913, James Larkin visited the London offices of the *Monitor* for an extensive interview. Larkin dismissed the notion that the Irish Parliamentary Party held any genuine interest in the needs of the Dublin workers and argued that the workers themselves must forgo their reliance on politicians (and publicans). Larkin told the *Monitor*, 'the Irish people have been described as happy-go-lucky. I should not describe them as happy-go-lucky; I should describe them as hopeless.' He continued, 'the next battle will be for education, and in learning self-respect, self-restraint, and self-reliance, they are undertaking the real resurrection of Ireland, for Ireland will eventually be freed and become a nation, through the efforts of her people to overcome their own failings, and not through the intrigues of politicians.'[4]

In contrast to the sympathetic tone of the *Monitor*, a *Washington Post* editorial in early September denied that the 'Dublin riots' related to issues pertaining to the Irish 'national question' and compared James Larkin and the Irish Transport and General Workers Union to Bill Haywood and the radical Industrial Workers of the World.[5] According to the *Post*, the fact that Larkin disguised himself to evade police and his association with the Scottish socialist and Labour MP, Keir Hardie, damaged his reputation and proved that 'the riots did not grow out of Irish politics, but a semi-political movement of more sinister design and execution than anything the liberals and unionists are accusing each other of conspiring to do. The Larkins court police brutality just as the Haywoods do, and for the same reason – to gain public sympathy.'[6]

In November 1913, Irish Parliamentary Party MP, T.P. O'Connor produced a series of articles about the Lockout for the *Chicago Tribune* which the *Irish World* subsequently reprinted.[7] As the only Irish Party MP to represent an English constituency (the Scotland Division in Liverpool), O'Connor enjoyed good relations with leading Liberal politicians and British trade union leaders, as well as being a member of the inner circle of the United Irish League in Britain, and a key fundraiser for the party in the US. O'Connor conceded that the 'horrors of labour conditions in Dublin', including substandard housing and malnutrition contributed to the 'unrest'. In mid-November, he claimed that Larkin's activities had 'produced such universal symptoms of unrest throughout the working classes as to seriously imperil the whole future of the Liberal program'. 'Politicians,' O'Connor claimed, 'had cause for grave reflections as socialists gained in popularity among the formidable shifting of the working class vote and the working class ideals.'[8] O'Connor objected, in particular, to Larkin's 'intemperate speech' and claimed his enthusiasm for radical syndicalism alienated him from 'sane' labour leaders in Ireland and England. Although conditions in Dublin 'impressed the national imagination', Larkin, O'Connor stressed, failed to distract the public from the important work of John Redmond, who had recently embarked on a speaking tour of England.[9]

Many American newspapers drew comparisons between Jim Larkin and Bill Haywood – the leading organiser of the Industrial Workers of the World. Haywood visited Ireland and England in November and December 1913 and spoke in Dublin, London, Manchester and Liverpool, sharing platforms with Larkin and Connolly, as well as leading English trade unionists.[10] In

December 1913, the *Irish Times* called Haywood 'The American Rebel' while the *Los Angeles Times* described Larkin as the 'Haywood of England'.[11] Haywood subsequently published an article about James Larkin in the *International Socialist Review*. First published in 1900, the Chicago-based monthly published articles written from members of various factions among American socialists.[12] Haywood recounted his speaking tour in England and his 'very instructive and interesting' tour of Dublin, praising, in particular, the efforts of Dora Montefiore, Delia Larkin and Lucille Rand to temporarily foster the children of Dublin's strikers with sympathetic families in England. In this respect, according to Haywood, the 'Dublin Kiddies Scheme' reflected the tactics of the IWW during recent strikes in Paterson, New Jersey and Lawrence, Massachusetts.[13]

The Irish World and The Gaelic American

By the 1890s the *Irish World* boasted 125,000 subscribers, along with 20,000 readers in Ireland, while by the turn of the century, the *Gaelic American* claimed a circulation of approximately 30,000.[14] Despite their divergent political traditions, Patrick Ford, the ardent home ruler, and John Devoy, the republican revolutionary, employed similar strategies to craft their own particular brands of Irish-American nationalism. As historian Edward T. O'Donnell has written, the *Irish World* represented the 'coming-of-age in Irish-American thought'.[15] The *Gaelic American* may also claim this distinction, however. Similar to Ford, Devoy continually emphasised the connections between the major contemporary social issues in the United States – education, labour unionism and business reform – to the challenges facing the Irish political establishment. In this respect, the constitutional and Fenian traditions in the United States were not distinct political ideologies and in the decades preceding the Lockout, the analysis presented in their respective newspapers shared many major assumptions.

In the spirit of the contemporary progressive era in American politics, both traditions within Irish-American political culture constructed a 'useable past' to link national histories of injustice and social deprivation with a contemporary agenda of social reform that allowed the 'exiled Irish' to achieve their civic and economic potential in the 'land of opportunity'.[16] Both the *Irish World* and the *Gaelic American* responded to the 1913 crisis by arguing that Irish self-government represented the only panacea to the issues connected with urban deprivation and emphasised the 'respectability' and competence that self-governance would introduce into Irish political culture.[17] Both newspapers downplayed the radical leadership of Jim Larkin and tended to divert their readers' attention to the perceived role of English misrule in exacerbating the conflict. Both editors employed commentary on the crisis that explicitly evoked allusions to the Great Famine, tenant evictions during the nineteenth century and so-called 'souperism'.[18]

Irish-American nationalism at the turn of the twentieth century reflected the deepest impulses of the age of progressive reform, as well as the inherent tensions that shaped the transatlantic politics of the Irish diaspora.[19] The Irish in America increasingly emphasised their self-identification as 'respectable citizens' who embraced 'New World Liberty' – in contrast to their rejection of the colonial excesses and inherent injustices of the 'Old World' they left behind.[20] Rooted in the philosophies of American pragmatist intellectuals, such as William James and John Dewey, American educators, urban planners and social workers studied the ideas and methods of their contemporaries in Europe and European models of governance increasingly influenced public policy and social service institutions in the United States.[21]

To avoid marginalisation in this era of progressive politics, Irish-Americans increasingly emphasised the centrality of Irish immigration to American national history. The wretched social conditions endured by Dublin's poor vividly exposed by the Lockout engaged the Irish-American social conscience, as they increasingly turned their gaze to the brutal industrial conflicts taking place in the United States. Class conflict in the United States in the opening decades of the twentieth century raised fundamental questions about the role of 'the immigrant' in American society while the conflict in Dublin revealed previously obscured contours to the national question in Ireland that could no longer be ignored. These twin political impulses influenced Irish-American nationalism in two fundamental ways. Firstly, it prompted Irish-Americans to embrace their identification by progressive-era politicians as an 'old immigrant' group who had proved themselves more respectable and willing to assimilate than the seemingly more problematic 'new immigrant' arrivals. Secondly, it helped inspire Irish-Americans to increasingly emphasise that Irish self-government was the only progressive solution to Ireland's social ills.

Both the *Irish World* and the *Gaelic American* mingled nationalist symbols that reflected American and Irish patriotism to emphasise the shared experience of historic struggle for independence from England. Ford, who served in the Union Army during the Civil War and fought in the Battle of Fredericksburg, regularly published articles on American military history, which he juxtaposed with the lyrics of contemporary Irish patriot ballads, such as Thomas Davis's, *A Nation Once Again.*[22] Likewise John Devoy frequently published articles championing the American constitutional political tradition and the endeavour of Irish-Americans in the Continental Army. By explicitly linking the inherent superiority of American progressivism with a shared history of resistance to English misrule, both editors helped establish a pattern for Irish-American political rhetoric for decades to come.

Through *Irish World*, Patrick Ford emphasised that home rule represented the ultimate realisation of the aptitude for independence and self-government that the Irish in America had demonstrated through the positive contributions they made to the American Republic since the eighteenth century. Patrick Ford was born in Galway in 1837, and emigrated to Boston with his family in 1845. In 1852, Ford began working for the abolitionist William Lloyd Garrison in the printing office of Garrison's radical newspaper, *The Liberator*. This launched his lifelong career as a journalist and editor. Ford established the *Irish World and American Industrial Liberator* in 1870. This weekly newspaper contained populist coverage of domestic and international news, educational articles pertaining to history and religion, as well as articles promoting various Irish American and Catholic causes. Ford collaborated with leading Fenians John Devoy and Jeremiah O'Donovan Rossa to launch a 'skirmishing fund' in the pages of the *Irish World* to finance militant Fenian activities in Britain in the 1870s, but fell out with Devoy over the use of the funds. He later orchestrated the American tours of Charles Stewart Parnell, John Dillon and Michael Davitt and launched 2,500 branches of the Land League in the United States between 1881 and 1882.[23]

Ford never returned to Ireland, but he nevertheless helped to develop a robust transnational political network through the United Irish League of America (UILA), with the *Irish World* acting as its mouthpiece. The UILA was founded in 1902 with the ambition to raise a 'million dollar fund' for home rule. Their rhetoric during the home rule crisis in 1912 emphasised the transnational importance of Irish independence and its significance as reprieve from political exile for Irish emigrants throughout the diaspora. In April 1912, following a mass home rule demonstration in Dublin attended by members of the UILA, Ford wrote, 'One felt with Mr Redmond that this, indeed, was Ireland. But it was not the languishing Ireland of sorrow; it was a proud, self-conscious Ireland. It was Ireland in her pride, Ireland in health. For one day at least, we were a nation.'[24] With

Home Rule officially on the statute books, albeit deferred for two years due to the veto powers of the House of Lords, the *Irish World* published letters of congratulations to John Redmond and the Irish Party from Theodore Roosevelt, along with dozens of United States Senators, Congressmen and diplomats.[25]

Although John Devoy excoriated the United Irish League of America and the *Irish World* in the pages of the *Gaelic American*, his experiences as a Fenian fugitive turned newspaper editor established his reputation as an embattled and cantankerous figure in transnational republican politics. He was born in 1841 in County Kildare, and joined the Irish Republican Brotherhood in 1861. He enlisted in the French Foreign Legion the same year, and was discharged in 1862 after serving in North Africa. After his discharge, he returned to Kildare to recruit for the IRB, and was tried and imprisoned for his Fenian activities between 1865 and 1871, when he was exiled from British territory.[26] He left for New York along with other leading Fenians, including Jeremiah O'Donovan Rossa, who were collectively known as the 'Cuba Five'.[27] In 1879 he met with Charles Stewart Parnell and Michael Davitt during a secret visit to Ireland to discuss a political alliance between his Clan na Gael organisation and the Parnellites. He would not return to Ireland for another forty-five years. In 1903, he assumed the editorship of the *Gaelic American* newspaper, which he used as his political anchor throughout the fractious history of Irish-American republican organising.[28]

With notable exceptions, United States immigration history has tended to overlook how immigrants in the nineteenth and early twentieth century maintained political connections with their homelands and integrated American political mores into their support for nationalist movements abroad.[29] Many historians have emphasised how progressive era reformers stifled the nationalist impulses of recently arrived immigrants in a climate of 'coercive Americanisation'.[30] Other scholars have traced the connections between this era of social reform with western imperialism, with perceived progressive intentions frequently used to justify the subjugation of non-white populations.[31] Yet, as the example of Irish-American nationalism suggests, both Patrick Ford and John Devoy argued that mass immigration from Ireland to the United States in the nineteenth century represented a crucial step towards achieving an Irish nationalist consciousness in the twentieth century. The upward mobility of the Irish in the US frequently underpinned the claim that social inequality was fundamentally a product of British rule in Ireland. In February 1913, a *New York Times* article reflected this notion in a report on a shortage of agricultural labourers in Ireland, the paper claimed, 'the steady stream of able-bodied Irishmen to America to become policemen, politicians and law-abiding thrifty citizens generally is proving very embarrassing to the big farmer and land owner of their native land'.[32]

'Foreign menaces' of socialism and anarchism

After two decades of peak immigration, the 1910 United States census reported approximately 13.5 million foreign-born respondents, representing 14.6 per cent of the total population. The majority of the approximately 23 million 'new immigrants' who emigrated between 1880 and 1920 arrived from southern and eastern Europe, and frequently encountered mistrust for their perceived sympathies for the 'foreign menaces' of socialism and anarchism.[33] In 1911, under the auspices of the congressional Dillingham Commission, the United States Federal government attempted to grapple with the 'immigration problem' and developed a novel distinction between 'old' and 'new' immigration in a 'Dictionary of Races or Peoples'. This transnational sociological study examined the national origins of European immigrants and characterised their political behaviour in the United States. The final report of the Dillingham Commission depicted Irish-Americans as more compatible with the values of American democracy than 'new immigrant' groups, who, it was claimed, frequently demonstrated a dangerous enthusiasm for radical labour organisations and a proclivity for socialism and anarchism. The report concluded that the United States must establish limits on immigration because of the social and political risks posed by the 'new' immigrants and supported the exclusion of Asian immigrants in its final recommendations.[34]

Both Ford and Devoy seized upon popular contemporary prejudices and characterisations of immigrant life in the United States and incorporated similar motifs into their political commentary. They lived through a period of unprecedented immigration between 1880 and 1920 and shared the common popular distaste for social radicalism. The *Gaelic American* and the *Irish World* criticised other 'newer' immigrant groups for their perceived 'subversive sympathies' and published anti-Semitic conspiracy theories pertaining to supposed Jewish control of global finance.[35] The political rhetoric employed by Ford and Devoy was frequently underpinned by the notion of a continuous upward trajectory of socioeconomic attainment by respectable, upwardly mobile Irish-American citizens.[36] These comparisons between 'old' and 'new' waves of immigration reinforced an Irish reputation for respectability and patriotism. The Dillingham Commission concluded that European immigration was 'largely a migration from country to city of people who are unfamiliar with urban conditions' and unprepared for the expectations of American citizenship.[37] In the *Irish World,* Irish-American journalists argued that the Irish assimilated into the American political landscape more successfully than the 'new' immigrants. In a March 1912 article on a strike of textile workers in Lawrence, Massachusetts, Robert Ellis Thompson claimed that recently arrived 'Hebrew', Russian, Polish and Italian immigrants 'are very often imbued with socialist and anarchist opinions, and come to America with entire readiness to overthrow the industrial and political order of the country'.[38] By contrast, Thompson claimed, the Irish and 'old German' workers conformed to American values and represented a model for other immigrants. Thompson claimed that widespread illiteracy among southern Italians hindered their assimilation into American society and explained their enthusiasm for the 'simplification of government' offered by socialists 'of all shades and degrees of inflection'.[39]

Mindful of contemporary anxieties about the role of the immigrant in American society, both Ford and Devoy struggled to find examples of progressive ingenuity in the Irish capital and Dublin consistently failed to captivate American social and political reformers in the same way as many other major European cities. Dublin's inadequate sewage systems and collapsing tenements, in particular, failed to inspire American progressives as models of civic innovation in the same way as Glasgow's city-owned streetcars or London's philanthropic housing companies.[40] As Pádraig Yeates has noted, 'at the beginning of the twentieth century Dubliners shared little of the confidence and municipal pride that existed among even the poorest working-class denizens of other cities, including Belfast'.[41] To explain away such obvious social and municipal deficiencies, both Ford and Devoy tended to point the finger of blame firmly at the inefficiencies and excesses of British rule as the root cause of Dublin's myriad social problems.

James Connolly and Elizabeth Gurley Flynn

In contrast to the rhetoric of the *Irish World* and the *Gaelic American* some Irish labour leaders in the US reflected more positively on the implications of European immigration for the American labour movement.[42] Both James Connolly and Elizabeth Gurley Flynn merged conventional labour radicalism with emotive appeals to the ethnic nationalism of immigrant workers, while urging them to simultaneously transcend the exclusivity of their ethnic identity and actively embrace the values of the wider American proletariat. In this respect, Connolly's experience in American was formative in helping shape his thinking regarding the synthesis of nationalism and socialism in Ireland.

Before returning to Ireland in 1910, Connolly warned Irish-Americans in his monthly newspaper, *The Harp*, to beware of 'invertebrate Irish American politicians who cynically brandished their ancestry in time for Election Day'.[43] Emphasising their traditional role as stalwarts of the Democratic Party, Connolly implored Irish-American workers to reject their 'aggressive insularity' and recognise their shared struggles with, 'that Polack, whose advent in the workshop you are taught to view with such disfavour'.[44] Connolly distributed *The Harp* in New York under the banner of the Irish Socialist Federation (ISF) an organisation he established in co-operation with Irish-American radicals. In the inaugural issue of *The Harp* published in January 1908, Connolly outlined the international and universalist Declaration of Principles of the Irish Socialist Federation,

> The Irish Socialist Federation is composed of members of the Irish race in America, and is organised to assist the revolutionary working-class movement in Ireland by a dissemination of its literature, to educate the working-class Irish of this country into a knowledge of Socialist principles and to prepare them to co-operate with the workers of all other races, colours and nationalities in the emancipation of labour.[45]

In his editorials, Connolly rejected the existence of 'pure races', and encouraged his readers to reflect on the commonalities amongst immigrant workers. He applied this principle to his version of Irish nationalism, writing in January 1908 that 'the modern Irish race is a composite blending – on the original Celtic stock have been grafted shoots from all the adventurous races of the continent'.[46]

Connolly co-founded the ISF with his neighbour from the tenements of the South Bronx, Elizabeth Gurley Flynn – frequently referred to in labour publications as 'the girl orator of the Bowery'. Flynn adopted Connolly's blend of traditional Irish republicanism and doctrinal socialism as an organiser for the Industrial Workers of the World and made sympathetic appeals to the ethnic nationalism of immigrant workers despite her own anarchistic sympathies. She was born in 1890 in New Hampshire. Her mother, Anne

Gurley emigrated from the Loughrea district to Boston in 1877; her father, Thomas Flynn, was born to Irish immigrants living in Maine in 1859. Her father was an itinerant cartographer during her youth, bringing her into contact with the everyday brutalities of America's industrial centres. Her family settled in a grim cold-water flat in Mott Haven, in the South Bronx in 1900, and the family first came into contact with James Connolly in 1907 when he was organising workers in the Singer Sewing Machine Company in Newark, New Jersey. Her parents imbued her with a devotion to Irish separatism and an appreciation for Irish participation in American labour organisations, including the Knights of Labor and the Western Federation of Miners.

As a teenager, Gurley attended meetings organised by German socialists eager to attract their English-speaking neighbours.[47] At 16, she delivered her first lecture to the Harlem Socialist Club (on women and socialism) and was first arrested (for lecturing without a permit and blocking traffic on Broadway). After her encounter with radical socialism in the tenements, her 'horizons broadened, beyond the South Bronx and the struggle for Irish freedom'.[48] In his folk anthem dedicated to Elizabeth Gurley Flynn, Joe Hill, the bard for the Industrial Workers of the World, wrote that 'The only and thoroughbred Lady is the Rebel Girl.' As Hill's lyric suggests, Flynn simultaneously challenged notions of femininity and American citizenship through her radical politics.[49] She exemplified the tensions within the American labour movement at the time, especially the challenge of realising the IWW ideal of 'One Big Union'. In April 1908, the New York Times described Flynn as the 'Anarchistic Joan of Arc', and claimed the appealing spectacle of her soapbox speeches transcended lines of ethnicity, class and sex.[50]

During the spring and summer of 1913, Flynn helped the IWW organise 25,000 striking textile workers and their families in the 'Silk City' of Paterson, New Jersey. After factory owners staged a Flag Day and festooned the city with stars and stripes (one of the main exports of Paterson's textile mills) in order to appeal to the patriotism of their workers, the strikers carried signs that read, 'we wove the flag, we dyed the flag, we live under the flag, but we won't scab under the flag!' In June, the strikers paraded with American flags to Madison Square Garden where an estimated 1,000 strikers re-enacted the events of the strike and sang labour anthems in English, German and Italian.[51] Flynn regarded the Paterson strike as a failure, echoing many who witnessed the Dublin Lockout. It ended on July 29 1913, with a shop-by-shop settlement restricting negotiations to the individual mills. In a

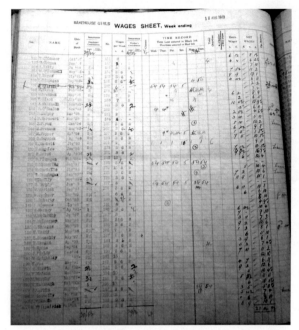

A page from the Wages Book of Jacob's Biscuit factory with an entry for Rosie Hackett, Number 169. She earned 9s for a six-day week. Contrary to popular myth she did not work in the factory in 1911 or lead the women's strike of that year. (National Archive of Ireland)

ICA veterans taking part in the 1916 Commemoration thought to be in the 1950s. The man at the front beside the flag bearer is Captain Christopher Poole, who was second in command of St Stephen's Green garrison in 1916. (Courtesy of Michael Poole)

Photograph of the Irish Citizen Army Pipe Band:

Standing at back , from left:- Pipe Major P. Lawlor, J.Crimmins, G. Campbell, Christy ? (known as Dead Meat), Robert de Coeur (in uniform of Irish Citizen Army), Jack Murphy , ? Carroll, Dan King, unknown, unknown, E.Tuke.
Seated at front: Ned Mallon, F. McCabe. (Young boy unknown)

The man in the background standing between the fourth and fifth band member from the left is Bob de Coeur. He was one of the earliest putative founders of the Irish Citizen Army. He organised a group of ITGWU members, armed with hurleys, to protect the band from the police attacks during the early days of the Lockout. Note the traditional Irish costumes adopted by band members. Over half of them participated in the Easter Rising. (Courtesy of Fintan Lalor Pipe Band)

COLLAPSE OF THE BRIDGE.

PEACE—" And I was just about to cross over!"

Reinstatement of ITGWU members locked out in 1913, and members of other trade unions who came out in sympathy with them, was something the employers never conceded. Distance sometimes lent perspective. 'Spex', or John Fergus O'Hea, was a London-based artist whose cartoons tended to be more detached than those of Dublin contemporaries. (Dublin City Library Archive)

(4) Number four is called William, the lion of the hour;
Either tram-tracks, or Corots, or strikes he'll devour.

(6) Six is Jim the white elephant, that breaks each contract,
And all things knocks down with which he's in contact.

William Martin Murphy and Jim Larkin depicted as a Lion and White Elephant respectively by S. H. Y.

The trade union pest metamorphosed from obstreperous worker to insect, by S.H.Y.

Jim Larkin as 'an old patched up gas-bag' by S.H.Y., Frank Reynolds, who regularly supplied cartoons to the *Leprachaun*. This humorous magazine sought to present a neutral stance during the Lockout but lampooned Labour leaders to a much greater degree than their opponents. (All images this page courtesy of Dublin City Library Archive)

In Dublin we have a balloon,
With ambitions as high as the moon;
It's a patched-up affair,
Full of bad gas and air—
'Twill burst, we believe, very soon.

'The Real Strikers' of the DMP and RIC depicted by 'Spex' shocked visitors such as Liberal MP Handel Booth and British Labour leaders such as George Barnes and James Seddon. Support for the Dublin strikers in Britain was as much due to revulsion at the brutality of the police and vindictiveness of the employers as to any sympathy for Larkin's syndicalist message.

THE REAL STRIKERS

On August 30 and 31 the Dublin Metropolitan Police and the R. I. Constabulary ran "amok" in the City of Dublin. Result: Two men batoned to death and several hundred men, women and children badly beaten, whose ages range from one week to ninety years.

"DEAR, DIRTY DUBLIN."
WANTED A PUBLIC HEALTH DEPARTMENT.

This cartoon by 'Fitz', Thomas Fitzpatrick, predates the Lockout by five years but eloquently identifies the civic inertia that was a breeding ground for social unrest as well as disease. (All images this page courtesy of Dublin City Library Archive)

When the crew on one Guinness barge repeatedly refused to handle 'tainted goods' delivered by strike breakers they were dismissed. James Connolly wrote to Ernest Guinness seeking the reinstatement of two men with sixteen children and forty years' service between them. Guinness was inclined to accede to the request but his father, Lord Iveagh, decided the men must serve as examples of the price of insubordination. (Diageo Archive, Guinness Archive)

Helena Molony was a leading figure in the Lockout and early years of the Labour and Women's movements but lived long enough to be deeply disillusioned by the Irish Free State that followed the struggle for independence. (Courtesy of Irish Congress of Trade Unions)

The Lockout revolutionised commercial transport in Dublin. The Guinness Brewery was not involved in the dispute, but it led the way in mechanising its fleet when many of its haulage subcontractors could not provide a service because they had locked out carters who were members of the ITGWU. One truck could do the work of nine horse-drawn vehicles. It marked the beginning of the end for the traditional carter with his horse and dray. (Guinness Archive, Diageo Archive)

The vast majority of school children went to work by the time they were 14, and thousands left much earlier. A Catholic Working Boys Technical Aid Association was established in 1914 but there was little uptake for classes because many youngsters were too tired to attend after work. (Dublin City Library Archive)

A Night School for Working Boys,

WILL OPEN

ON MONDAY, 29th SEPTEMBER, 1913,

At Boys' Schoolroom, Exchange Street,

At Half-past Seven o'clock.

The Committee desire to inform Parents and Guardians of boys, who may be engaged at work during the day, or who from various other reasons cannot attend day schools, that this School is organised specially to give them the benefit of an education they would not otherwise receive.

The Classes will begin at half-past seven each evening, at which time boys are requested to be ready to start work, and will terminate at ten o'clock.

These Schools will be lighted and heated, and this very fact should be an inducement to boys to attend regularly, as the Classes will be held during the winter months.

The School is free of charge, and is for boys living in the Parishes of SS. Michael and John, Exchange Street, and St. Audeon's, High Street ; it is carried on under the supervision of members of St. Audeon's and SS. Michael and John's Conferences.

No boy under 14 years of age will be admitted, but any person over 14 may attand.

Remember the School opens on Monday night, 29th September, at half-past seven o'clock, at which time a large attendance is expected.

MONEY PRIZES will be distributed for good attendance.

Re-enactors on O'Connell Street during State Commemoration in August 2013. (Courtesy of SIPTU)

Bottles of Guinness graced the managers' dining hall at St James's Gate. Jobs in the brewery were eagerly sought across all occupations because of the superior conditions. Larkin recruited less than 20 per cent of the 2,500-strong workforce and refused to bring them out, or call for a boycott of its beverage. Although he was a teetotaller he knew that both would be counterproductive. (Diageo Archive, Guinness Archive)

William Martin Murphy was not a popular figure during the Lockout. He was burned in effigy in some slum areas, provided with police protection, and targeted in placards such as this, after he declared that 'Larkin must go' from the leadership of the ITGWU before the dispute could be settled. (Courtesy of the National Library of Ireland)

speech to the New York Civic Club Forum the following January, Flynn described, 'English-speaking conservative elements' in the strike committee as a 'complicating factor' who strained finances and morale. On the Dublin Lockout, Flynn displayed an uncharacteristic naivety,

> In Ireland today there is a wonderful strike going on and they are standing it beautifully. Why? Because they have had half a million dollars since the thirty-first of August (five months) given into the relief fund, and every man that goes on the picket line has food in his stomach and some kind of decent clothes on his back.[52]

The *Irish World* emphasised the inherent compatibility between Irish and American social values, focusing on shared ideals of hard work, as well as a commitment to equality, individual liberty and upward mobility. In contrast to the radicalism of Connolly and Flynn, the *Irish World* showcased the work of respectable and professional Irish-American social reformers in New York City. In August 1913, the *Irish World* featured an illustrated article on Irish-born, Sarah W.H. Christopher, or 'The Fire Lady of New York'. The City Fire Commissioner appointed Christopher as a fire inspector in the wake of the Triangle Shirtwaist Factory Fire in Lower Manhattan in March 1911. After factory owners locked the stairwells and factory doors, 146 garment workers, mostly immigrant women, perished as they attempted to escape a blaze on the shop floor.[53] In order to prevent similar catastrophes, Christopher taught factory workers municipal safety requirements and evacuation procedures. The *Irish World* reported, 'without any word of the vote' Christopher was able to 'stand on her own' and contribute to 'civic welfare' because of her Irish lineage. Through her impeccable expertise in municipal policy and her aversion to the women's suffrage movement, the *Irish World* insinuated that Christopher proved herself an ardent Irish nationalist noting, 'the first thing that greets the visitor is the flag of Erin upon the walls of her living room'.[54]

Cian McMahon has noted that the Irish-American press often identified avarice as the lowest common denominator of British oppression.[55] The *Irish World* frequently emphasised the perceived machinations of Ulster Unionists and other 'Anglo-American conspiracies' in obstructing progressive social change while fuelling social division in Ireland. In January 1913, the newspaper featured a front-page illustration with the caption, 'Who Wants Equality?' The cartoon depicted a portly Ulster Orangeman seated at the table at a modest Irish cottage, devouring hot soup from a bowl emblazoned with the Union Jack. Erin, characterised as an emaciated mother, looks on as she cradles her four children, Leinster, Munster, Connacht and Ulster – the latter held closest to her bosom.[56]

Irish-American impressions of the Lockout

The *Irish World* frequently focused its ire on the international philanthropy of steel magnate, Andrew Carnegie. The paper published numerous articles criticising the Carnegie Endowments for International Peace and attacking the summit meetings they sponsored with representatives from the major international powers. Carnegie impeded Irish nationalism, the paper claimed, as it compromised the patriotism of American and Irish workers. Carnegie famously spent his fortune funding 2,811 public libraries throughout the English-speaking world.[57] According to the *Irish World*, Carnegie's endeavours inspired an alarming level of pro-British feeling among elected officials and ordinary American citizens alike 'in a grand rush for Carnegie's gold'.[58] In May 1913, the paper published an interview with German émigré and Harvard Psychology Professor, Hugo Muensterberg, who attended a Carnegie Endowment's conference in New York City on the subject of 'Anglo-American Peace'. Referring to the conference organisers, Muensterberg stated that despite their emphasis on British connections with the United States, 'in their heart they know that *all Europe* is the Mother Country, and that English and Irish, Germans and Swedes, and all stand at the same level'.[59] The influx of Carnegie's cash, the *Irish World* claimed, polluted American democracy by supporting Anglo-American diplomatic alliances. This represented nothing less, the paper claimed, than the denigration of Irish-American demands for Irish self-government, as well as the downplaying of the contribution of Irish-Americans to American history and society.[60]

Early reports about the Lockout in the *Irish World* claimed that the dispute held 'no political significance', because striking workers and business owners alike, including William Martin Murphy, supported Irish self-government. Con O'Leary, a native of Cork and the Ireland correspondent for the *Irish World*, maintained that unionists and the 'Tory Press' conspired to distort the facts of the Lockout, in order to 'prejudice home rule'. The paper assured Irish-Americans that 'nationalists view the situation in different ways, inclining to one side or the other, or holding themselves neutral, just as persons would act in any city in the world in similar circumstances'.[61]

The *Irish World* portrayed the Lockout as a threat to the future of Home Rule and to the delicate political coalition that sustained it and threatened to undermine the image of the Irish Parliamentary Party crafted by their editors. The paper contrasted the actions of the ITGWU with the perceived reputation that 'home rulers' in the United States cultivated as respectable, law-abiding 'citizens-in-waiting' who would rely on legislative and constitutional measures to address their nationalist grievances. As Con O'Leary put it at the end of November 1913, 'the dark cloud over Dublin depresses us all, especially when we need our capital to be in prosperity as the great national foil to Belfast and to be ready to take her place as the metropolis of the Irish race under Home Rule'.[62]

As the situation grew more desperate for striking workers, O'Leary and other correspondents for the *Irish World* acknowledged the consequences of the Lockout for the Home Rule campaign. In a November 1913 column entitled 'Industrial Conflict' Robert Ellis Thompson mused, 'the present year has been a period of conflict of Labor and Capital throughout a large part of the civilised world'. According to Thompson, both the strikers and the Dublin business owners had 'managed [the strike] in a clumsy way'. The indictment of James Larkin for 'using seditious language' seemed to him 'a page out of the earlier doings of Dublin Castle'. In Thompson's estimation, Asquith displayed weakness in its handling of the unions in Ireland and England, and placed the Liberal majority – and therefore Home Rule – in jeopardy.[63] Thompson compared the actions of the Dublin Metropolitan Police toward the workers to the attitudes of law enforcement officials in Paterson, New Jersey during the silk-workers strike the previous summer.[64] As for the ITGWU, the paper claimed they 'evaded the law' by halting transportation services in Dublin, and failed to understand that 'no mechanical contrivance will suffice to solve moral problems'.[65]

The *Irish World* identified exploitative industrial capitalism and Anglo-American friendship as the greatest threat to Irish independence. 'Exposés' of Carnegie, labelled by the *Irish World*, the 'prince of Anglo-Manicdom' accompanied accounts of the 'Dublin tram car strike', in September 1913. Carnegie's 'million dollar conspiracy' paralleled the machinations of the well-heeled leaders of Ulster Unionism and elements among the Conservative Party who, the paper claimed, 'utilised' the Lockout to their political advantage.[66] On 7 September, the first *Irish World* editorial on the Lockout warned readers to treat reports from the Associated Press with suspicion as 'The Tories and Unionists are in control of the news service, which is exaggerating all accounts of the troubles between the employers and the employees, and are trying to make a huge profit out of the encounters between police and strike sympathisers.'[67] An illustrated historical article on the same page told of Andrew Carnegie's brutality toward striking United Steel Company workers during an industrial dispute in Homestead, Pennsylvania in July 1892, considered one of the most serious labour disputes in American history. Carnegie refused to recognise the Amalgamated Iron and Steel Workers and his company contracted the Pinkerton National Detective Agency to provide private security. The paper reminded its readers, 'the Pinkerton thugs, armed with Winchester rifles, promptly set to do their master's bidding. As a result the sun rose on the seventh day July, 1892, not to rise and greet an Anglo-American Union, but to witness the bodies of American workmen strewn along the banks of the Monongahela River – The Victims of Carnegie's Greed for Gold.'[68]

In contrast to the *Irish World*, John Devoy's republican *Gaelic American* newspaper placed the action of the locked-out workers within the republican tradition of an armed citizenry with an emphasis on translating popular dissatisfaction into civic participation and political reform.[69] Devoy argued that the actions of the Dublin Corporation and the Metropolitan Police represented an affront to the dignity of Dublin's citizens and demanded independent inquiries into the behaviour of the police. In his weekly front-page report from Dublin, Belfast Fenian Bulmer Hobson, frequently described the Lockout as 'inevitable', considering the long-standing wage stagnation, substandard housing and the high cost of living in Dublin.[70] On 27 September, the paper reprinted an open letter from Thomas Clarke, later one of the executed leaders of the 1916 Rising, to the Dublin newspapers in which he condemned 'Dublin Castle and its idea of Law and Order'. Clarke described the social conditions that he observed during his time in Belfast, New York City and 'London's underworld', where he witnessed clashes between the police and the public – including a fight between 'Bowery hooligans and the New York Police'. The Dublin Metropolitan Police, Clarke claimed, behaved with 'downright, inhuman savagery', as they bludgeoned strikers on the streets and 'wrecked the homes of some of our citizens'. Clarke concluded that the people of Dublin must demand an independent inquiry into actions of the DMP, rather than any investigation sponsored by Dublin Castle in 'the interests of the city, the lives and property of the citizens – not to speak of national dignity and the dictates of common humanity'.[71]

The *Gaelic American* extensively covered a mass meeting on 11 January 1914 on O'Connell Street to demand a citizen's inquiry into the events surrounding the crisis.[72] The coverage of the Lockout petered out in the weeks to follow replaced by coverage of the growth of the Irish Volunteers, under headlines such as 'to organise and protect liberties'.[73] With this emphasis on self-reliance and the failure of state-sponsored institutions, the *Gaelic American* sought to expose well-heeled philanthropists in Dublin as agents of British subjugation of the Irish people. After Bloody Sunday 1913, they focused their ire on Ishbel Hamilton-Gordon, or Lady Aberdeen, the former President of the International Council for Women and prominent Dublin philanthropist.[74] Lady Aberdeen worked with her husband, John Campbell Gordon, Lord Lieutenant of Ireland, on a variety of social issues in Dublin, including public health programmes and intervention in industrial disputes. In an article entitled 'Police-Made Riots in Dublin' Devoy ridiculed the activities of Lady Aberdeen and her 'nincompoop husband' during the clash between strikers and the police on O'Connell Street on Bloody Sunday 1913. As the Viceregal Lodge hosted 'distinguished nonentities from England' and other 'visiting swells', Lord Aberdeen, the *Gaelic American* claimed, dispatched the DMP to 'maim and murder unoffending citizens'.[75]

The *Gaelic American's* contempt for Lady Aberdeen contrasted with the warm treatment she received in the *New York Times* the same month. The *Sunday Magazine* ran an illustrated feature on Elizabeth Burchenal, a New York City schoolteacher who travelled to Dublin as a guest of Lady Aberdeen. The previous August, she arrived in Ireland to instruct 500 Irish schoolteachers in folk dancing. Burchenal reflected many contemporary female middle-class reformers and as the executive secretary of the Girls' Branch of the Public Schools Athletic League she organised mass dance lessons for an estimated 7,000 New York City schoolchildren and teachers in Central Park.[76] On the subject of the Dublin Lockout, the *Times* quoted a wistful Burchenal, 'people used to say they wished the strike sufferers could have come in and got cheered up. Really I think it would have cheered up anybody'.[77]

The *Gaelic American* continued to deride Lady Aberdeen's endeavours in philanthropy and social reform throughout the dispute, referring to 'Her Tuberculosian Ladyship', and Devoy satirised her new project, the Welcoming Club, as an outgrowth of her 'fake Health Organisation'. She hoped, the paper claimed, that 'Irish-American millionaire toadies' would finance her charitable endeavours and realise, 'England's fostering care of the Irish people and its consistent promotion of Irish industries.' Similar to when the *Gaelic American* likened Lady Aberdeen to their rivals in the Irish Parliamentary Party knew in her 'ability to open the American breeches pocket or tap the American till is the supreme test of Irish leadership'. One article attacked Lady Aberdeen's supposed condescension towards visiting Irish-Americans, noting that it was up to Lady Aberdeen to explain 'the evictions and the clearances that were the instruments through which the British Providence worked to make the Irish people happy and turn them into millionaires in America'.[78]

Irish-American nationalists sustained political and familial connections between the United States and Ireland and developed an expectation that an independent and republican Ireland would somehow encompass the diaspora, and offer some form of redemption from the challenges of emigration. Yet, this period of solidarity was ultimately followed by a period of fracture and alienation over the role of the Irish diaspora in an independent Ireland. The transmission of American capital across the Atlantic in support of Irish nationalists shaped thinking throughout the diaspora regarding the social question, and American money was to play an immense role throughout the revolutionary period.

The United Irish League of America began to unravel at the end of 1913, with the deaths of its chief fundraiser, John O'Callaghan, and its leading publicist, Patrick Ford.[79] The *Irish World* eulogised Ford in October 1913 for awakening, 'Irish-America to a consciousness of itself as a separate entity', and for incorporating the Irish question into American politics and for drumming up political support for Home Rule in the US.[80] The deaths of O'Callaghan and Ford offered a point of reflection for conservative Irish nationalists in the US and coincided with the escalation of the activities of more militant republicans led by John Devoy. In early 1914, Devoy and Clan na Gael launched a series of fundraising campaigns for organisations in Ireland, firstly for Patrick Pearse's, St Enda's College Fund, and later to provide arms and supplies for the Irish Volunteers. Each week, the paper published the names of contributors, listed according to the amount they donated. The fundraising pivoted on lectures by key figures in Irish republicanism, including Roger Casement and Pearse himself. During his tour of America from February to April 1914, Pearse told his American audiences that Irish independence represented a 'pathway to necessary and practical social reforms in education, governance, and the workplace'.[81]

On 28 February 1914, the *Gaelic American* published an article praising St Enda's for 'its broad literary program, its courses in manual training, and, in short, its linking of the practical with the ideal at every stage of its work. We are convinced that we are training useful citizens for a free Ireland, and we believe further that we are kindling in our pupils something of the old spiritual and heroic enthusiasm of the Gael.'[82] This republican emphasis on the link between education and citizenry reverberated across Irish-American nationalist circles and complemented their focus on 'respectability' as an indicator of upward mobility. It also highlights the importance of fundraising in the emerging milieu of Irish-American nationalism.

Conclusion

A number of historians have highlighted the links between the 1913 Lockout and the Easter Rising, as 1913 crisis helped radicalise urban workers and highlighted the need for political change and municipal reform.[83] Yet, the Irish-American reaction to the 1913 Lockout and contemporaneous labour disputes in the US suggests that notions of the 'rising respectability' and upward mobility of Irish-Americans in the face of industrial unrest, dominated the analysis of Irish-American events in Dublin. Both the *Irish World* and the *Gaelic American* facilitated political and financial connections between nationalists in Ireland and in the United States and engendered a developing sense of interdependence between communities and events on both sides of the Atlantic. The coverage in the *Irish World* and in the *Gaelic American* emphasised the brutality of events in Dublin and conjured uneasy associations between the 'old world' and the 'new' and challenged Irish-American perceptions about the role of social class and the meaning of nationhood.

Both the republican and nationalist traditions in the United States avoided the uncomfortable realities of the Dublin Lockout. The *Irish World* and the *Gaelic American* shared a common strain of analysis that identified British misgovernment as the root cause of the exceptional poverty in Dublin. Both journals shared the assumption that home rule would prevent such economic disputes and that independence would remedy the grievances of the poor. Their focus on 'Anglo-American conspirators' such as Lady Aberdeen and Andrew Carnegie reinforced the notion that social conflict in Ireland had alien origins. In contrast to John Devoy and Patrick Ford, James Connolly and the Irish Socialist Federation chose to place Irish-American workers within the perspective of an international proletariat, rather than emphasise the exceptionalism of the Irish in America. Connolly sought to appeal to Irish nationalist sentiments as he emphasised the union of all workers from across America's ethnic spectrum, to include 'new immigrants' and 'old immigrants' alike. Thus, while the Lockout signalled a moment of introspection, ultimately, the analysis in traditional Irish-American newspapers avoided uncomfortable analysis of the social chasms that events in Dublin 1913 graphically exposed, in pursuit of a historical narrative that focused on the extraordinary upward social mobility of the Irish in the United States – an enduring notion of Irish-American prosperity that persists to the present day.

Endnotes

1   'America's debt to Ireland', *Freeman's Journal*, 4 Apr. 1913, cited in Joseph P. Finnan, *John Redmond and Irish Unity*, (Syracuse: Syracuse University Press, 2004), p. 164.

2   For example, see 'Dublin strikers rioting', *New York Times*, 31 Aug. 1913; 'Dublin strike marked by fierce rioting', *Atlanta Constitution*, 31 Aug. 1913; 'Fierce riot in Dublin streets', *Boston Daily Globe*, 1 Sept. 1913; 'Hundreds injured as strikers riot in Dublin streets', *Detroit Free Press*.

3   Rennie B. Schoeplin, 'Christian Science' in Paul Boyer (ed.) *Oxford Companion to United States History* (Oxford: Oxford University Press, 2001).

4   'One hope for Ireland held out by Dublin labour leader', *Christian Science Monitor*, 9 Oct. 1913.

5   'Dublin riot promoters', *Washington Post*, 2 Sept. 1913.

6   Ibid.

7   Owen McGee, 'O'Connor, Thomas Power' in *Dictionary of Irish Biography*.

8   Thomas Power, T. P. O'Connor, 'Larkin as factor in Home Rule', *Chicago Tribune*, 16 Nov. 1913.

9   'Home Rule Bill Gains Steadily, Says O'Connor', *Chicago Tribune*, 24 Nov. 1912.

10   'Larkin in Manchester', *Irish Times*, 22 Nov. 1913; 'Mr. Larkin's welcome at Liverpool', *Manchester Guardian*, 2 Dec. 1913.

11   'Larkin in Liverpool', *Irish Times*, 6 Dec. 1913; 'Strikes and strikers of this busy world', *Los Angeles Times*, 18 Jan. 1914.

12   Melvyn Dubofsky, 'Haywood, William Dudley' in *American National Biography*.

13   William D. Haywood, 'Jim Larkin's call for solidarity', *International Socialist Review*, xiv, 8 (Feb. 1914), pp. 469–74; See also: Caroline Nelson, 'Jim Larkin', *International Socialist Review*, xiv, 6 (Dec. 1913), pp. 335–7; William E. Bohn, 'The fiery Cross in England and Ireland', *International Socialist Review*, xiv, 7 (Jan. 1914), pp. 389–91; William D. Haywood, *The Autobiography of William D. Haywood* (New York: International Publishers, 1929), pp. 272–4.

14   Edward T. O'Donnell, 'Though not an Irishman, Henry George and the American Irish', *American Journal of Economics and Sociology*, lvi, 4, (Oct. 1997), pp. 407–19; p. 409.

15   O'Donnell, 'Though not an Irishman', pp. 407–19.

16   Kathleen Sprows-Cummings, *New Women of the Old Faith: Gender and American Catholicism in the Progressive Era* (Chapel Hill: University of North Carolina Press, 2009), pp. 17–58.

17   On the notion of respectability in Irish-American nationalism, see James P. Rodechko, 'An Irish-American journalist and Catholicism: Patrick Ford of the *Irish World*', *Church History*, xxxix, 4, (Dec. 1970), pp. 524–40.

18   For example, see 'To corral Irish visitors from America', *Gaelic American*, 6 Sept. 1913; Con O'Leary, 'Full steam ahead, Ireland's rallying cry', *Irish World*, 29 Nov. 1913.

19   On progressivism, American Catholicism and immigration, see John T. McGreevy, *Catholicism and American Freedom: A History* (New York: W.W. Norton, 2003), pp. 127–65.

20   Daniel T. Rodgers, *Atlantic Crossings*, pp. 34–5.

21   On the transnational character of progressivism, see Daniel T. Rodgers, *Atlantic Crossings: Social Politics in a Progressive Age* (Cambridge: Cambridge University Press, 1998).

22   For example see, *The Irish World*, 1 Apr. 1912.

23   Maureen Murphy, 'Ford, Patrick,' in *Dictionary of Irish Biography*.

24   'Greatest of Irish demonstrations', *Irish World*, 20 Apr. 1912; 'The origins and character of Irish-American nationalism', *The Review of Politics*, xviii, 3, (July, 1956), pp. 327–58; Francis M. Carroll, 'United Irish League of America' in Michael Funchion (ed.) *Irish American Voluntary Organizations* (Westport, 1983), pp. 272–6.

25   See for example, 'Congratulations to Redmond', *Irish World and American Industrial Liberator*, 20 Apr. 1912.

26   Patrick Maume, 'Devoy, John', *Dictionary of Irish Biography*; Funchion, 'Clan na Gael', *Irish American Voluntary Organizations*, pp. 74–93; p. 90; Terry Golway, *Irish Rebel: John Devoy and America's Fight For Irish Freedom* (New York: St Martin's Press, 1998).

27   The Cuba Five refers to the Fenian leaders – John Devoy, Jeremiah O'Donovan Rossa, Charles Underwood O'Connell, Henry Mulleda and John McClure – who were released from British prisons in 1871 on the condition that they remained in exile from British territory. They sailed for New York aboard the *Cuba* steamship, and arrived in the United States to great acclaim.

28   John Devoy wrote of his trip to Ireland in 1871 as a tourist guide which was published in 1882: see John Devoy, *The Land of Éire* (New York: Patterson and Neilson, 1882).

29   Rudolph J. Vecoli, 'Contadini in Chicago: A Critique of *The Uprooted*', *Journal of American History*, li, 3 (Dec. 1964), pp. 404–16.

30   See Oscar Handlin, *The Uprooted: The Epic Story of the Great Migrations That Made the American People* (New York: Little, Brown, 1951); Gary Gerstle, 'Liberty, coercion and the making of Americans', *Journal of American History*, lxxxiv, 2 (Sept. 1997), pp. 524–58.

31 Kristin L. Hoganson, *Fighting for American Manhood: How Gender Politics Provoked the Spanish–American and Philippine–American Wars* (New Haven: Yale University Press, 2000); Matthew Frye Jacobson, *Barbarian Virtues: the United States Encounters Foreign Peoples at Home and Abroad, 1876–1917* (New York: Farrar, Straus and Giroux, 2001).

32 *New York Times,* 2 Feb. 1913.

33 For United States census figures, see Campbell J. Gibson and Emily Lennon, 'Historical Census Statistics of the Foreign-Born Population of the United States, 1850–1990', *Population Division, U.S. Bureau of the Census* (Washington, D.C., 1999), Aristide Zolberg, *A Nation by Design: Immigration Policy in the Fashioning of America* (Cambridge: Cambridge University Press, 2006), pp. 461–5.

34 Frederick C. Croxton and William Dillingham, *Reports of the Immigration Commission: Abstracts of Reports of the Immigration Commission* (Washington, D.C., 1911) pp. 23–48.

35 Kevin Kenny, *The American Irish: A History* (New York: Routledge, 2000), p. 192.

36 Kerby A. Miller, *Emigrants and Exiles, Ireland and the Irish Exodus to North America* (Oxford: Oxford University Press, 1998), pp. 492–555.

37 Ibid.

38 Robert Ellis Thompson, 'The Lawrence strike', *Irish World*, 9 Mar. 1912.

39 Robert Ellis Thompson, 'The elimination of "unconditional arbitration"', *Irish World*, 23 Mar. 1912.

40 Rodgers, *Atlantic Crossings,* pp. 181–208.

41 Pádraig Yeates, *Lockout: Dublin 1913* (Dublin: Gill & Macmillan, 2000), p. xxi.

42 See Miller, *Emigrants and Exiles*, pp. 345–555; David Brundage, 'American Labour and the Irish Question, 1916–1923', *Saothar*, xxiv, (1999), pp. 59–66.

43 James Connolly, 'To Irish wage workers in America', *The Harp*, May 1908.

44 James Connolly, 'Harp Strings', *The Harp*, Jan. 1908.

45 James Connolly, 'Declaration of Principles of the Irish Socialist Federation', *The Harp*, Jan. 1908.

46 James Connolly, 'Harp Strings', *The Harp*, Jan. 1908.

47 Rosalyn Fraad Baxandall, *Words on Fire: The Life and Writing of Elizabeth Gurley Flynn* (New Brunswick: Rutgers University Press, 1987), pp. 1–20.

48 Elizabeth Gurley Flynn, *Rebel Girl: An Autobiography, My First Life (1906–1926)* (New York: Masses & Mainstream, 1955), p. 46–7.

49 William A. Adler, *The Man Who Never Died: The Life, Times, and Legacy of Joe Hill, American Labor Icon* (New York: Bloomsbury, 2011), pp. 12–13.

50 'Girl Anarchist to speak', *Detroit Free Press*, 6 Apr. 1908.

51 Elizabeth Gurley Flynn, *Rebel Girl*, pp. 167–1.

52 Flynn refers to the Lockout in her speech, 'The truth about the Paterson strike' delivered before the New York Civic Club Forum on 14 Jan. 1914, reprinted in Joyce L. Kornbluh (ed.) *Rebel Voices: An I.W.W. Anthology* (Ann Arbor: PM Press, Charles H. Kerr Press, 1964), pp. 215–26.

53   See Nan Enstad, *Ladies of Labour, Girls of Adventure: Working Women, Popular Culture and Labour Politics* (New York: Columbia University Press, 1999), pp. 84–160; Richard A. Greenwald, '"The burning building at 23 Washington Place": the triangle fire, workers and reformers in Progressive era New York', *New York History*, Vol. lxxxiii, 1 (winter, 2002), pp. 55–91.

54   'The fire lady of New York', *Irish World*, 16 Aug. 1913.

55   Cian McMahon, 'Caricaturing Race and Nation in the Irish American Press, 1870–1880: A Transnational Perspective', *Journal of American Ethnic History*, Vol. xxxiii, 2 (winter, 2014), pp. 33–56.

56   'Who wants equality?' *Irish World*, 18 Jan. 1913.

57   Joseph Frazier Wall, 'Carnegie, Andrew' in Susan Ware (ed.) *American National Biography* (Oxford, 2000); Brendan Grimes, 'Carnegie libraries in Ireland', *History Ireland*, 4 (winter 1998), pp. 26–30.

58   '"Peace" societies in grand rush for Carnegie's gold', *Irish World*, 20 Jan. 1912.

59   'All Europe the mother country of America', *Irish World*, 24 May 1913.

60   Ibid.

61   Paul Rouse, 'O'Leary, Con' in *Dictionary of Irish Biography*.

62   Thomas Power, T.P. O'Connor, 'Full steam ahead, Ireland's rallying cry', *Irish World*, 29 Nov. 1913.

63   Robert Ellis Thompson, 'Industrial conflict', *Irish World*, 22 Nov. 1913.

64   Ibid.

65   Ibid.

66   Con O'Leary, 'Tories utilize the Dublin riots', *Irish World*, 20 Sept. 1913.

67   'Dublin tram car strike', *Irish World*, 7 Sept. 1913.

68   Ibid.

69   Fearghal McGarry, *The Rising: Ireland, Easter 1916* (Oxford: Oxford University Press, 2010), pp. 44–52.

70   Bulmer Hobson, 'Talk of compromise on Home Rule', *Gaelic American*, 27 Sept. 1913.

71   'Dublin Castle's savage bludgeon men', *Gaelic American*, 27 Sept. 1913.

72   Bulmer Hobson, 'Dublin calls for fair public inquiry', *Gaelic American*, 31 Jan. 1913.

73   'Organize and arm to protect liberties', *Gaelic American*, 13 Dec. 1913.

74   Dame Ishbel Maria Gordon (Lady Aberdeen) (1857–1939) was a devoted philanthropist and ardent in Liberal politics, with special attention to women's issues and public education. G.F. Barbour and Matthew Urie Baird, see 'Dame Ishbel Maria Gordon, marchioness of Aberdeen and Temair', *Oxford Dictionary of National Biography*.

75   'Police-made riots in Dublin', *Gaelic American*, 6 Sept. 1913.

76   Elizabeth Burchenal founded the American Folk Dance Society, which later expanded to the American Folk Arts Centre in New York City. She published fifteen books on the subject of traditional dance and physical education, and served as a delegate at the First International Congress of Folk Arts convened by

the League of Nations in 1928. She died in Brooklyn in 1959. 'Obituary: Miss Burchenal, Folklorist, Dead,' *New York Times,* 22 Nov. 1959.

77 'American girl teaches folk dancing to Ireland', *New York Times,* 28 Sept. 1913.

78 'To corral Irish visitors from America,' *Gaelic American,* 6 Sept. 1913.

79 Patrick Maume, 'O'Callaghan, John', *Dictionary of Irish Biography.*

80 Con O'Leary, 'How Ireland Received the Sad News', *Irish World,* 11 Oct. 1913; for obituaries of Patrick Ford, see, *Irish World,* 27 Sept. 1913.

81 J.J. Lee, 'Pearse, Patrick Henry', *Dictionary of Irish Biography.*

82 'St Enda's College Doing National Work for Ireland,' *Gaelic American,* 7 Mar. 1914.

83 McGarry, *The Rising,* pp 38–9; Yeates, *Lockout,* pp. 571–87.

CHAPTER FIVE

Insult and the Locked-Out Workers of 1913

John White

Prejudice based on social class-dominated depictions of the striking workers and the urban poor during the 1913 Lockout. Those involved were continually portrayed within a framework of moral degeneracy, representative of the deep social chasm that existed between 'respectable' Ireland and the urban poor of Dublin's slums. The antagonism often shown towards the strikers' plight within contemporary political discourse was illustrative of the wider contempt for the urban poor based on their perceived moral and spiritual inadequacies. The Lockout became a class battle that played itself out, not only on the streets of Dublin but also within contemporary newspapers and publications. Leading journalists such as W.P. Ryan, writing some years after the Lockout, noted how the press, the professions, clerics and most politicians agreed that Larkin and his kind 'should be treated as outlaws'.[1] Throughout the dispute the striking workers were persistently labelled in print by respectable Catholic opinion as 'scum', 'roughs', 'parasites', 'corner-boys' and 'thugs' from amongst 'the lowest sinks of humanity'.[2] By placing the urban poor outside of the common culture of respectable Gaelic Catholic Ireland, the dominant discourse of the period facilitated opponents of the strikers to label the dispute a product of a degenerate Anglo-centric and materialistic culture, incubated by the city's slums.

In contemporary newspaper terms 'socialism', 'syndicalism' and 'Larkinism' were pejorative labels used to discredit the grievances of the striking workers and played upon the genuine fear of social upheaval. In turn, Larkin's *Irish Worker* labelled Murphy and other employers as 'vipers' and 'vampires'.[3] With Home Rule pending, nationalist politicians were greatly concerned with cultivating an image of national respectability, an image the grievances of the Dublin urban poor threatened to undermine.[4] Likewise, advanced nationalists such as Patrick Pearse were sceptical of Larkin's methods while Arthur Griffith of Sinn Féin attributed the root of poverty in Dublin to 'foreign domination' by England.[5]

Dublin's decline from being one of the most prodigious to one of the most depressed cities in Europe has been well documented.[6] Throughout much of the eighteenth century the city 'set the tone for contemporary Anglo-Ireland'.[7] The great architectural masterpieces of Georgian Dublin stood as a testament to the heights to which many of the wealthier patrons of the city had ascended. However, throughout the nineteenth century, Dublin saw a rapid decline in terms of its political, social and economic status. The passing of the Act of Union coupled with the crippling effects of the Great Famine and a lack of industrial development left the city a shadow of its former self.[8]

Over the course of the nineteenth century, much of Dublin's traditional Protestant elite left for more dynamic cities such as London. The social and political vacuum left by this exodus was replaced by a rising, post-Famine, Catholic middle class, who, by the turn of the twentieth century, were poised to become the dominant social group in independent Ireland.[9] This emerging generation had neither the financial resources nor the incentive to live within the traditional boundaries of the city centre and its deteriorating facades.[10] An influx of rural poor to the urban centres following the Great Famine served to increase the number of semi-destitute in Dublin.[11] The benefits of extended rail and tramway lines in the nineteenth century ensured that those who could afford to do so began to vacate the city for the more salubrious and spacious suburbs. Independent townships such as Pembroke, Rathmines, Dalkey and Kingstown to the south of the city, along with Drumcondra, Kilmainham and Clontarf to the north, offered cheaper rates on land and property. It is estimated that over 50 per cent of all suburban residents lived in the two neighbouring suburbs of Rathmines and Pembroke, which by 1911 included the areas of Rathgar, Harold's Cross, Milltown and Terenure, with the population reaching 38,000.[12] This almost wholesale evacuation of the upper and middle classes from the inner city to the suburbs led to what Disraeli termed a 'gap of two worlds' between the rich and the poor.[13]

The abandoned and vacant Georgian houses of the city were bought at greatly devalued prices and most were converted into tenement housing by slum landlords.[14] The location of these properties proved convenient for the working classes who needed to live in close proximity to the main avenues of employment concentrated in the heart of the city. However, these 'infernos of degradation' soon became a structural symbol of the chronic poverty that underlined the lives of many of Dublin's working classes as housing once built and designed to serve a single household now served several.[15] In 1836 a Poor Law Inquiry showed that the tenement system in Dublin had by then been well established north of the Liffey with many houses once held 'by respectable people ... now in a wretched condition'.[16] Over forty years later, in 1879, a 'Royal Commission on Sewerage and Drainage' noted that close to 70 per cent of the city's working-class population occupied only 30 per cent of all housing. The majority of them lived in either tenements or second and third-class housing.[17] Conditions within the tenements were the worst seen in any city of the United Kingdom and amongst the worst in the world.[18] Arnold Wright, who chronicled the lockout for the employers of Dublin, was forced to concede that Dublin's inner city was 'a maze of streets physically and morally foul'; a place where 'men and women live[d] like beasts of the field ...'.[19]

A government housing inquiry into the living conditions of the working classes carried out in late 1913 estimated that the population of Dublin City was 304,802, the majority of whom (63 per cent) were members of the Catholic working class.[20] Over a third of this figure, 118,000 people, lived within 5,322 tenements, the vast majority of which were deemed 'unfit for human habitation'.[21] Over two-thirds of tenement families lived in single-roomed accommodation, and Dublin had by far the highest number of one room dwellings throughout the United Kingdom.[22] A single water-tap in the yard often served as the sole source of water within a tenement and a communal water closet was also situated in the yard, which was used not only by the numerous occupants of the tenement but also by passers-by off the street. The Inquiry found that 'in nearly every case human excreta is to be found scattered about the yards and on the floors of the closet and in some cases even in the passages of the house itself'.[23] Such overcrowding and unsanitary conditions inevitably led to the spread of contagious diseases and Dublin had one of the worst infant and child mortality rates in Europe at this time.[24] Infectious diseases such as tuberculosis, pneumonia, cholera, and typhoid predominated amongst the working poor. According to Cormac Ó Gráda, the death rate per thousand was 16.5 per cent amongst the professional classes, 17.5 per cent amongst the middle classes and 40.2 per cent amongst the working classes.[25] Tuberculosis, in particular, was a major contributing factor to the high adult male death rate at this time. Between 1912 and 1914 over half of those affected by tuberculosis were aged between 15–35 with the vast majority coming from the lower strata of society.[26]

The predominance of casual work and underemployment augmented the problems of inadequate housing and sanitation. Unlike Belfast, with its thriving industries of linen, shipbuilding and metal works, Dublin had relatively few skilled workers, with most manual workers concentrated in the transport, brewing, distilling and confectionary sectors. The city's lack of industrial development led to a decline in the need for skilled manual labour and the oversupply of an unskilled workforce.[27] By 1913 the city had primarily become a receiving and distributing centre for the rest of the country.[28] It was estimated that 24,000 men, more than a quarter of the adult male population, were engaged in unskilled manual labour in the city at this time. This work was often seasonal, casual and difficult to obtain. Wages were low, on average between 15 to 18s per week, the vast majority of which went on rent, clothing and food supplies. Even when times were relatively good and work was on-going, debts still had to be repaid or possessions that had been sold or pawned had to be bought back. Charles A. Cameron, Dublin's Medical Officer for Health, had assertained that some years prior to the Lockout 2,866,084 pawn tickets had been issued in the City of Dublin in a single year.[29] As a result many families and labourers fell into a poverty trap of working to pay-off debts incurred.[30] The oversupply of labouring men left unskilled workers vulnerable to exploitation by employers who could replace them at will from a vast pool of desperate workers.[31]

The social and economic degradation of the urban poor in terms of housing, health and underemployment never became a political priority for the Irish Parliamentary Party and its supporters.[32] Apart from the privately sponsored Dublin Artisans Dwellings Company and Iveagh Trust schemes which built a limited number of labourers' cottages and artisans' dwellings in the latter half of the nineteenth century, there was relatively little done at a local government level to accommodate the city's poor. The rents required by both schemes were often too high for the very poor who were simply forced to uproot and re-house in alternative accommodation, thereby exacerbating the housing problem in the city.[33] Dublin Corporation was hampered by a lack of rates to fund the building of alternative accommodation for Dublin's tenement dwellers but the corporation's failure to ensure that slum landlords addressed the structural and unsanitary shortfalls of their premises compounded the misery of the inner city.[34] The reluctance of the corporation to adequately confront the housing crisis can be partially explained by the fact that a significant number of prominent slum landlords were themselves members of Dublin Corporation. In 1913, seventeen out of eighty elected members of Dublin City Corporation were slum landlords.[35] Moralistic and supercilious tones dominated notions of the deserving and undeserving poor. Contemporary attitudes often meant that tenement dwellers were blamed for their own circumstances due to moral failings on their part.[36] The unemployed were frequently labelled as being 'work-shy', 'wasters' and 'loafers'.[37] Such comments and ridicule intensified during the Lockout where class antagonism deepened the already existing social gulf between the haves and the have-nots.[38]

The arrival of James Larkin in Dublin in 1907 and the subsequent formation of the Irish Transport and General Workers' Union (ITGWU) in 1909 dramatically changed the face of Irish trade unionism. Existing 'craft' unions catered almost exclusively for skilled workers who traditionally occupied a privileged place within the hierarchy of Dublin industry. The ITGWU sought to organise the unskilled workers, aiming to lift them from the morass of poverty and despair generated by the predominance of casual working hours and underemployment. Larkin used his union as 'a revolutionary instrument' in the hopes of bringing about both economic change and social advancement for the poor.[39] He envisaged a new working class liberated from the tyranny of underemployment, which condemned unskilled workers to perpetual subservience and exploitation. His charismatic personality and leadership style, however, was exploited by his opponents who continually strove to present him as the embodiment of radical socialism and thereby discredit the grievances of the workers. William Martin Murphy and other employers sought to personalise the dispute by focusing on Larkin's personality, thereby seeking to 'kill Larkinism and what it stands for – Socialism and Anarchy'.[40] Likewise, Richard Shackleton, whose family owned a thriving flour mill in Lucan, claimed that 'If Larkin took a single ticket to Buenos Aires or Hong Kong we would not object to our men belonging to the Transport Union. What we object to is Larkinism, not legitimate trade unionism.'[41]

According to Emmet Larkin, the 'hysterical denunciation of socialism' simply served to awaken 'an Irish social conscience that had long been dormant with regard to the problem of urban poverty'.[42] The threat of Larkinism, which 'had become a catch-all to denote syndicalism, socialism, and any manifestation of either', became a genuine fear amongst wider public opinion.[43] The danger of 'ungodly' socialist doctrine 'infiltrating' and 'corrupting' Irish workers led the *Catholic Bulletin* to warn its readers that should 'the poison plant of Socialism ever take root here, all that is beautiful in the Irish national character must wither'.[44] The majority of Catholic clergy and hierarchy were profoundly alarmed by the perceived threat of socialism.[45] Revd F.E. O'Loughlin told his congregation in the suburb of Rathmines that Ireland had come under the influence of 'the Red Hand of Socialism'. He warned 'the Irish Roman Catholic workman' to be 'on his guard' against 'the storm of Socialism' that was 'sweeping over and devastating' much of Europe at this time and which was attempting to 'enkindle in their minds a hatred of the wealthy classes'.[46] In Sligo, the Revd A. Coleman told his congregation that 'the syndicalist took all classes and conditions of men into their ranks, unskilled labourers, petty or semi-criminals as well as corner boys'.[47] The *Irish Catholic* meanwhile implored Irish workers to 'break loose from the Socialist and consequently demonical influences which are dragging them to perdition and ruin'.[48] Nationalist MP, Timothy Healy, an advocate for the employers, spoke of how Larkinism was 'the most finished system of tyranny … ever started in any country'.[49]

Two Dublin weekly publications, in particular, devoted themselves solely to attacking Larkin and his 'demonic' teachings.[50] *The Liberator and Irish Trade Unionist,* which came into circulation on 23 August 1913, and *The Toiler,* whose first edition was issued on 4 October 1913. The former lasted only a few months ending publication on 23 November 1913 while *The Toiler* lasted until 12 December 1914. While both publications were seemingly united in their endeavours to 'crush' Larkin and socialism, an intense jealousy and bitterness underlay the relationship between the editors of each paper, Barney Doyle and Patrick J. McIntyre. Upon the demise of *The Liberator* the front page of *The Toiler* carried an editorial piece from McIntyre commenting on the 'death' of the paper. In it, McIntyre notes that *The Liberator* 'was useless to fight Larkin' being 'no more effective than a pop gun would be in modern warfare'. He claimed the 'men who ran the Liberator were only working for their salary' and were all former employees of Larkin who 'would be willing to work for Larkin tomorrow if the screw was big enough'. McIntyre personally accused Doyle of drinking away the paper's profits and claimed the success of *The Toiler* was due to the fact that those working for the paper had 'faith in the principles we preach'.[51] Throughout the pages of both newspapers Larkin was regularly labelled in varying terms as an 'atheist' and 'anti-Christ' whose 'cloven-footed' teachings had led the working classes astray and 'away from the straight path' of sound trade unionism.[52] *The Liberator* made a habit of deliberately misspelling Larkin's surname and referring to him as '£arkin', a visual wordplay used to question Larkin's alleged mishandling of union funds. Similarly, *The Toiler* accused Larkin of being an Orangeman, and questioned his familial origins by alleging that he was the son of James Carey, the informer who betrayed the Invincibles after the Phoenix Park murders in 1882.[53]

As public discourse surrounding the dispute became increasingly reduced to denouncing Larkin and the threat of socialism rather than a discussion of the endemic poverty of the inner city, it became easier for the employers to present the workers' grievances as irrational and merely the product of one man's radicalism. As James Connolly noted in the Glasgow socialist newspaper, *Forward*, in October 1913: 'the Dublin fight is more than a trade union fight; it is a class struggle, and recognised as such by all sides'.[54] The ability of Larkin and Connolly to gather in unison the collective strength of the working classes, both skilled and unskilled, was widely recognised at the time.[55] Internationally, Lenin even spoke of the 'miracle' Larkin had brought about in the advancement and organisation of the working classes of Dublin.[56] By incorporating the use of the sympathetic strike Larkin 'forged a cohesion between different classes of workers' that had not heretofore prevailed.[57] Nationalist councillor C.F. McNally told Carlow District Council in November 1913 that it was the use of the sympathetic strike that was proving 'destructive to all progress'.[58] The Liberal Unionist *Irish Times* also recognised the potential danger of employers yielding to the threat of the sympathetic strike, labelling them 'weak' and 'timid' in their attempts to crush 'the abominable' tyranny of the transport union.[59]

Employers portrayed the struggle for the betterment of workers' conditions as part of 'a far-reaching scheme' to advance 'the elimination of the capitalist'.[60] Throughout the Lockout the workers were portrayed in the national and local media as the 'misguided dupes' of Larkin, indicative of the unwillingness of most local and nationalist elites to see the lockout as stemming from genuine social injustice and their fight for their right to unionise.[61] An editorial piece in the *Connacht Tribune* (Galway) labelled Larkin as 'a mischief maker with a lot of plebeian fools to follow him'.[62] The *Irish Times* asserted that the workers were merely the 'frightened slaves' of the union organisers.[63] Some newspapers perceived the ITGWU as an organisation that harboured criminals. The *Meath Chronicle* (Navan) noted that those who joined the ITGWU were nothing more than 'a band of highwaymen' who 'sheltered' their 'insolence', 'disobedience', and 'laziness' under its banner.[64] The William Martin Murphy-owned *Irish Catholic* thought 'these bad, sad specimens of the human race have no interest in the cause of labour … they are not on strike, nor have they been locked out'.[65] The Mullingar *Midland Reporter* wrote of how 'the roughs of the

Dublin slums' were prone 'to rioting, stealing, and breaking shop windows to loot'.[66] The *Irish Times* agreed, claiming the organisation held 'tyranny over the working classes' and was 'an agency whose interest is agitation rather than settlement'.[67] In a letter to the editor of the *Irish Times* the journalist and pioneer of the urban town-planning movement, Ernest A. Aston, posed the question to employers on how certain they could be 'that their children would not learn to throw bottles at police if society had condemned them to the reeking nursery of the tenement house'.[68]

The Dublin slums, which housed the majority of working poor, were portrayed in much popular discourse, as incubators of moral decline and alien Anglo-centric tendencies. The republican trade unionist and ITGWU organiser, P.T. Daly, alleged the low wages paid to female employees at Jacob's factory 'was the cause of driving many of them onto the streets as prostitutes'.[69] Prostitution was indeed a contentious issue in Irish society throughout the nineteenth and early twentieth centuries.[70] The Dublin Metropolitan Police had estimated in 1901 that while female prostitution was decreasing there was still an estimated 1,677 women earning a living as prostitutes on the streets of the capital.[71] James Larkin was shocked by the living conditions of the poor in Dublin and during one of his initial visits to the city in 1907 he wondered why 'if Dublin men were so proud of their city, did they not look after the little children who were running about their streets hungry and dirty, and badly clothed'. He questioned why Dubliners did not put a stop 'to the disgraceful scenes in O'Connell Street, when fellows from the slums of London, in red uniform, were coming along with Irish girls on their arms, whom they would ruin in body and soul?'[72] *The Toiler* saw the slums as 'a very ancient organisation', a place where 'evil' must be 'alleviated'. An evil that was only recognised by 'philanthropists' and 'moralists' who failed to see that the poor themselves 'were not out against the tenements, as a grievance – they are out against work to pay for them. They do not, and never did, complain of them'. It blamed the conditions of the slums on the 'dirt and drunkenness of the men and women' that occupied them, 'people who would make a slum of a decent place in six months'. They had come from 'the rotten rookeries to the shades of respectability' and were 'not to "the manor born"'.[73] Father Phelan, writing in the *Catholic Bulletin* questioned the character of those workers who accepted food from English food ships to Ireland by the British Labour Party to help locked-out Irish workers. The 'greedy crunching' of the poor upon the 'begged crust' of 'the outsider' ran contradictory to those 'whose grandfathers gladly died on the roadside rather than accept the poorhouse taint'.[74]

Public commentators across nationalist Ireland often juxtaposed the insanitary conditions and perceived moral degeneracy of life in Dublin City with a romanticised view of country living. The *Catholic Bulletin* noted in October 1913 'young men and women are too easily lured from saintly country homes to aggravate Dublin's complicated labour problem' and 'they often fall prey to the vices of city life'.[75] The Lockout also served to focus attention on similar slum conditions in other parts of the country and *The Derry Weekly News and Tyrone Herald* noted:

The tenement houses in the towns are the analogue of the congested districts in the country. In such places human life festers and decays … Men are turned into beasts … In every urban slum, in every rural slum, in every poisonous and insanitary house, the divine laws and the natural laws are broken … It has made the publican and gombeen man and the owner of the slum property the rulers in our towns and made them the meanest and least ideal congregations of human life one could find anywhere.[76]

The Times of London claimed that nationalist politicians had always remained 'studiously silent' on the issues of poverty and neglect, claiming 'ardent members of Parliament are always streaming through Dublin, but they have never found time or inclination to expose such grievances'. The editor reproached 'the Churches, the employers of labour, the public men and the wealthy private folk, none can escape their share of blame'. It proclaimed that 'Dublin ought to be one of the healthiest cities in the world. It is swept by life-giving sea breezes. Yet people die like flies in its squalid slums, while even the broad expanse of the Phoenix Park remains for the most part deserted and desolate.'[77]

Irish Party MPs were indeed reluctant to address the escalating violence and deprivation generated by the dispute despite the apparent misgivings of a small number of party members.[78] Following the violence of Bloody Sunday 1913, Richard McGhee, M.P. for mid-Tyrone, wrote to John Dillon to express his concern that the Party had not yet condemned the attacks, 'I had expected to see a letter from you in the *Freeman* today denouncing the murderous attack upon peaceful citizens on Sunday last. It will be a serious mistake for our entire Irish Party to remain silent as if we approved of the devilish work.' McGhee noted that this would appear even more serious considering that 'the trade unions of Britain are stirred to the deepest indignation' over the attacks.[79] Instead, Dillon fantasised on how both sides annihilating each other might end the entire dispute and thereby solve the problem. In early October he told his close friend, T.P. O'Connor, Irish Party MP for Liverpool, 'it would be a blessing to Ireland' if both Murphy and Larkin 'exterminated each other'.[80]

Many nationalist MP's were publicly hostile to the strikers and David Sheehy's attempt to portray the workers as merely the dupes of Larkin was typical of the ambivalence amongst the political establishment to the genuine grievances of the urban poor. Sheehy declared 'there were a great many fine decent good men in Dublin out of employment, commanded out of employment by Mr. Larkin, under the feeling, under the threat of that ugly word "scab" being thrown at them, at their wives, or at their children as they go to school … even if Mr. John Redmond attempted tomorrow to assume the responsibility of Larkin, the conscience of Ireland would be so revolted that within a week he would be looked down upon, despised and ignored.'[81] In an open letter in the *Irish Worker*, Larkin rebutted Sheehy's remarks:

> The party of which you are a member have learned the truth and wisdom of the old proverb which tells us that 'Silence is golden,' especially when labour troubles are in the air. We know of course that you have been telling us all along that the Irish Parliamentary Party were devoted to the cause of labour. They lie awake at night thinking of our trials and troubles … but you, brave sir, have pulled them off the fence – into the ditch. You alone of all the Party were unwise enough to open your mouth about the present locking out, and you have put your foot in it![82]

While many ordinary Dubliners were sympathetic to the workers' plight, most advanced nationalists did not share the ideas of James Connolly who saw the struggle for Irish independence as indivisible from the fight for socialism.[83] Patrick Pearse did not know 'whether the methods of Mr. Larkin are wise methods or unwise methods (unwise, I think, in some respects)'. He did however recognise that there was 'a most hideous wrong to be righted, and that the man who attempts honestly to right it is a good man and a brave man'. Pearse, like many radical nationalists, saw the basis of the prevailing poverty of the slums as being entrenched in the national question, believing that 'the root of the matter' lay 'in foreign domination' rather than the exploitation of one class by another: 'a free Ireland would not, and could not, have hunger in her fertile vales and squalor in her cities'.[84] Arthur Griffith was in no doubt as to 'the wisdom' of Larkin's methods and portrayed him simply as a 'representative of English trade-unionism in Ireland'. Hostility to Larkin based on his English origins was reciprocated by the editor of the *Leader*, D.P. Moran, who noted how 'Irish Ireland does not stand for "hands across the sea," it stands for Ireland a self-contained entity ... We don't want to take our labour, politics, or our laws from England'.[85]

The so-called 'Save the Kiddies' scheme put forward by the English social worker, Dora Montifiore, in October 1913 further served to isolate and vilify the locked-out workers in the minds of established Irish society.[86] The plan, to house strikers' children within English homes for the duration of the lockout, was met with physical and verbal protest by Catholic clergy and laity alike who saw it as an attempt to proselytise impressionable Catholic working-class children to the Protestant faith. Montifiore and her 'socialist allies' were labelled as 'kidnappers', 'soul-snatchers', 'she-devils' and 'soupers' by the press.[87] During an attempt to board children on a train at Westland Row station on 22 October, both children and parents were met by angry protesters who flung mud at them amidst cries to 'Throw them in the Liffey.'[88] The Archbishop of Dublin, William Walsh, who up until then had been largely sympathetic to those on strike, was forced to issue a statement that was published in the various newspapers condemning the actions of Dublin mothers sending their children to England. According to Walsh, the women were being 'subjected' to a 'cruel temptation' to 'abandon their faith' and send their 'helpless offspring' abroad to be cared for in 'a strange land'. He warned those who did so that they could 'no longer be held worthy of the name of Catholic mothers'.[89] The episode highlighted the continued silence of the Irish Party who seemingly preferred to, as one contributor to the *Irish Times* put it, 'take refuge behind the apron of the Roman Catholic Archbishop of Dublin'.[90] George Russell (AE) maintained that the real reason why people were so outraged by the plan was that once children from the slums began 'getting full meals, they might be so inconsiderate as to ask for them all of their lives'.[91]

While William Martin Murphy's publication, the *Irish Independent*, served to vilify Larkin in the minds of the middle classes, Larkin's own publication made Murphy 'an ogre in the minds and folk memory of the workers'.[92] Larkin captured the popular imagination of the urban poor through the pages of the *Irish Worker* by expounding his anti-capitalist sentiments to the masses condemning and chastising employers through vitriolic and biting satire. William 'Murder' Murphy was constantly lampooned in the pages of the *Worker* as a 'tramway tyrant', 'industrial octopus' and 'blood-sucking vampire' of the poor.[93] His most recent biographer, however, has argued forcibly against such a biased interpretation but there can be no doubt that Murphy was ruthless in his treatment of the workers.[94] He realised fully that in not recognising the workers' right to unionise under the ITGWU he was forcing workers to 'fire their last cartridge' and go out on strike. He knew that while the employer would manage 'to get his three meals a day' the 'unfortunate workman and his family had no resources whatever except submission'. Murphy realised it would be 'extraordinarily' difficult to sit back and watch families of workers struggling to survive throughout the lockout but he did see it somewhat as his moral duty to 'teach' a 'lesson' to the workmen. As the *Freeman's Journal* noted upon his death in 1919, Murphy's 'views belonged to a world' that was by then 'passing away'.[95]

The exodus of Dublin's wealthier patrons from the inner city during the nineteenth century exacerbated the physical and cultural chasm between the urban poor and the Dublin middle classes. Social prejudices based on crude depictions of the urban poor were emblematic of a wider sense of disdain for the poor within contemporary notions of respectability. The tenor of much social commentary during the Lockout, despite a number of notable exceptions, denigrated public discourse and reduced complex social issues to mere caricature. The vast majority of politicians, priests and nationalists (both conservative and advanced) offered unsympathetic opinions on the locked-out workers. Theirs was a position of fear and trepidation brought about by a century of near neglect and ignorance of those who rose to try and meet them eye to eye.

Endnotes

1 Michael Wheatley, *Nationalism and the Irish Party: Provincial Ireland, 1910–1916* (London, Oxford University Press, 2005), p. 138.

2 M. Curran to Dr Walsh, 2 Sept., 1913 (Dublin Archdiocesan Archive, Priest Files, 1913); *Irish Independent*, 1, 4 Sept. 1913; *The Irish Catholic*, 6 Sept. 1913; *The Liberator and Irish Trade Unionist*, 23 Aug., 30 Aug., 6 Sep. 1913; *The Toiler*, 10 Jan. 1914.

3 Thomas J. Morrissey, *William O'Brien, 1881–1968, Socialist, Republican, Dáil Deputy, Editor and Trade Union Leader* (Dublin: Four Courts Press, 2007), p. 72.

4 James McConnel, 'The Irish Parliamentary Party, Industrial Relations and the 1913 Lockout', *Saothar*, 27 (2003), pp. 25–8.

5 *The Leader*, 4 Oct. 1913.

6 Mary Daly, *Dublin the Deposed Capital: A Social and Economic History, 1860–1914* (Cork: Cork University Press, 1984).

7   David Dickson, 'Capital and Country: 1600–1800', in Art Cosgrave (ed.), *Dublin Through the Ages* (Dublin: UCD Press, 1988), p. 73.

8   Jacinta Prunty, 'Dublin in the Nineteenth Century', in Joseph Brady, Anngret Simms (eds.), *Dublin Through Space and Time* (Dublin: Four Courts Press, 2001), p. 159.

9   Andrew Shields, 'Paul Cullen and the Irish Conservative Imagination', in Dáire Keogh and Albert McDonnell (eds), *Cardinal Paul Cullen and his World* (Dublin: Four Courts Press, 2011), pp. 205–15.

10   Ruth McManus, *Dublin 1910–1940: Shaping the City and Suburbs* (Dublin: Four Courts Press, 2002), p. 26.

11   Statistics show that while Ireland's population fell between 1841 and 1911, Dublin's population grew from 236,000 to 304,802 respectively. Mary Daly estimates that 29.67 per cent of these 304,802 people were born outside of Dublin City and county. See, Kevin C. Kearns, *Dublin Tenement Life: An Oral History* (Dublin: Penguin, 1994), p. 7; Daly, *Dublin, The Deposed Capital*, p. 4.

12   Daly, *Dublin, The Deposed Capital*, pp. 152–3.

13   Lydia Carroll, *In the Fever King's Preserves: Sir Charles Cameron and the Dublin Slums* (London: Four Courts Press, 2011), p. 190.

14   In July 1913, the *Irish Times* carried an advertisement for a north-side tenement house for £75 on a forty-two-year lease with an annual net profit of £40; McManus, *Dublin 1910–1940*, p. 28.

15   Enda Leaney, '"Infernos of Degradation": A Visual Record of Tenement Life in Dublin', in Francis Devine (ed.), *A Capital in Conflict: Dublin City and the 1913 Lockout* (Dublin: Four Courts Press, 2013), p. 145.

16   Jacinta Prunty, *Dublin Slums, 1800–1925: A Study in Urban Geography* (Dublin: Irish Academic Press, 1998), p. 284.

17   Joseph V. O'Brien, *Dear Dirty Dublin: A City in Distress, 1899–1916* (Berkeley: California University Press, 1982), p. 126.

18   Pádraig Yeates, *Lockout: Dublin 1913* (Dublin: Gill & Macmillan, 2000), p. xxiii.

19   Arnold Wright, *Disturbed Dublin: The Story of the Great Strike of 1913–14, with a Description of the Industries of the Irish Capital* (Dublin:Longmans, Green, 1914), pp. 3–4; p. 29.

20   *Report of the Departmental Committee Appointed by the Local Government Board for Ireland to Inquire into the Housing Conditions of the Working Classes in the City of Dublin* (1914), [Cd. 7273], pp. 2–4.

21   Ibid., pp. 2–4.

22   According to the report, the number of tenements of one-room accommodation per 1,000 total residents in Dublin was 329, this was followed by Glasgow, 200, and London, 134, with the remaining cities paling in significance. *Report of the Departmental Committee...* p. 3.

23   Ibid., pp. 2–4.

24   Peter Berresford Ellis, *A History of the Irish Working Class* (London: Pluto Press, 1985), p. 184.

25 Cormac Ó Gráda, 'Ireland, 1907–1947: The Socio-Economic Context', in Donal Nevin (ed.), *James Larkin: Lion of the Fold* (Dublin: Gill & Macmillan, 1998), p. 9.

26 Daly, *The Deposed Capital*, pp. 78; p. 246.

27 Mary Daly, 'Social structure of the Dublin working class, 1871–1911', *Irish Historical Studies*, 23 (Nov., 1982), pp. 121–33.

28 Emmet Larkin, *James Larkin, 1876–1947: Irish Labour Leader* (London: Routledge & Kegan Paul, 1965), p. 44.

29 *Irish Times*, 7 Mar. 1914; Charles A. Cameron, *How the Poor Live* (Dublin, 1904), p. 4.

30 Leeann Lane, 'George Russell and James Stephens: class and cultural discourse', *A Capital in Conflict*, p. 339.

31 See, O'Brien, *Dear Dirty Dublin*, p. 200.

32 McConnel, 'The Irish Parliamentary Party, industrial relations and the 1913 Lockout', pp. 25–8.

33 McManus, *Dublin 1910–1940*, p. 25.

34 Charles A. Cameron, *Reminiscences* (Dublin, 1913), p. 166.

35 *Report of the Departmental Committee … to Inquire into the Housing Conditions of the Working Classes in the City of Dublin* (1914), appendix 15 and 16; Arthur Mitchell, *Labour in Irish Politics, 1890–1930* (Dublin: Irish University Press, 1974), p. 47.

36 Brian Hanley, 'Lockout – 1913', *Look Left*, 2:14 (2013), pp. 22–7.

37 *Irish Independent*, 1 Sept. 1913; *The Toiler*, 10 Jan. 1914; *Housing Inquiry 1913*, p. 20.

38 Mary Daly, 'A Tale of Two Cities: 1860–1920', in Cosgrove (ed.), *Dublin through the Ages*, p. 116.

39 Emmet Larkin, *James Larkin, 1876–1947: Irish Labour Leader* (London: Routledge & Kegan Paul, 1965), p. xiv.

40 *Irish Independent*, 4 Sept. 1913.

41 *Irish Independent*, 15 Oct. 1913.

42 Emmet Larkin, 'Socialism and Catholicism in Ireland', *Studies: An Irish Quarterly Review*, 74 (spring, 1985), p. 67.

43 Pádraig Yeates, *Lockout*, p. xxiii.

44 *The Catholic Bulletin*, 1913, p. 701.

45 Joseph A. MacMahon, 'The Catholic Clergy and the Social Question in Ireland, 1891–1916', *Studies: An Irish Quarterly Review*, 70 (winter, 1981), pp. 263–88.

46 *The Irish Times*, 27 Aug. 1913; *Carlow Sentinel*, 13 Sept. 1913.

47 *The Liberator and Irish Trade Unionist*, 11 Oct. 1913.

48 *Irish Catholic*, 6 Sept. 1913.

49 *The Freeman's Journal*, 2 Oct. 1913.

50 *The Liberator and Irish Trade Unionist*, 23 Aug. 1913.

51 *The Toiler*, 6 Dec. 1913.

52 *The Liberator and Irish Trade Unionist*, 6 Sept. 1913; *The Toiler*, 4 Oct. 1913.

53 *The Toiler*, 25 Oct. 1913; 17 Jan. 1914.

54 Bill Moran, '1913, Jim Larkin and the British Labour Movement', *Saothar*, 4 (1978), pp. 35–49.

55 William O'Brien, 'Nineteen-Thirteen, Its Significance', *An Dion* (Dec., 1934), p. 3.

56 Andrew Boyd, *The Rise of the Irish Trade Unions, 1729–1970* (Dublin: Anvil Books, 1972), p. 90.

57 Emmet O'Connor, *Syndicalism in Ireland, 1917–1923* (Cork: Cork University Press, 1988), p. 12.

58 *Carlow Sentinel*, 5 Nov. 1913.

59 *The Irish Times*, 29 Aug. 1913.

60 Wright, *Disturbed Dublin*, p. 121.

61 Dermot Keogh, 'William Martin Murphy and the Origins of the 1913 Lock-Out', *Saothar*, 4 (1978), pp. 15–34.

62 *Connacht Tribune*, 22 Nov. 1913.

63 *The Irish Times*, 29 Aug. 1913.

64 *Meath Chronicle*, 13 Sept. 1913.

65 *Irish Catholic*, 30 Aug. 1913.

66 *Irish Independent*, 4 Sept. 1913.

67 *The Irish Times*, 26 Aug. 1913.

68 *The Irish Times*, 3 Sept. 1913.

69 Yeates, *Lockout*, p. 152.

70 Maria Luddy, *Prostitution and Irish Society, 1800–1940* (Cambridge, 2007).

71 O'Brien, *Dear Dirty Dublin*, p. 54.

72 *Freeman's Journal*, 12 Aug. 1907.

73 *The Toiler*, 8 Nov., 6 Dec. 1913.

74 *The Catholic Bulletin*, Nov. 1913, p. 771.

75 *The Catholic Bulletin*, Oct. 1913, p. 701.

76 *The Derry Weekly News and Tyrone Herald*, 20 Sept. 1913.

77 *The Times*, 22 Oct. 1913.

78 McConnel, 'The Irish Parliamentary Party', p. 28.

79 Richard McGhee to John Dillon, dated 15 Sep. 1913 (Dillon Papers, TCD, MS 6455–6909).

80 John Dillon to T.P. O'Connor, dated 1 Oct. 1913 (Dillon Papers, TCD, MS 6455–6909).

81 *The Freeman's Journal*, 23 Sept. 1913.

82 *The Irish Worker*, 4 Oct. 1913.

83 James Connolly, 'Socialism and Nationalism', *Shan Van Vocht*, Jan. 1897.

84 Patrick Pearse, 'From a Hermitage', *Irish Freedom*, Oct. 1913.

85 *The Leader*, 4, 11 Oct. 1913.

86 Pádraig Yeates, 'The Dublin 1913 Lockout', *History Ireland*, 9:2 (Summer, 2001), pp. 31–6.

87 *The Irish Catholic*, 1 Nov. 1913; *The Liberator and Irish Trade Unionist*, 25 Oct. 1913; *The Irish Times*, 31 Oct. 1913; *Butte Independent*, 15 Nov. 1913.

88 Yeates, *Lockout*, p. 267.

89 *Irish Times*, 21 Oct. 1913.

90 Letter to the editor from Major G.B. O'Connor, *Irish Times*, 29 Oct. 1913.

91   *The Irish Times*, 11 Nov. 1913.
92   Morrisey, *William O'Brien*, p. 72.
93   Dermot Keogh, 'William Martin Murphy and the Origins of the 1913 Lock-Out', pp. 15–34.
94   Morrisey, *William Martin Murphy* (Dublin, 2011).
95   Keogh, 'William Martin Murphy and the Origins of the 1913 Lock-Out', pp. 15–34.

CHAPTER SIX

'Into the Sun': Helena Molony's Lost Revolution

Fearghal McGarry

Introduction

Commemoration can be an unpredictable business. Anticipating the centenary of the Lockout, one historian predicted that it would be 'passed over for the most part by the mainstream media and political establishment', an omission that would demonstrate how the working class are 'written out of history'.[1] It was in fact marked by a remarkably comprehensive programme of conferences, documentaries, talks, exhibitions, publications, press supplements and arts and community initiatives, and by a formal state commemoration one hundred years to the day after 'Bloody Friday' (featuring a mass re-enactment of the Dublin Metropolitan Police's infamous baton-charge on protestors).[2] As ever, much of this commemorative activity was driven by vested interests, attesting in this case to the organisational abilities of the Irish trade union movement, but it also reflected a genuine public interest in the Lockout and working-class Dublin.

As always when collective memory collides with history, there were disconcerting facets of this commemorative binge. Strikingly, one of the most bitterly divisive events of early twentieth-century Ireland was recalled almost entirely without controversy. With the commemorative programme dominated by historians of (and from) the left, public attention – and sympathy – was focused on one side of the dispute; in contrast, the preceding year's centenaries of the Home Rule bill and Ulster Covenant witnessed a more vigorous contestation of the motives and actions of those on all sides of the conflict over Irish self-government. While Jim Larkin's significance as the embodiment of dignity for an oppressed people was emphasised, there appeared to be little awareness of the destructive legacy of the most divisive figure in Irish labour history.[3] Such was the tenor of the commemorative programme, it would have been easy to miss the fact that many Irish people – including the bulk of middle-class opinion and many advanced nationalists and republicans – had not supported the workers in 1913.

Despite the prominence of accomplished historians such as Emmet O'Connor, Pádraig Yeates and Brian Hanley, other aspects of the commemorative programme had the potential to mislead. The idea that the losing side remained hidden from history was frequently asserted, prompting a characteristically acerbic intervention from Kevin Myers, one of the few media voices to rain on the commemorative parade: 'Statues are not erected to the central figures of "hidden histories", nor are bridges named after them.'[4] Reflecting its function as a foundation myth for the modern labour movement,[5] the Lockout was depicted as a 'moral victory' – even a 'great turning-point'– that had laid the foundations for the future success of the trade union movement rather than a demoralising defeat.[6] With the centenary coinciding with a fraught round of public-sector pay negotiations, the Lockout was unsurprisingly depicted by the labour establishment as a struggle for the principles of trade union recognition and collective bargaining rather than one centred on sympathetic action and syndicalist class struggle.

In this latter respect, the significance of class *was* overlooked in 2013,[7] but this occurred as a result of how the Lockout was remembered rather than forgotten. Rather than highlighting the consequences of organised labour's defeat in a conflict that foreshadowed its marginalisation in an independent Ireland dominated by reactionary figures such as William Martin Murphy, the tone of much of the commemoration – uncharitably described by Myers as 'witless triumphalism' – did little to prompt reflection on the revolutionary decade's conservative legacy. While a welcome initiative, Dublin City Council's decision to name a new bridge after Rosie Hackett, a semi-mythologised striker plucked from obscurity, arguably testified less to the progressive instincts of contemporary Irish society than the manner in which overly consensual commemoration can distort understanding of the past by smoothing over its divisions.[8] The absence of female speakers at the official ceremony to open the bridge did nothing to allay such scepticism.[9]

Focusing on the life of Helena Molony, another trade unionist and rebel whose profile was raised as a result of recent commemoration,[10] this essay highlights more problematic aspects of the role of labour during the broader revolutionary period than those foregrounded by the centenary of the Lockout. Addressing a public meeting at Liberty Hall in 1913, Countess Markievicz declared that 'there were three great movements going on in Ireland at present – the National Movement, the Women's Movement, and the Industrial Movement. They were all really the same movements in essence, for they were all fighting the same fight, for the extension of human liberty.'[11] This uplifting sentiment, much in tune with public remembrance of the Lockout in 2013, was shared by many contemporary radicals – including Molony, a confidante of Markievicz. A more pessimistic evaluation of both women's revolutionary experiences suggests that they were largely mistaken: the cause of labour was trumped by nationalism, while women found themselves marginalised within both spheres. The demise of the radical vision espoused by labour activists like Molony demonstrates how tensions between progressive and conservative impulses were reflected not only in the rivalry between labour and nationalism but also by divisions within the labour movement. The setbacks and disappointments experienced by such activists points to the need for a more sober appraisal of labour's achievements during the revolutionary decade.

Before the Rising

Born at Coles Lane, off Henry Street, in 1883, little is known of Molony's early years; she reportedly experienced a difficult childhood following the death of her grocer father, due to a poor relationship with her stepmother.[12] Like many of her revolutionary generation, she attributed her politicisation to the cultural revival and the impact of the 1798 centenary, which she regarded as 'the starting point of the resurgence of real National idealism'.[13] As is the case in many autobiographical republican narratives, she could recall a particular moment of awakening:

> I was a young girl dreaming about Ireland ... when I saw and heard Maud Gonne speaking by the Custom House in Dublin one August evening in 1903. She was a most lovely figure, and she inspired me – as she did many others – with a love of Ireland ... I had been reading Douglas Hyde – his history and legends. She gathered all this up and made it real for me. She electrified me and filled me with some of her own spirit ... I went to join Inghinidhe na hÉireann.[14]

Family influences had also played a role in her politicisation; she was encouraged in this 'first active interest in politics' by her brother Frank.[15]

Molony became immediately embroiled in one of Inghinidhe's most celebrated protests. Calling at its offices to join up, she was directed to Maud Gonne's Rathgar home where she found dozens of men, armed with sticks and 'spoiling for a fight', preventing the police from seizing a black petticoat flying from the window. Ostensibly a tribute to the recently deceased Pope Leo XIII, this provocative gesture was intended to protest against King Edward VII's Irish visit. Many of the surrounding houses in this prosperous suburb were festooned with Union flags.[16] Well reported by the international press, the 'battle of Coulson Avenue' typified Inghinidhe's skilful efforts to exploit popular nationalist sentiment in support of its radical objectives. Following this 'baptism of fire', Molony considered herself a committed republican: 'After eleven o'clock that night I walked home on air, really believing that I was a member of the mystical Army of Ireland. I was at once given work to do, and plunged into it with the greatest enthusiasm.'[17]

Although the campaign generated public support, embarrassing Dublin Corporation and the Irish Parliamentary Party, Inghinidhe's commitment to physical-force republicanism confined it to the margins of nationalist politics.[18] So too did its status as a woman's organisation, one of the few to allow a public role to women who were denied the vote and largely excluded from cultural and political activism. While militant, Inghinidhe's feminist aspirations were firmly subordinated to its nationalist goals. Its activities were also gendered, focusing primarily on women and children. Originally formed to organise a 'patriotic children's treat' to reward children who had not participated in 'the orgy of flunkeyism' that marked Queen Victoria's 1900 visit to Ireland, it organised evening classes for poor Dublin children (teaching Irish language, history, games, dancing and music), and campaigned on maternal issues such as the provision of school meals.[19]

As with other advanced nationalist organisations that emerged during this seminal period, including Sinn Féin, culture – particularly theatre – played an important role within Inghinidhe. Its members comprised much of the cast in the first public performance of *Cathleen ni Houlihan* by Willie Fay's Irish National Dramatic Company, an initiative that led to the founding of the Abbey Theatre. A talented actor, Molony joined the Abbey in 1913, but she remained more at home within radical amateur troupes such as the Markieviczs' Independent Dramatic Company and James Connolly's Irish Workers' Dramatic Club whose object 'was to give dramatic expression to national political propaganda, as distinct from the "art for art's sake school"' associated with the Abbey's professional productions.[20]

Such developments demonstrated the impact of the cultural revival on radical nationalist politics by the early twentieth century. Inghinidhe aimed to discourage 'the reading and circulation of low English literature, the singing of English songs, the attending of vulgar English entertainments at theatres and music halls, and to combat in every way English influence'.[21] Problematically, from a feminist point of view, its approach was stridently moralistic. Railing against 'the sad sight of Irish girls walking through the streets with men wearing the uniform of Ireland's oppressor', Inghinidhe warned of the danger to women's 'purity and honour'.[22] Although more egalitarian than constitutional nationalism, the moralistic discourse of republicanism often reinforced conservative conceptions of gender roles.

At the same time the involvement of women in street politics also challenged prevailing values. Handing out leaflets to girls who consorted with British army soldiers was 'dangerous work', Molony recalled: 'soldiers at that time had the habit of taking off their belts and attacking civilians with them'. Many of her friends disapproved of her activism: 'it was not thought "becoming"', she recalled: 'women and girls were still living in a semi-sheltered Victorianism'.[23] Molony, in contrast, delighted in Inghinidhe's theatrical pranks. Approached by a police sergeant seeking her assistance in restraining youths from distributing seditious leaflets, one of the Gifford sisters recalled how Molony, 'pretending to sympathise with his difficulties, clapped him on the back as she was leaving him, at the same time sticking on a notice which appealed to young Irishmen not to join the British armed forces'. On another occasion, she plastered the Lord Lieutenant's official car with anti-recruitment leaflets.[24]

A committed agitator and effective public speaker Molony became a prominent activist, although she usually played supporting roles to more dominant figures throughout her life: elected secretary of Inghinidhe, she effectively represented Maud Gonne who was frequently absent from Ireland.[25] In 1908 she established a journal, *Bean na hEireann*, distinguished not only by its separatist outlook but its feminism. Viewing Sinn Féin's social conservatism and advocacy of non-violence as 'dull, and a little bit vulgar', it was for several years the only newspaper to advocate republican violence:

It was a mixture of guns and chiffon. The national position and international politics was front page news. But we also had fashion notes (written in the interest of Irish manufactured fabrics), gardening notes, written by Countess Markievicz, and a Children's Corner, with a serial fairy story, anti-recruiting articles (some from Arthur Griffith) and good original poems from Pearse, J. Plunkett, MacDonagh ... It was a funny hotch-potch of blood and thunder, high thinking, and home-made bread. We were the object of much good-natured chaff. Friendly newsagents would say 'Bean na hEireann? That's the woman's paper that all the young men buy'.[26]

As editor, responsible for soliciting contributions from the leading writers and activists of the day, Molony exercised some influence within separatist circles. Constance Markievicz 'came into national things through our paper', Molony claimed: 'I was more or less political mentor to the Countess at that time.' She helped found Markievicz's militant scouting organisation, Na Fianna Éireann, which had been planned in her brother Frank's Sherrard-street house: 'Every Sunday evening, we had a few friends in. A good deal of things were hatched there.'[27] Molony helped drill the boys (although, like Markievicz, she had to contend with their ungrateful attempts to expel her on the grounds that 'a physical force organisation is no place for women').[28] The medical campaigner, Dr Kathleen Lynn, attributed her politicisation to Molony who had convalesced at her Belgrave Road home: 'We used to have long talks and she converted me to the national movement. She was a very clever and attractive girl with a tremendous power of making friends.'[29]

It was not merely as women in the masculine world of physical-force separatism that Molony's circle challenged conventions. Molony participated in Maud Gonne's mystical Celtic ceremonies at remote locations like Island's Eye. With Countess Markievicz and their IRB mentor, Bulmer Hobson, she established a commune in north Dublin in 1909. Consisting of a large wreck of a house with seven acres, stables and a walled garden, the profits from Belcamp Park's produce were intended to support the coming revolution. Despite the involvement of Donnchadh Ó hAnnagain, a graduate of Albert Agricultural College (and subsequent leader of the East Limerick IRA), it failed due to lack of expertise: although *Bean na hÉireann*'s gardening correspondent, Markievicz's column was more metaphorical – 'root out weeds, as you want to root out British domination' – than practical.

The unorthodox setup at Belcamp Park gave rise to scurrilous rumours, with Molony's alleged relationship with Hobson – and Markievicz's estrangement from her husband – becoming the subject of Dublin gossip. Hobson quickly jumped ship, leaving Markievicz and Molony to cover the venture's liabilities.[30] The feminist republican Rosamond Jacob, who subsequently stayed with Molony and Markievicz at the latter's unkempt

Rathmines home, was struck by the bohemian nature of life at Surrey House, noting the pair's fondness for smoking and their unconventional attitudes to relationships: 'She [Molony] seems to regard men, as men, more as the relaxation of an idle hour than in any more serious light, does not appear to believe much in the one love of a lifetime, but rather in one minor flame after another. She prefers women and Madame prefers men.'[31]

By now Molony had begun to practice – as well as preach – revolution, prompting complaints from within the increasingly inactive Inghinidhe that she was 'attracted more by violence than editorial work'.[32] The final issue of *Bean na hÉireann* was published in 1911; the appearance of the IRB-backed *Irish Freedom* had diminished the demand for a woman's journal advocating violent republicanism.[33] In 1911, Molony became the first female political prisoner of her generation after smashing an illuminated portrait of King George V and Queen Mary ('smug and benign, looking down on us') during their royal visit.[34] Although ashamed by her arrest – 'no one but rowdies went to the police station' – she was dismayed when released from Mountjoy jail after payment of her fine by Anna Parnell. As Áine Ceannt noted of her brief incarceration: 'She was let out – as a matter of fact she was put out.'[35] Molony was, however, re-arrested for denouncing George V as 'a scoundrel' at a demonstration to welcome her release: 'That was marvellous; I felt myself in the same company as Wolfe Tone.'[36] Although she and Markievicz (who assaulted the police) were convicted for breaching the peace, no sentence was imposed 'on account of their sex'.[37]

Molony found herself increasingly drawn to the labour movement: 'I knew little of Labour ideas. But I was always on the side of the underdog.'[38] Her *Bean na hÉireann* column, 'Labour Notes', had brought her to the attention of James Connolly, then in the United States, who sought to recruit her to organise Belfast's mill girls.[39] Although supportive of revivalism, Connolly was critical of its bourgeois chauvinism, questioning how Inghinidhe could 'shed bucketfuls of tears over the sorrowful fate of the Children of Lir' while supporting 'a system condemning thousands of the children of Irish workers to miseries'.[40] Molony's writings did at times suggest a rather narrow nationalism: she declared, for example, that 'love of Ireland and of everything great and small that belongs to Ireland because it belongs to Ireland' should provide 'the great driving force' of cultural and political activism.[41] Following Connolly's return to Ireland, she developed a more socialist perspective. 'I was fumbling at the idea of a junction between labour and nationalism – which Connolly worked out clearly,' she recalled: 'Labour and the Nation were really one.' Like many radical women, she was drawn to Connolly's egalitarianism: 'Connolly – staunch feminist that he was – was more anxious to include women into the ranks on equal terms with men.'[42]

The Lockout also proved critical in her shift from physical-force republicanism to revolutionary socialism. She helped run the soup kitchen set up at the ITGWU's Liberty Hall headquarters to feed unemployed workers and their families.[43] She also put her theatrical expertise to use, disguising Jim Larkin as an elderly gentleman to facilitate his dramatic appearance on the balcony of the Imperial Hotel to address a public meeting in defiance of the police.[44] She had, nonetheless, little time for Larkin, describing him as 'a blatherskite ... who was all froth'. She recalled in her witness statement to the Bureau of Military History that 'the sympathy of the Irish Ireland movement was with the strikers but not all of us were in sympathy with James Larkin, or his outlook, which was that of a British Socialist'. Rosamond Jacob recorded Molony expressing similar sentiments at the time: 'we agreed most enthusiastically about the revolting unwholesome Englishness of Larkin & the strike'.[45] As within left republicanism generally, the tensions between socialism and nationalism that characterised her outlook were not easily reconciled.

The Lockout, Molony believed, 'profoundly affected the whole country', producing 'a sort of social and intellectual revolution' whose effects included the formation of the Irish Citizen Army. This is debatable but it certainly contributed to a personal breakdown, leading Molony to spend much of the following year convalescing in France with Maud Gonne. On her return to Ireland, she worked more closely with Connolly. Acting in the Abbey by night, she spent her days running the workers' co-operative store, which had been established during the Lockout. She also succeeded Delia Larkin as general secretary of the Irish Women Workers' Union (IWWU), which was close to collapse following the Lockout, and became the registered proprietor of Connolly's *Workers' Republic* newspaper.

Swept along in the wave of militarism that accompanied the Lockout and home rule crisis, Molony organised 'the girls as a unit of the Citizen Army', overseeing their training at the miniature rifle range in Liberty Hall.[46] She viewed the Citizen Army as a more radical organisation than the Volunteers (whom she dubbed the 'fan go fóills' due to its reluctance to commit to a policy of insurrection) and the Fenians who she dismissed as 'old maids'. Her attitude to the latter changed, however, in January 1916 when Connolly was persuaded of the IRB military council's determination to rise.

Molony's Eden Quay co-operative, which adjoined Liberty Hall, became a meeting place for the military council, allowing her to observe at first hand the preparations for the rebellion. 'Volunteer leaders dropped in to discuss plans two or three times a week,' she recalled:

In a little office at the back of the shop, and leading to the printing works, Connolly, after hours, could be free of union business, but available for private visitors. As secretary to the co-op, I was always on hand to identify such callers. Pearse called many times, also Joe Plunkett and Tom MacDonagh. These men were all intimate friends of mine, so it seemed quite natural for me to encourage them to buy socks and ties from us.[47]

Her own willingness to use violence – 'I always carried a revolver' – was demonstrated by her role in foiling a police raid on the co-op shortly before the Rising. The printer Christopher Brady described how he watched 'through a little door with two spy holes' as Molony prevented the police from seizing copies of a republican newspaper:

Connolly came down quickly, walked quietly to the counter with drawn gun in his hand. A few feet away Miss Molony was already covering the police with her automatic. Connolly looked sternly at the police and gave his command to them: 'Drop these papers or I will drop you' ... At once they changed their tune and said 'Of course we are only doing our duty and we have no warrant for this raid'. With this they beat a quick retreat.[48]

Had they not, Molony insisted, 'Connolly would have fired and I would have fired on the other man.'[49] From this point until the mobilisation on Easter Monday, Liberty Hall remained under armed guard: 'the atmosphere', she recalled, 'was like a simmering pot'. Unwilling to risk missing the rebellion which Connolly had hinted was imminent, she slept 'at night on a pile of men's coats in the back of the shop'. Christopher Brady's account conveys her intimate involvement in the last-minute preparations for the insurrection: 'When the printing of the Proclamation was completed I made up two parcels of the printed copies, 1,250 in each, and brought them to Miss Helena Molony who was lying on a couch in the co-op shop room in Liberty Hall. She told me to put them under her pillow. She was armed with a revolver.'

Revolution

Molony recalled the moment of insurrection in euphoric terms: 'When we walked out that Easter Monday morning we felt in a very real sense that we were walking with Ireland into the sun.'[50] Her comrades were nonetheless mocked by Dubliners as they filed up Dame Street: 'Here's the Citizen Army, with their pop-guns!'[51] Molony was among a group of thirty rebels that her Abbey Theatre colleague, Seán Connolly, led in an audacious attack on Dublin Castle. The ease with which they infiltrated the headquarters of the British authorities in Ireland would come to symbolise the humiliating unpreparedness of Augustine Birrell's regime.

Finding their entry to the Castle blocked by a solitary unarmed policeman, Connolly fired one of the first shots of the Rising, killing Constable James O'Brien. After hesitating briefly – whether due to shock or confusion – the rebels advanced into the Castle grounds, overwhelming the guardroom and briefly occupying the Upper Castle yard before fleeing. For a rebellion whose impact was primarily propagandistic, the failure to seize the Castle was a missed opportunity: 'It breaks my heart – and all our hearts – that we did not get in.'[52] However, their orders were to occupy City Hall rather than the Castle, which had initially been targeted for 'psychological effect' but was considered too large to hold.[53]

The experiences of women in the Citizen Army are often contrasted with those in Cumann na mBan who were confined to more strictly gendered roles or, in some cases, not permitted to participate in the rebellion.[54] Conscious of how the participation of women in the struggle for independence was marginalised in subsequent accounts, Molony emphasised her combatant role: 'I had my own revolver and ammunition,' she recalled: even 'before the Russian Army had women soldiers, the Citizen Army had them'.[55] It was, she insisted, 'the first army in the world where men and women were on equal terms'.[56] But although James Connolly had armed Molony and other women on Easter Monday, he had also ordered them not to use their revolvers 'except in the last resort'.[57] In reality, only one woman (the trouser-wearing, cigarette-smoking Countess Markievicz) was formally recorded as belonging to the Citizen Army prior to the Rising; the other female members were generally referred to as 'the women's section.'[58] Aside from a few exceptional individuals such as Margaret Skinnider – a Glaswegian teacher who cited the Proclamation in defence of her right to hurl a grenade through the window of the Shelbourne Hotel – women in the Citizen Army were also confined to roles such as cooking and first-aid.[59]

Whether because of their experience of police brutality during the Lockout, or their more radical outlook, the Citizen Army adopted a more ruthless attitude to the police than the Volunteers. Molony's account of the raid on Dublin Castle nonetheless suggests unease about the first killing of the Rising. An account she provided in the mid-1930s emphasised both the rebels' restraint and the momentous import of their actions:

> They reached the gate of the Castle, and Sean Connolly, who was in command ordered the policeman on duty to stand aside. He refused. Connolly insisted and warned him, presenting the revolver. But this blind tool of imperialism could not believe that the Irish people were demanding their own. Connolly shot him dead, and that bullet destroyed the *status quo* in Ireland.[60]

Her subsequent witness statement to the Bureau of Military History (recorded, in 1950, in the knowledge that it would remain confidential until her death) described O'Brien's killing more humanely:

> When Connolly went to go past him, the Sergeant put out his arm; and Connolly shot him dead ... When I saw Connolly draw his revolver, I drew my own. Across the road, there was a policeman with papers. He got away, thank God. I did not like to think of the policeman dead ... I think the policeman at the gate was killed instantly, because they were quite close. The police did not think the Citizen Army were serious.[61]

The rebels took up positions on the balustraded parapet of City Hall; overlooked by Dublin Castle's clock-tower, the position proved lethal. Within hours Seán Connolly – fatally wounded by a sniper's bullet – lay dying in Molony's arms: 'He was bleeding very much from the stomach. I said the Act of Contrition into his ear.' She was lucky not to share his fate: the officer who subsequently captured Molony told her that 'he very nearly "got me" on the roof once or twice'.[62] Like many of the rebel positions, City Hall was poorly chosen. Unable to prevent British reinforcements from streaming into the Castle, the rebels withdrew into the building: 'there was nothing to do, only sit', Molony recalled, 'the men fired desultory shots all day'. Peering through a window, Molony observed what she initially mistook for sleet before realising it was a hail of bullets: 'through the windows on the ground floor of the City Hall, there were machine gun bullets pouring in', she recalled: 'From the ceiling the plaster began to fall.'[63] They were quickly overwhelmed: 'A window was smashed at the back, and then we knew they were pouring in.'[64]

Molony spent the remainder of Easter week confined, with other female prisoners, to an 'old, dirty room' in Ship Street barracks: although 'we were all covered with vermin', she recalled, the 'soldiers were decent enough to us'. They remained defiant, rejoicing when food supplies to the soldiers (and themselves) were cut off. Following the surrender, she was moved to the grim disused prison at Kilmainham where the women were jeered by soldiers, some reportedly drunk, as they used the toilets. Their distress was compounded by their knowledge of the fate of the Rising's leaders at the stonebreaker's yard: 'I heard the shots every morning at dawn,' she recalled, 'and knew that that meant they were executing our men.' She was profoundly shaken by the experience: 'Connolly was dragged out, unable to stand, and murdered. After that life seemed to come to an end for me.'[65]

Following a spirited attempt to tunnel out of Kilmainham with a spoon, Molony was moved to more congenial environs at Mountjoy jail where the women were 'hailed with joy by the wardress' on the grounds that they were 'interesting prisoners' rather than 'ordinary criminals'.[66] They were allowed parcels, visitors, exercise and free association. Despite refusing to disavow their actions, all but six of the seventy-nine women prisoners were released within weeks on the grounds that they had been led astray by the men rather than acted on their own convictions. General John Maxwell, the commander-in-chief in Ireland, recorded his delight at finding himself rid of 'all those silly little girls'.[67] One of only five women among the 2,500 men interned in England, Molony received exceptional treatment – although Maxwell faced resistance from Downing Street and the Home Office in his efforts to intern this tiny handful of women whom he described as 'older, better educated and real believers in a free Ireland'. Similar political sensitivies were reflected by the decision not to execute Countess Markievicz 'on account of her sex'.[68]

The plight of the imprisoned republicans aroused greater public sympathy than their actions during Easter week. Molony's internment was raised in the House of Commons by Irish MP T.M. Healy who objected to the arrest of 'a number of women in Ireland, the offence of one being that she had played at the Abbey Theatre'.[69] Dublin Trades' Council also protested against Molony's detention which it attributed to her involvement in the labour movement.[70] Molony was equally aware of the propaganda opportunities arising from their plight. Despite the good conditions at Lewes prison, Marie Perolz recalled that 'Helena Molony said that we should not admit we were well treated.'[71] Transferred to Aylesbury prison, a gloomy Victorian jail in Buckinghamshire, Molony continued to create difficulties, taking advantage of a visit by an Irish MP's wife to smuggle an article exposing the conditions in which foreign women were held to Sylvia Pankhurst's Workers' Suffrage Federation. Recalling this period decades later, Molony dwelled not on the tribulations of imprisonment but the emotional impact of the executions which may have contributed to her depressive tendencies: 'After 1916 the colour went out of life for me.'[72]

In December, the new prime minister, David Lloyd George, eager to draw a line under the insurrection's fallout, declared a general amnesty for internees. Released from Aylesbury, Molony picked up the threads of her old life, albeit in more straitened circumstances. 'Marie Perolz and Helena Molony came to us after their release,' an Irish National Aid activist recalled, 'We did what we could for them.'[73] Although they returned as heroes – 'Failure was greater than triumph and victory less than defeat' – Molony recalled the period as a demoralising one: 'we were defeated; nobody thought we would rise up again'.[74] In contrast to those republicans determined to learn strategic lessons from the debacle of the Rising, Molony remained unrepentantly militant: 'For us, it was only a matter of taking up the gun again.'[75]

After the Rising women initially gained a more substantial role within the republican movement, particularly the prisoners' aid organisations that provided the first evidence of popular support for republicanism. Molony's radical circle – 'Cumann na mBan, the Plunkett girls and boys, well-known extremists' – were prominent in commemorating the Rising's first anniversary, flying tricolours from the rebel garrisons and pasting copies of the Proclamation throughout the city: 'I remember one poster in Grafton Street stayed up for six or eight months. Paste, mixed with glue, dries like china.'[76] After the police seized one of their banners ('James Connolly Murdered – May 12th, 1916'), Molony and other Citizen Army women barricaded themselves into Liberty Hall, unfurling another banner on the roof.[77]

Such activities placed Molony, as ever, in the revolutionary vanguard. She recounted indignantly how their efforts were opposed by the IRB which, with many convicted republicans still imprisoned, had its own reasons for a less confrontational commemoration. Similar tensions existed at Liberty Hall where her union colleagues were unenthusiastic about her decision to stage another symbolic act of defiance in a building only partially restored following its shelling by the *Helga*. In her witness statement Helena wrongly attributed their hostility to Larkinite influence: 'The Union was in the hands of Larkin's section. The Hall was in their hands too. We knew we had unsympathetic members in the back, and enemies in the front.'[78] In reality, the union was led by the Connollyites William O'Brien and Tom Foran who revered their predecessor's memory without seeking to emulate his sacrificial tactics. After 1916, organised labour would play a more peripheral, and non-violent, role in the struggle for independence. Molony's revolutionary politics also saw her sidelined within the IWWU as more moderate colleagues, such as the pacifist Louie Bennett who replaced her as general secretary in 1918, came to exert greater influence within the labour movement.

The focus in Molony's lengthy witness statement on her activism before the Rising may in part reflect her marginalisation following the emergence of republicanism as a mass movement. As a member of the League of Women Delegates, which represented Cumann na mBan among other women's organisations, she campaigned for women to be represented within the republican movement that was coalescing in late 1917. Molony and Countess Plunkett had been hastily added to the Mansion House Committee in April 1917 when Molony denounced its exclusion of women.[79] However, following the merger between Sinn Féin and its principal rival, Count Plunkett's Liberty Clubs, in June, women were again excluded from the leadership. Despite pointing out 'the risk women took, equally with the men, to have the Republic established', the League's demands for representation on Sinn Féin's executive were ignored. Molony and three other women were eventually co-opted but on the condition that they represented Sinn Féin branches, a measure intended to prevent 'the formation of an organised feminist caucus'.[80] Only twelve female delegates attended the thousand-strong Sinn Féin convention: although four women were elected to the new executive, only two were nominated for election in 1918. There was clearly little appetite for a prominent political role for women within the emerging new Ireland.

Although a pale shadow of the pre-1916 militia, Molony played a minor role within the Citizen Army during the revolution, supporting the sporadic efforts by workers to occupy factories and establish revolutionary 'soviets'. She served as a judge in the Ministry of Labour's arbitration courts in Rathmines, 'settling disputes, wages and that'.[81] She nominally enrolled as a member of Cumann na mBan but refused to wear its uniform. Much in demand as a public speaker, Molony remained active in prisoners' campaigns, a traditional sphere of female activism. During the Civil War, she was involved in the usual range of women's activities: first aid, procuring and concealing weapons, supporting prisoners' dependents, and publicity work.[82] Her prominent profile ensured unwelcome police attention. Described by a senior Dublin Castle official as 'the most dangerous woman in Ireland', she was kept under observation by the British – and then Free State – authorities, as well as receiving more overt attention: 'I was raided constantly. It would be easier to record the times I was not raided.'[83]

Aftermath

After the revolution Molony sought to resist the erosion of the egalitarian principles of the Proclamation as a conservative Catholic nationalist ethos that valued women as wives and mothers rather than citizens gained ground. Acknowledging that the feminist impulse was 'now unhappily long spent', she complained that although women had won the right to vote they retained 'their inferior status, their lower pay for equal work, their exclusion from juries and certain branches of the civil service, their slum dwellings and crowded, cold and unsanitary schools for their children'.[84]

Denouncing what she saw as the hypocrisy of the Labour Party's efforts to identify itself with Connolly's revolutionary ideals while advocating mild social democratic reforms, she condemned the party's acceptance of the 'imperialist' Treaty settlement, viewing its deputies' willingness to swear an oath to the Crown as a betrayal of the Republic.[85] She unsuccessfully sought to maintain the party's commitment to workers' control of industry.[86] She was equally scathing about the status accorded to women within the party: referring to a 'sorry travesty of emancipation', she urged its members to study Connolly's writings.[87] More moderate colleagues, in turn, resented Molony's efforts to commit the party – for which she was 'not prepared to go out and fight' – to unrealistic policies.[88]

As a trade union official Molony devoted much of her career to largely unsuccessful efforts to organise domestic workers. She also opposed measures such as the 1935 Conditions of Employment Act (which permitted the state to exclude women from certain occupations) and those aspects of the 1937 Constitution that sought to confine women to the home. She believed such discriminatory measures were prompted by reactionary impulses rather than concerns for women's welfare. These campaigns won little support among the Labour Party and wider trade union movement. Reflecting the interests of its overwhelmingly male membership, many trade union officials opposed the demand for equal pay and gender equality: 'Woman is the queen of our hearts and of our homes,' declared one Irish Trade Union Congress delegate faced by Molony's motion against the Conditions of Employment Bill, 'and, for God's sake, let us try to keep her there.'[89]

An articulate feminist, Molony highlighted the contribution of women to the revolution in support of her demands for equality. She chastised Sean O'Faolain, for example, for his unsympathetic portrayal of Countess Markievicz's motivations in his biography (for which she had been interviewed):

> It is a curious thing that many men seem to be unable to believe that any woman can embrace an ideal – accept it intellectually, feel it as a profound emotion, and then calmly decide to make a vocation of working for its realisation. They give themselves endless pains to prove that every serious thing a woman does (outside nursing or washing pots) is the result of being in love with some man, or disappointed in love of some man, or looking for excitement, or limelight, or indulging their vanity. You do not seem to have escaped from the limitations of your sex.[90]

Ironically, O'Faolain was no less opposed to the Free State's narrow Catholic ethos. His writings, which had been censored, sympathetically addressed 'the barren state of those who have become misfits in a restrictive society', but Molony's comments reflected an understandable frustration at the marginalisation of women's revolutionary role.[91]

During the same period, she entered into a lengthy dispute with the Military Pensions advisory committee due to its refusal to classify much of her revolutionary activism as military service: 'Women were recruited into the Citizen Army on the same terms as men. They were appointed to the duties most suitable to them – as were men – and these duties fell naturally into dealing with Commissariat, Intelligence, First Aid and advanced Medical Aid, but their duties were not confined to these.'[92] She was 'not primarily concerned with a pension', she told the committee, 'but with the recognition of women's services rendered to the Republic'.[93] Ill-health compelled her to drop her objections in 1937 but she continued to criticise the state's narrow definition of military service:

> when I was presiding at a meeting in O'Connell St ... (under Army orders) one woman was shot dead, and a boy standing beside me shot through his head, and six others wounded. It is difficult for the ordinary person to understand how such things are not classified as 'military

service'. In any regular Army in any civilized country, I never heard of such no[n]-combatants as Army Service Corps, or Intelligence Dept. – being classified as non-Military.[94]

Molony was involved in many of the lost causes of the 1930s: she helped found the Friends of Soviet Russia, spoke at the League against Imperialism's public meetings, campaigned for the Prisoners' Defence League, and supported anti-fascist agitation. Although a Catholic who could quote papal encyclicals in support of her political views, Molony's criticism of the Vatican provoked controversy.[95] Her radicalism saw her out of step not just with the state and the labour movement but with her own trade union: she was forced by the IWWU to resign from the IRA's political front, Saor Éire, in 1931. Her visit in the same year to the Soviet Union as part of a labour delegation saw her further marginalised. Refusing to purchase copies of the delegation's report, her own union passed a motion regretting how the 'principles of religion or liberty' were not upheld in the Soviet Union.[96] Despite being elected president of the Irish Trade Union Council in 1937, only the second woman to hold the office, she was forced to retire from trade union activity in 1941.

While attributed to illness, Molony's alcoholism and her links to the wartime IRA contributed to her early retirement. Her support for Coras na Poblachta, a pro-German IRA front, brought her to the attention of military intelligence during the Emergency. Along with Maud Gonne's daughter, Iseult Stuart, she was one of a circle of republicans who protected the German spy Hermann Goertz from the police by arranging shelter in safe houses, including her own. Although she was frequently under surveillance during this period, the police uncovered nothing more compromising than her bouts of heavy drinking, depression, and impecunious circumstances.[97] Awarded a small disability allowance by the IWWU on her retirement, she relied on appeals to her former trade union, and the kindness of friends, to make ends meet.[98]

Molony's close relationship with psychiatrist Evelyn O'Brien, with whom she lived from the 1930s until her death, has prompted speculation about her sexuality. Romantically linked (without firm evidence) to both Bulmer Hobson and Seán Connolly, Molony has also been claimed by feminists as a member of an influential lesbian network prominent in feminist, labour and republican circles.[99] Others included the Citizen Army rebels Kathleen Lynn and Madeleine ffrench-Mullen (who founded St Ultan's hospital); Cumann na mBan activists Julia Grennan and Elizabeth

O'Farrell (who conveyed Pearse's letter of surrender to the British military); and her IWWU colleagues Louie Bennett and Helen Chenevix. Although these women struggled and lived together, and (in some cases) were buried together in Glasnevin's Republican plot, this dimension of their lives has until recently remained hidden from history: whatever the precise nature of these intimate relationships,[100] they are inadequately acknowledged in, for example, the *Dictionary of Irish Biography*'s fleeting references to their unmarried status or close friendships with other women. As Roy Foster has noted, the whitewashing of revolutionaries' sexual lives, along with the suppression of their feminist, socialist, and secularist ideas, formed part of the 'post-revolutionary stabilisation and re-clericalisation of Irish Society'.[101]

When Molony died, at the age of 84, in 1967 there remained sufficient veterans from the depleted ranks of the Citizen Army, old IRA and Cumann na mBan to form a guard of honour to escort her coffin to Glasnevin's Republican plot. The Defence Forces sounded the Last Post as 'a cluster of Helena's nearest friends wept quietly'. Describing her as 'one of the great patriotic women of the time', Éamon de Valera delivered a generous oration: 'With James Connolly and Countess Markievicz she worked for Irish freedom, for the Irish worker and for the poor. She stood firmly for the rights of women and their political equality with men in our society.'[102] The same could not have been said of the president whose patriarchal vision of society proved so much more representative of his times.

Legacy

Revolutions, like political lives, frequently end in disappointment. Irish republicanism triumphed after 1916 but the state that emerged from Sinn Féin's revolution fell short of the radical vision for which Molony had struggled. The failure to transform society was partly a result of 'the contraction of political options that came with world war, revolution, and partition',[103] as the optimism and energy of the cultural and separatist revival culminated in a conservative state that prioritised power over liberation. It reflected also the ideological incoherence of republicanism, and the limited appeal of the radical vision that inspired a tiny minority before 1916. 'Perhaps the time was not ripe for success,' Molony later conceded: 'Our people had not a widespread economic knowledge to cope with social evils. I should have hated to see Padraic Pearse as President of an Irish Republic if the misery and wretchedness of the tenements had still gone on.'[104]

Molony's experiences highlight how the abstraction that was the Irish nation was shaped by the harsh realities of class, gender and power. Fitting 'uneasily in the well-established narratives that prescribe women as symbol, icon or emblem of the nation', the contribution of activists like Molony faded from view as the Irish state constructed a narrative of its liberation that reflected Catholic nationalist values.[105] Their absence from the historical record was as much a product of post-independence attitudes as their marginalisation prior to it, as is evident from recent research on such figures as Alice Milligan, Kathleen Lynn and Rosamond Jacob.[106]

As a result of the scandals and economic crises of recent years, the extent to which the state has failed to realise the progressive vision of the 1916 Proclamation is increasingly openly acknowledged. Alongside more celebratory commemorative narratives, the revolution's limitations might usefully be considered during the 'decade of centenaries'. Rather than simply re-enacting the past, the most successful forms of commemoration – as was demonstrated by the appropriation of 1798 by Molony's revolutionary generation – allow for the possibility of drawing on its energies to open up possibilities of alternative futures.[107] It seems apposite that the most successful protest movement to emerge from the centenary of the Easter Rising – the 'Waking the Feminists' campaign for gender equality in the theatre – occurred in response to the Abbey Theatre's Waking the Nation programme which celebrated 'the words of Helena Molony, Abbey Actress and Abbey Rebel' while simultaneously excluding contemporary women's voices from the stage of the National Theatre.[108]

Despite the poignant gap between her aspirations and the revolution's outcome, Molony did not regret her attempt to change the world. Writing two decades after 1916, by which time the myth of the Easter Rising as a Christ-like blood sacrifice had been firmly established, she continued to articulate a different narrative of struggle:

> 1916 has been represented as a gesture of sacrifice. It is said that those in it knew they would be defeated ... I know how we all felt. We thought we were going to do this big thing, to free our country. It was like a religion – something that filled the whole of life. Personal feelings and vanities, wealth, comfort, position – these things did not matter ... Everyone was exalted and caught in the sweep of a great movement. We saw a vision of Ireland, free, pure, happy. We did not realise this vision. But we saw it.[109]

Endnotes

1   David Convery, 'Uniting the working class: history, memory and 1913', in idem, *Locked Out: A Century of Irish Working-Class Life* (Dublin: Irish Academic Press, 2013), pp. 23–4.

2   See, for example, the programme of activities recorded in http://1913committee.ie/blog/.

3   On Larkin's evolving legacy, see John Cunningham, 'From *Disturbed Dublin* to *Strumpet City*: the 1913 "history wars", 1914–1980', in Francis Devine, *A Capital in Conflict: Dublin City and the 1913 Lockout* (Dublin: Four Courts Press, 2013), pp. 353–77. For Larkin's divisive impact, see Emmet O'Connor, *Big Jim Larkin: Hero or Wrecker?* (Dublin: University College Dublin Press, 2015).

4   *Sunday Times*, 6 October 2013.

5   Emmet O'Connor, 'Larkin's Road to Revolution', *Irish Times*, 11 September 2013.

6   On the myth, see Pádraig Yeates, *Lockout: Dublin 1913* (Dublin: Gill & Macmillan, 2000), p. xi; Joseph Connell, 'The Great Lockout of 1913', *History Ireland*, 21, 4 (July/August 2013), p. 66.

7   Brian Hanley, 'Class Dismissed?', *History Ireland*, 21, 4 (July/August 2013), pp. 10–11.

8   Legion of Mary founder, Frank Duff, a shoe-in during an earlier era, trailed in last on the council's shortlist (*Irish Times*, 3 September 2013). On distortion of Hackett's biography, see Pádraig Yeates' letter to the *Irish Times*, 11 September 2013.

9   *Irish Times*, 20 May 2014 (http://www.irishtimes.com/news/ireland/irish-news/why-did-no-women-speak-at-the-rosie-hackett-bridge-opening-1.1802908).

10 While the role of women received unprecedented attention in 2016, Molony was particularly prominent. Her story featured in theatrical productions by ANU and Smashing Times, and the RTÉ documentary *Seven Women*, as well as partly inspiring the character of Elizabeth Butler in the RTÉ drama *Rebellion*. She was one of six women whose images were displayed on buses and trains across the capital. For more on Molony and her legacy, see Fearghal McGarry, *The Abbey Rebels of 1916: A Lost Revolution* (Dublin: Gill & Macmillan, 2015).

11 *The Irish Citizen*, 27 September 2013, cited in Pat Quigley, *The Polish Irishman: The Life and Times of Count Casimir Markievicz* (Dublin: The Liffey Press, 2012).

12 Frances Clarke and Laurence White, 'Helena Molony', *Dictionary of Irish Biography* (Cambridge: Cambridge University Press, 2009).

13 B[ureau] of M[ilitary] H[istory] W[itness] S[tatement] 391 (Helena Molony), Military Archives, p. 1.

14 R.M. Fox, *Rebel Irishwomen* (Dublin: Talbot Press, 1935), p. 120. For recent valuable work on Inghinidhe, see Senia Pašeta, *Irish Nationalist Women, 1900–1918* (Cambridge: Cambridge University Press, 2013) and Lauren Arrington, *Revolutionary Lives. Constance and Casimir Markievicz* (Princeton NJ: Princeton University Press, 2016).

15 BMH WS 391 (Helena Molony); Fox, *Rebel Irishwomen*, p. 119.

16 Fox, *Rebel Irishwomen*, pp. 120–1; Margaret Ward, *Unmanageable Revolutionaries: Women and Irish Nationalism* (London: Pluto Press, 1983), pp. 63–4.

17 BMH WS 391 (Helena Molony), p. 6.

18 Senia Pašeta, 'Nationalist responses to two royal visits to Ireland, 1900 and 1903', *Irish Historical Studies*, 31:124 (Nov. 1999), pp. 488–504.

19 BMH WS 391 (Helena Molony), p. 1.

20 Ibid., p. 6.

21 Ward, *Unmanageable Revolutionaries*, p. 51.

22 'Irish girls' handbill, n.d., BMH CD 119/3/1.

23 BMH WS 391 (Helena Molony), p. 4.

24 BMW WS 909 (Sidney Czira), p. 10.

25 Penny Duggan, *Helena Molony: Actress, Feminist, Nationalist, Socialist and Trade-Unionist* (Amsterdam: International Institute for Research and Education, 1990), pp. 7–8.

26 BMH WS 391 (Helena Molony), p. 10.

27 Ibid., p. 57.

28 Duggan, *Molony*, p. 8.

29 BMH WS 357 (Kathleen Lynn), p. 1.

30 Marnie Hay, *Bulmer Hobson and the Nationalist Movement in Twentieth-Century Ireland* (Manchester: Manchester University Press, 2009), pp. 79–81; Duggan, *Molony*, p. 9.

31 Rosamond Jacob diary, 4 Nov. 1911, cited in Leeann Lane, *Rosamond Jacob, Third Person Singular* (Dublin: University College Dublin Press, 2010), p. 64.

32 Samuel Levenson, *Maud Gonne* (London: Reader's Digest Press, 1976), p. 271.

33 Ward, *Unmanageable Revolutionaries*, pp. 74–5.

34 BMH WS 391 (Helena Molony), p. 16.

35 BMH WS 264 (Áine Ceannt), p. 6.

36 Duggan, *Molony*, p. 10.

37 'Helena Moloney', Personalities file, CO 904/201/305, National Archives (London).

38 Fox, *Rebel Irishwomen*, p. 122.

39 BMH WS 909 (Sidney Czira); BMH WS 919 (Ina Heron).

40 Cited in Ben Levitas, 'Plumbing the Depths: Irish Realism and the Working Class from Shaw to O'Casey', *Irish University Review*, 33:1 (Spring-Summer 2003), p. 136.

41 Nell Regan, 'Helena Molony' in Mary Cullen and Maria Luddy (eds), *Female Activists: Irish Women and Change, 1900–1960* (Dublin: The Woodfield Press, 2001), p. 143.

42 BMH WS 391 (Helena Molony), p. 10.

43 Fox, *Rebel Irishwomen*, p.125; BMH WS 1670 (Seamus Kavanagh), p. 10.

44 BMH WS 909 (Sidney Czira), p. 16.

45 Rosamond Jacob diary, 11 Dec. 1913, cited in Lane, *Jacob*, p. 66.

46 BMH WS 391 (Helena Molony), p. 21.

47 Fox, *Rebel Irishwomen*, p. 125.

48 BMH WS 705 (Christopher Brady), p. 3.

49 BMH WS 391 (Helena Molony), p. 27.

50 Duggan, *Molony*, p. 16.

51 BMH WS 1,746 (Matthew Connolly), p. 5.

52 BMH WS 391 (Helena Molony), p. 35.

53 BMH WS 421 (William Oman); BMH WS 391 (Helena Molony), p. 33.

54 Fearghal McGarry, *The Rising: Ireland: Easter 1916* (Oxford: Oxford University Press, 2010), pp. 161–2.

55 BMH WS 391 (Helena Molony), p. 33.

56 'Sworn statement by Helena Moloney', 3 July 1936, Military Pension file (11739), Military Archives.

57 BMH WS 391 (Helena Molony), p. 33.

58 Ann Matthews, 'Vanguard of the revolution? The Irish Citizen Army, 1916', in Ruán O'Donnell, *The Impact of the 1916 Rising: Among the Nations* (Dublin: Irish Academic Press, 2008), pp. 28–9.

59 Idem, *Renegades: Irish republican women, 1900–1922* (Dublin: Mercier Press, 2010), pp. 129–30.

60 Fox, *Rebel Irishwomen*, pp. 128–9.

61 BMH WS 391 (Helena Molony), p. 35.

62 BMH WS 391 (Helena Molony), p. 37; Fox, *Rebel Irishwomen*, p. 131.

63 R.M. Fox, *The History of the Irish Citizen Army* (Dublin: James Duffy, 1943), p. 154; BMH WS 391 (Helena Molony), p. 38.

64 Charles Townshend, *Easter 1916: The Irish Rebellion* (London: Penguin, 2005), p. 164.

65 BMH WS 391 (Helena Molony), p. 41.

66 R.M. Fox, *Green Banners: The Story of the Irish Struggle* (London: Secker and Warburg, 1938); BMH WS 357 (Kathleen Lynn), p. 4.

67 Michael Foy and Brian Barton, *The Easter Rising* (Stroud: Sutton, 1999), pp. 225–6.

68 Townshend, *Easter Rising*, pp. 285–6.

69 *The Kerryman*, 3 Jun. 1916.

70 Mary Jones, *These Obstreperous Lassies: A History of the IWWU* (Dublin: Gill & Macmillan, 1988), p. 21.

71 BMH WS 246 (Marie Perolz), p. 11.

72 Fox, *Rebel Irishwomen*, p. 131.

73 BMH WS 826 (Maeve MacGarry).

74 Duggan, *Molony*, p. 16; BMH WS 391 (Helena Molony), p. 47.

75 BMH WS 391 (Helena Molony), p. 42.

76 Ibid., p. 45.

77 Ward, *Unmanageable Revolutionaries*, p. 122.

78 BMH WS 391 (Helena Molony), p. 47.

79 Ward, *Unmanageable Revolutionaries*, p. 124.

80 Margaret Ward, 'The League of Women Delegates and Sinn Féin', *History Ireland*, 4:3 (Autumn 1996), pp. 37–41.

81 BMH WS 391 (Helena Molony), p. 51.

82 'Sworn statement', 3 July 1936.

83 'Helena Molony', Personalities file, CO 904/201/305, National Archives (London); BMH WS 391 (Helena Molony), p. 52

84 Helena Molony, 'James Connolly and women', *Dublin Labour Year Book*, 1930.

85 Duggan, *Molony*, p. 21.

86 Clarke and White, 'Molony'.

87 Rosemary Cullen Owens, *Louie Bennett* (Cork: Cork University Press, 2001), p. 81.

88 Duggan, *Molony*, p. 23.

89 Jones, *Obstreperous Lassies*, p. 129.

90 Helena Molony to Sean O'Faolain, 6 September, 1934; BMH WS 391 (Helena Molony).

91 Maurice Harmon, 'Sean O'Faolain', *Dictionary of Irish Biography*.

92 Molony to Advisory Committee, 14 July 1936, Military Pension File (11739).

93 Ibid., 18 Nov. 1936.

94 Ibid., 11 Oct. 1937.

95 Duggan, *Molony*, p. 33.

96 Clarke and White, 'Molony'.

97 'Moloney, Miss Helena', G2/3364, Military Archives.

98 Jones, *Obstreperous Lassies*, p. 204.

99 Katharine O'Donnell, 'Lesbianism', in Brian Lalor (ed.), *The Encyclopaedia of Ireland* (Dublin: Gill & Macmillan, 2003), p. 624.

100 Marie Mullholland, *The Politics and Relationships of Kathleen Lynn* (Dublin: The Woodfield Press, 2002), pp. 6–19.

101 R.F. Foster, *Vivid Faces: The Revolutionary Generation in Ireland, 1890–1923* (London: Penguin, 2014), pp. 115–43.

102 *Irish Times, Irish Independent, Irish Press*, 30 Jan., 1 Feb. 1967.

103 Ben Levitas, *The Theatre of Nation: Irish Drama and Cultural Nationalism, 1890–1916* (Oxford: Oxford University Press, 2002), p. 228.

104 Fox, *Rebel Irishwomen*, p. 127.

105 Karen Steele, *Women, Press and Politics during the Irish Revival* (Syracuse NY: Syracuse University Press, 2007), p. 201.

106 Lane, *Jacob*; Catherine Morris, *Alice Milligan* (Dublin: Four Courts Press, 2012); Margaret Ó hÓgartaigh, *Kathleen Lynn: Irishwoman, Patriot, Doctor* (Dublin: Irish Academic Press, 2006).

107 Declan Kiberd, 'Disappearing Ireland', Theatre of Memory symposium, Abbey Theatre, 18 Jan. 2014.

108 See https://www.abbeytheatre.ie/waking-the-nation-2016-at-the-abbey-theatre/; http://www.wakingthefeminists.org/.

109 Fox, *Rebel Irishwomen*, pp. 131–2.

CHAPTER SEVEN

Glorious Forever? The Political Evolution of the Irish Citizen Army, 1913–1921

Conor McNamara

Many, no doubt, preferred Caithlin Ni Houlihan in a respectable dress than a Caithlin in the garb of a working woman.

Sean O'Casey, *The Story of the Irish Citizen Army.*[1]

The Irish Citizen Army went through several re-incarnations during the Irish Revolution, from a loosely organised workers' protection force, to a socialist republican militia committed to violent revolution, and finally, a militant micro-group on the margins of the republican movement. The Citizen Army was founded at the height of the Lockout in November 1913 as a means of raising striking workers' morale and to provide protection at pickets and political meetings. The Lockout generated sustained violence with street fighting and riots erupting across the city throughout the period.[2] Street violence between semi-organised gangs had long been a feature of working-class culture and the absence of an organised militia in the early phase of the Lockout did not mean that workers were helpless in the face of the violent excesses of the DMP.[3] The Citizen Army, however, represented a new development in working-class culture as the organisation was conceived as a conventional and disciplined force whose presence was designed to act as a deterrent to the DMP, ensuring the safety of workers while intimidating their perceived persecutors. The movement played a small role in the Lockout and James Larkin took little interest in the day-to-day running of the organisation.

Following the conclusion of the Lockout the Citizen Army partially collapsed but was revived under the leadership of James Connolly and

Michael Mallin – who, through sheer force of personality – transformed the organisation into a pragmatic and serious minded revolutionary group. Given Larkin's disdain for the Irish Volunteers, it is ironic that it was the involvement of around two hundred Volunteers of the Citizen Army in the 1916 Rebellion that assured the movement's place in modern Irish history. The ICA's role in the Rising, however, has tended to obscure the failure of the movement to garner popular support among Dublin workers and the internal implosion of the movement following the Rising. This chapter examines the foundation and evolution of the Citizen Army in the context of the persistence of internal disputes, both within the organisation, and in the wider Irish Labour movement, over what role, if any, the Citizen Army should play within the Irish Trade Union movement. A dearth of leadership following the execution of Connolly and Mallin; the death of Séan Connolly, who was killed on the first day of the Rising on the roof of City Hall and the death of William Partridge from Bright's disease contracted in Frongoch in 1917 were key reasons for the decline of the force. The Citizen Army ultimately failed to play a meaningful role in the War of Independence due to the apathy of its own membership, the disinterest of the working-class community and the opposition of the trade unions. The dramatic decline of the ICA must be considered in the context of the inexorable growth of the Irish Volunteers and the overwhelming tendency for trade union members to join the rival organisation, aggravated by the failure of the Citizen Army leadership to provide coherent strategy.

Historiography

The historiography of the Citizen Army is problematic. Sean O'Casey's brief account of the organisation, *The Story of the Irish Citizen Army*, published in 1919 was motivated by personal spite towards former comrades whom he accused of abandoning socialism for 'the high creed of Irish nationalism'.[4] O'Casey was briefly the secretary of the ICA but left in 1914 after failing to gather support for his motion to expel Countess Markievicz, whom he despised on account of her social class and association with the Irish Volunteers, and Cumann na mBan. The book reveals much about O'Casey's character but little about the ICA and throughout the later chapters, Captain Séan Connolly is referred to as Shaun Connolly and Michael Mallin as Michael Mallon. An officially sanctioned history of the movement, *The History of the Irish Citizen Army*, was published by R.M. Fox in 1943 at the behest of the ICA Old Comrade's Association.[5] The spur to commission an officially sanctioned history arose from controversies connected to the 1916 Roll of Honour compiled by the IRA Old Comrades organisation in 1936.[6] *The History of the Irish Citizen Army* provides important information about the early development of the movement while indulging the fantasy that the organisation played a meaningful role in the Irish revolution after 1916.[7] At the behest of the Citizen Army veterans, Fox pursued the fiction that the Citizen Amy was in the vanguard of the revolution during the period 1919–23 and lionises the leadership of its members.[8]

Much of Fox's official history of the movement was contradicted by Frank Robbins, a former member of the organisation's army council and a veteran of Easter Week, who published a personal account of his involvement in the Citizen Army in 1977.[9] *Under the Starry Plough: Recollections of the Irish Citizen Army* is an honest, warts-and-all account of the Citizen Army and pulls no punches about the decline of the movement after the Rising and the role of personality clashes and elitism that ultimately ruined the organisation. Robbins' forthright account includes details of many divisive episodes in the movement's history and while his memoir is not without spite towards those he blamed for the failure of the organisation to which he was devoted, his honest analysis is an important counterpoint to Fox's hagiography.[10]

Following the establishment of the Free State veterans of the Citizen Army were reticent to have their experience of the movement recorded, while the Free State was ambivalent about preserving them. The Bureau of Military History showed limited enthusiasm to record accounts from Citizen Army members and statements by former activists number less than ten.[11] The dearth of reliable accounts was compounded by the refusal of many senior veterans, including Stephen Murphy, Walter Carpenter and Seamus McGowan to facilitate the Bureau's requests for information.[12] In terms of the small number of accounts that were recorded, interviews conducted by the Bureau were concerned with the role of the ICA during the 1916 Rising and, to a lesser extent, the Lockout, and the movement's activities afterwards, along with other potentially divisive events are largely ignored. In terms of the movement's later history and ultimate demise, Brian Hanley has been the only historian to seriously ask the question 'Whatever happened to the Citizen Army?' in an important article published in 2003.[13] Hanley's article examines the movement's evolution until the 1930s and emphasises the organisation's decline into a social club where members were hidebound by a weak leadership and the petty application of formal discipline.

Foundation and early development

With 'Carson's Army' dominating newspaper headlines and public calls for the establishment of a nationalist Volunteer movement gathering momentum, it was not unforeseeable that a workers' defence force was mooted in November 1913. In the initial phase of its development, the Citizen Army represented an unrealised aspiration, lacking a coherent role, structure or purpose. Its formation was largely symbolic and neither Larkin nor Connolly made a sustained effort to create a popular, disciplined force. As the Lockout entered its third month, the faltering morale of the workers was beginning to become a source of anxiety to the union leadership and the idea of a workers' protection force provided much-needed succour for the increasingly desperate strikers and their families.

While Larkin and Connolly realised the value such a force provided for the morale of their followers, it was left to a most unlikely figure to organise and train the new force. Captain James R. White, DSO, of the Gordon Highlanders, only son of Field-Marshal Sir George White, VC, hero of Ladysmith, was a Protestant supporter of the Home Rule movement, and came to Dublin from Broughshane, County Antrim, on the outbreak of the strike.[14] In his autobiography, he explained, 'In the North I had raised a protest against the perversion of Protestantism to deny physical freedom to a subject nation. In the South I broke away from politics down to the real fight in indignant horror at the perversion of Catholicism to deny even the freedom to control their own children to an economically subject class.'[15]

White formally proposed the formation of a worker's militia at a meeting of the Civic League, the moderate successor to the Industrial Peace Committee, held in the Antient Rooms in Trinity College in early November. Formally proposing the setting up of a workers' militia, White announced his intention to offer his services to the ITGWU as a former military officer. James Connolly subsequently endorsed White's proposal and told the striking workers at a public meeting that an enrolment of a Citizen Army 'was another feature of their programme' and 'a time was coming when that blow would have to be struck, for engaged in a revolutionary movement as they were, they would pull down civilisation itself and go down with it rather than surrender or be beaten'.[16] Both Connolly and Larkin recognised the political leverage that an organised workers' militia potentially represented, in terms of displaying to the authorities the latent power of the mass of locked-out men. White, on the other hand, envisaged the new movement as a means of raising the morale of the striking men by introducing them to drill, military discipline and martial comradeship, believing 'It was just the thing to put the heart into them.'[17]

The prospects for a popular workers' militia were initially positive, as large numbers of striking men turned out for weekend parades from Liberty Hall to Croydon Park in north Dublin.[18] The ITGWU had purchased a lease to the park and it became the centre of the Citizen Army's manoeuvers and training until 1916. In the second week of December 5,000 men marched from Liberty Hall and were told by Jim Larkin to 'wait for a short time and you will be fully armed; and we'll see then who will resist us'.[19] Citizen Army men appeared at pickets and meetings across the city, identifiable by their ICA armbands and armed with hurls and sticks. Units were not only organised in the city but in Finglas, Lucan, Leixlip, Baldoyle, Swords, Dun Laoghaire and other centres in County Dublin. The appearance of these squads boosted the morale of striking workers and saved many from the brutal excesses of the DMP.

The idea that they were forming a workers' revolutionary militia was not shared by many ICA members, however, and as Fox has noted, for ordinary strikers the 'Citizen Army resolved itself simply into the idea of shaping a club with which to belabour their enemies'.[20] White's endeavours to train the men proved fruitless as most saw little benefit in route marches and tedious drill, leaving White, as he later admitted, 'alternatively in rage and despair at the difficulty of getting the members to see the necessity of regularity in drill and training'.[21] Sean O'Casey concluded that the major obstacles the organisation faced were 'the frequent arrests of the Labour leaders; the gradual and humiliating weakening of the workers' resistance to the pressure of the employers; the malignant penalising of the Irish Transport Union by the hierarchy of commerce; and the establishment in the Rotunda Rink on 25th October 1914 [sic] of the Irish National Volunteers'.[22]

White remained a perpetual outsider in the movement by reason of his class, religion, profession and lack of diplomacy. He endured suspicion, indifference and even hostility, and was publicly humiliated by Larkin in January 1914 when he attacked White's connection with the British army on a public platform.[23] He later recalled, 'In moments I saw the clear revolutionary principle; at others I was repelled by the bitterness of a philosophy fighting against the whole established order, imputing sinister motives to every "bourgeois action" including my own.'[24] In retrospect, White concluded that he had been used by Connolly and Larkin 'as a useful sideline to keep the men busy when they weren't doing anything else, and as a good publicity stunt'.[25] Frustrated by the disinterest of ordinary workers and the suspicion and distrust of the union's leaders, he quit the organisation in the summer of 1914.[26]

The appearance of the ICA on picket lines and at meetings played a valuable role in boosting the morale of the strikers but hopes that the ITGWU was intent on building a popular organised militia were an illusion sustained by Larkin's violent rhetoric. These large early gatherings were essentially shows of force by the ITGWU with thousands of angry workers caught up in the glamour and excitement of public spectacle. Very few of the men who paraded were willing to give the time needed for training and discipline, and even fewer were motivated by orthodox socialist doctrine.[27] As embittered workers sought to return to work in January 1914 they had even less inclination to continue training and many did not want to be associated publicly with the movement for fear of discrimination by potential employers. The decline in numbers attending parades was dramatic and on one occasion White arrived for a parade only to find '... when I arrived on the ground at the time appointed, I was literally alone.'[28]

Reorganisation of the ICA

After the collapse of the Lockout in January 1914, the Citizen Army no longer had a clear role in the labour movement and it needed to reinvent itself or fade away. Along with several prominent supporters, Jack White and Sean O'Casey revived the organisation at a meeting in March 1914 and for the first time a formal constitution and ruling council was approved.[29] An army council was elected with White as chairman; Jim Larkin, P.T. Daly, William Partridge, Thomas Foran and Francis Sheehy-Skeffington as vice-chairmen; and Richard Brannigan[30] and Countess Markievicz became treasurers.[31] Although he attended meetings, James Connolly was not a member of the first army council and he did not take formal control of the movement until the departure of Larkin to America. Larkin continued to support the Citizen Army until his departure, but following his exit, the ICA became tighter, more committed and smaller.

A fundamental break with the original purpose of the movement commenced with the departure of Jim Larkin for the United States in November 1914, and his replacement as the head of the union by James Connolly and Thomas Foran. After Larkin's departure, Connolly, with Michael Mallin as his deputy, took complete control of the ICA and both men came to be revered by their committed band of followers. Mallin was a native Dubliner and was formerly a British soldier and had served in India. An inspired motivator, he was a silk weaver by trade, and was secretary of their union during a bitter dispute in early 1913. Resigning subsequently, he opened a small shop in the Liberties, only to lose his business and employment due to the Lockout, subsequently becoming a full-time organiser for the ITGWU.[32]

The influence of James Connolly over the union and the Citizen Army following Larkin's departure was deeply resented by a coterie of union members centred around Jim Larkin's sister, Delia.[33] Before his departure for the United States, Larkin had intended to appoint P.T. Daly as his replacement, however, through the intervention of the union's general president, Thomas Foran, Connolly was brought from Belfast and elected through a democratic ballot of the union's committee. Delia Larkin and some of her supporters were outraged at what they saw as a usurpation of Jim Larkin's preferred candidate for the leadership and for a period attempted to undermine Connolly. With her brother gone, Delia, who had worked heroically during the Lockout to provide meals for strikers' families, was no longer allowed free rein of Liberty Hall and the unchallenged use of the union's resources. So hostile was the feeling that for a time Connolly was reduced to leaving Liberty Hall by a side door to avoid scuffles and verbal abuse from her supporters.[34] Without her brother's protection, Delia Larkin eventually left the union with characteristic acrimony in 1915 and departed for Liverpool.[35]

With no pickets or meetings to protect, the new incarnation of the Citizen Army was to be the vehicle for the advancement of Connolly's emerging political philosophy of violent revolution, a vision he promoted in *The Irish Worker* newspaper. Connolly's new political doctrine signified a movement away from doctrinal socialism to an alignment of class and national politics into a singular philosophy espousing a socialist republican state. He told his followers, 'an armed organisation of the Irish working class is a phenomenon in Ireland. Hitherto the workers of Ireland have fought as parts of the armies led by their masters, never as members of an army officered, trained, and inspired by men of their own class. Now, with arms in their hands, they propose to steer their own course, to carve their own future.'[36] As part of Connolly's new philosophy, the ICA was steadily brought into an alignment with the Irish Volunteers, relations with whom, largely thanks to Larkin's invective, had been strained. With Larkin in America, Connolly was free to build fraternal relations with the hard-line elements in the Irish Republican Brotherhood, promote greater comradeship between the ICA and the Volunteers, and nurture the commitment of his small band of followers.

Older, less committed members that had drifted away from the movement, were now replaced by younger, more determined fighters, committed to Connolly's philosophy of violent insurgency. For ordinary members the most immediate difference between the new movement and its previous incarnation was the imposition of formal command structures, the degree of personal commitment demanded and a new focus on the use of arms. Members were expected to become accustomed to handling rifles, purchasing uniforms and equipment from their own resources, participating in lectures on street fighting and taking part in mock battles on the city's streets. A boys' section was founded by Walter Carpenter, often marching with the Volunteers and the Fintan Lalor Pipe Band.[37] Connolly and Mallin made clear to prospective members that Volunteers were required to commit themselves entirely to an army intent on violent revolution, in which they would be required to prove their dedication to a socialist republic through personal sacrifice. Connolly told his followers:

> The Irish Citizen Army in its constitution pledges its members to fight for a Republican Freedom for Ireland. Its members are, therefore, of the number who believe that at the call of duty they may have to lay down their lives for Ireland, and have so trained themselves that at the worst the laying down of their lives shall constitute the starting point of another glorious tradition – a tradition that will keep alive the soul of the nation.[38]

Connolly's merging of nationalist doctrine with his commitment to socialism was a product of his personal pragmatism and commitment to making his movement relevant to ordinary working people. In this respect, Jack White noted that Connolly 'realised that the national movement was the reservoir of the nation's subconscious power, that amalgamating with it he could tap mines of energy, which would ultimately produce the true revolutionary ore in Ireland, even if mixed with a mass of sentimental dross'.[39] In the *Irish Worker* Connolly explained that the new Citizen Army was committed to meaningful action rather than the endless theorising and hopeless factionalism that characterised socialist groups in Ireland. For Connolly, a profound sense of urgency was generated by the outbreak of the World War in July 1914, which he argued, presented an unprecedented opportunity to strike at the British Empire. Through force of character, he steadily won the respect of the leadership of the Volunteers and the two groups publicly put their hostility behind them during the elaborate ceremonies surrounding the funeral of the Fenian, O'Donovan Rossa in August 1915. Connolly used his article 'Why the Citizen Army Honours O'Donovan Rossa' in the official funeral programme to explain the unprecedented opportunity the war offered Irish revolutionaries: 'We are neither rash nor cowardly. We know our opportunity when we see it, and we know when it has gone.'[40]

The Citizen Army, unlike the Irish Volunteers, admitted women as full members, and in theory the sexes were treated equally. In reality, while women played an important role in the organisation, it was generally in an auxiliary capacity to male Volunteers, and they tended to act as nurses, cooks and messengers. Nonetheless, by contemporary standards the inclusion of women was remarkable, demanded immense personal commitment and a number of remarkable women played significant roles. Volunteer Helena Molony recalled that involvement in the movement was not considered proper and 'the hurly-burly of politics, particularly the kind which led to the risk of being involved in street rows, was certainly not thought "becoming"'.[41]

After the outbreak of the war in July 1914 Connolly steadily prepared the ground for violent insurrection though a process involving several inter-related strategies. While he shared the Republican Brotherhood's determination to stage a violent insurrection before the war ended, he despised the secrecy and elitism of the IRB. Rather than adopt the cautious tone of the Volunteer leadership, Connolly began to openly preach revolution in the pages of the *Irish Worker*, declaring his determination to bring about an insurrection and goading the Irish Volunteers over their cautiousness. Simultaneously, Connolly succeeded in bringing the two movements closer together through fraternal solidarity and joint manoeuvres at political demonstrations and public processions, while preparing the Citizen Amy for urban warfare through the imposition of military discipline, political indoctrination, and the incremental acquisition of small amounts of arms and ammunition.

Despite claims by Sean O'Casey that the Citizen Army had at one time over one thousand members, active membership of the new ICA rarely exceeded three hundred staunch Volunteers.[42] Along with the level of commitment demanded, there were many impediments to joining the movement, chief among them being social snobbery and public ridicule, heightened by the superior attitude of the Irish Volunteers. Frank Robbins recalled being taunted by 'corner boys' for being a member of the 'run-away-army': 'Such remarks were made on several occasions. They used to burn inside and I often felt like taking to task the persons making them.'[43] The anti-Larkinite tabloid, *The Toiler*, published a satirical verse ridiculing the new force, coining the term 'run-away-army', after an incident on O'Connell Street when members of the ICA were attacked by the DMP:

> With stave and broom in every hand,
> They were a motley gang,
> And with oaths galore each bowsey swore
> That they would dare and hang.
>
> But when the row it did commence,
> They trembled with dismay,
> And some were seen at Dolphin's Barn,
> Five minutes from the fray.[44]

Despite the wide circulation of the *Irish Worker* most ordinary workers held aloof from joining the movement. The difficulty in recruiting members was exacerbated by the low morale and suspicion of workers who had suffered great deprivation due to their association with the ITGWU during the Lockout. Social snobbery and the appeal of the more glamorous Irish Volunteers, combined with what O'Casey identified as the elitism of skilled workers towards the unskilled workers stunted the movement's growth: 'The old lingering tradition of the social inferiority of what were called the unskilled workers, prompted the socially superior tradesmen to shy at an organisation which was entirely officered by men whom they thought to be socially inferior to themselves.'[45]

The Citizen Army after 1916

The contribution of the Citizen Army to the 1916 Rebellion and James Connolly's role on the secret military council that planned the insurgency has been well documented.[46] Two hundred and twelve Volunteers, including twenty-seven women, fought at the City Hall and Stephen's Green garrisons, and alongside the Volunteers in the GPO.[47] Eleven members were killed in the fighting and Commanders Mallin and Connolly executed, thus ensuring the movement a place among the nationalist pantheon of heroes.[48] The history of the movement after the Rising has received little academic attention, however, and Brian Hanley has been the only historian to examine the decline of the organisation.[49]

With Connolly as commandant, it had been difficult for senior members of the ITGWU who saw the Citizen Army as a distraction from 'genuine union work' to vocalise their opposition. Following the Rising, however, as Desmond Greaves has noted 'the sober non-belligerents who controlled the movement were determined that the organisation was not going to be shattered for a third time'.[50] The aftermath of the Rising was challenging for the burgeoning trade union movement on several levels. Leading union activists including P.T. Daly, William O'Brien and Thomas Foran, who had taken no part in the insurrection were deported. Ballaghadereen native, William Partridge, one of the foremost leaders of the Lockout, died from Bright's disease contracted in prison in July 1917. While the loss of James Connolly and Michael Mallin was obvious, other leading activists, Peadar Macken of the Painters Union and Richard O'Carroll of the Bricklayers, who were both senior Volunteers, were also killed in the Rebellion. Liberty Hall was severely damaged and the ITGWU's files confiscated by military.

On a political level labour needed to tread carefully as endorsing the Rebellion would fracture the movement along sectional and sectarian lines.[51] Under such circumstances, Thomas Johnson's priority as head of the Irish Trade Union Congress was to give impetus to the development of an Irish Labour Party and his address to the ITUC&LP annual conference in August represented a balancing act between supporting the union's imprisoned members, while mollifying more conservative and predominantly Protestant craft unions in the north east by honouring members who died in the World War.[52] Congress's response at their annual conference was to offer condolences to all union members who had died, both in the Rising and on the battlefields of Europe, while lobbying for the release of union leaders. Johnson told the annual meeting in August:

> As a trade union movement we are of varied mind on matters of history and political development, and consequently this is not the place to enter into a discussion as to the right or folly of the revolt. But we may say that those amongst the rebels who have been associated with us in the past, who have led and inspired some of us with the love of their country and their class, resolved to act as they did no selfish thought, but purely with a passion for freedom and a hatred of oppression.[53]

Johnson balanced his praise of the union members involved in the insurrection by paying equal tribute to those members 'who had laid down their lives in another field for what they believe to be the cause of liberty and democracy and for love of their country'.[54]

In the absence of the leadership provided by Seán and James Connolly, William Partridge and Michael Mallin, the growing distrust of the wider labour movement and the determination of the ITGWU to distance itself from the Citizen Army, issues revolving around personal rivalries and political ideology that had hampered the growth of the ICA since its foundation became overwhelming. After the Rising the Citizen Army was consumed by infighting and elitism, content to linger on the margins of the revolution, irrelevant to working people. From its inception, the ICA was viewed with suspicion, and even hostility, by many members of the ITGWU but now it was treated by many committed union officers as an obstacle to the conventional purpose of a trade union, by threatening to involve the organisation in debilitating conflicts with the authorities that would sap the union's ability to function.[55]

The memory of Connolly and Mallin inspired reverence from Easter Week veterans to the extent that would have been impossible for any new leader to emulate, and the movement did not produce any new charismatic organisers. The lack of leadership was exacerbated by the dramatic re-organisation of the Irish Volunteers in 1917 and the unprecedented rise of the movement under a leadership that contained a coterie of charismatic and inspirational figures. James O'Neill, a building contractor and carpenter, became commandant of the ICA in February 1917 after the last of the prisoners returned home from incarceration in Frongoch. O'Neill's leadership was cautious to the point of virtual inaction, and the movement played almost no meaningful role in the War of Independence. For militant members such as Frank Robbins, O'Neill's leadership was responsible for the decline of their movement and 'When questions of policy arose O'Neill's attitude was to procrastinate rather than take the line which would have been taken by Connolly or Mallin, were either there to lead.'[56] O'Neill was not the cause of the decline of the movement, however, but a manifestation of the wider apathy of the membership and the minute book of the ICA's army council during 1919 and 1920 reveals an organisation content to rest on the laurels earned during Easter Week, hampered by internal rivalries, an obsession with procedure and the fundamental apathy of its declining membership.[57]

From 1917 onwards, the Citizen Army was steadily marginalised at Liberty Hall, as the union sought to disassociate themselves from their activities and the menacing attention it brought from the Crown Forces.

In early 1917, a large drill room that had been occupied by the Citizen Army since its inception was made unavailable and R.M. Fox noted, 'the days when the army could wander down to their room at will were over'.[58] Helena Molony recalled 'we were defeated; nobody thought we would rise up again. Liberty Hall was mainly a Trade Union headquarters. They were not at all patriotic. Some of the Dublin workers were ex-British soldiers. After the rebellion the premises was largely in their hands.'[59] In his history of the ITGWU, Desmond Greaves claimed that the hoisting of a tricolour over Liberty Hall by the ICA following the election victory of Count Plunkett in 1917 marked the beginning of a period of friction between the union and the ICA and argued 'the swing of public opinion towards militant separatism had infected them with a touch of republican arrogance'.[60]

While the Citizen Army could count on between two and three hundred committed members before the Rising, only 120 members voted in a membership election in June 1919.[61] The laxity of the membership prevented the movement from carrying out basic training, and manoeuvres planned for St Patrick's Day 1919 were called off after only nine members signed up to participate.[62] Constant complaints about the failure of officers to mobilise, take drill, roster guard or attend meetings occupied meetings of the army council. In July 1919, it was noted that 'the night was nearly taken up taking numbers of absentees and excuses for not attending'.[63] Discussions regarding a re-organisation of the movement were regularly held and in April 1920 Seamus McGowan 'gave in detail the decline of the army since 1917' and presented a plan for reorganisation.[64] Frank Robbins had put forward proposals for a re-organisation in January and Seán McLoughlin proposed the council be abolished in October 1919.[65] None of these schemes were endorsed and McLoughlin, a Volunteer of considerable character who had distinguished himself in Easter Week, subsequently left the movement.[66] The elitism of the organisation was highlighted in May by the army council's refusal to send members to a public protest at the imprisonment of James Larkin in New York. The council informed the Irish Workers' Club that they would not participate and that 'any action we would take would be of a physical nature'.[67]

Under these circumstances, many dedicated activists such as William Oman, who played an important role in the development of the movement, and who wished to fight in the escalating struggle against the Crown Forces, left to join to Volunteers.[68] A significant number of senior officers remained, however, ensuring a strong degree of continuity; Robert de Couer, Christy Poole, Mick Donnelly, James O'Neill, Richard McCormack, Seamus McGowan, Madeleine ffrench-Mullen, Jennie Shanahan, Countess

Markievicz, Frank Robbins, John Hanratty and Michael Kelly were all veterans of the Rebellion and had spent time in prison, yet, without firm leadership and coherent political direction, old comrades increasingly turned against one another, often in petty disputes.

A further important change that occurred after the Rising was the declining role of women. Countess Markievicz, while still representing Sinn Féin in Dáil Éireann retained her place on the ICA army council. For many women members who remained, the Citizen Army became a less welcoming movement. Jennie Shanahan, a veteran of Easter Week, told the army council in March 1919, 'the girls were not wanted only when there was dirty work to be done ... some girls doing their best were always being snubbed.'[69] The army's nightly card game was off limits to 'the girls', forcing female members to linger in the hallways of Liberty Hall while the men lounged in their rooms.[70] The army council subsequently warned the 'girls' in March 1919 'about being in the passages and carrying on disorderly'.[71] Easter Week veteran, Margaret Skinnider, was charged with drilling the 'girls' in August 1919 but in March 1920 Madeleine ffrench-Mullen 'expressed her dissatisfaction with the council for not trying to organise the girls better'.[72] In April, Captain White, who briefly re-joined the movement, requested that women be allowed to attend a proposed Connolly memorial concert. His suggestion gained support but with the proviso that 'the stuff called jazz would be strictly forbidden'.[73] The concert was subsequently cancelled due to the apathy of the membership and the council recommended it be 'dropped rather than prove a farce'.[74] In August 1920, the council discussed the 'case of the neglect of the girls' and it was reported that they had no instructor.[75]

In the absence of meaningful military action, infighting dominated the energies of some senior officers with members routinely making charges against each other of a personal or trivial nature: Jennie Shanahan was reported by Bob de Couer for 'impertinence' in February 1919 and John Buddes was reported for using bad language at the same meeting;[76] Commandant James O'Neill tendered his resignation in October 1919 in protest at gossip regarding him circulating among members. Captain Michael Kelly tendered his resignation at the same meeting claiming that another officer had told his wife that he was 'a disgrace';[77] Captain Richard McCormack reported senior member Michael Donnelly to the council for stating that he 'wanted to break up the army';[78] Donnelly, in turn, objected to the presence of Easter Week veteran Christy Poole at an officer meeting, claiming he was not entitled to attend – Poole subsequently walked out, taking a group of members with him;[79] Frank Robbins reported Richard McCormack for drawing a weapon on a shop steward in a personal dispute;[80] and two drill instructors offered their resignations in protest at older members talking about 'the like of them instructing'.[81] Countess Markievicz told the army council that 'such rows were only personal issues', advising them to 'stick strongly to the constitution of the army'.[82]

With dwindling numbers and weak leadership, the movement faced two options: to continue on as a separate force, and rebuild its structures and membership, or build closer ties with the Irish Volunteers and participate in attacks on the Crown Forces. The leadership was split on the issue: Frank Robbins and others favoured closer co-operation with the Volunteers, while Mick Donnelly and James O'Neill zealously promoted the independence of their movement. Donnelly told the council in January 1920 'the Sinn Féin movement was making for political independence and we are making for a workers republic' and that it was 'illogical for our members to be members of Sinn Féin clubs'.[83] In the end, the army council chose neither path, remaining aloof from the Volunteers, reduced to spectators in the War of Independence, while engaging in futile internal disagreements. Efforts by members to bring about closer unity between the Volunteers and the Citizen Army were continually rebuffed by the leadership and dismissed by O'Neill as just 'another effort by the IRB to capture the organisation'.[84]

During the Truce that followed the War of Independence there were tentative moves by the ITUC&LP to use the ICA as a basis for a broader armed formation affiliated to the trade union movement, but these foundered over the question of who would control the new body. During the Civil War a significant number of ICA members fought with the anti-Treaty forces, while a smaller number joined the National Army.

Conclusion

With the collapse of the Lockout in January 1914, the Irish Citizen Army ceased to have an obvious role in the trade union movement. From late 1914 until the Rising, it reinvented itself as Connolly's private militia with an ambiguous relationship with the ITGWU. The men and women of the ICA performed valiantly in Easter Week and were involved in some of the most intense fighting of the Rebellion. Following Connolly's execution, however, the movement lacked any clear political direction and charismatic leadership, as thousands of union members rushed to join the Irish Volunteers.

The movement failed to play an active role in the War of Independence due to the apathy of its membership and the elitism of its leadership. The ICA was not entirely passive during the period 1920–21: members acting on their own initiative passed on information to the Volunteers, provided logistics, and famously, stole a large consignments of weapons and ammunition from US supply ship *The Valiant* in November 1918.[85] New branches were briefly established in Cork, Drogheda, Limerick, Monaghan and elsewhere but it is not clear how long these survived. The intention and capacity for a concerted campaign of military action did not exist after 1916 and was not discussed at army council meetings, let alone attempted. The organisation struggled on, more as a social club for old comrades than a military force.[86] The persistence of structures, military titles, chains of command and grandiose declarations of intent, however, should not be extrapolated into the persistence of a desire or capacity for violent revolution.

Without a clear political strategy, its members drifted away, or joined the Volunteers, and their inability to organise a Connolly memorial concert in May 1920 was a painful reflection of their limitations. That the movement existed at all was a tribute to the charisma of James Connolly, Seán Connolly, William Partridge and other early leaders, and their ability to engender immense loyalty from their small band of followers. Ultimately, the mistrust of the trade union movement inhibited the Citizen Army from developing beyond the fringes of the revolution, exacerbated by the limitations of its post-1916 officers. With the unprecedented rise of the Volunteers, a movement replete with considerable talent and ability, the support for a separate revolutionary force simply did not exist.

Endnotes

1   Sean O'Casey, *The Story of the Irish Citizen Army* (London: Maunsel, 1919), p. 9.

2   For examples see: Finglas, *Freeman's Journal*, 8 Nov. 1913 p. 8; The Quays, *Freeman's Journal*, 8 Nov. 191, p. 9; Francis Street, *Freeman's Journal*, 6 Nov. 1913, p. 20; Inchicore, *Freeman's Journal*, 5 Nov. 1913, p. 10; Ringsend, *Irish Independent*, 29 Nov. 1913, p. 6.

3   For details of the culture of street violence in Dublin tenements, see, Kevin C. Kearns, *Dublin Tenement Life: An Oral History of the Dublin Slums* (Dublin: Gill & Macmillan, 1994), pp. 51–7.

4   O'Casey, *The Story of the Irish Citizen Army*, p. 52.

5   The ICA Old Comrades Committee responsible for the book was composed of Seamus McGowan, Sean Byrne, John Hanratty, Stephen Murphy, Martin King, Walter Carpenter, James O'Shea, George Tully and Meave Cavanagh McDowell.

6   BMH/WS 96 (John Hanratty), p. 4.

7   R.M. Fox, *The History of the Irish Citizen Army* (Dublin: James Duffy, 1943).

8   Diarmuid Lynch published a series of comments on the details of Easter Week provided in Fox's account, *The IRB and the 1916 Insurrection* (Cork: Mercier Press, 1957), pp. 55–81.

9   Frank Robbins, *Under the Starry Plough: Recollections of the Irish Citizen Army* (Dublin: Academy Press, 1977).

10   Other published accounts of the Citizen Army include Anne Matthews, *The Irish Citizen Army* (Dublin: Mercier Press, 2013); 'Vanguard of the Revolution? The Irish Citizen Army, 1916' in Ruán O'Donnell (ed.), *The Impact of the 1916 Rising Among the Nations* (Dublin: Irish Academic Press, 2008), pp. 24–36; John W. Boyle, 'Connolly, the Citizen Army and the Rising' in Kevin B. Nowlan (ed.) *The Making of 1916: Studies in the History of the Rising* (Dublin: Stationary Office, 1969), pp. 51–70; R.M. Fox, 'The Irish Citizen Army' in multi-authored, *Dublin's Fighting Story, 1913–1921* (Tralee: The Kerryman, 1948), pp. 24–8; Donal Nevin, 'The Irish Citizen Army, 1913–1916' in Nevin (ed.) *James Larkin, Lion of the Fold* (Dublin: Gill & Macmillan, 1998), pp. 257–65; 'The Irish Citizen Army' in Owen Dudley Edwards, Fergus Pyle (eds), *1916, The Easter Rising* (London: MacGibbon & Kee, 1968), pp. 119–21.

11   The most revealing accounts include: BMH WS 96 (John Hanratty); BMH WS 391 (Helena Molony); BMH WS 357 (Kathleen Lynn); BMH WS 546 (Rosie Hackett); BMH WS 543 (Martin King); and BMH WS 258 (Meave Cavanagh McDowell).

12   BMH WS 545 (Stephen Murphy); BMH WS 583 (Walter Carpenter); and BMH WS 542 (Seamus McGowan).

13   Brian Hanley, 'The Irish Citizen Army after 1916', *Saothair*, 28 (2003), pp. 37–47.

14   White was to become the inspiration for the character 'Jim Bricknell' in D.H. Lawrence's 1922 novel, *Aaron's Rod*. See also Leo Keohane, *Captain Jack White: Imperialism, Anarchism and the Irish Citizen Army* (Dublin: Irish Academic Press, 2014).

15   Captain Jack White, *Misfit: An Autobiography* (London: Jonathan Cape, 1930), p. 138.

16   *Irish Times*, 19 Nov. 1913, p. 7.

17   White, *Misfit, an Autobiography*, p. 156.

18   For reports of Citizen Army processions see: *Irish Times*, 10 Nov. 1913, p. 7; *Irish Times*, 24 Nov. 1913, p. 9; *Irish Times*, 22 Dec. 1913, p. 8; *Irish Times*, 1 Dec. 1913, p. 6.

19   *Irish Worker*, 13 Dec. 1913.

20   Fox, *History of the Irish Citizen Army*, p. 46.

21   Ibid., p. 47.

22   O'Casey, *The Story of the Irish Citizen Army*, pp. 8–9. (The Volunteers were founded in 1913 not 1914.)

23   For an account of the incident see, White, *Misfit*, p. 177.

24   White, *Misfit*, p. 170.

25   White, *Misfit*, p. 172.

26   For details of White's adventures in later life, see, Andrew Boyd, *Jack White, First Commander, Irish Citizen Army* (Belfast: Donaldson Archives, 2001).

27   Fox, *History of the Irish Citizen Army*, p. 8.

28   White, *Misfit*, p. 171.

29   The text of the constitution was reproduced by O'Casey, *The Story of the Irish Citizen Army*, p. 71.

30   Andrew Boyd states that Brannigan was in fact Richard Braithwaite, a former Orangeman from Belfast who had served time in prison for a sectarian attack on a Corpus Christi procession in north Belfast in 1901. He subsequently left the Independent Orange Order in 1904 and renounced sectarianism, see, Boyd, *Jack White*, pp. 20–1.

31   Nevin, 'The Irish Citizen Army' in Dudley Edwards, Pyle (eds), *1916, The Easter Rising*, pp. 119–21.

32   Michael Mallin's brother, Thomas, left a brief account of his brother's life see, BMH WS 382 (Thomas Mallin).

33   For an account of the influence of Delia Larkin see, James Curry, 'Delia Larkin: "More harm to the big fellow than any of the employers"?', *Saothar*, 36 (2011), pp. 19–36. The episode discussed here is not mentioned.

34   For an account of this period, see, Robbins, *Under the Starry Plough*, pp. 25–34.

35   See Curry, 'Delia Larkin', p. 23.

36   'For the Citizen Army', *Workers' Republic*, 30 Oct. 1915.

37   The pipe band was formed in 1912 by Robert de Couer, an ITGWU activist and ICA Volunteer and originally practiced at a hall on Aungier Street and was a particular target for the DMP while on procession.

38   'Why the Citizen Army Honours Rossa', Rossa Souvenir, (Dublin, 1915).

39   White, *Misfit*, p. 161.

40   'What is our Programme?', *Workers' Republic*, 22 Jan. 1916.

41   BMH WS 391 (Helena Molony), p. 4.

42   O'Casey, *The Story of the Irish Citizen Army*, p. 31; O'Casey's claim was contradicted in Fox, *History of the Irish Citizen Army*, p. 8.

43   Robbins, *Under the Starry Plough*, p. 35.

44   *The Toiler*, 11 April 1914. The song was signed H. Barnton and consists of several more verses. Accounts of this incident are given by White, *Misfit*, pp. 189–90 and Robbins, *Under the Starry Plough*, pp. 35–6.

45   O'Casey, *The Story of the Irish Citizen Army*, p. 9.

46   For the most coherent accounts of the ICA's involvement in the fighting of Easter Week, see, Charles Townshend, *Easter 1916, the Irish Rebellion* (London: Penguin, 2005), pp. 152–82; Fearghal McGarry, *The Rising: Ireland: Easter 1916* (London: Oxford University Press, 2010), pp. 120–66; Michael T. Foy and Brian Barton, *The Easter Rising* (Stroud: Sutton, 1999) pp. 72–97.

47   The ICA's official Roll of Honour lists the strengths of the Easter Week garrisons as: GPO (31); GPO reinforcements to City Hall (8); Stephens Green (118); City

Hall, including outposts (43); Imperial Hotel (8); Metropole Hotel (2); Four Courts (1); Boland's Mill (1). Fox, *History of the Citizen Army*, pp. 227–32.

48   John Adams, Louis Byrne, Philip Clarke, Sean Connolly, James Corcoran, Charlie Darcy, James Fox, George Geoghegan, James McCormack, Sean O'Reilly, Frederick Ryan. For details see, Ray Bateson, *They Died by Pearse's Side* (Dublin, 2010).

49   Hanley, 'The Irish Citizen Army After 1916', pp. 37–47.

50   C. Desmond Greaves, *The ITGWU: The Formative Years* (Dublin: Gill & Macmillan, 1982), p. 181.

51   The ICA was officially endorsed by the Dublin Trades Council in April 1914, see, Seamus Cody, John O'Dowd, Peter Rigney, *The Parliament of Labour, One Hundred Years of the Dublin Council of Trade Unions* (Dublin, 1986), p. 116.

52   J. Anthony Gaughan, *Thomas Johnson, 1872–1963: First Leader of the Labour Party in Dail Éireann* (Dublin: Kingdom Books, 1980), p. 69.

53   Address by Johnson to delegates attending Irish Trades Congress, Sligo, August 7–9, 1916 (printed) with typescript draft bearing ms. annotations and associated news cutting (Thomas Johnson Papers, NLI, MS 17,205).

54   Ibid.

55   See, Greaves, *ITGWU*, pp. 181–3.

56   Robbins, *Under the Starry Plough*, p. 202.

57   ICA Minute Book, Jan. 1919 – Sep. 1920, Irish Labour History Archive.

58   Fox, *History of the Irish Citizen Army*, p. 214.

59   BMH WS 391 (Helena Molony), p. 47.

60   Greaves, *The ITGWU*, p. 181.

61   ICA Minute Book, minutes dated 30 Jun. 1919.

62   Ibid., minutes dated 3 Mar. 1919.

63   Ibid., minutes dated 7 Jul. 1920.

64   Ibid., minutes dated 9 April 1920.

65   Ibid., minutes dated 5 Oct. 1919 and 4 Jan. 1920.

66   Charlie McGuire, *Sean McLoughlin, Ireland's Forgotten Revolutionary* (Pontypool: Merlin Press, 2011), p. 53.

67   ICA Minute Book, minutes dated 13 May 1920.

68   BMH WS 421 (William Oman).

69   ICA minute book, minutes dated 5 Feb. 1919.

70   Along with card playing, members participated in Irish language classes, amateur dramatics, and the movement had a football team and the Connolly and Mallin Athletic Club.

71   Ibid., minutes dated 9 Sept. 1919.

72   Ibid., minutes dated 4 Aug. 1919 and 8 Mar. 1920.

73   Ibid., minutes dated 11 April 1920. White subsequently joined the Irish Volunteers and became an organiser in Derry and Donegal. He published several pamphlets including *The significance of Sinn Féin* in 1919.

74   ICA Minute Book, minutes dated 1 June 1920.

75   Ibid., minutes dated 19 Aug. 1920.

76 Ibid., minutes dated 5 Feb. 1919.

77 Ibid., minutes dated 19 Oct. 1919.

78 Ibid., minutes dated 25 Jan. 1920.

79 Poole was an officer of longstanding and held in high regard. He was court martialled for a minor offence but found innocent, however, he resigned in disgust but later re-joined.

80 ICA Minute Book, minutes dated 26 Aug. 1920.

81 Ibid., minutes dated 8 July 1920.

82 Ibid., minutes dated 15 Feb. 1920.

83 Ibid., minutes dated 25 Jan. 1920.

84 Robbins, *Under the Starry Plough*, p. 204.

85 See, Fox, *History of the Citizen Army*, p. 206.

86 See, Hanley, *The Irish Citizen Army after 1916*.

CHAPTER EIGHT

'The Layers of an Onion': Reflections on 1913, Class and the Memory of the Irish Revolution

Brian Hanley

In the towns tuppence-ha'penny looked down on tuppence, and throughout the country the grades in social difference were as numerous as the layers of an onion.

Ernie O'Malley, *On Another Man's Wound.*[1]

The centenary of the 1913 Lockout has been marked by postage stamps, commemorative coins, re-enactments and conferences.[2] The year also saw the publication of several edited books dealing with the events.[3] Local groups have also published their own valuable collections.[4] Many of the better initiatives were those, such as the unveiling of a mural in Dublin's East Wall, which sprang from community efforts.[5] There was still a tendency to present the Lockout in a very traditional framework, as the one occasion in Irish history in which labour was central and better still, the 'good guys'. But dangers lie in commemorating the Lockout as the single most important moment in Irish labour history, and reducing it to a battle between good (Jim Larkin and the poverty-stricken Dublin proletariat) and evil (William Martin Murphy). Class struggle did not begin or end in 1913 and class relations are about more than lockouts or strikes. In a pamphlet commemorating the Lockout, journalist Martina Devlin, argued that 'the strikers weren't engaged in class warfare or demanding a redistribution of wealth – all they were seeking was a slender improvement in their lot.'[6] But while we cannot understand the Lockout without reference to Dublin's poverty, it was never simply about that. As Emmet O'Connor argues 'essentially, 1913 was about sympathetic action. It was a sympathetic Lockout to get rid of sympathetic action. Larkin's response was a campaign for sympathetic action. The slums had nothing to do with it, to begin with at least.'[7] Suggesting that the Lockout was only about poverty allows many who retrospectively lament the conditions workers faced in 1913 to claim, that in contrast, today's workforce have very little to protest about. Interestingly 2013 saw only half-hearted attempts to rehabilitate Martin Murphy's reputation as 'the tycoon who saved Dublin from anarchy'.[8] These gained little popular traction. While the modern trade union movement still wishes to see themselves as the heirs of Larkin and Connolly, it would seem Ireland's business leaders would rather forget Murphy. Yet this was a man who had been lauded by the Dublin Typographical Provident Society, in acknowledgement of the week's paid holidays printers at the *Irish Independent* enjoyed, for 'the spirit of fairness with which he has ever met them in Trades Union matters'.[9] Murphy did *not* object to 'respectable' craft unions but to Larkinism and the organisation of the unskilled. That Murphy was a Catholic nationalist leading an overwhelmingly Protestant unionist group of employers was also highly significant. He represented the future; but it is easier to present him as an aberration than to see Ireland's modern capitalist class as his descendants.

In the long run the most positive result of the centenary has been a new interest in the importance of class division in Ireland. This is particularly welcome given that this has been a neglected topic of investigation. There has been a prevalent view that while class certainly mattered under British rule, it ceased to be as important after independence. In 1972 Fianna Fáil's Brian Lenihan contrasted Northern Ireland with 'the type of society which we have evolved here ... which is almost totally nonsectarian, classless and devoted to the common good and the achievement of justice'.[10] His colleague, Charles Haughey, would later dismiss socialism as 'an alien gospel of class warfare, envy and strife ... inherently un-Irish and therefore unworthy of a serious place in the language of Irish political debate'.[11] Yet long before independence Irish society was extremely class conscious. As Virginia Crossman explains of the 1800s:

> Irish people had a very clear idea of their place in society relative to other people, and the importance of maintaining this. If landowners tended to see all tenants as members of the lower classes broadly defined, middling and large tenant farmers regarded themselves as belonging to a very different social category from small tenants and labourers, and

were anxious to enforce this sense of difference through adherence to concepts such as respectability. The poor, and more particularly the destitute, were regarded by the better off as almost beyond class …[12]

In the early 1900s, Irish-Irelander, D.P. Moran, complained that class distinction in Ireland was 'ridiculously minute and acute'.[13] Ernie O'Malley's description of the grades in social difference as being as numerous as the 'layers of an onion' indicates something of this. Quite apart from the relationship between the 'Big House' and its tenants, post-Famine Ireland saw new divisions emerge. Donegal Cooperative organiser, Paddy Gallagher, claimed in the pre-independence era that the rural poor had 'two enemies', the British, and the 'Gombeen man' and asserted that 'whenever the Gombeen man is fighting the English, we are with him in that fight, but as soon as we are rid of you (the English), we will tackle him, and believe me, he will not last seven years, never mind seven hundred'.[14] Class divisions were also felt within the police, drawn largely from the Catholic farming and lower middle class. By 1914 there were complaints that recent recruits to the RIC were of 'a very inferior class, and there would be no chance of their being taken into the police some years ago at all … they come from labourers now, and some years ago the great majority of them were all farmers' sons.'[15] The turn of the century Gaelic Athletic Association, often seen as evidence of the egalitarian nature of Irish nationalism, had a disproportionate representation from the commercial and agricultural classes, with unskilled workers, farm labourers and the industrial class in general under-represented. Tom Hunt found that the early GAA was 'dominated by the lower middle classes' and 'those from farming communities'.[16] After independence rural Ireland retained its social hierarchy, exemplified in many areas, by the separate seating places for farmers and labourers at Sunday mass.[17] A survey of farming communities in east Limerick conducted in the late 1950s graphically illustrated the gap between farmers and those they employed. A common theme in farm owners' complaints was that the education system was creating unrealistic expectations among labourers. As one farmer put it 'education is ruining them; it gives them airs above their station'.[18]

The poorer residents of Ireland's towns and cities were seen as very different. While Dublin's inner-city poverty was particularly dire, there were similar areas around the 'lanes' and backstreets of most Irish towns. Aoife Bhreatnach has identified how 'the term "lane" was itself a significant class signifier'.[19] When church property was destroyed in the early stages of the

Civil War in Limerick a disgusted Limerick bishop complained that 'neither the sacred character of the Nuns nor their work for suffering humanity was considered by the crowds from the back lanes of Kilmallock'. His audience would have known immediately what kind of people he meant.[20] The language used about slum dwellers, whether in connection with the 1913 Lockout, or in clashes during the revolutionary era, tells us much about how class framed discourse.

Reporting on the riots that shook Dublin in late August 1913 (during which at least three people died as a result of police violence) the *Evening Herald* explained that it was

> towards nightfall, when the roughs and wastrels and the lowest dregs of the lanes ... usually congregate around Liberty Hall and its branches ... when these 'citizens' of Dublin get properly charged with drink, that the rioting commences. During the morning time these discreditable elements are not to be seen, for the very good reason that they are sleeping off the effects of their previous night's debauch or engaged in mending their broken heads caused in a good many instances not by the baton of police, but by their own broken bottles.[21]

A priest who had witnessed the fighting that weekend described how 'large groups of people, chiefly women and children, of a degraded class ... lost all control of themselves and behaved like frenzied lunatics ... Not only men, but women with hair all disheveled, and even young girls of fifteen or sixteen, rushed and surged around the police ... one obsessed creature seized an empty coal-bag from a cart and belaboured the constable to the utmost of her power.' For this cleric 'the only redeeming feature of what was for a Dublin citizen a really humiliating and disgusting spectacle' was the behaviour of the police.[22]

During the rioting police raided and wrecked tenement homes. The testimony of Foley Street residents seeking compensation for this destruction illustrated what Joseph V. O'Brien called the 'combative spirit and verbal resourcefulness' of inner-city Dubliners. When challenged by counsel for the Corporation, one woman was asked:

> 'Are you a peaceable woman yourself?'
> She replied 'I am.'
> But the counsel continued, 'did you get 14 days' imprisonment last year for assault?'

'I did sir, for my sister' she answered.
'You didn't think it any harm to assault your sister?
Not in the least. When she deserved it, why not give it to her?
I believe the weapon you used on your sister ... was a red-hot poker?
It was not red-hot.
I apologise, but was it hot?
I could not tell you.
You forget, I suppose.
I don't forget my 14 days.'[23]

These women were probably not members of a trade union. But they came from communities in which distrust and hostility towards the police was a given. However, there were substantial differences among those affected by the Lockout. As the *Irish Worker* complained in September 1911:

> the existence of class distinction among the women workers of Dublin is deplorable. Each different section of workers keep entirely to themselves ...You find the girl who earns her living as a typist stands icily aloof from the girl who works in the shop and the trades' girl: they in their turn look down haughtily on the factory hand and again you do not find the factory girl associating with the girls who hawk their goods in the streets.[24]

Social divisions within the working class were also apparent in the formation of the two militias that emerged in the midst of the Lockout. The male membership of the Irish Citizen Army was largely drawn from unskilled members of the Transport Union. Inchicore foundry worker, James O'Shea, described how within two hours of a mobilisation order in March 1916, ICA members were:

> running out of foundries, fitting shops, forges and building jobs. Carters left horses in the street and ran for their rifles and equipment ... when we got to the (Liberty) Hall it was a glorious sight to see men in all conditions of clothes, some with whips hanging to their belts, others in smocks all full of grease, mud, coal or cement, showing the various jobs they were on ... the only one respectably dressed was Seán Connolly who came from City Hall ... we had a great laugh listening to stories of what their different bosses thought of the mobilisation.[25]

Seán O'Casey would contend that one reason for the lack of support for the ICA among the craftsmen of Dublin was 'the old lingering tradition of the social inferiority of what were called the unskilled workers [which] prompted the socially superior tradesmen to shy at an organisation which was entirely officered by men whom they thought to be socially inferior then themselves'.[26] When the Irish Volunteers were launched in late November 1913, members of the ITGWU disrupted the event, protesting at the presence of prominent Home Ruler, Laurence Kettle, who they accused of strike-breaking. But the Volunteers themselves included substantial numbers of trade unionists, such as Peadar Macken of the painters and Richard O'Carroll of the bricklayers. Both these men had represented Labour on Dublin Corporation and large numbers of skilled workers were active in the Irish Republican Brotherhood and the Gaelic League.[27]

After the Bachelor's Walk massacre in 1914 the *Irish Worker* described the regiment responsible, the King's Own Scottish Borderers, as the 'sweepings of Scotch slums'.[28] There was an assumption in Ireland that those who joined the British Army were likely to be 'corner boys'. Prior to 1914 the typical Irish recruit was either an unskilled man from a city or town, or alternatively, a member of the Protestant landed gentry. As a result the Irish were over-represented in both the lower ranks *and* the highest echelons of the British army.[29] This tradition of service meant several thousand Transport Union men were called up as reservists in 1914.[30] As the *Irish Worker* lamented in August that year 'some of our best comrades are leaving the North Wall to fight for the glory of England'.[31] But after 1914 the nature of army recruitment became much more diverse, as Ernie O'Malley observed, 'before the war, scapegoats, those in debt or in trouble over a girl joined the ranks: now all trades, professions and classes were found there'.[32] Yet class still mattered. British enlistment officers complained that in Ireland 'a much larger number of recruits could be obtained from the (farming and commercial classes) if it were not for their reluctance to enter upon their training with recruits from the labouring classes. This class prejudice is probably much more pronounced in Ireland than elsewhere in the United Kingdom.'[33] Some Irish officers did not hide this prejudice. Lieutenant Moorhead of the 10th Dublin Fusiliers (Commercials Battalion) told the Galway Women's Recruiting Committee that the 'ranks' was 'not a very pleasant place for men of education and refinement to be huddled together with men who had probably not washed for a couple of months. He came to the conclusion that there was a large number of men who did not join because they did not care to be mixed up with the corner boys.'[34]

Another feature of the War years was the number of clashes between urban crowds and supporters of the separatist movement.[35] In general, republicans blamed these conflicts on those with relatives in the British army, the so-called 'separation women' who, they claimed, were active supporters of the Home Rule party. This helps contextualise the well-known examples of hostility encountered by the 1916 rebels in inner-city Dublin. In 1915 a Volunteer parade, made up of men from across Munster, was assailed as it paraded through Limerick's lanes. Mick Quirke recounted how 'we got an awful hiding ... from the mob of the city, who used bottles, bricks and stones, and pots full of urine'.[36] Tom Clarke reputedly remarked that he had 'always wondered why King William couldn't take Limerick. I know now'.[37] Republican descriptions of their opponents emphasised their heavy drinking and unrespectable behaviour. Denis F. Madden claimed that in Waterford during 1918 'drink was flowing ... to see that fanatical, separation-money mob, one could not help thinking what Daniel O'Connell thought when he said: "You should know the animals I was supposed to make a nation out of".'[38] John Flanagan recalled of Ennis in 1917 that 'the women were kept well plied with drink by a number of the publicans who were supporters of the Irish party and in their drunken condition they were a frenzied and ferocious crowd to deal with. On a couple of occasions the volunteers were obliged to use the ash plant in order to protect Sinn Féin supporters from being mauled by these infuriated females.'[39] Michael S. O'Mahony described those who clashed with republicans in Tullamore as 'the rabble of the town-wives whose husbands were in the British army and people like that'.[40] Laurence Nugent explained how:

> the women and children in two districts of the town of Longford were very rough. There were also a goodly number of young men (roughs) who had not yet joined the British Army. The people here mentioned were in receipt of Separation Allowances. Their husbands (mostly tinkers or militia men) were in the British Army. These people were violent supporters of the I.P.P. ...[41]

Many of those who took part in the Easter Rising also spoke of being 'attacked by the rabble in Bow Lane' or 'the rabble of the city'.[42] John Dorney is one of the few to have examined this relationship and has argued that by 1919 much of the urban poor had been won over to Sinn Féin.[43] But why does there seem to have been a base for the Home Rule party among them? How much of the violence was due to suspicion of outsiders? Many of the Volunteers parading through Limerick's poorest areas in 1915 were from the Munster countryside. Sinn Féin's canvassers came from across Ireland to campaign in Longford, Waterford and Clare but the Home Rule party's supporters seem to have been predominantly locals. Were republican descriptions of drunken separation women accurate or were they influenced by class (and gender) prejudice?[44] The use of the term 'tinker' is also instructive. Any discussion on class in Ireland must include Travellers and the references to Travellers in the Bureau of Military History Witness Statements give some indication of contradictory attitudes to them in the revolutionary era.[45]

While many tend to see the Lockout as naturally foreshadowing the Easter Rising (as in the lyrics of Donagh MacDonagh's song, 'Dublin city in 1913') there were fundamental differences between the two events. The Lockout involved over 20,000 workers and their families. In contrast around 1,800 people were 'out' in 1916. Most ordinary Dubliners, large numbers of whom participated in the Lockout, were observers in 1916 and could not have been otherwise.[46] It is almost certain that some of those who had fought the police in 1913 were among the 'rabble' who turned on the rebels during and after Easter Week. How republicans compared themselves and their enemies also tells us something about perceptions about class. British soldiers were the 'pale, puny anaemic products of English factory towns' while the Volunteers were 'the pick of Irish manhood, the product of our Irish soil, clean-limbed, strong and wholesome'.[47] Many assumed that the brutality of the Black and Tans was related to their being composed of 'the criminal classes and the dregs of ... English cities ... the offscourings of English industrial populations'.[48] It was widely accepted that the 'Tans' were comprised of the 'scum of English jails, the Lumpen-Proletariat and Professional Thug'.[49] In fact, recent research suggests a comparative lack of criminal records among the Black and Tans, who were mainly ex-servicemen from skilled and unskilled working-class backgrounds.[50] Ironically, urban myth in contemporary Limerick seeks to rid the city of its embarrassing association with organised crime by claiming that local feuding gangs are not really Irish at all but descendants of 'the Tans'.[51] Yet critics of the IRA sometimes also ascribed low social status to them, asserting that they were 'loafers' or 'corner boys'.[52] Urban unskilled backgrounds, and or criminal records, were clearly markers of depravity. The idealisation of rural life and suspicion of urban living produced the type of prejudice implicit in the statement by Hugo Flinn of Fianna Fáil when discussing youth unemployment during the 1940s that 'the country does not breed loafers of the kind found in cities'.[53]

The class composition of the revolutionary movement is significant. Sixty-five per cent of the members of the First Dáil and 58 per cent of the Second Dáil's TDs came from the commercial and professional classes. This was a huge over-representation of those categories in comparison to their numbers in wider society (around 10 per cent). Farmers were underrepresented, while there were no unskilled urban and rural labourers at all. Around 60 per cent of TDs in 1921 had attended secondary school and perhaps a quarter university, again numbers far in excess of the general population.[54] The Sinn Féin party was substantially middle-class compared to the Volunteers, whose makeup was more diverse. But while there were unskilled workers involved in the IRA, in proportion to their numbers in society they were still underrepresented, particularly among the officer class. IRA officers tended to be 'upwardly mobile members of the skilled working class, white-collar workers and lower professions' with a sprinkling of students.[55]

Until relatively recently most historians seem to have agreed with Kevin O'Higgins' self-serving claim that the Irish republicans of his generation were the 'most conservative minded revolutionaries that ever put through a successful revolution'.[56] Tom Garvin has suggested that since the Irish working class 'scarcely exists, or ever has existed, outside Belfast, as a classic industrial working class' there is little point in seeking evidence of the potential for radical social change.[57] Yet it is quite obvious that the revolutionary period saw intense class struggle and that the labour movement was acknowledged to be an important force. The unionist *Irish Times* asserted after the general strike against conscription of April 1918 that 'it was the voice of Labour, not the voice of religion or politics, which yesterday stopped the wheels of industry … We think that April 23rd will be chiefly remembered, not as the day when Nationalist Ireland proclaimed her spiritual and moral isolation, but as the day when Labour found itself.'[58] The story of labour in this period is not just about events like the 'Limerick Soviet' but the far more numerous local strikes and occupations.[59] There is strong evidence of political support too, with Labour winning 324 seats in local elections during 1920, second only to Sinn Féin.[60] 1920 also saw more agrarian outrages than any year since 1882, as what has been called the 'last Land War' took place. Fergus Campbell has shown how despite land reform, small farmers, their sons and landless labourers, remained predisposed to land agitation. In Co. Galway this added an extra dimension to the struggle for independence.[61] During the early 1920s the expectations of farm labourers would see thousands join the ITGWU and resistance by farmers to their demands produce violent, if largely forgotten, struggles.[62] An indication of changing attitudes was dramatically expressed by the RIC *Gazette* in 1920, which lamented how once the police officer had been 'a vastly superior man to the railway porter and the agricultural labourer, and yet, behold how they have advanced!'[63]

The reaction of republicans to these trends was mixed. Dáil Éireann's official account worried that land agitation had seen 'the mind of the people … diverted from the struggle for freedom by a class war'.[64] The labour movement for its part, publicly at least, could claim the confidence to assert after the Treaty that 'whatever form of government may be established, whatever name it may assume, Free State or Republic, unless it realises (Labour) aspirations it is not a Republic in the eyes of the workers'.[65] Most republican accounts suggest Labour was enthusiastically pro-Treaty. The general strike against militarism of April 1922 is perceived as 'directed in fact against … the anti-Treaty movement'.[66] But this strike had mass support and included sectors 'not covered by the General Strikes of 1918, 1919 and 1920' including the 'Post Office and the Great Northern Railway'.[67] The rhetoric of the strike was explicitly critical of *both* pro and anti-Treaty sides, complaining that 'since the Truce we have seen grow up in the ranks of the IRA … a spirit of militarism in sheer imitation of the militarism of the British, French, German, American and other armies'. Both pro and anti-Treaty forces were accused of committing acts

> which we who are not at all opposed to the use of arms, never have been and never shall be, can only describe as sheerest militarism. These acts, on both sides, are a direct copying of the worst methods of British imperialism and its army of occupation in Ireland … we are witnesses of the arrogance of 'regulars', who use the revolver as their only weapon of argument and their only authority. They are modelling themselves upon, and taking their example from, the ordinary militarist armies of other countries, the coercive armed forces of the State … perhaps the incidents on the other side (Anti-Treaty) are more numerous and perhaps they are more truly due to lack of central control. That makes them no less and no more heinous (and) as foolish as anything the armed militarists of England have ever committed.[68]

The success of the general strike suggests widespread working-class dissatisfaction with *both* sides, as does the Labour vote in June 1922 when seventeen out of eighteen candidates were elected, five of them topping the poll. Two seats were won in each of the Waterford/East Tipperary, Wexford, Kildare and East Cork constituencies. Labour candidates took 50 per cent of vote in Laois/Offaly.[69] Much of the support reflected recent strikes among local farm workers with union organisers elected in Waterford and Tipperary.[70]

The Communist Party, despite its strong opposition to the Treaty (and support for IRA resistance to it) was 'glad to note the sweeping victories of the Labour Party'. Optimistically they hoped that this showed:

> how easy it would be for a Revolutionary Labour Party to sweep the field clean of all adversaries and establish a Workers' Republic. It matters not for the moment that the successful candidates are all of the usual type of Labour-Betrayers and fakirs. They were elected because the workers believed in all their hypocritical declarations about the Workers' Republic and about James Connolly.[71]

As for the Treaty debate itself the CPI's *Workers Republic* also suggested that 'a big percentage of the Irish are apathetic to the struggle; this is particularly true of the landless peasants and the workers in the cities and big towns'. The CPI's ideas as to how republicans could offer something to workers would profoundly influence the thinking of Liam Mellows among others, and, thereafter, frame left-republican thinking on the Civil War. But the party was starting from a position of asserting that many workers were not interested in the Treaty.[72] Republicans have largely ignored this, tending to assume that because the 'stake-in-the-country people' supported the Treaty, that the poor automatically opposed it.

The debate on the class character of the Civil War is ongoing, with Gavin Foster's work revealing the importance of concepts such as social respectability and status to the participants.[73] What seems clear is that a sizeable number of workers did not take any part in the conflict. But large numbers of working-class young men did join the new National Army, a fact remembered by republicans as late as 1976 when *An Phoblacht* claimed that the Free State forces had been 'vastly inflated' by an 'army of youngsters from the garrison towns of the South'. Their fathers had been reared for the British Army, and for two years, had nowhere to go. The 'Civil War' was a god-send to them.[74] Echoes of the conflicts between republicans and 'the rabble' were also seen in clashes in Dublin's city centre in June 1973, when inner-city youth attacked supporters of Provisional Sinn Féin returning from Bodenstown. Bus windows were smashed, fights broke out and dozens were arrested as 'a three-way struggle between Northerners, Gardai and Dublin skinheads' took place.[75] There was no identifiable political reason for the trouble, though *An Phoblacht* claimed that the 'skinheads' had 'been indoctrinated against Republicans and their Movement'.[76] It was more likely that the fighting stemmed from 'outsiders' dramatically intruding on territory the youngsters regarded as theirs. Writing in 1975 the *An Phoblacht* columnist 'Freeman' asserted that the working class were not the majority in Ireland and not uniquely downtrodden; that in fact 'the people of Connacht ... suffer more oppression and have considerably less power'. In contrast, he asserted, many workers were highly paid, and some remained 'mentally more in England than in Ireland'.[77] But these comments drew angry responses and it was clear that much of the support for republicans in southern Ireland by then came from among the urban poor.[78] By the 1980s republican strategists would contend that their 'movement has to get into the large-scale politicisation of the young, especially the young people coming out of the ghettos of the larger cities and towns'.[79] The stereotypical republican activist of the 1980s was not a UCD student or a trainee teacher but an unemployed teenager or manual worker.[80] By 2013 protesting republicans at Leinster House were dismissed by hostile bloggers in terms redolent of those used about the poor in 1913, 'you'll probably have to wait until the afternoon when the Éirígí (a socialist republican group) maggots show up, their hang on skangers should be well oiled with Dutch Gold by then ... Isn't it sign on day? They'll have to get that out of the way first.'[81] When the *Sunday Independent* columnist John Drennan contended that Sinn Féin voters favoured a diet of 'chips, Dutch Gold and batter-burgers' he was leaving his readers in no doubt about where he thought these voters came from.[82]

Class was everywhere during the centenary of 1913. Not through the efforts of the trade unions or the left but because it informed everyday attitudes to a whole range of issues. The plight of the so-called 'squeezed middle' caused much angst throughout the recession.[83] Cabinet minister Leo Varadkar asserted the need 'to protect the middle-class' and lamented that many of our 'best and brightest', defined as doctors, lawyers, entrepreneurs and artists, were emigrating.[84] The suggestion was that the tragedy of emigration lay in the exodus of the educated. Implicitly then, the departure of 500,000 people during the 1950s did not represent either a 'brain drain' or as much of a calamity. This narrative goes mostly unchallenged because the working class is largely absent from modern Irish popular culture, except in caricature. The trade unions may still organise almost 700,000 people on this island but they are invisible in cultural terms. Television promotes a cult of business, where one can view *The Apprentice*, *Dragon's Den* and *The Secret Millionaire*, but there is unlikely to be a *Celebrity Shop Steward*. In his book *Chavs,* the British writer, Owen Jones, explored the demonisation of the British working class in an angry examination of stereotypes. Almost all of these would be familiar to Irish readers, even if our terminology of 'knackers', 'skangers' and 'skobies' is homegrown.[85] But perhaps even Jones would be shocked at how Irish television depicts working-class Dubliners in shows like *Damo and Ivor*, *The Centre* and even the acclaimed *Love/Hate*.

For those seeking an understanding of the impact of class conflict on Irish life, Emmet O'Connor's *A Labour History of Ireland* remains indispensable, as do the essays which appear regularly in *Saothar* (journal of the Irish Labour History Society). But the history of class is wider than that of organised labour and far broader than that of the left. Conor McCabe placed such analysis at the centre of his economic history *Sins of the Father*.[86] Newer studies are viewing it through the prisms of fashion, music and sport.[87] American historians Joshua B. Freeman, in *Working Class New York: Life and Labor Since World War II* and Jefferson Cowie in *Stayin' Alive: the 1970s and the Last Days of the Working Class* managed to place the story of workers at the centre of cultural upheavals.[88] Irish scholars might benefit from reading their work. In 1993 the absence of an E.P. Thompson or Eugene Genovese among the Irish historical profession was noted.[89] The emergence of a new generation of young historians will hopefully ensure that gap will soon be filled.

Endnotes

1   Ernie O'Malley, *On Another Man's Wound* (Dublin: Anvil, 1979), p. 24.

2   *Liberty*, Sept., Oct. 2013.

3   These include Francis Devine (ed.), *A Capital in Conflict: Dublin City and the 1913 Lockout* (Dublin: Four Courts Press, 2013); David Convery (ed.), *Locked Out: A Century of Working-Class Life* (Dublin: Irish Academic Press, 2013); Mary Muldowney (ed.) with Ida Milne, *100 Years Later: The Legacy of the 1913 Lockout* (Dublin: Seven Towers Press, 2013); *Socialist Party, Let Us Rise!* (Dublin, 2013).

4   Stoneybatter and Smithfield People's History Project, *The Church Street Tenement Collapse* (Dublin, 2013); Pádraig Mannion (ed.), *Lockout Centenary: Dun Laoghaire, 1913–2013* (Dun Laoghaire, 2013).

5   *Look Left*, 2:17 (winter, 2013).

6   Martina Devlin, 'Hell on Earth: but at least heaven was waiting for them', Mannion (ed.), *Lockout*, pp. 35–8.

7   Emmet O'Connor, 'Larkin's road to revolution', in 'Locked Out Special Supplement', *Irish Times*, 11 Sept. 2013.

8   The headline was misleading, as the article was a sober assessment of Murphy. Andy Bielenberg, 'Larkin's Nemesis', *Business Plus*, Sept. 2013, pp. 20–8.

9   Patrick Maume, 'William Martin Murphy, the Irish Independent and Middle-class Politics, 1905–19' in Fintan Lane (ed.), *Politics, Society and the Middle Class in Modern Ireland* (Basingstoke: Palgrave, 2010), pp. 230–48.

10   *Irish Times*, 4 Feb. 1972.

11   Diarmaid Ferriter, *The Transformation of Ireland, 1900–2000* (London: Profile Books, 2004), p. 697.

12   Virginia Crossman, 'Middle-class attitudes to poverty and welfare in post-Famine Ireland', in Lane (ed.) *Politics, Society and the Middle Class in Modern Ireland*, pp. 130–47.

13   Tony Farmar, *Ordinary Lives: Three Generations of Irish Middle Class Experience* (Dublin: Gill and Macmillan, 1991), p. 12.

14   Paddy 'the Cope' Gallagher, *My Story* (Dungloe, 1939), p. 139.

15   David Fitzpatrick, *Politics and Irish Life: Provincial Experience of War and Revolution* (Cork: Cork University Press, 1998), p. 6.

16   Tom Hunt, 'The GAA: Social Structure and Associated Clubs', in Michael Cronin, William Murphy, Paul Rouse (eds), *The Gaelic Athletic Association, 1884–2009* (Dublin: Irish Academic Press, 2009), p. 201.

17   Maura Cronin, 'Class and status in twentieth-century Ireland: the evidence of oral history', *Saothar*, 32 (2007), pp. 33–43.

18   Enda Delaney, *The Irish in Post-War Britain* (Oxford: Oxford University Press, 2007), p. 30.

19   Aoife Bhreatnach, 'Planning and Philanthropy: Travellers and class boundaries in urban Ireland, 1930–75' in Lane (ed.), *Politics, Society and the Middle Class in Modern Ireland*, pp. 249–70.

20   John O'Callaghan, *The Battle for Kilmallock* (Cork: Mercier Press, 2011), p. 117.

21   *Evening Herald*, 2 Sept. 1913, cited in Stoneybatter and Smithfield People's History Project, *The Church Street Tenement Collapse*, p. 6.

22   Joseph V. O'Brien, *Dear, Dirty Dublin: A City in Distress, 1899–1916* (Berkeley, University of California Press, 1982), p. 226.

23   O'Brien, *Dear, Dirty Dublin*, p. 227.

24   Ann Matthews, 'Poverty Paraded in the Streets, 1913: The Mothers and Children', in Devine (ed.), *A Capital in Conflict*, pp. 239–60.

25   BMH WS 733 (James O'Shea), p. 26.

26   Seán O'Casey, *The Story of the Irish Citizen Army* (London: Maunsel, 1919), p. 9.

27   Charles Callan, 'Labour Lives: Peadar Macken, 1878–1916', *Saothar*, 31 (2006), pp. 121–3.

28   *Irish Worker*, 1 Aug. 1914.

29   David Fitzpatrick, 'Militarism in Ireland, 1900–1922', in Thomas Bartlett, Keith Jeffrey (eds), *A Military History of Ireland* (Cambridge, 1996), p. 381.

30 Adrian Pimley, *A History of the Irish Citizen Army from 1913–1916*, (unpublished thesis, University of Birmingham, 1982), p. 92.

31 *Irish Worker*, 8 Aug. 1914.

32 O'Malley, *On Another Man's Wound*, p. 28.

33 Niamh Puirséil, 'War, Work and Labour', in John Horne (ed.), *Our War: Ireland and the Great War* (Dublin: RIA, 2008), pp. 181–94.

34 *Galway Express*, 15 Jan. 1916. (I am grateful to John Cunningham for this reference.)

35 John Borgonovo, *The Dynamics of War and Revolution: Cork City, 1916–1918* (Cork, 2013), pp. 62–5; pp. 142–44.

36 John O'Callaghan, *Revolutionary Limerick: the Republican Campaign for Independence in Limerick, 1913–1921* (Dublin, 2010), p. 37.

37 BMH WS 1,068 (Michael Brennan), p. 6.

38 BMH WS 1,103 (Denis F. Madden), pp. 10–11.

39 BMH WS 1,316 (John Flanagan), p. 4.

40 BMH WS 669 (Michael S. O'Mahony), p. 1.

41 BMH WS 907 (Laurence Nugent), p. 97.

42 BMH WS 307 (Thomas McCarthy), p. 19; BMH WS 147 (Bernard McAlister), p. 10.

43 John Dorney, 'The Rabble & the Republic', *Saothar*, 41 (2016) pp. 101–9.

44 Similar prejudices were also expressed in contemporary publications such as, *The Soldier Hunter*, 2 Mar. 1918.

45 See, BMH WS 1,328 (Philip Boyle), p. 6; BMH WS 1,241 (Michael Shalloe), pp. 2–3; BMH WS 1,398 (Michael Rock), p. 7.

46 John Newsinger, *Rebel City: Larkin, Connolly and the Dublin Labour Movement* (London: Merlin Press, 2004), pp. 145–7.

47 *An t–Óglác*, 30 Nov. 1918.

48 D.M. Leeson, *The Black and Tans: British Police and Auxiliaries in the Irish war of Independence* (Oxford: Oxford University Press, 2011), p. 85.

49 Communist leader, Michael O' Riordan, quoted in Michael Quinn, *The Making of an Irish Communist Leader, Michael O'Riordan, 1938–1947* (Dublin: Communist Party of Ireland, 2011), p. 37.

50 Leeson, *The Black and Tans*, p. 87.

51 *An Phoblacht/Republican News*, 11 Dec. 2008.

52 Peter Hart, *The IRA & its Enemies: Violence and Community in Cork, 1916–1923* (Oxford: Oxford University Press, 1998), pp. 135–6.

53 Bryce Evans, 'The Construction Corps, 1940–48', *Saothar*, 32 (2007), pp. 19–31.

54 J.L. McCracken, *Representative Government in Ireland: A Study of Dáil Éireann 1919–48* (Westport: Connecticut), pp. 93–101.

55 Pádraig Yeates, *A City in Turmoil: Dublin, 1919–21* (Dublin: Gill and Macmillan, 2012), p. 229.

56 J.J. Lee, *Ireland, 1912–1985: Politics and Society* (Cambridge: Cambridge University Press, 1989), p. 105.

57 Tom Garvin, 'Revolution? Revolutions are what happens to wheels – the phenomenon of revolution, Irish style', in Joost Augusteijn (ed.), *The Irish Revolution, 1913–1923* (Basingstoke: Palgrave, 2002), pp. 224–32.

58 *Irish Times*, 24 Apr. 1918.

59 Dominic Haugh, 'The ITGWU in Limerick, 1917–22', *Saothar,* 31 (2006), pp. 27–42.

60 Conor McCabe, 'The Irish Labour Party and the 1920 Local Elections', *Saothar,* 35 (2010), pp. 7–20.

61 Fergus Campbell, *Land and Revolution: Nationalist Politics in the West of Ireland, 1890–1921* (Oxford: Oxford University Press, 2005), pp. 226–85.

62 Emmet O'Connor, *A Labour History of Ireland, 1824–2000* (Dublin: UCD Press, 1992), pp. 105–7; pp. 119–22.

63 Fitzpatrick, *Politics and Irish life,* p. 6.

64 Ministry for Home Affairs, *The Constructive work of Dáil Éireann,* 1: *The National Police and Courts of Justice* (Dublin, 1921), p. 10.

65 *The Voice of Labour,* 14 Jan. 1922.

66 Charlie McGuire, *Roddy Connolly and the Struggle for Socialism in Ireland* (Cork: Cork University Press, 2008), p. 51.

67 *The Voice of Labour,* 29 Apr. 1922.

68 *The Voice of Labour,* 15 Apr. 1922.

69 McGuire, *Roddy Connolly and the Struggle for Socialism in Ireland,* p. 55.

70 O'Connor, *A Labour History of Ireland,* pp. 125–6.

71 *The Workers' Republic,* 24 Jun. 1922.

72 *The Workers' Republic,* 29 Jul. 1922.

73 Gavin Foster, *The Irish Civil War and Society: Politics, Class and Conflict* (Basingstoke: Palgrave, 2015), pp. 1–51.

74 *An Phoblacht,* 23 Jul. 1976.

75 *Irish Independent,* 11 Jun. 1973.

76 *An Phoblacht,* 22 Jun. 1973.

77 Ibid., 7 Mar. 1975.

78 Ibid., 14 Mar. 1975.

79 Pádraig O'Malley, *The Uncivil Wars: Ireland Today* (Boston: Beacon Press, 1997), pp. 278–9.

80 Though there was a visible republican presence at UCD throughout the 1970s and 1980s.

81 Comments from Broadsheet.ie, 'Dáil Lockout', Wed. 18 Sept. 2013.

82 *Sunday Independent,* 1 Dec. 2013.

83 *Irish Times,* 4 Feb. 2012.

84 *Irish Times,* 9 Sept. 2013; *Irish Independent,* 30 Sept. 2013.

85 Owen Jones, *Chavs: The Demonization of the Working Class* (London: Granta, 2011).

86 Conor McCabe, *Sins of the Father: The Decisions that Shaped the Irish Economy* (Dublin: The History Press, 2011).

87 See, Carole Holohan, 'Challenges to Social Order and Irish Identity? Youth Culture in the Sixties', *Irish Historical Studies*, 38:151 (May 2013), pp. 389–405.

88 Jefferson Cowie, *Stayin' Alive: The 1970s and the Last Days of the Working Class* (New York: The New Press, 2010); Joshua B. Freeman, *Working-Class New York: Life and Labor Since World War II* (New York: The New Press, 2000).

89 Cited in Campbell, *Land and Revolution*, p. 293.

CHAPTER NINE

1913: The Cinderella Centenary

Pádraig Yeates

Just over a hundred years ago Irish newspaper readers were treated to conflicting views of the 1913 Lockout. The perspective provided to the vast majority of people in the provinces was summed up in the weekly cartoon on the front page of the *Sunday Independent* of 31 August 1913, 'Bloody Sunday'. It showed a startled 'Eblana' watching a lance with 'Civic Duty' carved on its shaft being thrust into a slithering dragon, entitled 'The Strike Monster'. The newspaper's verdict on the disturbances that marked the start of Ireland's greatest industrial battle was that there had been 'a deliberate attempt to establish a reign of ruffianism in the city. Out of the reeking slums the jail birds and most abandoned creatures of both sexes have poured to vent their hatred upon their natural enemies, the police.' Many Dubliners, including growing numbers of a younger generation of cultural and political activists disillusioned with the seedy corruption of the Home Rule establishment in the city, would have seen for themselves who the authors of this 'ruffianism' were; but reports such as this, sedulously disseminated by the newspapers of William Martin Murphy's business empire, prompted local authorities across the country to pass motions that condemned the 'strike monster' and served to isolate its adherents.

It would be another 103 years before the police records that belied this version of events would surface. They would show that, while 205 people were arrested in the six days from the start of the DUTC strike on 26 August 1913 until Bloody Sunday, compared with thirty-eight over the same period covering the 1912 bank holiday, the type of person arrested and the offences involved were significantly different. All of those arrested in 1912 were for offences such as larceny, theft and housebreaking, whereas 179 of those charged in 1913 were for incidents related to the Tramway dispute and involved offences such as intimidation, rioting, attacks on trams, assaulting police officers and sedition. Men and juveniles invariably outnumbered women appearing in the police courts in this era, but in the week culminating in Bloody Sunday 1913 not only women but juveniles almost disappear from the Prisoners Books. Those coming before the courts were overwhelmingly adult males in manual occupations with high levels of unionisation, including tram workers and trade union officials. The latter two groups comprise a third of all those arrested before the widespread rioting on Bloody Sunday, but even on that day manual workers in unionised occupations predominated. These were not opportunist criminals out for mischief but militant workers in extremis; revolting against intolerable living and working conditions.[1]

Contrast the *Sunday Independent's* depiction of the rioters to that in the *Daily Mirror* with its photographs of civilian casualties and smashed homes, or with the *Daily Herald's* headline, 'Rioting in Dublin: Crown Cossacks bludgeon strikers, women and children alike, Irish bosses write in Blood'. They pose the question; would Dublin's urban working poor have been better off remaining in the United Kingdom with mass circulation newspapers such as the *Mirror* and *Herald*, or Home Rule Ireland with mass circulation newspapers such as the *Sunday Independent?*[2]

Burying Larkin

In January 2013 I attended the first formal commemoration of the Lockout Centenary Year in Glasnevin Cemetery, Dublin. It was to mark the anniversary of Jim Larkin's death and was the first formal commemoration of that event for fifteen years. James Connolly's death is marked by various organisations every year; a fact that poses questions about the way we prize the memory of those who died for Ireland over those who merely tried to make it a better place in which to live. Without Larkin there would have been no Connolly, for without Larkin there would have been no Irish Transport and General Workers Union, let alone an Irish Citizen Army and Connolly would probably have spent his latter years as a gifted propagandist of the labour movement in America. It was Larkin who founded the modern Irish trade union movement, who brought hope and the organisational means to battle for a better share of the nation's material wealth and deeper appreciation of its culture to some of the most marginalised people on this island.

Larkin's funeral had another significance for me. It was the first public event I ever attended. I was only eight months old at the time, so I cannot claim any recollection of it. But I do know that the following day my parents caught the mail boat from Dun Laoghaire and I can recall many miserable subsequent journeys going back and forth on the Irish Sea, when the mail, and cattle on occasion, were taken off before the passengers.

My parents knew the streets of Birmingham were not paved with gold. My mother had worked in a munitions factory during the Second World War and my father served in the British Army. Both were radicalised by their experiences then and during the great depression that preceded it. They had seen Britain transformed: Churchill's coalition cabinet of Conservatives, Labour and Liberals realised they had to tackle the deep-seated malaise that set in after 1918 when a land fit for heroes failed to materialise. To sustain public support for the sacrifices that a new war effort required meant offering more than the almost impossible prospect of military victory in 1940; they had to provide a vision of a better future made credible by practical pledges of intent based on how the War itself was waged. These included conscription (industrial as well as military), compulsory billeting, food rationing, taxes on excess profits and a 90 per cent surtax on high incomes (18s in the £). Unions and their members were given a voice in how industry was run, albeit with mixed results. The government took over the commanding heights of the economy, while the Beveridge Report was commissioned to outline the shape of a future welfare state. Wartime Britain was a more 'socialist' state, in real terms, than the Soviet Union. My father saw dramatic changes in Italy and France as the term 'collaborator' became short hand for the ruling class and, I suspect, my parents made the not unreasonable, if naïve, assumption that Ireland too must have changed. They were quickly disabused. The great storm had passed us by. I cannot help feeling the death of Larkin in 1947 quenched their last spark of hope that Ireland could become a country that offered a future to its working poor. My parents voted with their feet, as did hundreds of thousands of their contemporaries.

Redmondism and the urban poor

Their disillusionment and that of a generation begs the question posed at the beginning of this essay – Were people born in places such as Dublin's tenements, as my parents were in 1911 and 1912, destined to find their natural homes in Britain after scraping a living for almost thirty years, in what was, for them, a failed state?

While the 'Decade of War and Revolution' swept away the Home Rule elite of John Redmond, the values of neo-Redmondism lived on, more or less intact. Certainly, this was true in Dublin, where municipal corruption and a Catholic moral ascendancy cohabited quite comfortably. Efforts to salvage Redmond's political reputation in recent years are understandable given the importance of the northern peace process, but the fact remains that he failed to achieve Home Rule or reconcile unionists to the cause of constitutional nationalism.

Yet constitutional nationalism did have one lasting achievement to its credit; it secured the land of Ireland for the farmers of Ireland (including significant improvements in housing for agricultural workers). Unfortunately, these reforms did nothing for the capital, or other towns. Even the Town Tenants Association, another creation of constitutional nationalism, only protected the interests of the shop keeper and business tenant.[3] 'Dear, dirty Dublin' with its disease and its slums epitomised all that was worst about the Redmondite political regime for Unionists. Meanwhile the Irish Party's success in preventing us from being overrun by the nascent British welfare state offered confirmation that whoever else benefitted from Home Rule it would not be the working poor.

We tend to remember David Lloyd George as the man who sent the Black and Tans to Ireland but he also gave us old-age pensions and unemployment benefit. He would have given us the foundations of a national health service too but the twin elections of 1910, caused largely by his reforming zeal, gave the Redmondites the balance of power at Westminster and, with it, the capacity to protect the Irish ratepayer and taxpayer from the wilder extravagances of British socialism. Dublin's leading Catholic nationalist businessman, William Martin Murphy, was one of many witnesses who strenuously opposed the extension of health insurance to Ireland at hearings of the British Treasury Committee.[4] Apart from the burden on employers, Murphy claimed that 'In Ireland, and especially in a city like Dublin, with its hospital and dispensary system, there was no person wanting medical relief and medicine unable to pay for them who could not obtain them without any payment whatsoever.'[5]

The attitude of those providing the city's health care services belied such a philanthropic view. The voluntary hospitals were appalled at the impact the extension of the British 1911 Health Insurance Act would have on revenue streams predicated on private medicine, while many doctors saw the 'contract work' involved in the British scheme as 'demeaning and detrimental to their status'. Members of the medical profession interviewed by the Parliamentary Committee said that 'while not against the principle of medical benefits, [they] were wary of participating in a system that would hurt the earning power of the profession'. To prove their point, they demanded a 21s capitation fee to co-operate with it, treble the fees paid to doctors in London.[6]

The British disease

This is not to claim that Lloyd George was brimming with generosity for the working classes, but he was mindful of the rapidly emerging threat the Labour Party posed to Liberal hegemony and the advances that labour was making in the years leading up to the First World War. Legislation such as the 1906 Trade Disputes Act, which protected unions from being sued for damages caused by industrial action, was meant to demonstrate that the Liberals were the workers' friends. Instead, it unleashed a wave of pent-up militancy, driven by price inflation. After years of relative tranquillity when the average number of workers involved in strikes across the United Kingdom averaged 200,000 to 300,000, the figure jumped to 515,000 in 1910; 962,000 in 1911; and 1.46 million in 1912.[7] Murphy was therefore right to be fearful of the consequences of British social reform. One particularly dangerous innovation was the introduction of unemployment benefit in 1912. This would play a major role in sustaining the morale of workers locked out in 1913 who, having just qualified for the dole, believed that it would save them from destitution. In fact, it would be February 1914 before many of them would know the outcome of their claims.[8]

The British 'socialist disease' had taken a particularly virulent form in Dublin, called Larkinism; otherwise syndicalism. Syndicalism was a quasi-revolutionary ideology that sought to unite workers in 'One Big Union' to not alone secure better pay and conditions but overthrow capitalism through the agency of a general strike. This could be assisted by political action when appropriate, both parliamentary and extra-parliamentary. Larkin's support for Irish Home Rule, female suffrage, slum clearance and other reforms needs to be seen in the context of this world view.

While he was an advocate of rhetorical revolution, Larkin's practical approach to politics and trade unionism remained anchored to the wilder shores of British social democracy. It was his lieutenant, James Connolly who would venture out to embrace the Fenian variant of Blanquism and, like many European contemporaries, forge a revolutionary template based on nationalism, socialism or some variant of both, of which Lenin's Bolsheviks was the most spectacularly successful group.

'Murphyism' – the antidote

To meet the Larkinite threat Murphy created an antidote. He christened it, with all due modesty, Murphyism. If Jim Larkin's great achievement was to bring syndicalism to Ireland and raise Dublin's unskilled workers from their knees, Murphy's was to persuade his fellow employers that they could defeat the threat of a general strike with the reality of a general lockout.

Larkin did try to recruit the big battalions of British trade unionism to his cause in 1913, assisted by the incompetence and brutality of the Dublin Metropolitan Police and Royal Irish Constabulary in the riots surrounding Bloody Sunday on 31 August. The outrage generated in the British labour movement by this atrocity transformed a local strike over pay and conditions in Murphy's Dublin United Tramway Company into a battle over union recognition of national proportions. Larkin's call for sympathetic action in Britain received a ready response, especially from dockers, carters and railway workers in areas where he had strong personal connections and where there were concentrations of workers who had emigrated from Dublin. Goods were 'blacked' on Merseyside, in the West Midlands and South Wales.[9] However these incidents quickly degenerated into localised disputes about reinstating the men suspended or sacked because of their response to Larkin's call. The railway unions in particular were reluctant to sanction official action following their own bruising battle with the employers in 1911. As the general secretary of the newly formed National Union of Railwaymen, J.E. Williams pointed out, not only were railways statutorily obliged to accept all traffic offered but 'if the principle of the sympathetic strike is to be followed our members must always be involved'.[10]

Williams had a point; Larkin for all his threats of sympathetic strike action in Dublin rarely used it and the Dublin railway men worked throughout the Lockout, due to the defeat they had suffered at the hands of the Great Southern and Western Railway directors, who included William Martin Murphy, in 1911, when they took sympathetic action on behalf of their British comrades.[11] Board of Trade statistics confirmed what they had learnt the hard way, that sympathetic strikes rarely succeeded. While unions were completely successful in 31 per cent of sectional disputes and partially successful in another 48 per cent in this period, only 5 per cent of sympathetic strikes ended in victory for the workers.[12]

Larkin was not looking for a fight in the summer of 1913. He had already won a series of disputes in the city over the previous six months and was looking forward to the appointment of a conciliation board to

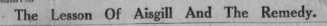

DAILY SKETCH.

No. 1,404.   LONDON, MONDAY, SEPTEMBER 8, 1913.   [Registered as a Newspaper.]   ONE HALFPENNY.

DUBLIN'S DAY OF FUNERALS PASSES OFF QUIETLY, BUT THE STRIKES GO ON.

The seven victims' bodies pass the scene of their death.   Inset are Byrne's wife and daughter.   Sergeant Woolfe, photographed just before the riot.

Dublin is still afraid of further rioting, but the police, apparently acting under instructions, are keeping as much out of sight as possible. The Irish capital was a day of sorrow on Saturday, when John Byrne, the second victim of the famous baton charge, was buried, but the city was also the scene of the funeral of the seven victims of the Dublin house collapse. Sergeant Woolfe, Dublin's biggest policeman—he is 7ft. 6in. high—was knocked out in the famous riot. He is so big that they say he is always the object of attack during strikes.

The collapse of two tenements in Church Street on 2 September 1913, causing seven deaths, highlighted the city's housing crisis. Among the dead was 17-year-old Eugene Salmon, a locked-out Jacob's worker who died trying to save his 6-year-old sister Elizabeth, who was also killed. British newspapers such as the *Daily Sketch* often provided better coverage of such events than their Irish counterparts, because they were uninhibited by local political considerations and a reluctance to show Dublin in a bad light on the eve of Home Rule.

The flag of the Irish Citizen Army was flown from the roof of William Martin Murphy's Imperial Hotel during the Rising on the instructions of James Connolly, to divert British artillery fire from the rebel headquarters in the GPO. It is now on display in the National Museum, Collins Barracks. (Courtesy of National Museum of Ireland)

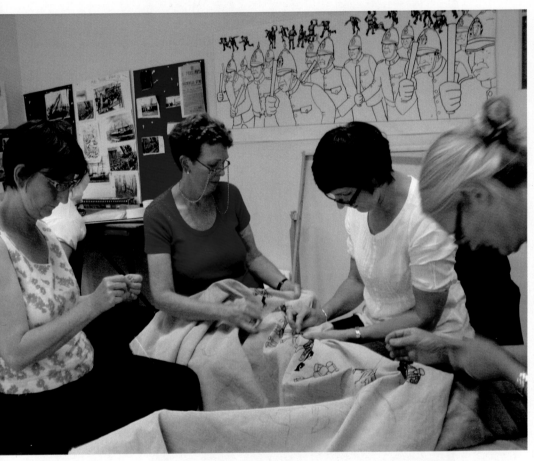

Patchwork Society members working on the Lockout Panel for the 1913 Centenary during 2012. This was one of many voluntary groups that came together to help create the 1913 Tapestry designed by Robert Ballagh and Cathy Henderson for the 1913 Committee. (Courtesy of SIPTU)

Bloody Sunday Panel for Lockout Tapestry design by Cathy Henderson captured the drama of the moment. Each small crowd figure in the background took two hours to stitch. This Panel was made by members of the Irish Patchwork Society. (Courtesy of SIPTU)

Members of Blanchardstown ICA Guild work on Lockout Panel depicting strikers' families using TUC Food Tickets to collect food. (Courtesy of SIPTU)

Completed panel, designed by artist Cathy Henderson, of TUC Food Tickets issued during the 1913 Lockout. (Courtesy of SIPTU)

Liberty Hall Wrap from Sir John Rogerson's Quay in 2013 with Robert Ballagh's depiction of Jim Larkin and the 'SOLIDARITY' message conveying one of the central themes of the Centenary. (Courtesy of SIPTU)

The continuity of socialist themes from the Lockout Centenary were extended in the 2016 Wrap to commemorate the 1916 Rising, highlighting the most radical passages in the 1916 Proclamation, which was printed in Liberty Hall and the central roles played by women activists and James Connolly. (Courtesy of SIPTU)

consolidate those gains. The evidence suggests Larkin was anxious to avoid a confrontation with Murphy in August 1913 and only sanctioned the strike when he was told that the workers in the Dublin United Tramway Company (DUTC) power house would come out in support of the ITGWU if even some trams stopped.[13] Instead they remained at their stations when Murphy drafted in strike breakers and threatened to dispense with their services. Ironically it was not Larkin, so often portrayed as the fiery instigator of industrial conflict, who scuttled the initiative of Dublin's Lord Mayor Lorcan Sherlock, to establish a disputes mediation body in the city, but William Martin Murphy.

The peace initiative, promoted in the background by the Catholic Archbishop, Dr William Walsh, had benefitted from the enforced absence of William Martin Murphy through illness in the first half of 1913. Murphy's return to health in July saw him systematically purge his enterprises of Larkin's union. The speed with which the tram strike escalated into a wholesale lockout – nine days – suggests that his undertaking was carefully planned and benefitted from the lessons learnt in previous lockouts such Cork in 1908, as well as the 1911 GSWR dispute. While mediation could avert strikes and lockouts, along with their unpredictable outcomes, Murphy realised that it would also allow Larkin to strengthen his grip on the city's transport network and consolidate his organisation of the city's unskilled in pursuit of a workers' commonwealth.

The proxy war

Although the Lockout is often portrayed as a heroic proletarian phase in the fight for national liberation it would not have happened if we had not been part of the United Kingdom. Without the Liberals' progressive social legislation and TUC support, the infant ITGWU might have been strangled at birth. Larkin and his allies on the Dublin Trades Council were totally unprepared for Murphy's onslaught. The appeal for British support was driven by material necessity as much as syndicalist ideology. While the British trade union movement was far more developed than its Irish counterpart, with four million members compared to 100,000, the British Trades Union Congress lacked both the organisational power and the political capacity to win Dublin's battles for it. The unions were simply outmatched by the employers. The figures speak for themselves. The TUC sent over £93,000 in strike pay and provisions to Dublin in 1913–14 and at least another £13,000 came from other sources; but lost wages in Dublin are estimated at £400,000.[14] Business suffered more in absolute financial terms and the overall cost of the dispute to the city's economy was approximately £2.3 million (including the £400,000 in lost wages). But these losses were widely spread and, as Murphy constantly reminded locked-out workers, the employers could still afford three square meals a day. The revenue of the Dublin Port and Docks Board, one of the enterprises most affected, only fell by 8.4 per cent.[15] The Murphy enterprise at the epicentre of the dispute, the DUTC, saw net profits fall by 16 per cent, but the annual dividend on ordinary shares was only cut by half a per cent.[16]

The cost of subsidising the Lockout for allies of Dublin's employers was less than £20,000, with the largest amounts coming from the British Shipping Federation, the Engineering Federation and Lord Iveagh, head of the Guinness dynasty.[17] In other words, for every £5 spent by the TUC on class war in Dublin, the enemy only had to spend £1 to maintain the Lockout. (Some historians, such as John Newsinger, calculate total British aid to the unions at £150,000 or £7.5 for every £1 spent by the enemy.)[18] Unlike the TUC funds, the employers' subsidies were kept secret. After all, it would have been difficult for Murphy to portray Dublin workers as unwitting cats' paws of the British TUC, being used to destroy Irish industry in return for bowls of soup, if it became known that he was receiving handouts from British employers. (Nor should we forget that Murphy's own business empire was founded on British government subsidies to develop Ireland's light rail network.)[19]

Separatism with a red hue

Ironically the intervention of the TUC accelerated the separatist urge within the Irish labour movement. Relations with the British leaders were seriously damaged by the dispute. Tensions over how it was waged between the TUC veterans funding it and the younger generation of local Dublin leaders who were running it was inevitable. When the TUC refused to contemplate extending sympathetic strike action to Britain, what began as a 'blame the Brits' strategy by Larkin and Connolly to explain away defeat, quickly evolved on the outbreak of the Great War into a leftist variant of militant separatism. Whatever chance there was of Larkin keeping the ITGWU and the newly formed Irish Citizen Army within the broader labour movement ended with his departure to America in October 1914. His successor as acting general secretary of the union and commander of the Citizen Army, James Connolly, led a group of committed militants into an alliance with kindred spirits in the Irish Republican Brotherhood.

The Citizen Army had been born out of the need to breed discipline and self-respect into the ranks of the ITGWU, as well as to protect workers in confrontations with the police. But it was the adoption of a constitution with the objective of vesting 'the ownership of Ireland, moral and material ... of right in the people of Ireland' that transformed the ICA into something more than other contemporary workers' self-defence forces that frequently emerged in such disputes. The ICA was by turns socialist, nationalist, internationalist and revolutionary in a peculiarly parochial Dublin way. Efforts to build it outside Dublin were largely unsuccessful but this tiny force, from which Connolly and his martinet of a chief of staff, Michael Mallin, weeded out the slack and the uncommitted, had an influence out of all proportion to its size. It was one of many phenomena, including the Lockout itself, which marked the emergence of Dublin, and the movements it generated, as the focal point of Irish politics for the next nine years. The alliance between radical socialists, radical nationalists and radical feminists nourished by the Lockout helped transform the capital into the cockpit of revolution. This was a role it would retain until the Truce in 1921, when Irish electoral politics once more became local. The Civil War was a military version of the same process of post-Truce adjustment. While the IRA, effectively a federation of local militias with national pretensions, faced rapid military defeat, its members would subsequently be an important factor in reasserting the traditional parochialism that characterised Irish politics.

The emergence of the Citizen Army and the Irish Volunteers in November 1913 marked a new development in the arena of street conflict. Another change in Dublin politics, however, was taking place at a deeper level from quite early on in the Lockout. This was the intervention by Dr Walsh, Archbishop of Dublin, on the side of the employers during the 'Dublin Kiddies' controversy.[20] It was all the more significant because Walsh was the most socially progressive member of the Catholic Hierarchy and, among other things, was an advocate of industrial relations mediation to avert conflicts such as the Lockout. In October 1913, he condemned unequivocally plans to take strikers' children to foster homes in England to be looked after in the homes of 'socialists, atheists, Protestants and suffragettes'. The women who sent them would 'no longer be held worthy of the name of Catholic mothers'. Worst of all, this 'fantastic scheme' would make children sent to England 'discontented with the poor homes to which they will sooner or later return ... That surely is by no means to be viewed with anything but abhorrence by anyone sincerely anxious for the welfare and happiness of the poor'.[21]

Archbishop Walsh accepted that the poor would always be with us: the important thing was that they be content with moderate ameliorations to their lot. Such attitudes would prevail throughout the decade of war and revolution, especially where children were concerned. By 1924 there were more of them in industrial schools in Ireland than in England, Scotland, Wales and Northern Ireland combined.[22]

It was the treatment of children in particular that horrified British trade union leaders during the Lockout, as it did Irish female suffrage campaigners, many of whom came from eminently respectable middle-class backgrounds such as Louie Bennett and Kathleen Lynn. They were drawn to the workers' cause initially by their concern for the plight of children. Cultural nationalists across the political spectrum were equally appalled, from Thomas Ashe and Patrick Pearse to Lady Gregory and W.B. Yeats. The grasping philistinism of Murphy and his allies would be immortalised in the poet's 'September 1913'.

Unionists and the Lockout

The demonstration of clerical power was not lost on over 92,000 Protestants living in Dublin city and county, most of them unionist. T.D. Rudmose-Brown, Professor of Romance Languages at Trinity College witnessed the success of mobs led by young Catholic clerics and Ancient Order of Hibernian stalwarts at Amiens Street station preventing children from being taken to foster homes in Belfast. He wrote that the scenes provided, 'an interesting foretaste of the joys of unfettered Home Rule to which we are hastening'. John Campbell, who was an MP for Trinity College put it more forcefully at an anti-Home Rule rally of Southern Unionists in Dublin's Theatre Royal a month later when he declared, 'I would rather suffer under the whips of Larkin than under the scorpions of Joe Devlin. I honestly believe that I would have a greater chance of liberty, of personal judgement and of conscience under Jim Larkin and the Irish Transport Union than I would under Joe Devlin and the Molly Maguires.'[23] Rudmose-Brown's views were echoed by T.M. Healy, who represented the employers at the Board of Trade (Askwith) Inquiry into the Lockout and was as near to a personal friend as Murphy ever had. In correspondence with his brother Maurice, he predicted that Redmond was losing Dublin and confided that, 'I should prefer Larkin to Devlin, and I told Murphy so.'[24]

Edward Carson is often credited with the reintroduction of the gun into Irish politics, but it was Dublin employers, Catholic and Protestant, unionist and nationalist, who used their status as Justices of the Peace to issue licensed revolvers to strike breakers, some of whom used them all too readily on the streets of the capital. Not one of these gunmen was given a prison sentence, even in cases where they caused serious and, in at least one instance, fatal injuries. (Fifteen-year-old Alicia Brady contracted tetanus and died from a ricochet wound after a strike breaker opened fire in Mark Street on a group of protesting women in December.) Meanwhile, Mountjoy was filled (the women's prison, as well as the men's) with strikers and their supporters.

Reinventing the Lockout experience

While Murphyism triumphed over Larkinism in 1913 its victory was far from complete. The ITGWU survived. Defeat in some situations is inevitable. What then becomes important is how it is handled and perhaps the most important service James Connolly ever did the Irish labour movement was his brilliant polemical defence of syndicalism in the aftermath of the Lockout. He convinced posterity that it was a draw, although all the evidence was to the contrary. In an article published by *Forward* on 9 February 1914, he described the support of the British working-class movement for Dublin as 'its highest point of moral grandeur', then castigated the TUC leadership:

> Could that feeling but have been crystallised into organic expression, could we but have had real statesmen amongst us who, recognising the wonderful leap forward for our class, would have hastened to burn behind us the boats that might make easy a retreat to the old ground of isolation and division, could we have found labour leaders capable enough to declare that now that the working class had found its collective soul it should hasten to express itself as befitted that soul and not be fettered by the rules, regulations and codes of organisations conceived in the olden outworn spirit of sectional jealousies; could these things have but been vouchsafed to us, what a new world could now be opening delightfully upon the vision of labour? Consider what Dublin meant to you all! It meant that the whole force of organised labour should stand behind each organisation in each and all its battles, that no company, battalion or brigade should henceforth be allowed to face the enemy alone, and that the capitalist would be taught that when he fought a

union anywhere he must be prepared to fight all unions everywhere ... But sectionalism, intrigues and old-time jealousies damned us in the hour of victory, and officialdom was the first to fall to the tempter.

And so we Irish workers must go down into Hell, bow our backs to the lash of the slave driver, let our hearts be seared by the iron of his hatred, and instead of the sacramental wafer of brotherhood and common sacrifice, eat the dust of defeat and betrayal. Dublin is isolated.[25]

What made the polemic all the more persuasive was that it appealed to the nobler instincts of the most visionary elements in the British and Irish labour movements. That it ignored the conundrum of how to build a more united movement without it becoming more bureaucratic, and that Connolly's only alternative strategy of maintaining spontaneity and militancy through the sympathetic strike had patently failed, has not diminished the potency of his message or the relevance of the questions posed. The reference to 'the sacramental wafer of brotherhood and common sacrifice' would prove ominous. Soon the mantle of martyrdom in 1916 would insulate Connolly from critical scrutiny on the revolutionary left, and the Irish revolutionary left in particular.

Even without Connolly's involvement in the Easter Rising, it was inevitable that mythology would embroider the drama of defeat. The most recent case has been the reinvention of Rosie Hackett, who worked for many years in the ITGWU and its Irish Women Workers' Union branch, as a leading figure in the Lockout.[26] This arose as part of the very successful campaign to have the newest bridge across the Liffey named after her. While the use of the occasion to celebrate the role of women in the labour and independence movement is very welcome the blatant distortion of the historical record is not. One of the worst examples of such unhistorical re-imagining was Mark Lawler's, 'Irishman's Diary' that appeared in the *Irish Times* on 19 August 2013. Writing of Rosie's role he told readers that:

The first event [leading to the Lockout] took place two years earlier at W & R Jacob and Co's Biscuit Company on Bishop Street. On August 22nd, 1911, 3,000 women came out on strike in support of their men – 'A procession of the strikers was then formed ... A great deal of excitement in vent of the strike spirit was manifested ... Shortly after noon, the strikers were reinforced by some 3,000 girls ... These latter formed in professional order and moved about.'

Jim Larkin opined that the conditions for the biscuit makers were 'sending them from this earth 20 years before their time'. The person who galvanised these '3,000 girls' was Rosie Hackett, an 18-year-old messenger at Jacobs, and her successful negotiations led to an increase in wages and better working conditions at the factory.[27]

There is no mention of Rosie Hackett in the *Irish Times* report cited. Nor is any other evidence presented by Lawler to support his claims. As the report implies it was Larkin who negotiated a return to work. The strike action began among boys, probably inspired by the Dublin newsboy's strike (see Chapter Three), who were joined by the 1,000 male operatives in the ITGWU. It was then that the 2,000 women, who were not unionised at the time, came out as well in pursuit of better pay and conditions. About half the women subsequently joined the newly formed Irish Women Workers Union but Rosie Hackett was not one of them because she only entered employment with Jacob's in 1913.[28]

Jacobs was certainly one of the first companies to lock out workers in 1913 but it was only after male employees, who were members of the ITGWU, took sympathetic action by refusing to accept 'tainted' flour from Shackleton's Mill in Lucan. On Monday, 1 September 670 of the 1,000 male workers came out in support of their colleagues but only 303 women out of the 2,000 did so. While this was the largest and most vocal group among the 840 women workers involved in the Lockout, Rosie Hackett does not appear in any contemporary accounts. In her own witness statement to the Bureau of Military History she says that 'It was as a result of the big strike in 1913 that I first became attached to Liberty Hall. A workroom was opened to assist girls who had lost their employment as a result of the strike.'[29] The extravagant claims made by Rosie Hackett's champions should serve as a warning against succumbing to the temptation of meeting the requirements of the day by replacing one historical myth with another.[30]

Dublin Port, Connolly's blunder and the Lockout in microcosm

The main focus of historical martyrology has been on Larkin and Connolly; Connolly the more so because of his subsequent execution in the cause of militant nationalism. His stewardship of the dispute during Larkin's imprisonment has rarely been examined. The decision on 12 November 1913, to bring out the dockers and close Dublin port 'tight as a drum' was a major blunder. Larkin had been holding his 1,000 members on the docks in reserve. They were able to seriously disrupt trade by guerrilla action, using the 'go-slow' to ensure ships missed the tide and selectively blacking 'tainted goods', while continuing to draw a week's wages and pay a week's union contributions. On the very day Connolly pulled the dockers out, the Shipping Federation delivered 300 free labourers or 'scabs' to the Alexandra Basin. The main effect of the ITGWU action was to drive all the port companies into the arms of the Federation and William Martin Murphy.[31] Connolly's call on the Irish in Britain to vote against Liberal candidates in bye elections for as long as Larkin was incarcerated proved more effective and helped secure the latter's early release, but many of the dockers were never reconciled with Connolly's leadership of the ITGWU.

The refusal of the Special Delegate Conference of the TUC on 9 December 1913, to endorse the proposal for sympathetic strikes in Britain in support of the locked-out men was therefore not the only cause of fragmentation and defeat in Dublin. Major miscalculations occurred in the city and many craft workers, from book binders and printers, to engineers and carpenters passed the pickets, while members of the most militant white collar union, the drapers assistants, were accused of doing the locked-out porters work in stores such as Arnotts and Clerys.

The use of the sympathetic strike tactic within Dublin could itself cause division and weakness, rather than strength. A case in point is the Dublin Port and Docks Board, which should have served as a warning to Connolly only ten days before he pulled out the dockers. The Board's *Namebook* lists every manual employee from 1895 to 1925.[32] During the Lockout there were 375 employees. On 20 October 1913, labourers refused to handle 'tainted' coal delivered by strike breakers for the Port and Docks power station. It was classic sympathetic action and would, if successful, have drastically affected the operation of the port. On 23 October the board decided to give the men until 27 October to return to work or face dismissal. News reports vary about the number of men who came out from 60 in Murphy's *Irish Independent* to 200 in the Irish Party's *Freeman's Journal*. The actual figure is 233, of whom the vast majority were labourers, dockers, sailors, firemen and 'hands' on floats.[33]

Less than a dozen of the skilled workers participated and over 140 passed the pickets. Seven strikers returned by the Board's October deadline, another seven in the run up to Christmas and a further twenty-seven a week or so before Larkin told men to seek reinstatement on 18 January 1914 at a mass meeting in the ITGWU's recreational centre at Croydon Park.

Larkin was acknowledging defeat and wanted to ensure as orderly a return to work as possible, rather than see the union turn into a retreating rabble with divisions that could last generations. As an experienced union leader, he knew an organised return to work was vital to the ITGWU's survival.

The evidence from the Port and Docks Board records shows that those who returned to work early received preferential treatment. They generally had their former service recognised, did not have their pay cut, and in a few instances, received pay rises and promotion. The early returnees included a ganger, a machinist, a pattern maker, a pavier and a craneman, while the rest were unskilled. Some unskilled workers, particularly the elderly or disabled, such as nightwatchmen approaching retirement did not come out at all for fear of losing their pensions. The vast majority of craft workers who passed the pickets would have their turn to strike in 1917, when they successfully secured significant pay rises in a booming war time economy.[34] On that occasion it was the labourers' turn to pass pickets. In fact, they never went on strike again between 1913 and 1925 because pay rises could be secured through negotiation once the War economy kicked in.

In 1913–14, however, things were very different. Fifty-one strikers were not taken back, including an apprentice and three boy labourers. The employer used the opportunity to punish and victimise militants, as well as get rid of men considered 'idlers', 'slackers' and trouble makers. One man who stayed out sick through the dispute came back armed with medical certificates only to find his job gone anyway. The Port and Docks Board was one of the better employers, possibly the best, in the port. It was a public body. Although shipping companies and other employers nominated the majority of board members, it included public representatives. During the Lockout the most prominent of these was William Field, the Irish Party MP for Dublin's Harbour Division who was most sympathetic to the workers' cause.[35] The Board also met in public so that its deliberations were tempered by what was thought to be measured responses to the conflict, rather than taking decisions that could be regarded as partisan or unfair. If this was the position taken on victimisation by such an employer, we can only speculate on the discussions that took place behind closed doors in other companies.

One interesting aspect of the dispute in the port, and elsewhere, was that there was relatively little violence. One fireman/engineer was injured by strikers on the first day, but just two strikers were convicted of assault over specific incidents during the three months it lasted. Both were subsequently re-employed. The other interesting feature of the *Namebook*, as noted above, is that the men who took sympathetic action in 1913 did not come out again, even during the engineers' strike of 1917. While the craft workers led the way in terms of militancy during the war years, the ITGWU managed to piggyback their efforts so successfully that it narrowed significantly the pay differentials with skilled tradesmen. Obviously both sides had learnt lessons from the Lockout.[36]

Workers and militarism

The level of violence in the city during the Lockout was surprisingly low, at least on the strikers' side, given the large numbers involved. Only one strike breaker was killed and that was towards the very end of the dispute. In fact, the murder of Thomas Harten, a strike breaker for the coal merchants, on 17 January 1914, when he was kicked to death on Eden Quay outside Liberty Hall, may have been a factor in Larkin's decision to call off the dispute next day.

What ultimately saved the ITGWU and transformed the labour market was the outbreak of War in August 1914. This sucked thousands of working-class British Army reservists out of Dublin's labour market, including 2,700 ITGWU members. The figure may have risen to 5,000 by 1917.[37] The British Government, whose new priority was to defeat Germany, told Redmond he would have to wait for Home Rule. Domestic peace took precedence over nationalist demands and domestic peace meant, above all, industrial peace. Arbitration structures were put in place to mediate on the conflicting demands of capital and labour in war industries. Inevitably pay rises in war industries set benchmarks for other sectors.[38] This did much to enhance union representation in the workplace, a factor still largely unacknowledged by many Irish historians in the growth of the labour movement. It is no coincidence that following the establishment of the Agricultural Wages Board by the British government in late 1917, ITGWU membership rose from 25,000 to well over 100,000 by 1919. The union became the recognised negotiator on pay and conditions for agricultural labourers, who joined in droves. Meanwhile, James Connolly's execution and transformation from political pariah to national martyr played an important role in the popular legitimisation of the union.

However, it was not his socialist principles, his Marxist interpretation of Irish history or his trade union activities in 1913 that gave Connolly his heroic stature – it was British bullets. Thanks to him, the Irish Citizen Army, born during the Lockout to protect pickets from police brutality, organised to instil discipline and self-respect in members, played a role out of all proportion to its numbers. Under Connolly's direction, from late 1914 onwards, it forced the pace of insurrection in 1916. Connolly's role in the Easter Rising was a blow against the imperialist war in Europe but it can also be seen as contributing to the rise of militarism at home which would, paradoxically, reach its height, north and south, in the so-called Truce of 1921–2.

The role of political violence has been pernicious in Ireland. In the years after 1913, and again after 1968 in the North, armed elites of one sort or another, which were in part a response to state repression, would inadvertently collaborate with the same state machine to drive popular movements off the streets. In such conditions the role of organised labour became increasingly marginalised, as did that of other civil society groups. The public space was occupied by power struggles between competing militias. Occasionally, as with the Munster 'soviets' and the eviction of anti-Treaty forces from the Ballast Office in Dublin in 1922, workers' power exerted itself; but such acts were sporadic and frequently brought trade unionists into conflict with the forces of the Republic, as well as those of the Crown.

The material cost of military conflict was high. As we have seen the five months of the Lockout cost the city's economy £2.3 million. The six days of the Easter Rising cost £2.5 million in damage to property alone.[39] The death toll of the Lockout was miniscule, thirteen direct deaths if we include the Church Street tenement collapse victims. Easter week, on the other hand, cost over 500 dead and over 2,500 injured.[40]

There was a method in Connolly's insurrectionary madness and his determination to make the Citizen Army the catalyst for revolutionary violence, even if it meant neglecting the ITGWU, whose membership had fallen from 30,000 in August 1913 to somewhere between 3,500 and 5,000 by 1916.[41] One of the most striking characteristics of twentieth-century history is the capacity of his international counterparts in various communist parties inspired by the Bolshevik variant of Blanquism to exploit military conflicts to assume leadership of patriotic struggles against foreign aggression or occupation. In countries as different as China, Korea, the Philippines, Malaya and Vietnam in East Asia, in Italy, Spain, Greece, Albania and former Yugoslavia in Europe, communist parties either seized state power or came within fighting distance of it on the same basis as Connolly's plan to fuse socialism with nationalism; they espoused the same thesis that the working class was the last, incorruptible bastion of patriotic national identity. Like Ireland, most of these countries were overwhelmingly peasant societies but, unlike them, Ireland was shielded by Britain from exposure to the worst excesses of the wars that engulfed Eurasia. British imperialism may thus, inadvertently, have done our own national bourgeoisie some service. In the decade of War and Revolution and again in the so-called Thirty Years War from 1968–98, the British army held the ring until its political masters and the other combatants were ready to negotiate a settlement.

A socially deferential revolution

The Russian revolution has coloured much of the left historiography surrounding 1913 and subsequent events, including the debate on whether Connolly was the Irish Lenin. Perhaps he was, but the Labour Party was certainly not an Irish version of the Bolsheviks. It owed far too much to British social democracy and Irish constitutional nationalism to have developed a ready-made revolutionary ideology; nor did it have the highly focussed leadership required for such a project. Connolly took a deep interest in the European revolutionary tradition but it had few other enthusiasts among his contemporaries. Irish socialists were also deeply influenced by religious beliefs and practices, on both sides of the confessional divide, to a degree that marked them out from the international revolutionary left.

The religious factor reinforced the deep division within the labour movement, north and south, on the constitutional issue. The Labour Party was very much an extension of local Trades Council networks that varied enormously in their politics. Nominations for Labour candidates were determined by these bodies, thereby ensuring the national organisation would be at least as parochial in its concerns as other parties. Nor should we confuse the ITGWU, important as it was, with the broader labour movement.

Much work still needs to be done at local level on the nature of the Irish Labour Party and Trade Union Congress between 1912 and 1923, but it seems clear that it was totally unprepared to assume political leadership at national level.[42] Dublin was the most politically radical citadel of labour in the South before the First World War. It was certainly an incubator for new ideas. But militant nationalism continued to gather momentum during the War, having a dampening effect on the radical feminist and labour movements which had emerged in the period culminating in the Lockout. The new, more militant breed of nationalist might be prepared to challenge the political orthodoxy of constitutional nationalism when it came to physical force, but not where the status of women or rights of the lower orders were concerned.

Whether women or workers would have fared better if they had been more united we will never know but both proved incapable of responding effectively to the resurgent power of militant nationalism through Sinn Féin and the Irish Volunteers. After 1916 these organisations managed to accommodate legions of 'yesterday's men', from publicans to priests in their ranks, as well as a younger breed of predominantly male, lower middle-class revolutionary. Cumann na mBan largely subsumed the activism of earlier women's movements in a subordinate role to men in the War of Independence, and the ILP&TUC could not obtain a viable mandate to contest seats in the 1918 election from its own affiliates – even in Dublin.[43]

On paper the Irish Labour Party & Trade Union Congress remained strong in the capital, but it was primarily strong industrially, not politically. Even with the aura of Connolly's martyrdom to sustain it and years of propagandising, Dublin Labour only polled 12 per cent of first preference votes in the municipal elections of 1920, compared with a national average of 18 per cent and just over 20 per cent in Belfast. [44] Whether that higher vote elsewhere reflected greater class consciousness or greater acceptance of the new nationalist consensus (or unionist consensus in Belfast) we don't know. Dubliners were certainly politically radical at the time, but it was the radicalism of militant nationalism that attracted them. The alienation of radical female activists and trade unionists from the avaricious, patriarchal consensus of neo-Redmondism was redirected at British rule as the fount of all evil. It is one of history's ironies that Connolly's participation in the Easter Rising helped ensure the 1916 Proclamation provided radical nationalism with a ready-made programme for social and economic justice, as well as for national liberation from British rule. Nothing in past Labour Party manifestos, which had been tailored to local elections, could rival it. It was like comparing poetry with outdated shopping lists.

Politically active women such as Hanna Sheehy-Skeffington, Countess Markievicz and Kathleen Lynn now identified closely with militant nationalism. Similarly, many workers, especially craftsmen, were more likely to be members of the Irish Volunteers, Irish Republican Brotherhood and Sinn Féin than Labour. The most important long-term industrial relations initiative undertaken by the Dail Éireann government, the creation of the Irish Engineering, Shipbuilding and Foundry Workers Trade Union, was very much an IRB project. Ironically, it was in rural Ireland that the growth of the ITGWU, in large part through absorbing agricultural labourers' proto-unions, saw greater class consciousness emerge, but it usually remained workplace bound.[45]

A residual legacy

In the context of the revolutionary decade, the legacy of the Lockout was residual. Nevertheless, it was the nearest thing we ever had in this country to a debate on the type of society we wanted in the twentieth century. The values that triumphed then have shed their religious foliage and blossomed into an unabashed brand of possessive individualism not very different from that of contemporary Britain – in the process neo-Redmondism has given way to neo-liberalism.

Social solidarity values were not totally eliminated. The 1916 Proclamation and the Democratic Programme of the First Dail were uniquely progressive documents informed by the experience of the Lockout, and ones to which socialists had a crucial input. The emphasis on women's rights and public ownership of natural resources is particularly noticeable. (Sean O'Casey can be considered one of its authors, with elements of the Irish Citizen Army's Constitution that he wrote, incorporated in the text.) Certainly, they could not have been written anywhere on this island except Dublin; but they were never subjected to public debate. The Treaty debate was consumed by the issue of the Oath and, to a lesser extent, partition.

The basic issues at stake in the Lockout, those of collective bargaining, the right to union representation, freedom of expression and assembly in the workplace remain unresolved. They are important because, apart from taxation, collective bargaining is the most effective means of redistributing wealth within a capitalist economy. The more the right to collective bargaining is restricted, the more imperfect its influence and the greater the risks of social inequality and political instability. By 1924 the Irish political superstructure may have changed dramatically but Dublin's slums remained intact. The only major housing project in the city was at Killester, where the British War Office was building homes for ex-servicemen. As we have seen, we had more children incarcerated in institutions than the United Kingdom we had just left.

This is not to deny that some form of self-government for the southern part of Ireland was well-nigh inevitable by 1912 and that southern labour leaders shared the nationalist consensus that Home Rule or some form of greater independence from Britain was an innately 'good thing'. This included, of course, many Irish women who chose to disregard the warnings by veteran Unionist suffrage campaigner Anna Haslam that their interests would be better served by remaining part of a liberal, urban democracy, than being left to the mercies of a predominantly church-dominated, peasant society.

It is hard to disagree with the verdict of that great revisionist, Karl Kautsky, in his 1922 commentary on the Irish Revolution when he concluded that:

> The deciding battles for Ireland's independence in recent years were won mainly because of the energy and devotion of her proletariat. And in spite of this, this proletariat is threatened by the independent state which it won, not with an improvement, but with a further decline of its position ... In an oppressed country the class contradictions are only too easily hidden and obscured by national contradictions.[46]

The Lockout was a foretaste of what the future held in store for this proletariat, for the working poor, for the marginalised generally and for emigrants, who were the most marginalised of all. If we cannot ask the question over a century later whether 1916 and all that followed was worth it, when can we ask it? For all these groups the Lockout, the Cinderella of Centenaries, is their 1916.

Endnotes

1 *Irish Independent*, 1 Sept. 1913. Records of the arrests made during the opening weeks of the Lockout are now available on line in the *DMP Prisoners Books*, Volume 3, https://digital.ucd.ie/view/ucdlib:43945. For a detailed analysis see Padraig Yeates, *Rioters, Looters, Lady Patrols & Mutineers* (Dublin: Dublin City Council, 2017), pp. 7–16.

2 *Sunday Independent*, 31 Aug. 1913; *Daily Mirror*, 1 Sept. 1913; *Daily Herald*, 1 Sept. 1913.

3 Conor McNamara, 'A Tenants' League or a Shopkeepers' League: Urban Protest and the Town Tenants' Association in the West of Ireland, 1909–1918', *Studia Hibernica*, 36 (2009–10), pp. 135–60.

4 For Murphy's evidence to Treasury Committee see, *Irish Times*, 8 Mar. 1913.

5 *Irish Times*, 8 Mar. 1913; *Irish Independent*, 8 Mar. 1913.

6 David Durnin, 'Medicine in the City: the impact of the National Insurance Act on health care and the medical profession in Dublin', in Francis Devine (ed.), *A Capital in Conflict: Dublin City and the 1913 Lockout* (Dublin: Four Courts Press, 2013), pp. 83–104.

7 *Reports on Strikes and Lockouts and on Conciliation and Arbitration Boards in the United Kingdom in 1913 With Comparative Statistics, Parliamentary Papers*, Vol. 36 (1914) [Cd., 7658].

8   Dublin Trades Council Minutes, Oct. 1913 to Mar. 1914; Minutes of the Executive Committee of the Drapers Association, 3 Sept. 1913; 7 Jan. 1914; Saint Vincent de Paul, *Bulletin*, May 1914.

9   Bill Moran, '1913, Jim Larkin and the British Labour Movement', *Saothar*, 4 (1978), pp. 35–49; *Irish Times*, 15–18 Nov. 1913; Shipping Federation Reports, Nov. 1913 (University of Warwick, TSF, MS 367); TUC Reports, 1911–15 (University of Warwick, TUC Papers, MS 292); C. Desmond Greaves, *The Irish Transport and General Workers' Union: The Formative Years, 1909–1923* (Dublin: Gill and Macmillan, 1982), pp. 103–4.

10 Pádraig Yeates, *Lockout: Dublin 1913* (Dublin: Gill & Macmillan, 2000), p. 151.

11 Greaves, *The Irish Transport and General Workers' Union*, pp. 60–6; Conor McCabe, 'The Context and Course of the Irish Railway Dispute of 1911', *Saothar*, 20 (2005), pp. 21–31.

12 *Reports on Strikes and Lockouts and on Conciliation and Arbitration …* vol. 36 (1914) [Cd., 7658].

13 Yeates, *Lockout*, pp. 12–6.

14 'Financial contributions by British unions and loss of earning', Dublin Food Fund Report, TUC Annual Reports 1914–15, Irish Labour History Society Archive; Minutes of the Parliamentary Committee of the TUC, 1912–15 (University of Warwick, TUC Papers, MS 292).

15 Tom Kettle, 'Effects on business', *Freeman's Journal*, Sept. 1913; TUC Annual Reports, 1914–15; Minutes of the Parliamentary Committee of the TUC, 1912–15 (University of Warwick, TUC Papers, MS 292); Dublin Port and Docks Board Annual Reports, Press Clippings Book, 1913–1915, Dublin Port Company Archives.

16 *Irish Times*, 4 Feb. 1914.

17 'Subsidies to employers', Shipping Federation Reports for 1913 (University of Warwick, TSF Papers, MS 367); Guinness Archive (GDB/COOP/24).

18 John Newsinger, *Rebel City: Larkin, Connolly and the Dublin Labour Movement* (London: Merlin Press, 2004), p. 90.

19 Dublin Port Company Archive for Port and Docks financial statement, *Irish Times*, 7 Feb. 1914; Dublin Chamber of Commerce Reports, 1913, 1914. See, Newsinger, *Rebel City*, for an academic exposition of the TUC 'betrayal' argument.

20 Dr William Walsh, 'The Dublin Children's Distress Fund, Address to Society of St Vincent de Paul, 27 Oct., 1913' (Walsh Laity Papers, Dublin Diocesan Archive). For countervailing viewpoint, see, Thomas J. Morrissey, 'Archbishop Walsh and the 1913 Lockout', *Studies: An Irish quarterly review*, 102: 407 (2013), pp. 283–95.

21 The Archbishop's Statement, The Dublin Children's Distress Fund, Society of St Vincent de Paul (Walsh Laity Files, Dublin Archdiocesan Archive).

22 Mary Raftery, Eoin O'Sullivan, *Suffer the Little Children: The Inside Story of Ireland's Industrial Schools* (Dublin: New Island Press, 2001), p. 69.

23 *Irish Times*, 29 Nov. 1913.

24 Cited in Frank Callanan, *T.M. Healy* (Cork, 1996), p. 489.

25   *Forward*, 9 Feb. 1914.

26   The IWWU did not become an independent union until Louie Bennett became General Secretary. Significantly when the IWWU left Liberty Hall in 1918 Rosie Hackett remained with the ITGWU.

27   *Irish Times*, 19 Aug. 2013.

28   *Jacob's Wages Books*, National Archives, Ireland.

29   BMH WS 546 (Rose Hackett), p. 1.

30   See, Patricia McCaffrey, 'Jacob's Women Workers During the 1913 Lock-Out', *Saothar*, 16 (1991), pp. 118–29, for figures of number of Jacob's workers involved.

31   Yeates, *Lockout: Dublin 1913*, pp. 399–400.

32   Namebook, uncatalogued material, Dublin Port Company Archives, Damastown.

33   *Irish Times*, 21–4 Oct. 1913; *Irish Independent*, 21–4 Oct. 1913.

34   Pádraig Yeates, '"An injury to one is the concern of all": Dublin Port, the Namebook, the 1913 Lockout and the sympathetic strike', *Saothar*, 38 (2013), pp. 73–72.

35   Patrick Maume, 'William Field (1843–1935)', *Dictionary of Irish Biography*.

36   'Namebook', Dublin Port Company Archives.

37   William Partridge is quoted as the source of the 2,700 figure, David Fitzpatrick, 'Strikes in Ireland, 1914–1921', *Saothar*, 6 (1980), pp. 26–39; P.T. Daly, for the figure of 5,000, cited in the Irish Trade Union Congress Executive Report for 1917, p. 29.   http://centenaries-ituc.nationalarchives.ie/wp-content/uploads/2014/10/23rd-annual-report-1917.pdf

38   For the best description of the arbitration system, see, Humbert Wolfe, *Labour Supply and Regulation* (Oxford: Oxford University Press, 1923).

39   Report of Captain Thomas Purcell, Dublin Fire Brigade, 1916. (Dublin Corporation Reports).

40   Michael T. Foy, M and Brian Barton, *The Easter Rising* (Stroud; Sutton, 1999), pp. 210–11.

41   Membership roll, 1915 (ITGWU Papers, NLI, MS 3,097).

42   Seamus Cody, John O'Dowd and Peter Rigney, *The Parliament of Labour: 100 Years of the Dublin Council of Trade Unions* (Dublin: Dublin Council of Trade Unions, 1986), pp. 111–21; Arthur Mitchell, *Labour in Irish Politics, 1890–1930: The Irish Labour Movement in an Age of Revolution* (Dublin: Irish University Press, 1974), pp. 92–3; Thomas J. Morrissey, *William O'Brien, 1881–1968: Socialist, Republican, Dáil Deputy, Editor and Trade Union Leader* (Dublin: Four Courts Press, 2007).

43   Sarah Benton, 'Women Disarmed: The Militarization of Politics in Ireland, 1913–23', *Feminist Review*, 50 (Summer, 1995), pp. 148–172 (My thanks to Dr Katherine O'Donnell UCD for providing this article).

44   Mitchell, *Labour in Irish Politics*, pp. 92–3, Morrissey, *William O'Brien*, pp. 154–5; Cody, O'Dowd, and Rigney, *The Parliament of Labour*, pp. 111–21; Neil O'Flanagan, *Dublin City in an Age of War and Revolution*, (Unpublished MA thesis, UCD, 1985); Conor McCabe, 'The Irish Labour Party and the 1920 Local Elections', *Saothar*, 35 (2010), pp. 7–21; Pádraig Yeates, *A City in Turmoil: Dublin, 1919–21* (Dublin: Gill & Macmillan, 2012), pp. 70–81.

45 Pádraig Yeates, 'Craftworkers during the Irish Revolution, 1919–21', *Saothar*, 33 (2008), pp. 37–54.

46 Karl Kautsky, *Ireland: translated by Angela Clifford and published by the British and Irish Communist Organisation* (Belfast, 1974).

CHAPTER TEN

The Legacy of the Lockout: Lessons From Oral History

Mary Muldowney

This chapter is dedicated to the memory of Sarah Lundberg and John Moran, members of the 1913 Alternative Visions Oral History Group who died in 2014.

The 1913 Lockout occupies an important place in the collective memory in particular districts of Dublin, as well as in the consciousness of the trade union movement. It was not just the members of the Irish Transport and General Workers Union and the unions who supported them who felt the impact of the Lockout. In families who have relatives who participated in the Lockout, oral history has been passed down through generations, providing sometimes surprising insights. Many families have been silent on the subject, often because of the trauma they suffered during the period and because they did not feel they could celebrate the role played by their relatives. It is also probable that family stories have simply been forgotten. The latter is one of the problematic elements of researching events that predominantly affected so-called 'ordinary people', mainly because accounts that survived did so because they fitted a particular agenda. The scarcity of written records about those experiences is one reason why oral history is so valuable in challenging 'the condescension of posterity', facilitating the restoration of neglected accounts to the historical record.[1]

1913 Alternative Visions Oral History Group (Alternative Visions)

This chapter will outline the work of the 1913 Alternative Visions Oral History Group who came together to collect memories of the Lockout.

'Post memory' describes the relationship of second and later generations to powerful experiences that preceded their births but that were nevertheless transmitted to them so deeply as to generate memories in their own right.[2] When she first defined post memory in the late 1970s, Marianne Hirsch was exploring stories of the Holocaust, as told by the children of survivors who had not themselves directly experienced the suffering they were describing. Hirsch wrote that the notion of 'post-memory' usefully describes other second-generation memories of collective or cultural traumatic events and experiences.[3] The post memories elicited in the oral history interviews collected by the Alternative Visions group are used to explore the influence of the Lockout 'legend' on families and communities who had connections with the original actors in the Lockout story. In many cases, the stories are told by the third generation of particular families and traumatic memories have been filtered through the life experiences of the tellers. Hirsch first defined 'post-memory' in terms of images, such as the photographs of a Holocaust survivor's father as interpreted by his son. There are few photographs of the participants in the 1913 Dublin Lockout other than those of the main protagonists and the anonymous crowds who were frequently the subject of newspaper coverage of the key events. There are the famous illustrations of the poverty that was such a stark feature of Dublin tenements, however, captured by photographer John Cooke for the Dublin Housing Inquiry in November 1913. That Inquiry was held to examine the circumstances of the collapse of the Church Street tenements on 2 September 1913 and the photographs provide a valuable pictorial record of the housing conditions in which many Dublin workers and their families lived. None of the subjects of these photographs were named and if they were recognized by their descendants, such information is rarely documented.[4]

In September 2012, twenty people gathered in the training rooms of the Technical Electrical and Engineering Union (TEEU) in Dublin. They were all either trade union, community or political activists and they wanted to learn how to collect oral histories related, in the first instance, to the 1913 Dublin Lockout, and in the longer term to their trade unions and local neighbourhoods. Those present followed a training programme for six weeks before seeking out potential participants and conducting interviews.[5] Half of the group went on to write about their interviews and this is the work that was later published as *100 years later. The legacy of the 1913 Lockout*.[6]

In oral history, trust is the key to interviewing, especially when exploring emotionally or politically sensitive issues. It takes time and patience on the part of the interviewer to build a working relationship that allows the interviewee to open up. One of the advantages possessed by the Alternative Visions interviewers was that they had the trust of their interviewees, either through prior acquaintance or even closer relationship, or because of their mutual membership of an altruistic organisation, like a community group or a trade union.[7]

Oral history and understanding trade union activism

The themes that emerged from the interviews are not just relevant to examination of the Lockout and its significance to Irish society but relate to how we research and write about labour and working-class history in general. One of the advantages of oral history is its capacity to shed light on undocumented experiences, and, in terms of the influence of the 1913 Lockout, to explore the relationship between class consciousness and community and trade union activism. The members of the Alternative Visions group were broadly familiar with the events of the Lockout and several of them had been influenced by stories they had heard from members of their own families. They were not setting out to unearth new facts about the Lockout but to examine its legacy and to consider to what extent that heritage contributed to the development of Irish trade unions and working-class consciousness.

The focus of several of the interviews was on individuals who had been involved in the movement for many years and whose activism was driven by their belief that trade unions could contribute to the creation of a better and more equal society. Jim Quinn is one such individual; at 83 years of age he is a lifelong trade union member and political activist in the Labour Party who still participates in the activities of the retired members of SIPTU.[8] He was interviewed by Michael Halpenny. Both of Jim's parents were union members and activists and knew many of the major figures of the period. Jim was born in Ringsend and grew up on the South Quays of the Liffey where the docks were the main source of employment and the memory of 1913 still existed. Jim's family lived and worked in the area for generations although his maternal grandmother came from Boolavogue in Wexford, where his ancestors had 'been out in '98'.[9] The people of the Docklands suffered during the Lockout but they remained committed to trade union membership. Jim's father was a butcher who was also an organiser for the Workers' Union of Ireland (WUI) and a personal friend of Jim Larkin. Jim grew up listening to his father and James Larkin discussing politics and union activities. Another influence was Barney Conway, on whom the Mulhall character in James Plunkett's *Strumpet City* is thought to be based.[10] In the interview he gave to Michael Halpenny, Jim said 'I wasn't in the union to get money out of it. I was in the union because it gave me a say. It [allowed] me to call a meeting … to go up and talk to the boss and tell them what I thought … I'm on that side and that's it.'[11]

Other interviewees shared that altruistic interpretation of what motivated an effective union activist, whether they were speaking about their own involvement or that of influential figures in the evolution of their political philosophies. Interviewed by Alex Klemm, political activist and retired trade union official Des Bonass, recalled that his family had a tradition of republican activity. He was also inspired by Matt Merrigan, who was secretary of the Amalgamated Transport and General Workers Union when Des joined in the 1950s:[12]

> Matt Merrigan was a great believer in education and trade union activities, whatever they would be and certainly he was a left wing trade union official and was way ahead of his time … and I got involved in that and through Matt Merrigan's discussion and talk and education wise – not putting it down your throat or anything but certainly educating you on 1913.[13]

Trade union official, historian and singer Fergus Whelan, who was interviewed by Nora Shovelin about the role played by song and story-telling in the labour movement, also remembered Matt Merrigan as a positive force. However, he credited his parents for passing on their political beliefs in a manner that helped him to develop his own ideas but within the strong collective tradition to which they belonged:

> I had decided even then that what I wanted to do when I joined the workforce was to be a trade union official. And my father wasn't without contacts in the movement … Micky Mullen said I was welcome to a job as a porter down in Liberty Hall but he said that he wouldn't give anybody a job as a trade union official who hadn't, I'm not saying this was his term but it was a term that another trade union leader, Matt Merrigan, used to say 'who hadn't felt the lash of the employer on his back'.[14] The advice to me was, the strong advice to me was to go out into the workplace, find out what it's like to be a worker, and then, in time, apply for a job in the trade union movement. And that's precisely

what I did. I worked as a bricklayer for 10 years … And all through that time, I was involved in trade union affairs.[15]

Seamus and Martin Fitzpatrick spent years as activists in IMPACT[16] and the National Union of Journalists respectively, and although they are both retired they are still involved with trade unions.[17] They told Mary Muldowney that they were strongly influenced by their father John, who was blacklisted by the Dublin Grand Canal Company after the Lockout but maintained his lifelong admiration for Larkin. John was more involved in republican activity than the labour movement after the Lockout ended. He became a member of the IRA and during the War of Independence served as an intelligence officer with the Dublin Brigade. Martin spoke of his father's deeply felt Catholicism, which did not clash with his belief in physical force republicanism.

> As far as he was concerned the only solution to any problems that we had was the restoration of a true republic … [he] had no compunction about going off and taking arms against people, even including their own friends. And I always thought that was a very difficult one to get your head around [laughs] but he never seemed to have any difficulty with it … He didn't challenge that particular paradox, which is a paradox of militant Irish republicanism. You can impose your view on people whether they like it or not.[18]

Both James Connolly and James Larkin were practising Catholics, as were many others who were involved in the Lockout who persisted in their activities despite the Church hierarchy's hostility to the ITGWU. After the publication of Pope Leo XIII's encyclical *Rerum Novarum* in 1891, Catholic theologians and priests believed they had a valid role in relation to strikes. *Rerum Novarum* taught that strikes were caused by 'evil principles' and should not be permitted.[19] The practice of preaching against striking by Catholic priests continued up to more recent times, and Bernard [Barney] O'Connor, a former dock worker and union organiser in Dublin, told Sarah Lundberg and Joe Mooney about the parish priest in East Wall's Catholic parish of St Joseph the Worker, chastising dockworkers for striking in the 1960s, leading to a walkout from Mass of strikers and their families.[20]

Although the influence of the Catholic Church was strong and the majority of the ITGWU members in 1913 were devout Catholics, in cases of conflict between their loyalty to their fellow workers and their obedience to their priests, the choice was to support their union. The ITGWU leaders were careful to distinguish between matters of faith and morality as being the territory of priests and the secular interests of the members, which were the responsibility of the union. Larkin used the pages of the *Irish Worker* to condemn the hypocrisy of priests who neglected their moral duty to care for the poor and abused the strikers for their refusal to give in to the Employers' Federation. He and Connolly were particularly angry when the children of strikers were refused benefit from Archbishop Walsh's relief scheme.[21]

Memories of family trauma

In Des Dalton's interview with Úna Ó Callanáin, granddaughter of Michael Mallin, she talked about her grandfather's early life and the influences that led him to play a central role in the trade union movement.[22] She attributed at least some part of his strong sense of social justice to his religious beliefs and his commitment to the Catholic Church. Michael Mallin's last letter to his wife included the instruction that at least one of his children should be dedicated to the priesthood.[23] Una was told about her grandfather's life and death by her father Seamus, Mallin's eldest son, whose early life was framed by the loss of his father and by his own political involvement. For a long time, Seamus was silent about his father and this is reflective of others in that second generation to which Úna belonged who found their parents were reluctant or even unwilling to talk about the traumatic events that indelibly marked their lives.

Alan MacSimóin interviewed Moira Crawford, a relation of James Nolan, who was killed by a member of the Dublin Metropolitan police.[24] She said that Nolan's children never recovered from the trauma of their father's loss and the impact it had on his family. Nolan was severely injured in a police attack on people walking from Liberty Hall along Eden Quay on Saturday, 30 August 1913. Several sworn statements from eye-witnesses noted that at least some of the group of policemen were drunk but no action was taken against the men who attacked James Nolan.[25] He had two sons and a daughter and James Larkin seems to have tried to help the family by arranging for the ITGWU to give Mrs Nolan the lease of a shop. Moira Crawford's great grandmother, who only died when Moira was 16 years old, was the sister of James Nolan's wife. Mrs Nolan died three years after her husband and is buried with him in Glasnevin Cemetery:

When she died her two sons were put into Artane School and my great grandmother took in her niece, Christina … Now the story was that Artane School was very severe and George wet the bed and he got terrible hassle for it whereas Christy was in the Artane Boys Band so he kind of got out a little bit.[26] Now my grandmother and my great grandmother said that they used to go for a walk up Malahide Road to see the children on a Sunday and you couldn't speak to them and you couldn't visit them but she used to slip them – you know the threepenny bars of chocolate?[27]

George Nolan left Ireland when he was released from Artane and joined the British Army. His side of the family blamed Larkin for what happened to their relative while Christy and Christina's descendants revered him. It seems that the greater hardship that George experienced as a result of his father following Larkin's leadership (as he saw it) created a bitterness that has lasted through generations. Other stories referred to the admiration and love that Larkin's name still elicits in areas of Dublin that experienced significant hardship because of the Lockout with blame assigned to the employers.

In her interview with the great-grandson of someone who is generally thought of as a hate-figure for his role in the 1913 Lockout, Ida Milne found that Gerry Murphy thought his ancestor, William Martin Murphy should be remembered for creating jobs in Ireland.[28] He spoke in his interview about his membership of the union representing the sales and marketing staff in the *Irish Independent* where he worked for years. In an RTÉ television documentary, he also questioned the portrayal of his great-grandfather as the chief villain of the Lockout.[29] This suggests that his primary loyalty is to his family and explains his reluctance to acknowledge his ancestor's ruthlessness in his dealings with the ITGWU and its members and their families:

It's given me a pride in the business he formed, the employment he gave, and the way he ran his businesses … William Martin Murphy invested in Irish business. He was a patriot. After the *Risen People*, the play, there was a review in a paper, and she [the critic] called him [the William Martin Murphy] character 'an old knacker'.[30] William Martin Murphy committed the greatest crime any Irish person could commit. You were Irish, Catholic and successful. You were not prepared to kowtow to foreigners investing in this country or taking their money away from this country. That was my thought anyway. He was a patriot, a true patriot, a practical patriot.[31]

In the same chapter, Ida Milne writes that Stella Larkin McConnon remembers her grandfather as an amiable man, although other people who knew Larkin personally remember his frequent irascibility. She was only 12 years old when he died but she remembers going with him to canvass when he was standing for election and the outpouring of love and respect that he got from Dubliners. Her testimony also describes some of the hardship that Larkin's family endured in the course of the Lockout that was similar to the suffering experienced by locked-out workers, including being evicted from their home after Larkin instigated a rent strike in protest at the eviction of people for being unable to pay their rent from strike pay.

Women and the Lockout

John Gibbons interviewed political activist and former Lord Mayor of Wexford David Hynes about the Wexford Lockout in 1911. The chapter includes a reference to a shop lease being given by the ITGWU to the widow of a worker killed by police.[32] In September 1911 Michael Leary was an innocent bystander coming out of a shop in Wexford at the same time as locked-out foundry workers were being baton charged by members of the Royal Irish Constabulary (RIC). He died of septic meningitis as a result of his injuries several days afterwards and his funeral was described 'as the largest seen in the town for many years'.[33] The police had been brought in to Wexford to protect the blackleg labour imported to run the foundries that were at the centre of the Lockout. In that case, it was James Connolly who arranged for the shop to be assigned to Mrs Leary but the provision sheds an interesting light on how women were viewed. It is clear that the ITGWU officers felt a responsibility for the widows of men who were killed as a result of union activity, even if they were not directly involved. What is not clear is why they were offered a business to support themselves when a job or a pension might have been more beneficial. Unfortunately, we do not know how Mrs Leary fared with her shop but James Nolan's descendants acknowledged that his widow knew nothing about business and that her shop failed.

Contemporary accounts neglected the role played by women in unions and in supporting their families and communities through the hardship of the Lockout. Too often the perception persists that they were passive observers of men's activities on their behalf. At the very least, they played a role in inspiring their families and ensuring that the message of class solidarity was passed on. Several interviewees explained that their mothers had been key figures in instilling their awareness of trade unions and the role they have played in Irish society. Speaking to Alex Klemm, political and trade union activist Mick O'Reilly recalled that he first heard about the 1913 Lockout at an early age:

> My mother was involved in the Irish Women Workers' Union and she was a shop steward in a company called Bagot Huttons. Now my mother was not a political person but she would have had great admiration for Jim Larkin and that was kind of mentioned in the house.[34]

In 1913, many of Dublin's women workers were single women, contributing to a household budget. Others were heads of households where there was no male earner. Over 1,000 tenement households were headed by charwomen.[35] Most women earned half or less of the average industrial wage, which at that time was £1 per week for men. This was despite the fact that a Board of Trade Survey in 1912 found that Dublin had the highest cost of living in the United Kingdom outside London, where wages were higher.[36]

Jacob's Biscuit Factory was the single largest employer of women in Dublin with 2,085 female employees, although only a small percentage of them were union members when the Lockout commenced.[37] Jacob's tried to force these women to sign the pledge to renounce their union. The women stayed out for the duration of the Lockout despite a management ultimatum that they would lose their jobs if they did not return to work. One of the best known of these women is Rosie Hackett, who was a member of the Irish Women Workers' Union (IWWU) from its foundation in 1911. The IWWU was launched at a public meeting in September 1911 as a semi-autonomous branch of the ITGWU. Jim Larkin was the Union's first president and his sister Delia was the general secretary. One of the IWWU's first activities was a successful pay dispute in Jacob's.

Rosie's family did not talk about her activities in 1913, according to her cousin Phil Crowley, who was interviewed by Mary Muldowney.[38] Phil was only told about Rosie's involvement in the Irish Citizen Army (ICA) and the 1916 Rising:

> My father used to tell me that's Auntie Rosie and she was in the 1916 Rising and she was carrying guns. Now I don't know who it was for

she was carrying the guns and my Daddy used to say the guns were bigger than her, which I can now appreciate.[39] And he always told me that she'd have a State funeral … My mother went and I was asking her about it, was it a State funeral as we know it? And she said 'well no, [but] she had the Tricolour over her coffin'.[40]

When Phil was a child she was fascinated by Rosie Hackett's tiny stature. She also remembered that Rosie was very religious:

There used to be forty hours' adoration of the Sacred Heart – now I'm going back to when I was a child, and it was literally forty hours' adoration and it would be in different churches and she used to go to every one of them. No matter where they were in Dublin she would go to the forty hours' adoration.[41]

Other accounts of Rosie Hackett are consistent about her heartfelt Catholicism, which did not prevent her from taking part in activities that were frowned on by the Catholic Church. She remained single throughout her life, which may have been one of the reasons she was able to spend sixty years in service to the trade union movement, for which she was awarded a gold medal. In 1913 and for many decades later, Irish women were defined by their marital status and there was little provision for childcare outside the home so that it was difficult for mothers to continue the activism of their younger years. In her review of the Bureau of Military History Witness Statements[42] for memories of the 1913 Lockout, Alex Klemm found that the women who gave statements tended to stress their marital status as did the men who referred to them.[43]

The impact of the Lockout on community relationships

Aileen Morrissey told Mary Muldowney that her family have been active trade unionists since the 1913 Lockout, when her grandfather was jailed for attacking a man who was strike breaking at Jacob's Biscuit Factory.[44] Her grandparents lived in the Bride Street tenements in Dublin and they worked in Jacob's, as did most of their neighbours. Living in such close quarters meant that it was difficult to be discreet if a resident was tempted back to work:

Everybody knew what you were doing. Everybody knew if you had a bit more on the table and if you did, how and what happened. Nobody could keep that kind of thing secret, or private … If you were willing to have your children do without food and the person next door to you, their children were getting food, it's horrible, very difficult.[45]

Aileen has been a union activist and a full-time trade union official for years and she is very conscious that going on strike is not an easy option:

There's never a right time to strike. There's always going to be the economic difficulties people are going to encounter when they do take that final action, the only resort left to them is to withdraw their labour and the consequence of that for them and you realise that it could be brother against brother, or sister against sister or father against son and the fact they were living in tenements and all living in close proximity to each other, it must have been horrendous.[46]

The perceived diminution of class solidarity in the hundred years since the Lockout was referred to frequently in interviews. The levels of support given by families to striking members, by working-class communities, particularly in the tenements, to neighbours who were locked out and by other unions to the ITGWU indicate a collective consciousness of shared interests that many of the interviewees suggested no longer exists. John 'Miley' Walsh told Sarah Lundberg and Joe Mooney that he went to work as a docker in the East Wall area when he was 17 years old and immediately joined the union.[47] The tradition of union membership was passed on to him from his father and uncles:

That brings me to thinking now, that if the unions begin to see a little weakness in themselves or in their workforce, then the workforce has been brought up wrong. It worked well for me, because I was in a docker's family, and it was like our religion. Everyone would listen to what the Da would say; you didn't dare criticise him or argue with him until you knew exactly what you were talking about … A little bit of that needs to happen today because over the last number of years, the last couple of years, the only people that I see that have got anything from really bad redundancy situations are those that stuck together …

The strength of the union is in the men. If they stand together, no employer can beat them. And it was like that for us.

Miley remembered acting as a mentor for younger dockers when he got older and stressing the need for solidarity in the workforce. The issue of strike-breaking was considered at length by Sarah and Joe in their exploration of how the Lockout is remembered in the close-knit East Wall community in which dockers and related workers were mainly loyal to their unions, at both great personal cost and communal loss. The houses on Merchants Road in East Wall were built by the Merchants Warehousing Company as housing for their employees, adjacent to their East Wall premises. In December of 1913 over sixty workers' families were evicted, and their homes were handed over to strike-breakers.

One of the questions that was asked of most of the interviewees concerned the extent to which the unity that featured so strongly during the Lockout still exists. The answers varied but there was an underlying theme which suggested that union members have become 'softer' and would be less willing to make sacrifices and to act collectively. There was a general perception that a leader of Larkin's calibre would make a positive difference to the confidence of union members and their capacity to take action to protect their own interests and those of other workers. Mick O'Reilly said that was not the only point of remembering the 1913 Lockout:

> I think it's not so much the events that we do, it's what we stir in people to go and read about and study and learn what Larkin was about, what he stood for – I don't mean just what Larkin was about, what's important about Larkin is what he was able to stir in the ordinary people. Because it was the ordinary people in this city that stood up in 1913 – he wasn't there on his own, there were thousands of people with him.[48]

In terms of class solidarity, Des Bonass stressed the importance of the massive support shown by members of British unions, whose generosity in sending food and funds helped to sustain many families in Dublin. He believed Irish workers repaid that debt during the Miners' strike in Britain in 1984 and made a conscious connection between donating funds then and reciprocity for the support in 1913:

> It would be very difficult to put your finger on the exact amount of money, but we raised hundreds of thousands of pounds: there's no

doubt about that. Scargill has said, and I think he's right, that Ireland's contribution per capita, per trade unionist, would have been bigger than any other donations they got throughout the world[49] ... Not alone were there collections, but there was linkage towards the trade union movement. You were doing something that identified the workers here in Dublin with the NUM dispute that was taking place.[50]

Eimear Ging interviewed members of the IMPACT Dublin Hospitals Branch Executive who were involved in the ballot for the Haddington Road negotiations in 2013. The Haddington Road Agreement was an agreement made between the Irish Government and various public service unions, guaranteeing no further pay cuts or compulsory redundancies in the public service in return for no industrial action and co-operation with wide ranging reforms intended to decrease employee numbers, increase efficiency and reduce costs. It was negotiated after an earlier agreement Croke Park 2 was rejected by union members. Eimear wondered what, if anything the anniversary meant 'for those who might be considered the natural heirs of that legacy, the workers who make up the membership of modern day trade unions'.[51] Eimear found that most of her interviewees were not clear about the details of the 1913 Lockout but they shared a belief that it is a source of inspiration for present-day trade union activists, if not necessarily directly transmitted. Tony Martin who was Branch Chairman when he was interviewed, outlined how he got most of his information – an experience likely to be shared by many Irish people over a certain age:

Well, I think, probably for most people of my generation ... unless you had that [trade union] culture in your family or you were working in an organisation which was unionised, which I didn't until about 1997 ... most people would have got it from *Strumpet City*.[52] Most people my age would have watched *Strumpet City* ... it was iconic ... But that would have probably been my first, and in fact thinking back, there wasn't really exposure to it during the school curriculum or any books or history books. I could be wrong; I just have no memory of it.[53]

There was very little examination of the 1913 Lockout for the first fifty years after it took place. In 1963, the executive of the Workers' Union of Ireland (WUI) decided that the story of the Lockout had been neglected. The WUI was the union founded by Jim Larkin in 1924 after he failed in his attempt to oust members of the Executive of the ITGWU. The story of the Lockout had in fact been distorted to the extent of excluding Larkin's importance but also in positioning the Lockout as part of the narrative of the independence struggle rather than the labour movement. As John Cunningham has outlined, the suggestion that the Lockout was in some way a precursor to the national struggle was introduced quite soon after 1913.[54] Cunningham traced the evolution of that link to the animosity between Larkin and O'Brien, who became more prominent in the ITGWU after Connolly's death in 1916.[55] During the twenty-first anniversary commemoration in 1934, O'Brien wrote a pamphlet entitled *Nineteen Thirteen – Its Significance*, in which he did not mention Larkin at all.[56] In 1963 the WUI decided to publish a book about the events of 1913 'so that the present and future generations of trade unionists might learn and understand something of the heroic struggles of those who built our Irish trade union movement'.[57] The first part of the book reproduces a chapter from W.P. Ryan's book on the Irish labour movement and the second part contains articles, speeches and verse relating to the events of 1913 and 1914.[58]

Conclusion

How does the testimony in the interviews collected by the Alternative Visions group contribute to a broader understanding of working-class consciousness, in 1913/14 and later? It indicates the extent to which so-called 'ordinary' members of the working class have been sidelined in the writing of Irish history. Taking the historiography of the 1913 Dublin Lockout as an example, it was not until 2000 that Padraig Yeates's comprehensive book was published.[59] The centenary year witnessed the publication of a number of volumes on the Lockout, ending the previous neglect, including *Locked Out: A Century of Irish Working-Class Life*.[60] Many of the essays in *A Capital in Conflict: Dublin City and the 1913 Lockout* also focus on the impact of the Lockout on ordinary citizens.[61] Editor Francis Devine questions whether a social audit in 2013 would show that workers 'are in credit' after a century of trade union efforts to achieve a more equal society.[62]

The struggle in 1913 was essentially about the right of all workers to belong to the trade union of their choice and for employers to be obliged to recognise and negotiate with that union. It is not a battle that had been won when the strikers were forced to return to work in the spring of 1914 but neither was it a war that was lost. The employers, even with the full force of the State at their beck and call, abjectly failed to destroy the trade union movement, although full recognition rights have not been secured 100 years later. The many improvements in workers' employment rights that were achieved during the 100 years since the Lockout owe much to the agency of 'ordinary' trade union members. Oral history can give voice to those frequently unsung heroes and heroines and can thereby play a valuable part in restoring the role of the working class to its rightful place in the contemporary historical record.

Contributors

Des Dalton is a long-standing political and trade union activist and a leading member of Republican Sinn Féin. He is a regular contributor to independent media. He secured a postgraduate degree in History from Trinity College Dublin subsequent to his involvement in the 1913 Alternative Visions Oral History group.

John Gibbons is a retired member of the TEEU and a keen local historian. He is currently studying for an undergraduate degree in history at University College Dublin as well as working on a number of research projects.

Eimear Ging is an activist in IMPACT trade union working in the Dublin Hospitals Branch. She holds the HETAC Certificate in Trade Union Studies and postgraduate degrees in both History and Heritage Management.

Michael Halpenny has retired as a SIPTU official but continues to be active politically. He was closely involved in organising many of the commemorative events for the centenary of the 1913 Lockout. Michael writes regularly for SIPTU's *Liberty* newspaper.

Alex Klemm works in communications for UNITE the Union. She was one of the organisers of the re-enactment events organised for the centenary celebrations, including the baton charge on 31 August 1913 and the arrival of the SS *Hare* food ship.

Sarah Lundberg was a historian, poet and independent publisher who died in 2014. With Joe Mooney she worked with the East Wall local history group, collecting oral histories of the area. She also taught creative writing to secondary school students.

Alan MacSimóin is a political activist and was a shop steward in SIPTU for many years until he was made redundant. Subsequently he has worked as a tour guide and leads regular historical walking tours. He writes regularly in independent media and he is the director of the Irish Anarchist History online archive.

Ida Milne is a social historian, with a particular interest in the impact of epidemic disease on Irish society. She has also published on the history of the *Irish Independent* newspaper, where she worked for twenty years.

Joe Mooney is a community activist in the East Wall area of Dublin, which was central to the 1913 Lockout. He has a long history of campaigning on behalf of the people in his area and is an active member of the East Wall History Group.

John Moran was a photographer who died in 2014. His work is not featured in this chapter but it was an important part of the 1913 Alternative Visions project. John created a significant photographic record of community and trade union events, particularly in Dublin city.

Mary Muldowney is an independent historian who works with oral history to explore labour and working-class history, with a particular interest in women's involvement. She is also an adult education consultant working with community groups and trade unions.

Nora Shovelin is a retired secondary school teacher and member of the ASTI who has a particular involvement in the history of Irish music and how song has been used to disseminate political ideas. She worked as a presenter and researcher in the Irish language community radio station Raidió na Life.

Endnotes

1   This is the phrase coined by E.P. Thompson in his magisterial *The Making of the English Working Class* (London: Victor Gollancz Ltd, 1963) to describe his restoration of the lives of ordinary working people to the written history of eighteenth and nineteenth-century England.

2   Marianne Hirsch, 'The Generation of Post Memory', *Poetics Today*, 29:1 (spring 2008), http://www.columbia.edu/~mh2349/papers/generation.pdf downloaded 15.3.2013.

3   Marianne Hirsch, *Family Frames: Photography, Narrative and Post Memory* (Cambridge: Cambridge University Press, 1997), p. 22.

4   The full collection of photographs is reproduced in Christiaan Corlett, *Darkest Dublin: The Story of the Church Street Disaster and a Pictorial Account of the Slums of Dublin in 1913* (Dublin: Wordwell Press, 2008).

5   The programme was designed and delivered by Mary Muldowney and Ida Milne and was based on best practice in oral history interviewing, as advocated by the Oral History Network of Ireland (www.oralhistorynetworkireland.ie/), the Oral History Society (www.ohs.org.uk/⊠) and the Oral History Association (www.oralhistory.org/). It was generously sponsored by the Technical Engineering and Electrical Union (TEEU).

6   Mary Muldowney (ed.) with Ida Milne, *100 Years Later: The Legacy of the 1913 Lockout* (Dublin: Seven Towers, 2013).

7   There are brief biographical notes about the interviewers in an appendix to this chapter.

8   Michael Halpenny, 'Jim Quinn: "Decline to Report"', *100 Years Later*, pp. 55–64.

9   Jim's family connections were named Murphy. Father John Murphy of Boolavogue is credited in the ballad of the same name with being one of the leaders of the 1798 rebellion in Wexford. The ballad was written for the centenary in 1898 by which time the historiography of the rebellion had shifted to promote the role of Catholic clerics in the leadership.

10   James Plunkett (Kelly) wrote *Strumpet City*, a novel about the lead up to and the events of the Dublin Lockout in 1913/14. He grew up in Dublin's inner city. His father was an ITGWU member and Plunkett himself worked for Larkin in the WUI between 1946 and 1947. *Strumpet City* was his greatest success but he also wrote plays and short stories. James Plunkett, *Strumpet City* (Dublin: Hutchinson, 1969).

11   Halpenny, 'Jim Quinn: "Decline to Report"', p. 64.

12   Matt Merrigan (1922–2000) was Regional Secretary of the Amalgamated Transport and General Workers Union (ATGWU) in the Republic of Ireland. He was a member of the Labour Party from the 1950s until his expulsion in 1977 for his opposition to the party's coalition policies. He had stood unsuccessfully for election as a Labour candidate on several occasions. In 1977, Merrigan and Dr Noel Browne went on to found the Socialist Labour Party with other left-wing former members of the Labour Party but it was dissolved in 1982 after failing to make the impact its founders had hoped to achieve.

13   Alex Klemm and Mary Muldowney, 'A Spirit of Defiance, Commemorating Larkinism and the Trade Union Movement' in *100 Years Later*, p. 171.

14   Michael (Mickey) Mullen (1919–1982) was General Secretary of the Irish Transport and General Workers Union (ITGWU) from 1969 to 1981. He had also been a Labour alderman on Dublin Corporation and a Labour T.D. for Dublin North West. During his lifetime he was known as a 'fighter for the underprivileged' and in 1977 he arranged for his Dáil pension to be divided between the Irish Council for

Civil Liberties and organisations assisting handicapped children. Francis Devine, *Organising History, A Centenary of SIPTU* (Dublin: SIPTU, 2009), pp. 967–8.

15   Nora Shovelin, 'Celebrating 1913: Mobilisation and Reconstruction of Tradition in Song', *100 Years Later*, pp. 155–68.

16   IMPACT (Irish Municipal, Public and Civil Trade Union) is Ireland's largest public sector union. Members also include workers in the community and voluntary sector and in commercial sectors such as aviation and telecommunications. In 1991, the Local Government and Public Services Union merged with the Union of Professional and Technical Civil Servants to form IMPACT. The new union was also joined that year by the members of the Irish Municipal Employees Trade Union.

17   Mary Muldowney, 'Following in the Footsteps of a "Larkin Man"' in *100 Years Later*, pp. 87–99.

18   Ibid., p. 90.

19   *Rerum Novarum, Encyclical of Pope Leo XVIII on Capital and Labour*, 1891 (Points 20 and 38).

20   Unrecorded interview with Barney O'Connor (used with permission).

21   John Newsinger, *Rebel City: Larkin, Connolly and the Dublin Labour Movement* (London: Merlin Press, 2003), p. 74.

22   Des Dalton, 'A Disciplined Soldier: Michael Mallin', *100 Years Later*, pp. 65–76.

23   Michael Mallin's last letter to his wife is quoted in, B. Hughes, *16 Lives, Michael Mallin* (Dublin: The O'Brien Press, 2012), pp. 230–3.

24   Alan MacSimóin, 'James Nolan: a Lockout Martyr', *100 Years Later*, pp. 48–54.

25   Donal Nevin (ed.), *1913 Jim Larkin and the Dublin Lock-Out* (Dublin: Workers Union of Ireland, 1964), pp. 31–2.

26   St Joseph's Industrial School was state funded and run by the Christian Brothers in Artane, Dublin from 1870 to 1969. The Commission to Inquire into Child Abuse investigated allegations of abuse at Artane and found that sexual abuse of children by members of the Christian Brothers was 'a chronic problem'. It also found that the school 'used frequent and severe corporal punishment', which was 'systemic and pervasive', and that even when a child behaved it was still possible for him to be beaten. Clothing was poor quality, institutional and patched, despite there being a cash surplus in school accounts. Final Report of the Commission to Inquire into Child Abuse, 20 May 2009, p. 115.

27   MacSimóin, 'James Nolan: A Lockout Martyr', p. 52.

28   Ida Milne, 'Living with 1913: Descendants of the Leaders Reflect' in *100 Years Later*, pp. 77–86.

29   *My Lockout*, directed by Brian Hayes and produced by Rhenda Sheedy, was shown on RTÉ1 on 16 Dec. 2013. It examined the Lockout from the perspective of the families of protagonists on both sides of the dispute.

30   *The Risen People* was written by James Plunkett and was first produced in the 1950s as a radio play although it has had several revivals as a stage play in the intervening years. The story is based on the events of the 1913 Lockout and many of the characters were further developed in *Strumpet City*.

31   Milne, 'Living with 1913: Descendants of the Leaders Reflect', p. 80.

32   John Gibbons, 'Freedom's Pioneers: The Wexford Lockout of 1911–1912', *100 Years Later*, pp. 38–47.

33   Michael Enright, *Men of Iron: Wexford Foundry Disputes, 1890 & 1911* (Wexford, 1987), p. 24.

34   Klemm, Muldowney, 'A Spirit of Defiance', pp. 169–79.

35   *Census of Ireland 1911 General Report* (London, 1913), p. 112.

36   Theresa Moriarty, '"Who will look after the Kiddies?" Household and Collective Action during the Dublin Lockout, 1913' in Jan Kok (ed.), *Rebellious Families: Household Strategies and Collective Action in the Nineteenth and Twentieth Centuries* (New York: Berghahn Press, 2002), p. 112.

37   Patricia McCaffrey, 'Jacob's Women Workers during the 1913 Lock-Out', *Saothar*, 16 (1991), pp. 118–29.

38   Mary Muldowney, 'Looking for their rights, Women and the influence of the Lockout', *100 Years Later*, pp. 141–54.

39   Rosie was in Michael Mallin's ICA garrison in St Stephen's Green during the 1916 Rising.

40   Muldowney, 'Looking for their Rights, Women and the Influence of the Lockout', p. 149.

41   The forty hours' devotion is a Catholic practice in which the 'Blessed Sacrament', a host representing the Body of Christ, is exposed on the altar of a church as the focus for prayer.

42   Between 1947 and 1957, the Bureau of Military History gathered 1,773 statements from over 1,600 witnesses. The statements included eyewitness accounts of the Lockout, but also a snapshot of political and social attitudes – not just in 1913, but in the late 1940s and early 1950s when the statements were taken.

43   Alex Klemm, 'Witnessing the Lockout', *100 Years Later*, pp. 16–37.

44   Mary Muldowney, 'A bit of trouble – dealing with a scab. Aileen Morrissey's story about her grandfather, John Conalon' in *100 Years Later*, p. 123.

45   Ibid., p. 152.

46   Ibid., p. 151.

47   Sarah Lundberg and Joe Mooney, 'An injury to one (Part One)' in *100 Years Later*, p. 105.

48   Klemm, Muldowney, 'A Spirit of Defiance', p. 169.

49   Arthur Scargill was president of the National Union of Mineworkers from 1982 to 2002. He was the focus of much of Margaret Thatcher's hatred of trade unions.

50   Ibid., p. 175.

51   Eimear Ging, 'Pass it on? A glimpse of the perceived relevance and legacy of the 1913 Lockout one hundred years on for present day trade union activists' in *100 Years Later*, p. 180.

52   This was the TV drama made by RTÉ in 1980, based on James Plunkett's *Strumpet City*. The script was adapted from the novel by playwright Hugh Leonard.

53 Eimear Ging, 'Pass it on? A glimpse of the perceived relevance and legacy of the 1913 Lockout one hundred years on for present day trade union activists', p. 188.

54 John Cunningham, 'From *Disturbed Dublin* to *Strumpet City*: the 1913 "history wars", 1914–1980' in Francis Devine (ed.), *A Capital in Conflict: Dublin City and the 1913 Lockout* (Dublin: Four Courts Press, 2013), pp. 353–78.

55 William O'Brien (1881–1968) began his working life as a tailor but soon became involved in trade union and political activity and was a member of James Connolly's Irish Socialist Republican Party in the 1890s. He supported Larkin in founding the ITGWU and the Labour Party and helped in the planning of the 1916 Rising. He became Secretary of the ITGWU in 1918 and was a leading figure in the organisation until his retirement in 1946. When Larkin returned from the United States in 1923, O'Brien organised a change in the Union's rules to significantly curb the former's powers as general secretary.

56 Cunningham, 'The History Wars', p. 359.

57 Introduction to Donal Nevin (ed.), *1913, Jim Larkin and the Dublin Lockout* (Dublin, 1964), p. 5.

58 In 1913 W.P. Ryan was assistant editor of the radical newspaper the *Daily Herald* and he reported on the events of the Lockout. In 1919 he published *The Irish Labour Movement From the 'Twenties to Our Own Day* (Dublin: The Talbot Press, 1919) in which he traced the development of the labour movement through the previous 100 years.

59 Pádraig Yeates, *Lockout: Dublin 1913* (Dublin: Gill & Macmillan, 2000).

60 This is a collection of essays which traces how class conflict in Ireland was ignored throughout the twentieth century as the interests of the labour movement and the working class were submerged by the dominant nationalist narrative and the concerns of the capitalist class that emerged victorious from the independence struggle. David Convery (ed.), *Locked Out, A Century of Irish Working-Class Life* (Dublin: Irish Academic Press, 2013).

61 Devine (ed.), *A Capital in Conflict*.

62 Ibid., p. 20.

CHAPTER ELEVEN

An Introduction to Manuscript Sources on the Irish Citizen Army

Conor McNamara

A limited volume of archival material pertaining to the Irish Citizen Army is available to researchers. This chapter offers an introductory guide and examines published and archival sources pertaining to the Irish Citizen Army, along with archival sources held by the National Library of Ireland, the Military Service Pensions Board and the Bureau of Military History, in particular. This guide is not intended to be exhaustive but to serve as a starting point for researchers.[1]

Contemporary published sources

First-hand accounts of the Citizen Army are few and only a small number of personal accounts by former members have been published. An officially sanctioned, *History of the Irish Citizen Army* by R.M. Fox was published in 1943 and three personal accounts, notable for their passion and partisanship, chart the history of the movement – Sean O'Casey's scathing, *The Story of the Irish Citizen Army 1913–1916* (1919); Jack White's idiosyncratic memoir, *Misfit: An Autobiography* (1930); and Frank Robbins', *Under the Starry Plough: Recollections of the Irish Citizen Army* (1977).[2] The split within the wider labour movement between Larkinites and Connollyites is mirrored in the historiography of the organisation as their respective partisans seek to enhance the status of Connolly and Larkin at the expense of each other. O'Casey's eulogising of James Larkin is only surpassed by his contempt for James Connolly. Robbins, on the other hand, treats Larkin's leadership as an irrelevance, lionising the charisma of Connolly.

In producing his official history, Fox was directed by senior ICA veterans who sanctioned the publication on behalf of the Old Comrades Association of the ICA. This committee consisted of Séamus McGowan, Séan Byrne, John Hanratty, Stephen Murphy, Martin King, Walter Carpenter, James O'Shea, George Tully and Maeve Cavanagh McDowell. Fox's narrative carefully skirts challenging issues, such as the saliency of internal divisions between rival leaders, indiscipline and the collapse of the movement after the Rising. Fox's detailed appendix lists the 212 Citizen Army members who fought in the Rising, their status within the organisation, and details of garrisons and command structures.[3]

O'Casey's peculiar book, *The Story of the Irish Citizen Army 1913–1916*, represents a deeply personal attack on James Connolly's leadership of the movement. O'Casey loathed what he perceived as the petty bourgeois nature of Sinn Féin and the Volunteers, and despised Arthur Griffith, in particular. For O'Casey, Connolly's alliance with militant republicanism from 1914 onwards represented a betrayal of the class struggle in favour of bourgeois nationalism. For O'Casey, the ICA coalition with the Volunteers signified that, 'Connolly had stepped away from the narrow byway of Irish socialism onto the broad and crowded highway of Irish nationalism.'[4]

Remarkably O'Casey's account of the Citizen Army's participation in the Rebellion occupies only three pages. Seán Connolly, who led the attack on City Hall and was shot dead on Easter Monday, appears disparagingly as 'Shaun' Connolly; Michael Mallin, executed for his role in the Rebellion, appears as 'Michael Mallon'. O'Casey's judgement on Connolly is acerbic: 'In Sheehy-Skeffington, and not in Connolly,' he concludes, 'fell the first martyr to Irish socialism.'[5] His final verdict is equally dour: 'A Citizen Army can only be formed from a class conscious community of workers, and the Irish workers still slumbered on in the dark shade of unawakened thought.'[6] Ultimately, however, even O'Casey was forced to concede the transformative nature of the Rising: 'The breath of death which had swept over poor Dublin carried with it the seeds of a new life, which, falling in different parts of Ireland, began to appear as green blades of new thought and new activities.'[7]

Frank Robbins fought in the 1916 Rebellion as a senior member of the Citizen Army in the Royal College of Surgeons. In his witness statement to the Bureau of Military History, extensively re-written and published as, *Under the Starry Plough: Recollections of the Irish Citizen Army* (Dublin, 1977), he accused R.M. Fox and O'Casey of giving distorted accounts of the Citizen Army. He attacked O'Casey's, 'personal antipathy to Connolly', and Fox's 'lack of knowledge'.[8] Robbins' assessment of Larkin is rounded: 'I came under the powerful influence of Larkin. Some years later, my faith in Larkin was destroyed, but at the time Jim Larkin radiated for me an aura of magnetism.'[9] Robbins singled out Michael Mallin's appointment as a transformative development within the movement: 'with their [Connolly and Mallin] appearance came the determination of new and more earnest men, women and boys to do the work that lay ahead'.[10]

Robbins offers a sober appraisal of Connolly's posthumous fame: 'During his lifetime he was not considered in any way worthy of such tribute. In fact, apart from the Irish Citizen Army and a very limited number of members of the Union, including some of the leading officials and some outside friends, he was practically ignored and unknown.'[11] While Robbins was to the right of the Labour struggle and garnered many enemies in the Trade Union movement in the ensuing decades, his treatment offers a corrective to Fox's sanitised account. Robbins writes, 'The socialistic ideals expressed in the constitution of the Irish Citizen Army, were not understood by the workers and where understood, were not acceptable. The hardcore of the Irish Citizen Army who remained loyal to Connolly embraced the ideal of Irish Independence as expressed in the very definitive terms of the *Workers Republic*.'[12]

Jack White dedicated a brief section of his autobiography, *Misfit: An Autobiography*, published in 1930, to the Citizen Army and offers an intimate portrayal of Dublin during this period. White came to Dublin after the commencement of the Lockout believing, 'the present state of the workless poor in Dublin, and the callous apathy with which it is being met, is a blot on civilisation and an outrage in the name of Christ'.[13] White paid for the initial supplies, uniforms and boots of the Citizen Army himself, much of which he later alleged, 'found their way to the pawn shop'.[14] He resigned from the movement in 1914, however, frustrated by Larkin's contempt for him and by his own inability to organise a credible fighting force. White's account generously defends Connolly's subsequent control of the movement: '[Connolly] was a realist,'[15] he claimed while, of Larkin, 'It is Jim at his worst which perpetually dogs Jim at his best. In those days, at the height of his influence he was, what God meant him to be, great.'[16] Arthur Griffith on the other hand was 'an unpleasant little man' who 'seemed to emanate the suspicion of the professional Gael towards the foreign or Protestant interloper in the "movement"'.[17]

Manuscript sources in the Bureau of Military History

Veterans of the Citizen Army were reticent to record their experience in projects controlled by the Free State, while the Bureau of Military History showed limited enthusiasm in recording ICA accounts and only collected a limited number of testimonies from Citizen Army members and associates.[18] Many senior figures, including Stephen Murphy, Walter Carpenter, James O'Neill and Séamus McGowan refused the Bureau's requests for interviews.[19] The Bureau's primary concern during interviews was with the role of the ICA during the 1916 Rising and discussion of the Lockout was noticeably sidelined.[20]

James Larkin Junior (BMH WS 906) used his witness statement to reinforce the centrality of the Lockout to the perceived resurgence of working-class militancy after 1913. He noted that the elite craft unions' 'main hope and purpose was to keep themselves above the swarming mass of casual unskilled labourers'. 'The unskilled workers had been given up as incapable of organisation by the older trade union leaders, and trade union solidarity was not considered as extending to the lower ranks of labour.'[21]

Maeve Cavanagh McDowell (BMH WS 256), a member of the Citizen Army in her own right, was the sister of Ernest Kavanagh, the gifted cartoonist for the *Irish Worker* who was shot dead by the military on the steps of Liberty Hall during Easter Week. She wrote,

> [Larkin] was concerned about temperance and hated the idea of the men spending their time and money in public-houses, so he started to organise concerts. He asked me would I help and we started the concerts at the time the public-houses would open. Larkin told the men to bring their wives and babies and that the babies could cry all they wanted. I used to play the piano and sometimes I got a lecturer for them and helped in any way I could. When I was speaking once to Connolly about Larkin, he said, 'Jim is able to attract a crowd', but I always thought that Connolly himself could attract a better type of man. When I heard Larkin was going to America I asked him why would he go now when the Revolution was coming off – we all knew it was coming – at first we thought it was to be Good Friday in commemoration of Brian Boru's victory. He said the real work was to be done in America. I felt that things at Liberty Hall had become strained and that it was a relief that he went. Connolly was the man for the Revolution.[22]

Frank Robbins (BMH WS 585) left the most thorough account of the Citizen Army with the Bureau of Military History. His statement illuminates the experience of the ordinary membership. Recalling O'Casey's botched attempt to have Countess Markievicz expelled, he recalled, 'O'Casey handled the matter so tactlessly for himself by declaring in the course of his speech that he was afraid of no man, physically or morally, not even of Jim Larkin. This immediately brought the latter to his feet, and he poured forth his vituperation against O'Casey.'[23]

Robbins' most acute observations concern the decline of the Citizen Army. Following the Rebellion, the old divide between the followers of Larkin and Connolly infected the wider labour movement: 'There was a distinct cleavage after Easter Week between a certain section of the ICA who were used against the Irish Transport and General Workers' Union for the personal aims of certain individuals.'[24] After returning from Frongoch, Robbins believed that the new recruits lacked 'the same spirit, the understanding and the discipline which was there before'. He attributed this to the women who had taken part in 1916 leaving the Citizen Army, because the new women recruits 'had very obnoxious pasts as far as trade union matters were concerned: at least one of them had actually scabbed during the strike'.[25]

Before joining the Citizen Army in 1913, Helena Molony (BMH WS 391) had been a central member of Inghinidhe na hÉireann, editing their journal, *Bean na hÉireann*, and organising free school meals in the inner city. Her conversion to the Citizen Army was inspired by the Lockout, when 'Jim Larkin had galvanised that most under of underdogs – the unskilled labourer – into a consciousness of his rights and dignity.'[26] She subsequently became a staunch admirer of Connolly: 'Connolly – stanch feminist that he was – was more than anxious to welcome women into the ranks on equal terms with men, and to promote them to such rank as they were suited for.'[27]

Molony's witness statement details her involvement with Delia Larkin's co-operative shop at Liberty Hall, established to provide work for girls victimised by employers following the Lockout. She subsequently became involved in first-aid classes as part of the ICA women's corps. Of these women, she recalled, 'Eventually they all fought in the Rebellion, and, as far as I know, not one of them is a penny the better for her part in either fight. They served their country without desire or hope of gain or reward.'[28] The ICA women distributed anti-recruitment literature, and encouraged girls not to socialise with soldiers, exposing them to danger on Dublin's streets:

'Any hesitation or delay would lead to a mobbing, and soldiers at that time had the habit of taking off their belts and attacking civilians with them if they thought there was any hostility towards them.'[29]

Disdainful of the moderate element within the Irish Volunteers – personified by Éoin Mac Néill and Bulmer Hobson – Molony was contemptuous of their ingrained caution: 'in our case there would be no backing down on the part of our leaders, but we were not so sure about the leadership of the Volunteers'.[30] She regarded Connolly as a more gifted leader than Larkin: 'He was a man of character and brains – not a blatherskite like Larkin who was all froth. If he had to go out fighting alone, he would have done so.'[31]

Marie Perolz (BMH/WS 246) spent Easter Week delivering despatches for Connolly across Dublin and Munster. Her account is colourfully forthright, Tomás Mac Curtain was a 'brat'[32] and prominent Citizen Army member, William O'Reilly 'an awful cod, but a nice cod'.[33] Upon learning of the countermand, Perolz and her comrades were distraught, 'That day I didn't want to live any longer. We were all in a state, Tom [Hunter] cried like a baby.'[34] Arrested upon her return to Dublin, she was imprisoned in Lewes jail, where she recalled that 'we were well treated'.[35]

Rosie Hackett (BMH WS 546) was one of several women Volunteers who admired Helena Molony: 'She always had a gun, and was always prepared.'[36] Hackett worked tirelessly in Liberty Hall throughout the Easter Weekend, preparing food for the Citizen Army billeted under Connolly's orders. Hackett assisted Madeleine ffrench-Mullen throughout the week. Following the order to surrender, Hackett vividly recalls a despondent Michael Mallin: 'He took my hand, and did not speak, he was terribly pale. I thought his face was drawn and haggard. The worry was there.'[37] Hackett resented that the Citizen Army was overlooked after the War of Independence: 'Historically, Liberty Hall is the most important building that we have in this city. Yet it is not thought of at all by most people. More things happened there, in connection with the Rising, than in any other place. It really started there.'[38]

James O'Shea (BMH WS 733), a foundry hand, joined the ICA at its inception. O'Shea's absorbing testimony recounts the actions of the ICA in the Stephen's Green/College of Surgeons garrison. O'Shea, a confidante of Mallin, was arrested in 1915 for making steel bars at his Inchicore works to be used by the ICA for housebreaking. An unnamed informer was subsequently shunned by fellow workers, subjected to attacks and intimidation, and eventually confined to an asylum.[39] Resentful at the presence of employers among the Volunteers, O'Shea joined the Citizen Army as: 'Jim Connolly meant business; what kind, we did not know':[40]

> We had also something that was worth more than anything else since or before, a peculiar comradeship that had no limits. It meant you stood by your mates against all comers, friend or foe. We were like a big family when you got the swing of it. Home or nothing else mattered. It made for a carelessness in danger and a happy-go-lucky devil-may-care comradeship that I had never experienced before.[41]

O'Shea categorised the complex political loyalties in Dublin:

> At that time, Dublin was a different place to what it is now. There was the 'extreme', the 'not too extreme', those whose sympathy we had, people who thought we were lunatics, and others who thought our place was in France. There were also two other elements – the loyalists made up of the police and their touts, and last but in no way least, the soldiers wives who thought we should all be shot as we were only playing soldiers and annoying the nice English soldiers and gentlemen.[42]

O'Shea and his workmates armed in advance of meetings in support of striking workers and inevitable confrontation with the 'peelers': 'I had men coming from all over the works that day for handy bolts, pieces of irons bars, etc.'[43] O'Shea recalled the collapse of the Lockout with brutal honesty, 'There was resentment and seething rebellion everywhere; there was also plenty of cowardice.' Members, he recalled, openly avoided the union hall because 'they afraid to be seen ... At this time, everything was at its lowest ebb'.[44]

Matthew Connolly (BMH WS 1,745) was one of several brothers, who, along with their father, took an active part in the Rebellion. Matthew fought at City Hall under his brother, Sean's command, and witnessed his sibling's death. His account describes the build-up to the Rising at Liberty Hall, 'it was quite a common thing, on entering the armoury room, to find a man sitting over the fire; brewing a can of tea on one side of it, while melting a pot of lead on the other side; two or three men at a bench, making repairs to a rifle, while at the same time, two or three others were stretched on the bare floor, snoring fast asleep'.[45]

Fr Thomas O'Donoghue (BMH WS 1,666) was a founding member of both Na Fianna Éireann and the Citizen Army. He objected to women in the ranks: 'I had a horror of ladies in uniform and masquerading as soldiers.'[46] His account of training exercises is unsentimental: 'I had very little respect for the ability of the officers of the Citizen Army. The fundamental reason was that the majority of them, as trained soldiers of the British Army, lacked initiative and the practical knowledge of strategy and tactics.'[47]

William Oman (BMH WS 421) recounted the final days leading up to the Rebellion in Liberty Hall, where he liaised with ICA leaders, James Connolly, Michael Mallin and Seán Connolly. Oman provides details of the attack on Dublin Castle and he was part of the unit led by Seán Connolly that occupied City Hall. Recalling the cancellation of manoeuvres on Easter Sunday, Oman wrote: 'Connolly gave us the impression that he was more-or-less despondent over the whole affair, that the Volunteers would not take part in the Rising, and that he was going out to act on his own and take the Castle.'[48] The discipline imposed by Michael Mallin at the College of Surgeons included a nightly rosary: 'We had to make down our own beds and, in the morning reveille, which was not sounded, of course, we had to make up our beds and fold them up, etc.'[49]

John Hanratty (BMH WS 96), an oven hand at Jacob's biscuit factory, joined the Citizen Army at its foundation. He missed taking part in the Rebellion after being accidentally shot in the leg at Liberty Hall two weeks previously. His statement alludes to the uneasy relationship between the ICA and the Volunteers, noting a 'mutual hostility due to the fact that each underestimated and misunderstood the other. This feeling, however, was gradually overcome by the efforts of James Connolly.'[50]

Dr Kathleen Lynn (BMH/WS 357) was one of a small group of extraordinary women who held a leadership role in the ICA.[51] A lecturer in first aid to both the ICA and Cumann na mBan, Lynn was a role model to the younger women lacking formal education who made up the bulk of both women's organisations. Recalling the leadership of Countess Markievicz, Lynn recalled, 'She was a grand soul. She was brimming over with enthusiasm and was not like other people. Although you might gather from her manner that she was fantastic, she was full of sound sense and was quite practical.'[52] Lynn was present during the fighting and subsequent capture of City Hall and wrote a detailed account of her subsequent imprisonment. All of the women contracted scabies while at Ship Street Barracks: 'We had dusty grey blankets which were all crawling with lice. I never slept during the time I was there. I could not. The scratching was not so bad in the daytime but in the night time it was perfectly awful.'[53] The women were later transferred to Mountjoy jail where they 'could hear the shootings in the mornings, and we would be told afterwards who it was. It was a very harrowing experience.'[54]

Thomas Mallin (BMH WS 382) brother of Michael Mallin, left an intimate account of his brother's life. He details his sibling's life in the British army, his radicalisation upon returning to Dublin, and his final visit with his family before execution, 'All the family had collected at my mother's. I found them all crying. My mother said "What is the use of crying – would it not be better for you to get down on your knees, and pray for him." I fell asleep.'[55]

William O'Brien Papers, National Library of Ireland

The William O'Brien Papers housed in the NLI are seminal to the history of the wider Labour movement in Ireland from 1898 to 1916, and in particular, to the contribution of James Connolly. O'Brien collected correspondence and papers of his comrades and associates including material pertaining to radical groups in Dublin from 1898 onwards, the Irish Socialist Republican Party of Ireland founded by James Connolly in 1898 and the Irish Citizen Army. O'Brien collected material relating to the 1913 Lockout and the Rising, the two seminal events of his political life, including primary documents (letters, organisational material, propaganda). He assembled papers about the publication of the *Worker's Republic*, and extensive correspondence concerning Connolly's endeavours in the United States from 1903 to 1910, letters from Connolly to his wife, and to his American comrades.

Table 1. Select material from the William O'Brien Papers (NLI)

Manuscript	Details
MS 34,937	Citizen Army notebook belonging to Michael Mallin containing notes on mobilisation, military exercises, accounts, names, addresses, munitions, flags, fundraising, c. 1914: list of his children with their birth dates.
MS 29,046	Irish Volunteers, the Irish Citizen Army, the 1916 Rising etc., 1909–16.
MS 15,672/1–2	Three notebooks listing members of the ICA, 1916.
MS 15,672/4	ICA member's card for Thomas Kain, 26 Charlemont St, Dublin, 1914.

Manuscript	Details
MS 15,672/8	Christmas card from Kathleen Clarke and Constance Markievicz, Holloway Jail, December 1918.
MS 15,673/1	Notes by William O'Brien on the ICA, 1913.
MS 15,673/2	Notes by William O'Brien on the ICA, 1914–47.
MS 15,673/3	Notes by William O'Brien on the ICA, mostly concerning James Larkin and Sean O'Casey, 1908–1938.
MS 15,673/4	Notes by William O'Brien on the ICA and the Dublin Industrial Peace Committee, 1913.
MS 15,673/5	Newspaper cuttings regarding the ICA, 1914–63.
MS 15,673/7/1	Typescript 'James Connolly: Ireland's Trotsky' by John Carson-Tozer, May 1941.
MS 15,673/8	Papers relating to the ICA, 1913–22.
MS 15,673/8/1	Recruitment form for ICA, c. 1913.
MS 15,673/8/2	Handbill 'Reasons Why you Should Join the Irish Citizen Army', c. 1913.
MS 15,673/8/3	Handbill 'A song for the Irish Transport and General Workers' Union', c. 1913.
MS 15,673/8/6	Circular about anti-conscription resolution adopted by the Dublin United Trades Council and Labour League, 25 Oct. 1915.
MS 15,673/8/20	Handbill 'Hymn on the battlefield': Dedicated to the Citizen Army by Constance de Markievicz, c. 1913.
MS15,673/8/10	Note from Kathleen Lynn and Andrew Conroy regarding their appointments as judges at the court martial of Commandant James O'Neill, 20 January 1922.
MS 15,673/10/3	Report by Sean O'Casey on a visit to Kingstown to form a branch of the ICA 16 July 1914.
MS 15,673/10/7	Letter from Constance de Markievicz regarding an accusation by Michael Mallin that she was a spy, reportedly made at an ICA meeting, 14 July 1917.
MS 15,673/10/1	'Full List of Members of Irish Citizen Army', with an X marked beside the names of those who fought in the Easter Rising, 1916, [c. 1916].
MS 15,672/4	ICA member's card for Thomas Kain, 26 Charlemont Street, Dublin, 1914.

Table 2. Printed material by the Irish Citizen Army (NLI)

NLI Reference	Details
LO P 112 [Item 2]	ICA Dramatic Class card advertising a concert and dramatic performance at 41 Parnell Square, 21 October 1917.
LO P 112 [Item 3]	Irish Citizen Army card advertising a smoking concert on Thursday 15 April 1915 in Liberty Hall.
LO P 115 [Item 10]	Balance sheet of the concert and fund held at St George's town hall, 3 Nov. 1914 for the benefit of the women and children of Dublin.
LOLB 163 (21)	Reasons why you should join the Irish Citizen Army (handbill).
LO P 109 [Item 31]	War: What it means to you (handbill urging Irish workers not to volunteer for service in the British forces).
LOLB 163 (41)	ICA, Member's card 1914.
LO P 115 [Item 52]	A Night in Mountjoy 1914, by William O'Brien (pamphlet).
EPH C82	Why Irish workers should not join the National Volunteers! (handbill).

Manuscript material pertaining to the Easter Rebellion

Senior ICA veterans were requested to supply the details of the membership and command structure of the organisation for the provision of military pensions. File MA/MSPC/10A in the archives of the Military Service Pension Board contains the details of Citizen Army membership from 1913 to 1922. These lists contain inconsistencies and disagreements pertaining to officer positions. In addition to the lists of members and time spent in the organisation, individual claims for pensions can be accessed to build a detailed picture of the ICA.

Citizen Army veterans of Easter Week disagreed over exact roles in the command structure during the Rebellion, and officer positions were fluid. Veterans Christopher Poole and John Hanratty supplied details of the command structure to the Bureau of Military Pensions in 1935.[56] There are discrepancies between the lists and those in Fox's official history. Séamus McGowan and Joseph Doyle do not appear on Poole's list, for example, but are included in Fox's.[57] While Kathleen Lynn was a senior member of the organisation, her name is not included on Poole or Fox's list, and

Helena Molony and Madeleine ffrench Mullen, also senior members, are likewise omitted. Fr Thomas Donoghue appears on Poole's list but not Fox's or Hanratty's. James O'Shea is mentioned as a Captain by John Hanratty but does not appear on other lists.[58]

Table 3. ICA Command structure, Easter 1916
(File MA/MSPC/10A)

General: James Connolly
Commandant: Michael Mallin
Staff Captain: Christopher Poole
Quartermaster: John Hanratty
Director of Munitions: Séamus McGowan
Surgeon General: Dr Kathleen Lynn
Captains: Sean Connolly; Richard McCormack; James O'Neill; Séamus McGowan
Lieutenants: Michael Kelly; Thomas Kaine; Robert DeCoeur; Thomas O'Donoghue; Peter Jackson; Countess Markievicz; Joseph Doyle; James O'Shea
Sergeants: George Norgrove; Joseph Doyle; Elliot Elmes; George Oman; Frank Robbins
Boy's Section: Commanded by Captain Walter Carpenter; assisted by Lieutenant Christopher Cruthers and Captain Matthew Connolly

Table 4. Bureau of Military Service pension applications;
Citizen Army, Easter 1916

Name	BMSP File	Address	1916 Garrison	After the Rising
Adams, John Francis*	1D317	109 Cork St.	Stephen's Green	Killed 25 April; labourer; married: one daughter
Allen, Mary, née Devereux	MSP34REF8867	54 Mountjoy Sq.	Sent home due to youth after two days	Rejoined ICA
Bannon, John	MSP34REF367	68 Foley Street	Stephen's Green	Rejoined ICA
Barrett, Kathleen, née Connolly	MSP34REF2198	14 Lower Rutland St.	City Hall	Cumann na mBan; Anti-Treaty; interned

Name	BMSP File	Address	1916 Garrison	After the Rising
Barry, John	MSP34REF1245	2 Spencer St.	Stephen's Green	Rejoined ICA
Beggs, Robert	MSP34REF1963	8 St Joseph's St.	Four Courts	Wounded in hip
Bermingham, Peter	MSP34REF1965	589 Wood View Tce., Rathfarnham	Stephen's Green	Evaded arrest; joined Volunteers
Bird, James	MSP34REF20471	4 Rutland Cottages	Four Courts	Member of IV and ICA in 1916
Boylan, John	MSP34REF33887	23 St Michael's Tce., Blackpits	Annesley Bridge	No further service
Bradley, Luke	24SP5856	Fordstown, Kells, Co. Meath	Stephen's Green	Joined National Army
Bradley, Patrick	MSP34REF5024	Newport, Tipperary	Stephen's Green	Joined Volunteers
Brennan, James	MSP34REF55143	59 Bride St.	Jacob's/ Stephen's Green	Took no further part
Bryan, Thomas	MSP34REF2435	Prosperous, Kildare	GPO (Imperial Hotel)	Rejoined ICA
Burke, Edward	MSP34REF1199	13 Park Terrace, Meath St.	Stephen's Green	Rejoined ICA; interned in Civil War
Buttner, Patrick	MSP34REF980	2 Swifts Row	Stephen's Green	Sent home due to youth; interned in Civil War
Byrne, Denis	MSP34REF1570	New Bride St.	Stephen's Green	Evaded arrest; rejoined ICA
Byrne, James	MSP34REF58980	Portrane Hospital	GPO	Suffered ill health
Byrne, John (Séan)	MSP34REF17897	31 Upper Wellington St.	City Hall	Rejoined ICA: senior officer

Name	BMSP File	Address	1916 Garrison	After the Rising
Byrne, Louis	1D312	47 Lower Gardiner St.	GPO	Evaded arrest; rejoined ICA; interned in Civil War
Byrne, Louis*	MSP34REF2068	23 Summerhill	City Hall	Killed 25 April; cabinetmaker; married: five children
Byrne, Patrick Joseph	MSP34REF452	60 Lower Dominick St.	City Hall	Wounded in Rising
Caffrey-Keeley, Christina	MSP34REF9970	17 Church St., North Wall	Stephen's Green	Went to Glasgow: remained active in Cumann na mBan
Campbell, George	24SP6503	20 Auburn St.	Stephen's Green	Joined National Army
Carpenter, Peter	MSP34REF14697	Tara Hall, Talbot St.	GPO (Metropole)	Joined Volunteers
Carpenter, Walter	MSP34REF8789	169 Parnell St.	GPO	Evaded arrest; rejoined ICA: active in Belfast; interned in Civil War
Carroll, Michael	MSP34REF52328	18 Upper Erne St.	Stephen's Green	Rejoined ICA
Carroll, Patrick	MSP34REF32621	116 Leix Rd, Cabra	Stephen's Green/GPO	Released account of youth; joined Volunteers; Anti-Treaty IRA: imprisoned
Carton, Eugene	MSP34REF809	21 Temple St.	Stephen's Green (Davy's)	Joined Volunteers; Anti-Treaty IRA; interned; hunger strike

Name	BMSP File	Address	1916 Garrison	After the Rising
Chaney, Patrick	MSP34REF1380	5 Northcourt Ave, Church Road	Stephen's Green	Wounded in action
Chaney, William	MSP34REF13552	3 Upper Rutland St.	Stephen's Green	Rejoined ICA
Charlton, Michael	MSP34REF60029	55 Saint Albans Rd	Stephen's Green	Rejoined ICA
Clarke, Philip* 1D162	1D162	65 Cork St.	Stephen's Green	Killed 25 April; married; eight children
Coates, Peter	MSP34REF615	2 Spenser St, North Strand	Stephen's Green	Rejoined ICA; very active
Colman Tuohy, Patrick	MSP34REF222	73 Bride St.	GPO	Rejoined ICA; Anti-Treaty IRA
Connolly, George	MSP34REF1284	13 Buckingham Tce.	City Hall (Castle Guard)	Anti-Treaty IRA; interned
Connolly, James*	1D178	36 Belgrave Sq, Rathmines	GPO	Executed 12 May; six children
Connolly, Joseph William	MSP34REF56783	Central Fire Station, Tara Street	GPO	Rejoined ICA
Connolly, Matthew	MSP34REF3803	Kilbarrack House, Raheny	City Hall	Released early due to youth; London IRA
Connolly, Roderick	MSP34REF38900	Inishowen, Bray Head	GPO	Rejoined Volunteers; Anti-Treaty IRA
Connolly, Séan*	1D205	3 Mountjoy Sq.	City Hall	Killed 24 April; corporation clerk; three children
Conroy, Andrew	MSP34REF20076	16 Pearse St.	GPO (Hopkins & Hopkins)	Wounded during Easter Week

Name	BMSP File	Address	1916 Garrison	After the Rising
Conroy, John	24SP3406	32 Upper Rutland St.	Stephen's Green	Joined Volunteers; National Army
Corbally, Laurence	MSP34REF1390	6 Upper Gloucester St.	GPO	Rejoined ICA; sentenced for armed robbery, 1922
Corbally, Richard	MSP34REF208	5 Upper Gloucester Place	GPO	Rejoined the ICA: interned
Corcoran, James*	1D301	2 Elizabeth Place, Oriel St.	Stephen's Green	Killed 25 April; labourer; three children
Corcoran, Mary Teresa, née O'Reilly	MSP34REF20325	45 Leix Road, Cabra	City Hall/ Jacobs	Associated with both the ICA and IV; interned in Civil War
Cosgrave, Edward*	1D304	65 Lower Dominick St.	GPO	Killed 25 April; rope maker; seven children
Costello, Edward*	1D261	3 Castle Lane, Lurgan, Co. Armagh	Church St.	Died 25 April; drapery manager; daughter
Courtney, Daniel	MSP34REF811	13 Upper Stephen's St.	GPO (Annesley Bridge)	Rejoined ICA
Coyle, Thomas	24SP602	8 Queens Sqe, Pearse St.	City Hall (Dublin Castle)	Wounded Easter Week; National Army
Crothers, Christopher	MSP34REF210	43 Connolly Gardens, Inchicore	Stephen's Green	Rejoined ICA; senior member;
Cullen, Patrick	MSP34REF1724	12 Parnell St.	Stephen's Green	Rejoined ICA

Name	BMSP File	Address	1916 Garrison	After the Rising
Darcy, Charles*	1D204	4 Murphy's Cottages, Gloucester Place	City Hall	Shop assistant; unmarried
De Couer, Robert	MSP34REF1658	80 Tolka Road, Ballybough	Stephen's Green	Rejoined ICA; interned in Civil War
Delaney, Michael	24SP8402	62 Brian Rd, Marino		Joined Volunteers; National Army
Devereux, Patrick	MSP34REF13565	49 Summerhill	GPO (Imperial)	Developed Traumatic neurasthenia
Donnelly, James	24SP9180	68 Amiens St.	Stephen's Green	Joined National Army
Donnelly, Michael	MSP34REF291	6 Hanover St. West	Stephen's Green (Harcourt St)	Rejoined ICA; senior member
Doran, Bridget, née Lambert	MSP34REF57178	Old Bridge House, Milltown	GPO	Released after Rising; joined Cumann na mBan
Doyle, Edward	MSP34REF60191	Iveagh House, Bride Rd	GPO (DBC, Hopkins)	Rejoined ICA
Doyle, Joseph	MSP34REF13569	37 Anner Rd, Inchicore	Stephen's Green (Davy's)	Rejoined ICA
Drury, Patrick	24SP1303	8 Annesley Sq, North Strand	GPO (Imperial Hotel)	Joined Volunteers; National Army
Dunne, Andrew	MSP34REF18903	208 Pearse St.	Stephen's Green	Ill health after imprisonment
Dunne, Margaret, née Ryan	MSP34REF10285	Buckingham Buildings	Stephen's Green	Evaded arrest; no further part

Name	BMSP File	Address	1916 Garrison	After the Rising
Dutton Cooper, John	MSP34REF52139	33 Lennox St., Portobello	GPO (D.B.C.)	No further service
Dwyer, James	MSP34REF723	4 Arran Quay	Stephen's Green	Rejoined ICA
Dwyer, Michael	24SP219	10 Buckingham Tce.	Stephen's Green/GPO	National Army
Dynan, Christopher	MSP34REF9612	25 Upper Cumberland St.	Stephen's Green	Evaded arrest; rejoined ICA
Egan, William	24SP859	Fairbrothers Fields, S.C.R.	Stephen's Green	National Army
Elmes, Elliott	MSP34REF866	23 St. Jarlaths Rd, Cabra	City Hall/ GPO	Rejoined ICA; interned Civil War
Eustace, Robert	1D461	24 Gloucester St.	GPO	Died 23 Aug. 1918
Farrell, Denis	MSP34REF229	6 Willett Place, Glorney's Buildings	City Hall	Rejoined ICA
Finegan, Michael	MSP34REF14715	2 Whites Cottages, Summerhill	GPO (Imperial)	Detained but not interned; no further service
Finlay, John	MSP34REF1635	5 Grenville St., Mountjoy Sq.	City Hall	Wounded
Fitzpatrick, Francis	24SP3651	2 Lower Kevin St.	City Hall (Evening Mail)	Evaded arrest; National Army
Flanagan, Mary [Marie], née Perolz	MSP34REF20982	Strand Rd, Sutton	dispatches	Interned in Kilmainham, Mountjoy & Lewis
Fox, James Joseph*	1D150	3 Altinure Tce, Cabra Park	Stephen's Green	Killed 25 April; shop assistant; unmarried

Name	BMSP File	Address	1916 Garrison	After the Rising
Foy, Martin	24SP1285	21 Little Denmark St.	Stephen's Green	National Army
Geoghegan, George*	1D43	27 Upper Dorset St.	City Hall	Killed 26 April; boiler maker; married
Gifford-Donnelly, Nellie	MSP34REF1386	39 Carlingford Rd	Stephen's Green	No further service
Goff, Bridget	MSP34REF8920	26 Little Mary St.	Stephen's Green	Imprisoned in Kilmainham; serious illness
Gough, James	MSP34REF8910	16 Station Rd, Baldoyle	Stephen's Green (Davy's)	Joined the Volunteers
Grange, Annie, née Norgrove	MSP34REF6982	12 Upper Grand Canal St.	City Hall	Detained at Ship Street Barracks & Kilmainham; rejoined ICA
Hackett, Rosie	MSP34REF20787	Croydon Park, Marino	Stephen's Green	Detained at Kilmainham; rejoined ICA
Halpin, William	MSP34REF1216	6 St Valentine's Tce.	City Hall	Rejoined ICA
Halpin, William*	1P161	12 Moore St.	City Hall/ GPO	Transferred to an asylum; died in hospital
Hand, Matthew	MSP34REF870	26 Summerhill	Stephen's Green	Rejoined ICA
Hanratty, Emily, née Norgrove	MSP34REF724	77 Eccles St.	City Hall	Released from Kilmainham 8 May; rejoined the ICA
Healy, Thomas	MSP34REF2337	23 Lower Oriel St.	City Hall (Synod House)	Rejoined ICA

Name	BMSP File	Address	1916 Garrison	After the Rising
Hendrick, John Joseph	24SP8147	173 Emmet Rd, Inchicore	Stephen's Green	Joined Volunteers in Glasgow; National Army
Henry, Francis	MSP34REF1685	5 Fennells Cottages, Charlemont St.	Stephen's Green	Rejoined ICA
Henry, Frederick	1D164	92 Lower Mount St.	Stephen's Green (Davy's)	Joined Volunteers; died 1921
Higgins, Peter	MSP34REF8947	9 Horseman's Road, Parnell St.	GPO	Evaded arrest; no further service
Hyland, James	MSP34REF22258	St Michael's Tce, Blackpitts	Stephen's Green	No further service
Jackson, Peter	24SP735	New Bride St.	Stephen's Green	Joined Volunteers; National Army
Jennings, Thomas	24SP4257	30 North William St.	Stephen's Green	National Army
Joyce, Edward	MSP34REF2252	4 High St., Dublin	Stephen's Green (Harcourt St.)	Rejoined ICA
Joyce, James	MSP34REF1243	51 Dominick St.	Stephen's Green (Davy's Pub)	Rejoined ICA
Joyce, Margaret	MSP34REF1861	51 Lr Dominick St.	Stephen's Green	Rejoined ICA
Kain, Thomas	MSP34REF13912	15 Old Camden St.	Dublin Castle	Rejoined ICA
Kelly, Annie	MSP34REF44682	Harold's Cross Rd	Stephen's Green	Rejoined ICA
Kelly, Elizabeth, née Lynch	MSP34REF1670	34 Devenish Rd	City Hall	Detained in Kilmainham

Name	BMSP File	Address	1916 Garrison	After the Rising
Kelly, Francis	MSP34REF4038	74 Marlborough St.	Stephen's Green	Joined Volunteers; interned in Civil War
Kelly, Hugh	MSP34REF873	23 Synnott Place	Stephen's Green (Davy's Pub)	Evaded arrest; joined Volunteers; Anti-Treaty IRA
Kelly, James	MSP34REF1518	39 Daniel Street, S.C.R.	Stephen's Green (Davy's Pub)	Evaded arrest; rejoined ICA
Kelly, James	MSP34REF22058	25 Newfoundland St.	Stephen's Green	Retained ICA connections
Kelly, John	MSP34REF59639	5 Swift's Row	Stephen's Green (Davy's Pub)	Injured during the Rising
Kelly, Joseph	MSP34REF874	93 Lower Dorset St.	Stephen's Green (Portobello)	Joined Volunteers; Anti-Treaty IRA; interned
Kelly, Martin	MSP34REF21852	16 Kildare Rd, Kimmage	City Hall (Evening Mail)	Evaded arrest; rejoined ICA; interned Civil War
Kelly, Mary, née Hyland	MSP34REF4547	364 Kildare St., Crumlin	Stephen's Green	Evaded arrest
Kelly, William	MSP34REF1506	9 Bishop St.	Stephen's Green	Rejoined ICA; interned Civil War
Keogh, Edward Patrick	MSP34REF1344	10 Park St., Inchicore	Stephen's Green (Portobello)	Joined Volunteers; interned Civil War
Keogh, James	MSP34REF1314	6 Hendrick St.	Stephen's Green	Rejoined ICA
Killeen, Robert	MSP34REF21154	16 St Joseph's Parade, Dorset St.	Magazine Fort/GPO	Rejoined ICA

Name	BMSP File	Address	1916 Garrison	After the Rising
King, Daniel	MSP34REF10992	67 Aungier St.	City Hall/ GPO	Wounded during Easter Week; evaded capture
King, Martin	MSP34REF1131	25 St. Ignatius Rd	Stephen's Green	Emigrated to Scotland
King, Samuel	MSP34REF1179	25 St. Ignatius Rd, Drumcondra	City Hall (Henry & James); GPO	Rejoined ICA
Lacey, Philip	MSP34REF219	10 Braithwaite St.	Stephen's Green	Wounded in Easter Week
Lalor, Patrick Joseph	24SP8028	1 Coburgh Place, Seville Place	Stephen's Green	Joined Volunteers; National Army
Largan, Michael	24SP1596	9 Parnell St.	GPO (Imperial)	National Army
Leahy, Thomas	MSP34REF321	657 Dumbarton Rd, Partick West, Glasgow	GPO	Joined ICA on his release from Frongoch; Interned in Civil War
Leddy, Peter	MSP34REF60219	Upr Buckingham St.	Stephen's Green	Rejoined ICA
Little, James	MSP34REF1293	6 Charlemont Mall	Stephen's Green	Took no further part
Lynch, Patrick*	DP754	North Cumberland St.	GPO	Killed 28 April; unmarried
Maguire, James	MSP34REF9992	32 St Michael's Terrace, Blackpitts	Stephen's Green	Rejoined ICA; interned Civil War
Mallin, Michael*	1D322	105 Ceannt's Fort	Stephen's Green	Executed 8 May; two children

Name	BMSP File	Address	1916 Garrison	After the Rising
Mannering, Edward*	1D452	10.5 Cuffe St.	Stephen's Green	Died 6 June 1923; widow denied pension
McAlerney, Lily, née Kempson	MSP34REF28861	Washington, USA	Stephen's Green	Emigrated to USA
McCormack, James*	1D66	13 Sutton Cottages	GPO	Killed 26 April; labourer; married
McCormick, Richard	MSP34REF2186	St Michan's House, Mary's Lane	Stephen's Green (Davy's)	Rejoined ICA: senior member
McDonagh, Joseph	MSP34REF17145	18 Station Rd, Baldoyle	GPO	Wounded during Rising
McDowell, Meave	MSP34REF10925	53 Larkfield Grove	Dispatches	Rejoined ICA
McGowan, Séamus	MSP34REF4289	19 Hardiman Rd	GPO	Rejoined ICA; senior member
McMahon, Daniel	MSP34REF1240	20 Summerhill	GPO	Rejoined ICA
Meagher, John W	MSP34REF51	6 Richmond Place	St Stephen's Green	Rejoined ICA
Molony, Helena	MSP34REF11739	51 Larkfield Grove	City Hall	Later Sinn Féin
Moore, John	MSP34REF11838	Newfoundland Street, North Wall	GPO (Imperial Hotel)	
Mulligan, Andrew	MSP34REF11831	4 Willitt Place, Rutland Street	GPO	Rejoined the ICA
Murphy, Bridget, née Brady	MSP34REF32618	12 Corporation Street	City Hall	Imprisoned in Kilmainham
Murphy, Frederick	MSP34REF34537	82 Lower Gardiner Street	Stephen's Green/Jacob's	Took no further part

Name	BMSP File	Address	1916 Garrison	After the Rising
Murphy, Martha, née Kelly	MSP34REF11828	1 Leinster Avenue, North Strand Road	GPO (Imperial Hotel)	Remained active with ICA
Murphy, Stephen	MSP34REF2052	3A Old Church St.	GPO/Jacob's	rejoined ICA; interned in Civil War
Nelson, James	MSP34REF1160	9 Middle Gardiner St.	Stephen's Green	Rejoined ICA
Nelson, Thomas	MSP34REF1238	34 North Great George's St.	City Hall (Castle)	Rejoined ICA
Nicholls, Henry	MSP34REF15964	70 St Stephen's Green	Stephen's Green	Associated with ICA and IV; no further service
Nolan, Patrick	MSP34REF21180	3 Beaver St.	Stephen's Green	Volunteers during Easter Week; wounded; joined ICA
Nolan, Shaun (John)	MSP34REF1615	13 Upper Mayor St., North Wall	GPO/City Hall	Joined Irish Volunteers; Anti-Treaty IRA
Norgrove, Alfred	MSP34REF1764	15 Strandville Avenue, North Wall	City Hall	Rejoined ICA; army council,1922
Norgrove, Frederick	MSP34REF204	26 St. Aidan's Park, Marino	GPO	Sent home due to youth; rejoined ICA
Ó Briain, Liam	MSP34REF2988	UCG	Stephen's Green	Joined Volunteers
O'Connor, John	24SP12177	18 Francis St.	Stephen's Green	National Army
O'Doherty, Michael*	1D92	10 Lower Mayor St.	Stephen's Green	Died of wounds 22 Dec. 1919

Name	BMSP File	Address	1916 Garrison	After the Rising
O'Donoghue, Henry Vincent	MSP34REF14026	Anascaul, Co. Kerry	Stephen's Green	Joined Volunteers; Anti-Treaty IRA
O'Donoghue, Thomas	MSP34REF13080	8 Ferguson Rd, Drumcondra	Stephen's Green	Joined Volunteers; Anti-Treaty IRA
O'Duffy, Brigid, née Davis	MSP34REF20583	32 Mobhi Rd, Glasnevin	City Hall	Detained until 9 May
O'Dwyer, James	MSP34REF1604	Tolka Rd, Clonliffe Rd	City Hall	Rejoined ICA
O'Keefe, John Christopher	MSP34REF2255	26 Little Mary St.	City Hall (Synod House)	Wounded; rejoined ICA
O'Kelly, Michael	MSP34REF17898	Liberty Hall, Beresford Place	Stephen's Green	Joined Volunteers; interned Civil War
O'Leary, David	MSP34REF2766	Fairview, Mount Avenue, Dundalk	St Stephen's Green	Evaded arrest; joined Volunteers; Anti-Treaty IRA
O'Leary, Philip	MSP34REF970	4 Middle Gardiner St.	City Hall (Castle Guard)	Rejoined ICA
O'Neill, James	MSP34REF8368	187 Malahide Rd	GPO	Commandant ICA
O'Neill, John	MSP34REF3713	61 Ballybough Rd	GPO	Rejoined ICA
O'Neill, Patrick Joseph	MSP34REF46307	Elmhurst, Long Island, New York	GPO	Rejoined ICA; interned Civil War
O'Reilly, John	MSP34REF1470	5E Ross Rd	City Hall	Rejoined ICA
O'Reilly, John*	1D151	12 Lower Gardiner St.	City Hall	Killed 24 April; carter; unmarried

Name	BMSP File	Address	1916 Garrison	After the Rising
O'Reilly, Joseph	MSP34REF1106	Spring Garden St., North Strand	GPO	Rejoined ICA
O'Reilly, Patrick	34E139	43 Geraldine St.	Unspecified	Rejoined the ICA
O'Reilly, Thomas*	1D291	43 Geraldine St.	City Hall/ GPO	Killed 27 April; electrician
O'Shea, James	MSP34REF150	15 Joyce Rd, Drumcondra	Stephen's Green	Rejoined ICA; Anti-Treaty IRA; imprisoned
O'Shea, Robert	MSP34REF9485	52 Lwr Mountpleasant Ave	Stephen's Green (Harcourt St.)	Took no further part
O'Toole, William	MSP34REF1108	19 Hanover St. East	GPO (Metropole)	Rejoined ICA
Oman, George	MSP34REF14740	16 Kickham Rd, Inchicore	GPO (Imperial Hotel)	Rejoined ICA
Oman, William	MSP34REF37	8 Joyce Rd, Drumcondra	City Hall/ Jacob's	Joined Volunteers; Anti-Treaty IRA; interned
Partridge, William*	1D303	3 Patriotic Tce., Rathfarnham	Stephen's Green	Died 26 July 1917; four children
Poole, Christopher	MSP34REF10145	108 Walsh Rd, Drumcondra	Stephen's Green	Rejoined ICA
Poole, John	MSP34REF22247	43 James's St.	GPO/City Hall	Joined Volunteers
Poole, Patrick	MSP34REF1261	41 Upper MacDermott St.	Stephen's Green	Rejoined ICA
Poole, Vincent	MSP34REF460	3 Ryders Row	GPO	Anti-Treaty IRA; interned

Name	BMSP File	Address	1916 Garrison	After the Rising
Quigley, James	MSP34REF25076	33 Newfoundland St.	St Stephen's Green	Evaded arrest; rejoined ICA; interned in Civil War
Redmond, Andrew	MSP34REF3719	7 Camac Place, Dolphin's Barn	GPO (Metropole)	Joined Volunteers
Redmond, Cathleen, née Seery	MSP34REF33364	9 Upper Sean McDermott St.	Stephen's Green	Wounded; imprisoned in Kilmainham
Redmond, John	1924A15	8 Templeogue Rd, Terenure	GPO (Imperial Hotel)	National Army
Robbins, Frank	MSP34REF17899	5 Fairview Tce, Croydon Park	Stephen's Green	Rejoined ICA; senior member
Rogan, Séan	MSP34REF63368	9 St Kevin's Parade	Stephen's Green	Evaded capture
Ronan, Fenton Christopher	24SP4901	52 Marlborough St., Dublin	GPO (Hopkins & Hopkins)	National Army
Ryan, Frederick*	1D105	3 High St.	Stephen's Green	Killed 27 April; labourer; unmarried
Scott, William John	MSP34REF1644	7 New Rd, Inchicore	Stephen's Green	Injured in Rising; evaded arrest; joined Volunteers
Seery, James	MSP34REF2279	15A Corporation Place	City Hall (Dublin Castle)	Evaded arrest; no further service
Seery, John	MSP34REF1566	2 Beresford Place	Stephen's Green	Rejoined the ICA
Shanahan, Jane	MSP34REF10154	71 Larkfield Grove	City Hall	Cumann na mBan
Shannon, Martin Joseph	MSP34REF1397	1 Emerald Street, Seville Place	Stephen's Green	Emigrated to Scotland

Name	BMSP File	Address	1916 Garrison	After the Rising
Shiel, Thomas	MSP34REF903	36 Moyelta Road, North Strand	Stephen's Green	Applied to join Volunteers
Skinnider, Margaret	MSP34REF19910	31 Waverley Ave, Fairview	Stephen's Green	wounded; Cumann na mBan; Anti-Treaty; interned
Smith, Charles	MSP34REF188	43 Foley St.	GPO (Imperial Hotel)	Injured; evaded arrest; no further service
Stynes, Ellen, née Lambert	MSP34REF56696	17 Farranboley Cottages, Windy Arbour, Dundrum	GPO/ Stephen's Green	joined Cumann na mBan; interned Civil War
Tuke, Edward	24SP3528	35 Fairview Strand	Stephen's Green	Joined National Army
Tully, George	MSP34REF57221	Gloucester Place	GPO/ Stephen's Green	Joined Irish Volunteers
Tuohy, Patrick	MSP34REF222	73 Bride St.	GPO (Imperial Hotel)	Subsequently joined the Volunteers
Wade, Michael	MSP34REF1375	41 Mountjoy Sq.	GPO	Joined Anti-Treaty IRA: interned
Whelan, John	MSP34REF731	Gloucester St.	Stephen's Green	Joined Anti-Treaty IRA: imprisoned
Whelan, Joseph	MSP34REF8978	Lower Gardiner St.	GPO (Metropole)	Joined the Volunteers
White, John	MSP34REF28572	Brent Green, Hendon, London	GPO/City Hall (Dublin Castle)	Returned to England; later imprisoned

*Indicates killed or died from wounds received.

Ancillary material

Citizen Army Captain, Séamus McGowan, deposited a collection of private and organisational material in the University College Dublin Archives. The Cowan Papers include material pertaining to the left-wing political activism of members of the Cowan family of Drumcondra, including Séamus McGowan's career in the Citizen Army. McGowan was one of a number of Protestants from Dublin's northside who played an important role in the organisation. Along with material pertaining to the Citizen Army, the Cowan Papers includes material relating to the wider labour movement in Dublin and related groups, including the Connolly–Mallin Social and Athletic Club, the James Connolly Workers' Club, the ITGWU, the Communist Party and the Labour Party. The papers are not currently available to readers.

The Irish Labour History Archive, located at Beggars Bush Barracks, Dublin, holds the Irish Citizen Army, Army Council minute book for the period February 1919 to September 1920. The book contains minutes of bi-weekly meetings of the Council and details of the activities of the organisation during the War of Independence. The book provides details of the political activities of the Citizen Army members who fought in the Rising and charts the inexorable decline of the organisation in the period after the Rising. There are also significant papers pertaining to the ICA held in Kilmainham Jail; these catalogues can only be viewed by appointment and no catalogue is publicly available.

Endnotes

1 A version of this paper was originally published in *Saothar, Journal of the Irish Labour History Society*, 41 (1916 Centenary Special Edition), pp. 145–64.

2 Fox, R.M., *The History of the Irish Citizen Army* (Dublin: James Duffy, 1943); Seán O'Casey, *The Story of the Irish Citizen Army* (London: Maunsel, 1919); Frank Robbins, *Under the Starry Plough: Recollections of the Irish Citizen Army* (Dublin: Academy Press, 1977); Captain Jack White, *Misfit: An Autobiography* (London: Jonathan Cape, 1930).

3 Fox lists 212 members who took part in the Rising and this list was endorsed by the ICA Old Comrades Committee in 1943, Fox, *History of the Irish Citizen Army*, pp. 227–32. Fewer members are listed on the 1936 Roll of Honour. Fox's list, however, is supported by the pension files and therefore more reliable than the 1936 list. O'Casey, *The Story of the Irish Citizen Army*, p. 52.

4 Ibid.

5 Ibid., p. 64.

6 Ibid., p. 8.

7   Ibid., p. 63.

8   BMH/WS 585 (Frank Robbins), p. 162.

9   Robbins, *Under the Starry Plough*, pp. 15–20.

10 Ibid, pp. 26–7.

11 Ibid, p. 33.

12 Robbins, *Under the Starry Plough*, p. 34.

13 White, *Misfit: An Autobiography*, p. 188.

14 Ibid, p. 184.

15 Ibid, p. 161.

16 Ibid, p. 174.

17 Ibid, p. 157.

18 The most lucid accounts include: BMH WS 96 (John Hanratty); BMH WS 391 (Helena Molony); BMH WS 357 (Kathleen Lynn); BMH WS 546 (Rosie Hackett); BMH WS 543 (Martin King) and BMH WS 258 (Maeve Cavanagh McDowell).

19 BMH WS 545 (Stephen Murphy); BMH/WS 583 (Walter Carpenter); BMH WS 542 (Séamus McGowan).

20 For details of the history of the movement after the Rebellion, see Brian Hanley, 'The Irish Citizen Army after 1916', *Saothair*, 28 (2003), pp. 37–47.

21 BMH WS 906 (James Larkin Jnr.), pp. 2–6.

22 BMH WS 258 (Maeve Cavanagh McDowell), p. 4.

23 Ibid, p. 23.

24 Ibid, p. 29.

25 Ibid, p. 157. This was a reference to the 1913 Lockout.

26 BMH WS 391 (Helena Molony), p. 19.

27 Ibid., p. 20.

28 Ibid., pp. 20–1.

29 Ibid., p. 4.

30 Ibid., p. 22.

31 Ibid., p. 24.

32 BMH WS 246 (Marie Perolz), p. 4.

33 Ibid., p. 6.

34 Ibid., p. 7.

35 Ibid., p. 11.

36 BMH WS 546 (Rosie Hackett), p. 2.

37 Ibid., p. 8.

38 Ibid., p. 11.

39 BMH WS 733 (James O'Shea), p. 23.

40 Ibid, p. 8.

41 Ibid, pp. 8–9.

42 Ibid, p. 33.

43 Ibid, p. 3.

44 Ibid, p. 5.

45 BMH WS 1,745 (Matthew Connolly), p. 3.
46 BMH WS 1,666 (Fr Thomas O'Donoghue), p. 3.
47 Ibid., p. 6.
48 BMH/WS 421 (William Oman), p. 5.
49 Ibid., p. 11.
50 BMH WS 96 (John Hanratty), p. 3.
51 Margaret Ó hÓgartaigh, *Kathleen Lynn: Irishwoman, Patriot, Doctor* (Dublin: Irish Academic Press, 2006).
52 BMH/WS 357 (Dr Kathleen Lynn), part 1, p. 2.
53 Ibid, part 2, p. 2.
54 Ibid, part 2, p. 3.
55 BMH WS, 382 (Thomas Mallin), p. 7.
56 List of ICA officers, Easter 1916 by Christy Poole (MA/MSPC/RO/10A, p. 30).
57 Fox, *History of the Irish Citizen Army*, p. 136.
58 List of ICA officers, Easter 1916 by John Hanratty (MA/MSPC/RO/10A, p. 4).

Contributors

Donal Fallon

Donal Fallon is a PhD candidate with the School of History and Archives at University College Dublin, researching republican commemoration in 1930s Dublin. He teaches the course 'Hidden Dublin: From the Monto to Little Jerusalem' with the Adult Education Department of the same university. His previous publications include a study of Dublin's 'Animal Gangs' in the 1930s, published in *Locked out: A century of Irish Working-Class Life* (2013) and he is co-founder of the Dublin history-focused website, *Come Here To Me* (www.comeheretome.com).

Peter Collins

Dr Peter Collins is a senior Lecturer in history at St Mary's University College, Belfast. Among his publications are *Nationalism and Unionism: Conflict in Ireland, 1885–1921* (1994) and *Who Fears to Speak of '98? Commemoration and the Continuing Impact of the United Irishmen* (2004).

Brian Hanley

Dr Brian Hanley has lectured in Irish history since 2002. He is the author of *The IRA, 1926–1936* (2002) and *The IRA: A Documentary History, 1916–2005* (2010) and co-author with Scott Millar of *The Lost Revolution: The Story of the Official IRA and the Workers Party* (2009). He has written extensively on radical politics in Ireland and is currently researching the impact of the Northern Ireland conflict on southern Ireland.

Fearghal McGarry

Fearghal McGarry is Professor of Modern Irish History at Queen's University Belfast. He has written widely on Irish history but his recent work has focused on Easter 1916 and the Irish revolution. He is the author of *The Abbey Rebels of 1916: A Lost Revolution* (2016) and *The Rising. Ireland:*

Easter 1916 (2010). With Richard Grayson, he edited *Remembering 1916: the Easter Rising, the Somme and the Politics of Memory.* He is currently leading an AHRC-funded project, *A Global History of Irish Revolution,* and researching a study of cultural anxieties in inter-war Ireland.

Conor McNamara

Dr Conor McNamara is the 1916 Scholar in Residence at Moore Institute, NUI Galway, for 2015/17. His research focuses on social and political upheaval in modern Ireland. He has written extensively on food shortage in the late nineteenth century, the social impact of political violence and the Irish revolution. He was formerly employed in the Manuscript's Department of the National Library where he archived the Mahon Papers, one of the largest collections of estate papers in the state. He was the senior researcher at the University of Notre Dame's 1916 Project.

Meredith Meagher

Dr Meredith Meagher completed her PhD in modern history at the University of Notre Dame. Her work has been supported by the Gilder-Lehrman Institute for American History, the Keough-Naughton Institute for Irish Studies, and the John F. Kennedy Presidential Library. She has written and contributed to publications on the impact of the Great Hunger in the United States, and the international dimension of the 1916 Rising. A native of New York City, Meredith is currently based in Dublin.

Mary Muldowney

Dr Mary Muldowney is an independent scholar who is the author of books, journal articles and presentations using oral history as a primary source. She is an organiser of the Stoneybatter & Smithfield People's History Project, whose focus is on highlighting working-class history in Dublin. She is also an adult education consultant, designing and delivering training courses for community groups and trade unions.

John White

John White is a school teacher who lives in Dublin. His postgraduate research has centred on social and political upheaval during the revolutionary period,

1913–23. A native of County Kildare, his research explores the intersection between class and political violence in the Irish midlands, and his most recent work has focused on the national context of the 1913 Lockout and perceptions of the role of class.

Pádraig Yeates

Pádraig Yeates is a member of the 1913 Committee. He is a journalist and author whose books include *Lockout: Dublin 1913* (2010), *A City in Wartime: Dublin 1914–1918* (2011), *A City in Turmoil: Dublin 1919–1921* (2012) and *A City in Civil War: Dublin 1921–1924* (2015). He previously edited the *Irish People* and worked for the *Irish Times* as Community Affairs and as Industry and Employment Correspondent. He served on the national executive of the Workers Party in the 1970s and 1980s, was national organiser for Clann na hÉireann and served as a lay officer in the National Union of Journalists for many years.

Select Bibliography

Books, book chapters and journal articles

Boyd, Andrew, *The Rise of the Irish Trade Unions, 1729–1970* (Dublin: Anvil Books, 1972).

Brady, Joseph and Simms, Anngret (eds), *Dublin Through Space and Time* (Dublin: Four Courts Press, 2001).

Carroll, Lydia, *In the Fever King's Preserves: Sir Charles Cameron and the Dublin Slums* (London: Four Courts Press, 2011).

Cody, Seamus, O'Dowd, John, and Rigney, Peter (eds), *The Parliament of Labour: One Hundred Years of the Dublin Council of Trade Unions* (Dublin: Dublin Council of Trade Unions, 1986).

Connolly O'Brien, Nora, *Portrait of a Rebel Father* (Dublin: The Talbot Press, 1935).

Convery, David (ed.), *Locked Out: A Century of Working-Class Life* (Dublin: Irish Academic Press, 2013).

Corlett, Christiaan, *Darkest Dublin: The Story of the Church Street Disaster and a Pictorial Account of the Slums of Dublin in 1913* (Dublin: Wordwell Press, 2008).

Cronin, Maura, 'Class and Status in Twentieth-Century Ireland: the evidence of oral history', *Saothar*, 32 (2007), pp. 33–43.

Cullen, Mary and Luddy, Maria (eds), *Female Activists: Irish Women and Change, 1900–1960* (Dublin: The Woodfield Press, 2001).

Cunningham, John, *Labour in the West of Ireland: Working Life and Struggle, 1890–1914* (Belfast: Athol Books, 1995).

Curry, James, 'Delia Larkin: "More harm to the big fellow than any of the employers"?' *Saothar*, 36 (2011), pp. 19–36.

Daly, Mary, 'Social Structure of the Dublin Working Class, 1871–1911', *Irish Historical Studies*, 23 (1982), pp 121–33.

– *Dublin the Deposed Capital: A Social and Economic History, 1860–1914* (Cork: Cork University Press, 1984).

Devine, Francis (ed.), *A Capital in Conflict: Dublin City and the 1913 Lockout* (Dublin: Four Courts Press, 2013).

– *Organising History, A Centenary of SIPTU* (Dublin: SIPTU, 2009).

Enright, Michael, *'Men of Iron': Wexford Foundry Disputes, 1890 & 1911* (Wexford, 1987).

Fagan, Terry, *Dublin Tenements: Memories of Life in Dublin's Notorious Tenements,* (Dublin: North Inner City Folklore Project, 2013).

Farmar, Tony, *Ordinary Lives: Three Generations of Irish Middle Class Experience* (Dublin: Gill and Macmillan, 1991).

Foster, R.F., *Vivid Faces: The Revolutionary Generation in Ireland, 1890–1923* (London: Penguin, 2014).

Fox, R.M., *The History of the Irish Citizen Army* (Dublin: James Duffy, 1943).

– *Rebel Irishwomen* (Dublin: Talbot Press, 1935).

Gaughan, J. Anthony, *Thomas Johnson: First Leader of the Labour Party in Dáil Éireann* (Dublin: Kingdom Books, 1980).

Gray, John, *City in Revolt: James Larkin and the Belfast Dock Strike of 1907* (Belfast: Blackstaff Press, 1985).

Greaves, C. Desmond, *The Life and Times of James Connolly* (London: Lawrence & Wishart, 1961).

– *The Irish Transport and General Workers' Union: The Formative Years, 1909–1923* (Dublin: Gill & Macmillan, 1982).

Hanley, Brian, 'Class Dismissed?' *History Ireland*, 21/4 (Jul./Aug. 2014), pp. 10–1.

– 'The Irish Citizen Army after 1916', *Saothar*, 28 (2003), pp. 37–47.

Horne, John (ed.), *Our War: Ireland and the Great War* (Dublin: Royal Irish Academy, 2008).

Jones, Mary, *These Obstreperous Lassies: A History of the IWWU* (Dublin: Gill & Macmillan, 1988).

Kearns, Kevin C., *Dublin Tenement Life: An Oral History of the Dublin Slums* (Dublin: Gill & Macmillan, 1994).

Keogh, Dermot, 'William Martin Murphy and the origins of the 1913 Lock-Out', *Saothar*, 4 (1978), pp. 15–34.

Keohane, Leo, *Captain Jack White: Imperialism, Anarchism and the Irish Citizen Army* (Dublin: Irish Academic Press, 2014).

Lane, Fintan (ed.), *Politics, Society and the Middle Class in Modern Ireland* (Basingstoke: Palgrave, 2010).

Larkin, Emmet, *James Larkin, 1876–1947: Irish Labour Leader* (London: Routledge & Kegan Paul, 1965).

Lynch, Diarmuid, *The IRB and the 1916 Insurrection* (Cork: Mercier Press, 1957).

Matthews, Ann, *Renegades, Irish Republican Women 1900–1922* (Dublin: Mercier Press, 2010).

McConnel, James, 'The Irish Parliamentary Party, Industrial Relations and the 1913 Lockout', *Saothar*, 27 (2003), pp. 25–8.

McGarry, Fearghal, *The Rising: Ireland: Easter 1916* (Oxford: Oxford University Press, 2010).

– *The Abbey Rebels of 1916: A Lost Revolution* (Dublin: Gill & Macmillan, 2015).

McManus, Ruth, *Dublin 1910–1940: Shaping the City and Suburbs* (Dublin: Four Courts Press, 2002).

McNamara, Conor, 'A tenants' league or a shopkeepers' league? Urban Protest and the Town Tenants' Association in the West of Ireland, 1909–1918', *Studia Hibernica*, 36 (2009–10), pp. 135–60.

Mitchell, Arthur, *Labour in Irish Politics, 1890–1930: The Irish Labour Movement in an Age of Revolution* (Dublin: Irish University Press, 1974).

Morgan, Austen, *Labour and Partition: The Belfast Working Class, 1905–23* (London: Pluto, 1991).

Moriarty, Theresa, '"Who will look after the Kiddies?" Household and Collective Action during the Dublin Lockout, 1913' in Jan Kok (ed.), *Rebellious Families: Household Strategies and Collective Action in the Nineteenth and Twentieth Centuries* (New York: Berghahn Press, 2002).

Morrissey, Thomas J., *William O'Brien, 1881–1968: Socialist, Republican, Dáil Deputy, Editor and Trade Union Leader* (Dublin: Four Courts Press, 2007).

Mary Muldowney (ed.) with Ida Milne, *100 Years Later: The Legacy of the 1913 Lockout* (Dublin: Seven Towers Press, 2013).

Nevin, Donal (ed.) *James Larkin, Lion of the Fold* (Dublin: Gill & Macmillan, 1998).

– *Between Comrades: Letters and Correspondence 1889–1916, James Connolly* (Dublin Gill & Macmillan, 2007).

Newsinger, John, *Rebel City: Larkin, Connolly and the Dublin Labour Movement* (London: Merlin Press, 2003).

– '"The devil it was who sent Larkin to Ireland": The Liberator, Larkin and the Dublin Lockout of 1913', *Saothar*, 18 (1993), pp. 101–6.

Ó hÓgartaigh, Margaret, *Kathleen Lynn: Irishwoman, Patriot, Doctor* (Dublin:Irish Academic Press, 2006).

O'Brien, Joseph V., *Dear Dirty Dublin: A City in Distress, 1899–1916* (Berkeley: California University Press, 1982).

O'Casey, Seán, *The Story of the Irish Citizen Army* (London: Maunsel, 1919).

O'Connor, Emmet, *Syndicalism in Ireland, 1917–1923* (Cork: Cork University Press, 1988).

– *A Labour History of Ireland, 1824–2000* (Dublin: UCD Press, 1992).

– *James Larkin* (Cork: Cork University Press, 2002).

– *Big Jim Larkin: Hero or Wrecker?* (Dublin: University College Dublin Press, 2015).

Patterson, Henry, *Class Conflict and Sectarianism: The Protestant Working Class and the Belfast Labour Movement, 1868–1920* (Belfast: Blackstaff Press, 1980).

Prunty, Jacinta, *Dublin Slums, 1800–1925: A Study in Urban Geography* (Dublin: Irish Academic Press, 1998).

Robbins, Frank, *Under the Starry Plough: Recollections of the Irish Citizen Army* (Dublin: Academy Press, 1977).

Saothar, Journal of the Irish Labour History Society, 41, 1916 Special Issue (2016).

Ward, Margaret, *Margaret Ward: Unmanageable Revolutionaries, Women and Irish Nationalism* (London: Pluto Press, 1983).

Wheatley, Michael, *Nationalism and the Irish Party: Provincial Ireland, 1910–1916* (London, Oxford University Press, 2005).

White, Captain Jack, *Misfit: An Autobiography* (London: Jonathan Cape, 1930).

Woggon, Helga, '"Not merely a labour organisation": the ITGWU and the Dublin dock strike, 1915–16', *Saothar*, 27 (2002), pp. 43–54.

Wright, Arnold, *Disturbed Dublin: The Story of the Great Strike of 1913–14, with a Description of the Industries of the Irish Capital* (Dublin: Longmans, Green, 1914).

Yeates, Pádraig, *Lockout: Dublin 1913* (Dublin: Gill & Macmillan, 2000).

– *A City in Wartime: Dublin, 1914–18* (Dublin: Gill & Macmillan, 2012).

– (ed.) *The Workers Republic: James Connolly and the Road to the Rising* (Dublin: SIPTU, 2015).

Newspapers

An Phoblacht/Republican News
Daily Herald
Forward
Freeman's Journal
Irish Catholic
Irish Independent
Irish Times
Irish Catholic
The Catholic Bulletin

The Irish Worker
The Liberator and Irish Trade Unionist
The Toiler
The Voice of Labour
The Workers' Republic

Parliamentary Reports

Report of the Departmental Committee Appointed by the Local Government Board for Ireland to Inquire Into the Housing Conditions of the Working Classes in the City of Dublin, parliamentary papers, vol. 19 (1914), [Cd. 7273].

Reports on Strikes and Lockouts and on Conciliation and Arbitration Boards in the United Kingdom in 1913 with Comparative Statistics, Parliamentary Papers, Vol. 36 (1914) [Cd., 7658].

Report of the Dublin Disturbances Commission, Parliamentary Papers, Vol. 8 (1914) [Cd., 7269]

Archival Collections

Belfast Trades Council Annual Reports 1889–1900, British Library of Political and Economic Sciences, London School of Economics

Bureau of Military Witness Statements

Dublin Chamber of Commerce Reports, National Archives

Dublin Corporation Reports, Dublin City Archives

Dublin Port Company Archives, Damastown, Dublin

Dublin Trades Council Minutes, National Archives

Irish Citizen Army, minute book, Jan. 1919–Sep. 1920, Irish Labour History Archive

ITGWU Papers, NLI

Jacob's Wages Books, National Archives

Sheehy-Skeffington Papers, NLI

Military Service Pension Records

TUC Papers, University of Warwick

Walsh Laity Papers, Dublin Diocesan Archive

William O'Brien Papers, NLI

Dublin Metropolitan Police (DMP) Prisoners Books, UCD, https://digital.ucd.ie/view/ucdlib:43945

Index

1913 Alternative Visions Oral History Group 185–7, 198

Abbey Theatre 104, 108, 110, 112, 119
Aberdeen and Temair, Ishbel Hamilton-Gordon, Marchioness of 77–8, 79
Aberdeen and Temair, John Campbell Hamilton-Gordon, Marquess of 77
Act of Union (1800) x, 30, 86
Æ *see* Russell, George
agricultural labourers: class divisions and 146; education and 146; Independent Labour Union 22; ITGWU and 153, 176, 179; ITGWU members locked out 9; reported shortage 68–9; riot in Finglas 7; St Lawrence estate, agricultural labourers' strike 7; strike-breakers and 18, 19; strikes and 7, 18; wage increases 4
Agricultural Wages Board 176
agriculture: attacks on farms 9, 18; land agitation 153; land reforms 164; 'last Land War' (1920) 152; strike-breakers employed 18, 19
Alexandra Basin 15, 25, 174
Amalgamated Carpenters and Joiners 32
Amalgamated Iron and Steel Workers 76
Amalgamated Society of Railway Servants 53
Amalgamated Transport and General Workers Union (ATGWU) 188
anarchism 69–70, 89
Ancient Order of Hibernians (AOH) 12, 13, 15, 18; attack on Sunday school party 36–7; Devlin and 19, 37; Dublin Lockout and 41–2; fostering scheme,

prevention of 41, 170; Ulster branches of 41–2
anti-Home Rule rally 170
anti-Semitism 69
Artane Industrial School 191
Askwith, Sir George 8, 9
Askwith Inquiry 56, 170
Asquith, Herbert Henry 75
Aston, Ernest A. 92
Aylesbury Prison 112–13

Bachelor's Walk massacre (1914) 149
Bean na hÉireann 105–6, 107, 209
Bekken, Jon 48
Belcamp Park commune 106
Belfast: attitudes to Dublin Lockout 34; blacklegs, police protection and 33; Catholic workers 34, 37; Catholics and 36; City Hall 31; Connolly and 34–6, 38, 43–4; dock strike 51; Dublin Lockout and 31, 39, 41, 42, 43; Home Rule Bill (1912) and 36; industrial unrest (1907) 33; industries x, 30; ITGWU and 34–5; labour movement 31; Larkin and 1, 33, 34; linen workers' strike 35; military aid 33–4; 'Mollies' 37; NUDL and 33, 34; population of 30; Protestants and 30, 32; sectarianism 33, 34, 44; SPI and 36; strikers 33, 34; women workers and 30
Belfast Corporation 32
Belfast Evening Telegraph 34, 43
Belfast Harbour Board 42, 43
Belfast Labour Chronicle 32
Belfast Newsletter 35
Belfast Protestant Association (BPA) 32

Index

Belfast Steamship Company 33
Belfast Trades Council 32, 37, 38, 39;
    ITGWU and 35
Belvedere Newsboys' Club xi, 58–9
Bennett, Louie 114, 118, 170
Birrell, Augustine 15, 16, 26, 110
Black and Tans 24, 151, 164
Blanquism 165, 177
Bloody Sunday xiii, 3, 5, 39; rioting 162,
    166; *Sunday Independent* and 161, 162
Board of Trade: inquiry 8, 170; Larkin and
    8; survey (1912) 193; sympathetic strike
    statistics 166
Bolsheviks 165, 177
Bonass, Des 188, 196
Brady, Alicia 23, 25, 27, 171
Brady, Christopher (printer) 109
British Army: class divisions and 149;
    Dublin reservists, WWI and 176;
    housing for ex-servicemen xvii, 180;
    recruitment post-1914 149; recruits,
    perception of 149; reservists, ITGWU
    members and 149, 176; 'separation
    women' 150; strike-breaking duties 8
British Mine Owners Association 8
British Socialist Party 8
British soldiers: Irish girls and 105;
    perception of xvi, 151
British War Office 180
Burchenal, Elizabeth 77
Bureau of Military History (BMH) 47, 54,
    57; Hackett's statement 173; ICA and
    126; ICA manuscript sources 208–13;
    Molony's statement 111, 113–14;
    newsboy strike 54; Travellers and 151;
    women's marital status 194
Burke, George 11–12
Byrne, James 7, 15
Byrne, John (labourer), DMP attack on 5
Byrne, John (Séan) 206, 217
Byrne-Perry Summer School (2013) ix

Cameron, Charles A. 88
Campbell, David Robb 35, 36, 37, 38, 40,
    43

Campbell, Fergus 152
Campbell, James, MP 19, 170
Carlow District Council 91
Carnegie, Andrew 74, 75, 76, 79
Carnegie Endowment for International
    Peace 74
Carpenter, Walter 25–6, 126, 131, 206, 208,
    216, 218
Carpenters' Union 26
Carson, Sir Edward 14, 17, 19, 39, 171
'Carson's Army' 127
Casement, Roger 78
Catholic Bulletin 89–90, 92, 93
Catholic Church: fostering scheme,
    opposition to 41, 95, 169–70; ITGWU
    members and 189–90; *Ne Temere Decree*
    and 31; *Rerum Novarum* and 189;
    socialism and 90; strikes and 189; trade
    unions and 189
Catholic clergy: behaviour of 13, 14;
    'deportation' of children, patrols and
    12, 170; food aid, criticism of workers
    and 92; Larkin and 11, 12, 13; strikers
    (1960s) and 189; strikers' children and
    11; sympathetic strike criticised by 15;
    syndicalism and 90
Catholics: lay groups 17; middle class and
    86
Ceannt, Áine 107
census (1911), newsboys and 51
Chenevix, Helen 118
Chicago Tribune 64
children: Christmas party for 25;
    deprivation and xii; fostering scheme
    and 10, 11, 12, 13, 41, 65, 95, 169–70;
    historiography of Lockout and xii;
    industrial schools and 170, 191;
    institutions and xvii, 180; poverty and
    92; relief scheme, Archbishop and
    190; street trading and 49–50; *see also*
    newsboys
Christian Science Monitor, The 63
Christian Union 25
Christopher, Sarah W.H. 73
Church Street tenements 6, 15, 177, 186

245

3

...ket Company 8

...15, 138, 154, 169

...18, 76, 150

class ... 45–6; British rule
and xv, 145; farming community and
145–6; GAA and 146; police force and
146; post-Famine Ireland and 146;
role of xvii; Travellers and 151; women
workers of Dublin and 148; working
classes and 148, 149; see also middle
classes; social class; working classes
class warfare xii; Lockout and xiii, 62,
91, 144; republicans' reaction to 153;
revolutionary period and 152
Coal Merchants' Association 7
Coghlan, Charles 10
Coleman, A., Revd 90
collective bargaining: Dublin Lockout and
xvii, 180; the right to xvii
collective memory xiii–xiv; Dublin Lockout
and xviii, 185
Collins, Peter x, 30–48
Communist Party of Ireland (CPI) 154, 233
Conditions of Employment Act (1935) 115
Connacht Tribune 91
Connolly, James 14, 70–1, 135, 189, 219;
anti-war speeches 43; arrest 5, 39;
background 34; Belfast and 34–6, 38–9,
40, 43–4; Belfast Corporation election
campaign 38–9; Catholic clergy and
35; Conciliation Board proposal 7;
death of Alicia Brady 25; DMP raid
and 109; dockers' strike and 16, 19,
173–4; Dublin Lockout and x, 91;
Easter Rising and x, 133, 172, 179,
216; execution xv, 112; female linen
workers and 35; Guinness boatmen,
plea for 22; hunger and thirst strike
7, 40; ICA and xv, 17, 124–5, 127,
129, 130–1, 169, 176–7; ideal of Irish
independence 207; imprisonment 40;
IPP and 36; Irish Labour Party and
37, 38; Irish Socialist Republican Party
and 34; Irish Textile Workers' Union
and 35; Irish Workers' Dramatic Club
104; Irish-Americans and 71, 79; ISF
and 71; ITGWU and 13, 16, 17, 34–5,
130, 168–9; Jacob's workers, plea for 22;
Larkin and 13–14, 16, 162; militarism
and 177; 'Mollies' and 37; Molony and
107–8, 115, 209, 210; nationalism 131;
O'Brien papers and 213; O'Casey's
views on 206; perception of 205, 207,
208, 210, 211; political activism 34, 36;
Protestant clergy and 35; release from
prison 7; socialism and 73, 130, 131,
165; Socialist Party of Ireland and 34,
36; syndicalism, defence of 171; TUC
conference and 21, 22; Ulster Unionists
and 36; US visit and 70–1; violent
revolution and 130, 131, 132, 165, 177,
178; Walkerites and 38–9; writings in
Harp, The xii, 62–3
Connolly, Matthew 211, 216, 219
Connolly, Nora 35, 42
Connolly, Seán xv, 135, 139, 219; City Hall
unit and 206, 212; death of 111, 125,
211; Dublin Castle attack 110, 111;
Easter Rising and 216
Connollyites 114, 205
Conservative Party 75
Constitution of Ireland (1937) 115
constitutional nationalism 164, 178
Conway, Barney 188
Cooke, John (photographer) 186
Cork docks strike (1908) 1, 167
Cowan, Kate 51
Cowan Papers 233
Cowie, Jefferson 156
Crawford, Lindsay 32
Crawford, Moira 190–1
Croke Park Agreement 197
Crossman, Virginia 145–6
Crowley, Phil 193–4
Croydon Park, Fairview 3, 25, 27; ICA
drilling 18, 23, 128; mass meetings 5,
27, 174

cultural revival 103, 104–5
Cumann na mBan 110, 113, 114, 117–18, 179, 212
Cunningham, John 198

Dáil Éireann: First Dáil 152, 180; industrial relations initiative 179; Second Dáil 152
Daily Herald 18, 24, 40, 41, 162
Daily Mirror 162
Daily Telegraph 48
Dalton, Des 190, 199
Daly, P.T. 14, 26, 39, 129, 134
Daly, Thomas 27
Davitt, Michael 48–9, 67, 68
de Couer, Robert 136, 137, 216, 220
de Valera, Éamon 118
'decade of centenaries' ix 119; commemorative programme xiii–xiv, 101–2; historians and xiv, 102
Derry newsboys strike (1907) xi, 51
Derry Weekly News 93
Detroit Free Press 63
Devine, Francis 198
Devlin, Joseph (Joe), MP 36, 170; AOH and 19, 37, 41–2; IPP and 36, 37
Devlin, Martina 144
Devoy, John 65, 67, 68, 69, 78; *see also Gaelic American*
Dickens, Charles 30, 49
Dickens Fellowship 49
Dictionary of Irish Biography 118
'Dictionary of Races or Peoples' 69
Dillingham Commission 69, 70
Dillon, John 36, 67, 93–4
Domestic Workers' Union 11
Donnelly, Charles 57
Donnelly, Henry 27
Donnelly, Michael (Mick) 136, 137, 138, 221
Dorney, John 150
Drennan, John 155
Dublin Artisans Dwellings Company 88
Dublin Castle: Board of Trade inquiry 8; DMP and 76; Easter Rising and 110, 111, 212; Hardie's warning and 6;

Molony and 115; Murphy's visit to 4; sedition charges and 14, 75
Dublin Chamber of Commerce 3, 6, 20, 28
Dublin City: Catholic middle class and 86; city centre tenements 86–7; class warfare and xii, 62; cockpit of revolution 169; cost of living (1912) 193; economic consequences of Lockout x 167–8, 177; economic decline x, 30, 86; employment and 30–1, 88; food manufactories 31; health care services 164; infant and child mortality rates 87; moral degeneracy and 93; newsboy strike (1911) xi, 52, 53–5; population (1913) 87; Protestant elite, departure of 86; railway workers' strike (1911) 52–3; riots, slum dwellers and 147; social problems and 70; street violence 22, 27, 147, 154–5; suburbs, growth of 86; unskilled workers 31, 88, 89; US perception of 70; women, employment and 31
Dublin City Council 102
Dublin Corporation 28, 76; housing crisis and 88–9; Inghinidhe na hÉireann and 104; Lockout and 5; slum landlords and 28, 88–9; Unemployed Workmen Act and 50
Dublin Disturbances Commission 26, 28
Dublin Employers' Federation 190; contingency fund 10, 15; donations and 10, 15, 16; ITGWU and 10; reward offered by 27; UKEDU, address to 17
Dublin Farmers' Association 4
Dublin Free Breakfasts for the Poor 17
Dublin Grand Canal Company 189
Dublin Housing Inquiry (1913) 186
Dublin Kiddies Scheme 65, 95; Archbishop Walsh and 169; objections to 13, 41; publication of parents' names 11; *see also* children, fostering scheme and
Dublin Lockout x–xi, 1; July (1913) 3; August (1913) 4–5; September (1913) 5–9; October (1913) 9–14; November (1913) 14–20; December (1913) 20–5;

January (1914) 25–8; February (1914) 28; June (1914) 29; aftermath 171; AOH and 41; attitudes towards strikers xiii; basic issues xvii; Belfast attitudes to 31, 39, 41, 42, 43; centenary, class and xv–xvi, 102, 144, 145; centenary publications 198; centenary xiii, xiv, 101–2, 103, 162; class battle 85; collective bargaining and xvii 180; death toll 177; Easter Rising and 79; economic consequences of x, 167–8, 177; effects of 108; English workers' support for 7; food relief shipments 7, 8, 9, 10, 24, 27, 40; Home Rule and 75, 85–6; ICA and xiv–xv, 108, 124, 138; impact on community relationships 194–8; IPP and 41, 64, 93–4; Irish-American perceptions of xii, 66, 73, 74–80; Larkin and 4, 145, 168, 198; legacy of xvi, 185–99; newsboys and 55–6; newspaper coverage and 161, 162; number of workers involved in xvi; 'official' interpretation of xvii; oral history xvii–xviii; reinvention of 171–3, 198; street violence and xiv–xv, 5, 124, 176; sympathetic action and 16, 42–3, 145; TUC support and 167, 168; union representation, right to xvii, xviii; unionists and 170–1; US coverage of 63–5; wages lost 167–8; women and 192–4; working-class militancy and 208

Dublin Metropolitan Police (DMP): AOH mob and 12; attacks by 5, 76, 190; baton-charges and 3, 4, 5, 101; Bloody Sunday and 3, 5, 77, 93, 161, 166; Bloody Sunday re-enactment xiii, 101; citizens' injuries and 5; ICA and xv, 124, 128, 133; Irish-American perception of 75, 76; Murphy and 4; newsboys, clashes with 53, 54, 55; perception of 76; port guarded by 15; prostitution and 92; raids and 4, 12; rally at Croydon Park and 5; rescue of strike-breaker 10

Dublin municipal elections (1913) 25–6; Larkinites and 26, 27; Nationalists (Irish Party) and 26, 27; results 26–7
Dublin municipal elections (1920) 179
Dublin Petty Sessions 8
Dublin Port: Connolly's decision and 173–4; dockers' criticism of Connolly 19; engineers' strike (1917) 175, 176; free labourers and 174; ITGWU and 176; ITGWU dockers and 16; Larkin and 174–5; return to work 20, 174, 175; strike pay 19; strike-breakers and 18; sympathetic action and 16, 174, 175
Dublin Port and Docks Board 23, 168, 175; *Namebook* of employees 174, 175–6
Dublin Trades Council 2, 3, 5, 6, 23; Industrial Peace Committee and 10; railway workers and 7; strike committee 17, 21; strike fund 24; TUC and 17, 21
Dublin Typographical Provident Society 145
Dublin United Tramway Company (DUTC) 2, 168; annual returns (1913) 28; company cottages, eviction threats and 11; dismissal of employees 2; incidents, arrests and 161–2; Larkin and 2, 166, 167; midnight meeting called by Murphy 2, 3; 'scabs' (strike-breakers) and 2, 4; strike (1913) 2, 167; strike (August 1913) 4; support for strikers 3; sympathetic action in Britain 166; tram crew threatened 20; trams, stoning of 25; workers begin returning to work 11
Dublin University Magazine 48
Dubliners: militant nationalism and 179; TV depiction of working class 156

Eason, Charles 24
Easter Rising (1916) x, xi, 44; aftermath 115–18, 134; centenary 119; City Hall 110, 111–12, 133; Connolly and x, 133, 172, 179; countermanding orders, Mac Néill and 210; death toll 177; Dublin Castle killing and 110, 111; Dubliners and xvi, 151; executions and 112, 113;

first anniversary 113; General Post Office (GPO) 57, 133; *Helga*, shelling and 113; ICA and xv, 40, 125, 126, 133, 138, 215; manuscript material 215–32; Molony and 109, 110, 111–12, 113, 119; newsboy, proclamation distribution and 57; number of people 'out' xvi; rabble, attacks by 150, 151

Edward VII, King 104

Ellis, Sir Thomas Ratcliffe 8

Elmes, Elliot 216, 222

emigration: during the 1950s xvi, 155; middle-class professionals and xvi, 155; Yeates family and 163

employers: demands for protection 15; Dublin Lockout and 91; issue of licensed revolvers by 171; Larkinism and 90; subsidies, Dublin Lockout and 168

Employment of Children Act (1903) 50

Engineering Federation 168

Ennis, County Clare 150

Europe, revolution and 178

Evening Herald 11, 53–4, 55, 56

evictions: rent strike and 192; strikers and 196; threat of 11

Fallon, Donal xi, 47–61

Farrell, John (newsboy) 56

Fay, Willie 104

feminism 117–18; *Bean na hÉireann* and 105; Connolly and 108; Jacob and 106; Molony and 114, 115, 116, 117, 119; Montefiore and 10, 41

Fenians 67, 108; 'Cuba Five' 68; Devoy and 68; *Gaelic American* and 63

ffrench-Mullen, Madeleine 117, 136, 137, 210, 216

Fianna Éireann, Na 106, 211

Figgis, Darrell 57–8

Fitzpatrick, John 189

Fitzpatrick, Martin 189

Fitzpatrick, Seamus 189

Flavin, Patrick, Revd 15

Flinn, Hugo 151–2

Flynn, Elizabeth Gurley 70–1; background 71–2; Connolly and 72; Dublin Lockout, perception of 73; ISF and 71; IWW and 71, 72; Paterson textile workers' strike 72–3; radical socialism and 72

food: bread shortages in Dublin 19; charitable institutions and 25; TUC shipments 24, 26

food ships 9, 10, 24, 27, 40; criticism of 92; *Fraternity, SS* 9, 40; *Hare, SS* 7, 8, 27, 40

Foran, Thomas (Tom) 26, 114, 129, 130, 134

Ford, Patrick xii, 62, 63, 65, 66–7, 69, 78; *see also Irish World and American Industrial Liberator*

Forster, E.M. 31

Forward 22, 36, 91, 171

Foster, Gavin 154

Foster, Roy 118

Fox, R.M. 136; *History of the Irish Citizen Army, The* 125, 126, 128, 205, 206, 207

'free labourers' 15, 19, 24; attacks on 27; Belfast and 43; Dublin Port and 174; Head Line steamers and 42, 43; lenient treatment by courts 24; *see also* strike-breakers (scabs)

Free State 115, 116, 126, 153, 154, 208

Freeman, Joshua B. 156

Freeman's Journal 56, 63, 93, 96, 174

Frongoch 125, 135, 209

Gaelic American xii, 62; anti-Semitism and 69; circulation 65; Dublin Lockout and 65–6, 76–7; Fenian movement and 63; immigration and 69; Irish self-government 65–6; *Irish World* and 65–9; Lady Aberdeen, criticism of 77–8, 79; nationalist symbols and 66; philanthropists, portrayal of 77; St Enda's School and 78–9

Gaelic Athletic Association (GAA) 146

Gaelic League 149

Gallagher, Patrick (Paddy) 146

Gallaher, Thomas 33
Galway, Mary 35
Garrison, William Lloyd 67
Garvin, Tom xvi, 152
Gas Workers and General Labourers' Union 8, 21
Gazette 153
General Election (1918) x, 179
General Election (1922) 153–4
General Federation of Trade Unions 20
Genovese, Eugene 156
George V, King 107
Gibbons, John 192, 199
Ging, Eimear 197, 199
Glasnevin Cemetery 162; Republican plot 118
Glencree Reformatory 56
Goertz, Hermann 117
'Gombeen man' 93, 146
Gonne, Maud 91, 103, 104, 105, 106, 108
Good, John 17, 24
Great Britain: Beveridge Report 163; Dublin Lockout and 167; health insurance legislation 164; immigration 163; industrial unrest 165; Larkin's propaganda campaign 16, 17; railwaymen's strike 52–3; strikes and 165; sympathetic action in 16; trade union movement 167; unemployment benefit 165; welfare benefits 164; working class, demonisation of 156
Great Famine 66, 86
Great Northern Railway Company (GNR) 43, 153
Great Southern and Western Railway (GSWR) 7, 166, 167
Greaves, Desmond 35, 39, 134, 136
Griffith, Arthur 85, 94–5, 105, 206, 207
Guinness brewery x, 7, 10, 15, 30
Guinness, Ernest 22

Hackett, Rosie 173, 193–4, 210, 223; memorial bridge 102, 172
Haddington Road Agreement 197
Halpenny, Michael 187, 188, 199

Hanley, Brian xiv, xv, xvi, 102, 126, 133, 144–56
Hanratty, John 137, 206, 212, 215, 216
Hardie, Keir, MP 6, 39, 64
Harland and Wolff 31
Harp, The xii, 62–3, 71
Harten, Thomas 27, 176
Haslam, Anna xvii, 180–1
Haughey, Charles J. 145
Haywood, William Dudley (Bill) 64, 65
Head Line Steamship Company 42, 43
Healy, Timothy M. 8, 90, 112, 170
Heiton & Company 10, 15, 27
Higgins, Patrick 25
Hill, Joe 72
Hirsch, Marianne 186
Hobson, Bulmer 76, 106, 117, 210
Hollwey, John 23, 24, 27
Home Rule Bill: centenary xiv, 101; third (1912) 36
Home Rule xii–xiii, 5, 163–4; anti-Home Rule rally 170; commercial dangers of 19; Dublin demonstration (1912) 67; Dublin Lockout and 75, 85–6; Irish-American newspapers and xii, 67–8, 74–5; Larkin and 165; nationalist consensus and 180; unionist opposition to 17, 19, 31, 33, 37, 39; urban poor and 164; WWI and 176
housing: Dublin Artisans Dwellings Company 88; Dublin Housing Inquiry (1913) 186; inquiry into housing conditions 15, 28; Iveagh Trust schemes 88; Killester housing project xvii 180; Merchants Warehousing Company 196; rents and 88; *see also* slum landlords; slums; tenements
Hunt, Thomas (Tom) 146
Hynes, David 192

immigration/immigrants: American labour movement and 70; anarchism and 69, 70; Asian immigrants 69; 'Dictionary of Races or Peoples' 69; European immigrants, perception of 70; Irish nationalism and 68; Italian immigrants, illiteracy and 70; 'old' and 'new' immigration 69–70; socialism and 69, 70; United States and 66, 68, 69; *see also* Irish-Americans

IMPACT 189; Dublin Hospitals Branch Executive 197, 199

Independent Dramatic Company 104

Independent Labour Party (ILP) 36

Independent Labour Party of Ireland (ILP (I)) 36

Independent Labour Union 22

Independent Newspapers 2, 4, 11, 58; *see also Evening Herald*; *Irish Independent*; *Sunday Independent*

Independent Orange Order (IOO) 32–3

Industrial Peace Committee 9, 10, 12, 13, 16, 17, 127

industrial schools 170, 191

Industrial Workers of the World (IWW) 64, 65, 71, 72

Inghinidhe na hÉireann: *Bean na hÉireann* and 105–6, 107; cultural revival and 104–5; Molony and 103–6, 107, 209; repubicanism and 104, 105

International Council for Women 77

International Socialist Review 65

International Workers of the World (Wobblies) 34

Ireland: health insurance/medical benefits 164–5; Irish-American perceptions and xii; political violence and 177; self-government and 65–6, 180

Irish Catholic 90, 91

Irish Citizen 6

Irish Citizen Army (ICA) x, 54; arms theft (*The Valiant*) and 139; army council 126, 129, 135, 136, 137, 138; Bureau of Military History sources and 208–13; Civil War and 138; command structure, Easter (1916) 216; Connolly and 17, 124–5, 127, 129, 130–1, 169, 176–7; decline of 125, 135, 136–8, 209; DMP and xv, 124, 128, 133; Dublin Lockout and xiv–xv, 108; early development

127–9; Easter Rising and xv, 40, 110, 125, 126, 133, 148, 177, 216; evolution of 124–39; foundation of xiv, 124, 127–9; historiography 125–6; history of, Fox and 205, 206; Irish Volunteers and 18–19, 128, 130, 131–2, 136, 138, 139, 212; ITGWU and 17, 129, 135, 169, 209; Larkin and xv, 127, 128, 129; manuscript sources 205–33; members of 148–9; military service pension applications 216–32; mobilisation order and 148; Molony and 108, 110, 113, 114, 116–17; O'Casey's story of 206; Old Comrade's Association 125, 206; police and 111; post-1916 133–9; reorganisation of 129–33; 'run-away-army' 132, 133; strikers and 128, 129; training/drilling and 18, 131; unskilled workers and 148, 149; War of Independence and 125, 135, 138; White, Captain and 40, 127–9; women and 110, 116–17, 132, 137, 209–10, 212

Irish Engineering, Shipbuilding and Foundry Workers Trade Union 179

Irish Freedom 107

Irish Independent 95, 145, 174, 191; newsboys and 52, 56

Irish Labour History Archive 233

Irish Labour History Society 156

Irish National Aid 113

Irish National Dramatic Company 104

Irish News 41–2

Irish Parliamentary Party (IPP) 8, 19, 36; Bloody Sunday attacks and 93; Catholic support for 37; Dublin Lockout and 41, 64, 93–4, 95; Inghinidhe na hÉireann and 104; Irish-American perception of 75; Larkin's views on 63, 94; urban poor and 88, 164

Irish Republican Army (IRA) 57, 106, 117, 169; Old Comrades 126; social status and 151, 152

Irish Republican Brotherhood (IRB) 106, 108, 113, 130, 132, 169; Devoy and 68;

Irish Freedom 107; militant nationalism and 179; skilled workers and 149

Irish Socialist Federation (ISF) xii, 63, 71, 79

Irish Socialist Republican Party 34, 213

Irish Textile Operatives' Society 35

Irish Textile Workers' Union 35, 40

Irish Times 21; attacks on Dora Montefiore 13; conscription (1918) 152; Derry newsboys strike (1907) 51; Haywood 'The American Rebel' 65; ITGWU and 91, 92; Jacob's strike (1911) 173; newsboys xi, 47, 48, 52, 55; Russell's (Æ) letter to 9; 'September 1913' (Yeats) 6; sympathetic strikes and 91

Irish Trade Council 117

Irish Trade Union Congress (ITUC) 26, 36, 37–8, 134, 178; Larkin elected President 29; Parliamentary Committee 38; Walker elected President (1904) 32; women's role and 115–16

Irish Trade Union Congress and Labour Party (ITUC&LP) 38, 134, 138, 179

Irish Transport and General Workers' Union (ITGWU) xv, xviii, 2; aftermath of Easter Rising 134; agricultural labourers and 176, 179; bakeries and 19; Belfast and 34–5, 42; Belfast Trades Council and 35; British Army reservists and 149, 176; Connolly and 13, 16, 17, 34–5, 130, 168; dockers return to work 20; Dublin Employers Federation and 10; Dublin Farmers' Association and 4; DUTC dismissals and 2, 3; files confiscated by military 134; ICA and 17, 129, 135, 169, 209; imprisonment and 24; Irish-American perception of 75; Jacob's and 5; Larkin and 2, 34, 52, 89, 168; Liberty Hall and 136; Murphy's strategy and 6; newsboys and 52; perception of 91; protest march 12; provincial press and 91–2; survival of 171; TUC support for 5, 21; unskilled workers and 89; widows of workers and 190, 192; women and 12; workers, pledges renouncing 28

Irish Volunteers xv, 56–7, 108, 109, 125, 138, 210; attacks on 150, 151; Clan na Gael and 78; class divisions and 152; Easter Rising and 133, 134; formation of 18, 128, 149, 169; hostility towards 150; ICA and 18–19, 128, 130, 131–2, 136, 138, 139, 212; Irish-American coverage and 76–7; membership 149; militant nationalism and 179; O'Casey's views on 206; perception of xvi, 151, 210; reorganisation of 135; War of Independence and xv; women and 132

Irish Women Workers' Union (IWWU) 23, 108, 114, 117, 172, 173, 193

Irish Women's Franchise League 7

Irish Worker 10, 24, 26–7, 47, 94, 208; army recruitment 149; Bachelor's Walk massacre (1914) 149; criticism of Catholic clergy 190; employers, labelling of 85; ICA and 133; lampooning of Murphy 95; newsboys and 47, 52, 55; readership 52; revolution, Connolly and 132

Irish Workers' Club 136

Irish Workers' Dramatic Club 104

Irish World and American Industrial Liberator xii, 62, 64; American military history articles 66–7; 'Anglo-American conspiracies' and 73; anti-Semitism and 69; Carnegie, criticism of 74, 75, 76, 79; circulation 65; Dublin Lockout and 65–6, 74–5; establishment of 67; eulogy for Ford 78; Fenian 'skirmishing fund' and 67; *Gaelic American* and 65–9; Home Rule and 67; immigration and 69, 70; Irish self-government 65–6; nationalist symbols and 66–7; social values/Irish and American 73; UILA and 63, 67; Ulster Unionists, depiction of 73–4

Irish-Americans xii; Connolly and 71, 79; Dillingham Commission and 69; Dublin Lockout and 66, 74–80; fundraising and 78, 79; Irish self-government and 65–6; nationalism and 66, 68, 73, 78, 79; newspapers and xii,

73; 'old immigrant' group 66; perceived as conforming 70; perception of Ireland xii, 62, 68; perception of Lockout xii 73; self-perception 66; upward social mobility and 68, 73, 79, 80

Iveagh, Edward Cecil, 1st Earl of 10, 15, 22, 168

Iveagh Trust 88

Jackson, Peter 216, 224

Jacob, George 5, 8, 22, 24

Jacob, Rosamond 106–7, 108, 119

Jacob's x, 5, 19; ITGWU workers locked out 5, 6; strike-breakers and 14, 194; women employed by 31, 92, 193; women workers' strike (1911) 172–3; workers locked out 6, 22, 173

Johnson, Marie 40

Johnson, Thomas 35, 36, 40, 43, 44, 134–5; Belfast Trades Council and 39; Dublin Lockout and 40; ITUC and 134–5

Johnston, J.A. 42–3

Joint Labour Board 20, 21, 23

Jones, Jack 21

Jones, Owen, *Chavs* 156

Kautsky, Karl 181

Kavanagh, Ernest (cartoonist) 208

Kelly, Michael 137, 216

Kettle, Andrew 18–19

Kettle, Laurence 18, 149

Kettle, Thomas (Tom), MP 9, 10, 17

Kiernan, Sergeant (DMP) 25

Kilmainham Jail 112

King, Carla 48

King, Martin 206, 226

Klemm, Alex 188, 193, 194, 199

labour movement: activism, oral history and 187–90; in Belfast 31; British 32; Dublin Lockout and xiv, xvii, xviii; Easter Rising and 134–5; employers and 198–9; Hackett, Rosie and 194; ICA and xv, 125, 138, 139; Larkin and 162; Larkinites/Connollyites split 205;

Molony and 107, 114; nationalism and 103; O'Brien papers and 213; socialism and 26; solidarity and 195–6; in US 70, 72; war industries and 176; women and 192–3; workers' rights and xviii, 198–9

Labour Party, British 6, 8, 92, 165

Labour Party, Irish 36, 37, 38, 115, 134, 152, 178; General Election (1922) 153–4

Land League, branches in US 67

Larkin, Delia 40, 41, 65, 108, 130, 193, 209

Larkin, Elizabeth 24

Larkin, Emmet 52, 89

Larkin, James (Jim) 190, 192; admiration for 189, 191, 193; aggressive tactics 52; allegations made against 90–1; anti-clericalism, accusations of 42; appeal to trade unionists 24; arrest of 3, 39; Belfast visit 1, 33, 34; Board of Trade inquiry and 8; clergy and 11, 12, 13, 190; commemoration of funeral 162–3; Connolly and 13–14, 16, 162; Cork docks strike (1908) 1; criticism of British union leaders 10, 34; criticism of 10, 22, 25, 90–1, 94; disguise and 108; DMP raid and 4; dockers and 19; Dublin Disturbances Commission 26; Dublin Lockout and 4, 145, 168, 198; Dublin Port tactics 174; DUTC strike and 2, 166; eviction and 24, 192; firearms and 23; fostering scheme and 41; fundraising tour in England 7; Haywood, comparisons with 64, 65; hostility to 94–5; ICA and xv, 127, 128, 129; imprisonment 1–2, 13, 16, 136; interview with the *Monitor* 63–4; IPP, views on 63, 94; Irish-American perception of 66, 75; ITGWU and 2, 34, 52, 89, 168; ITUC and 29; IWWU and 193; Joint Labour Board meeting 20; legacy of xiv, 101–2; mission of 7; Molony's views on 108; Murphy and 95, 167; nationalists and 86; newsboys and 52, 55, 56, 59; NUDL and 1, 51; O'Casey's regard for 205; oral history/memory of 187; perception of xiii, 64,

85, 108, 191, 192, 196, 207, 208, 210;
propaganda campaign in Britain 16,
17, 19, 41; proselytising, accusations of
12; release from prison 6, 16; religion
and 189; return to work advised by
27; sedition trial 12–13; speech from
Imperial Hotel 3; sympathetic strikes
and 91, 145, 166; syndicalism and
166; TUC and 9, 16, 17, 21, 24; TUC
leadership, attack on 18, 40; US tour
and 44, 129, 130, 168, 208; WUI and
197; *see also Irish Worker*
Larkin, James, Junior 208
Larkinism 35, 42, 89, 90, 145, 165, 171
Larkinites 26–7, 113–14, 205
Lawler, Mark 172, 173
Leader 95
League of Women Delegates 114
Leary, Michael 192
Lee, Alan J. 48
Lee, Edward 9
Lenihan, Brian, Snr 145
Lenin, Vladimir 91, 165
Leo XIII, Pope 104, 189
Lewes Prison 112, 210
Lewis, James 27
Liberal government 14, 16, 33, 64, 165
Liberator 10
Liberator and Irish Trade Unionist, The 90
Liberator, The (US paper) 67
Liberty Hall: co-op shop and 108, 109, 209;
DMP raids and 12, 109; Easter Rising
and 134, 210, 211, 212; Hackett, Rosie
and 173; *Helga*, shelling and 113; ICA
and 108, 135, 136; ITGWU and 136;
Larkinites and 113–14; mass meetings
4, 7; Molony and 113; soup kitchen 13,
108, 130
Limerick 146, 147, 150, 151
Limerick Soviet 152
Liverpool 8, 16, 33, 53
Lloyd George, David 113, 164, 165
Local Government Board 28
Los Angeles Times 65
Luddy, Maria 50

Lundberg, Sarah 185, 189, 195, 196, 199
Lynn, Kathleen 106, 117, 119, 170; Easter
Rising and 212, 215, 216; ICA and
212–13; militant nationalism and 179

McCabe, Conor, *Sins of the Father* 156
McCann, Agnes 31
McCann, Alexander 31
McCormack, Richard 136, 137–8, 216
Mac Curtain, Tomás 210
McDevitt, Danny 35, 36, 43, 44
MacDonagh, Donagh, 'Dublin city in 1913'
151
MacDonagh, Thomas 9, 106, 109
McDowell, Maeve Cavanagh 206, 208, 227
McGarry, Fearghal xiii, xiv, 101–19
McGhee, Richard, MP 93
McGowan, Seamus 126, 136, 206, 208, 216,
227, 233
McIntyre, Patrick J. 27, 90
Macken, Peadar 134, 149
McKenna, Lambert, SJ 58
McKeown, Michael 14, 34
McLaughlin, Henry 17
McLoughlin, Seán 136
McMahon, Cian 73
McNally, C.F. 91
McNamara, Conor x, xiv, xv, 124–39,
205–33
Mac Néill, Éoin 210
McPartlin, Thomas (Tom) 17, 21, 26
MacSimóin, Alan 190, 200
McWalter, James 5
Madden, Denis F. 150
Maguire, George 27
Mallin, Michael 135, 206, 213, 226; Easter
Rising and 133, 212, 216; ICA and 125,
129–30, 131, 169, 207; motivation 190;
newsboys and 54
Mallin, Seamus 190
Mallin, Thomas 213
Mansion House Committee 114
Markievicz, Constance, Countess 40, 103,
104, 105–7, 179, 212; *Bean na hÉireann*
and 105–6; Fianna Éireann, Na 106;

ICA and 110, 125, 129, 137, 138, 209, 216; imprisonment 112, 214; O'Casey and 125, 209; O'Faolain's portrayal of 116; Sinn Féin and 137

Martin, Tony 197

Maxwell, John, General 112

Meagher, Meredith xii, 62–85

Meath Chronicle 91

Mellows, Liam 154

'Men and Masters - The Great Lockout of 1913' (conference) ix

Mendicity Institution 25

Merchants Warehousing Company 196

Merrigan, Matt 188

Metropolitan Hall, protest meeting 17

M.H. Gill and Son 17

middle classes: death rate 87; Dublin Lockout and 1, 96; emigration and xvi, 155; rise of 86; 'squeezed middle' xvi, 155; trade unions and xvi

Midland Reporter 91–2

militant nationalism 178, 179

militarism: anti-Treaty forces 153; Connolly and 177; pro-Treaty forces 153; workers and 176–8

Military Service Pension Board 215; pension applications 216–32

Milne, Ida 191, 192, 200

Miners Federation 9, 22, 25

Miners' Strike (UK 1984) 196–7

'Molly Maguires' ('Mollies') 19, 37, 170; *see also* Ancient Order of Hibernians (AOH)

Molony, Frank 103, 106

Molony, Helena xiii, 102–19, 227; acting and 104, 108, 119; arbitration courts and 114; arrest 107; background 103; *Bean na hÉireann* and 107, 209; Belcamp Park commune 106; BMH witness statement 209–10; Civil War and 114–15; co-op shop and 108, 109, 209; Connolly and 107–8, 112, 115, 209, 210; cultural revival and 103; death of 118; Dublin Lockout, effects of 108; Easter Rising, aftermath 115–18; Easter Rising and 109–12, 113, 119; feminism and 114, 115, 116, 117, 119; funeral oration 118; ICA and 108, 109, 110, 113, 114, 116–17, 136, 216; Inghinidhe na hÉireann and 103–4, 209; internment 112–13; Irish Volunteers and 132; IWWU and 108, 114, 117; labour movement and 107–8, 115–16; Larkin's disguise and 108; marginalisation of 117; military service and 116–17; nationalism 107, 108; political activism 105; radicalism 103, 107, 113, 117, 118; raids and 109, 115; release from prison 113; Revolution and 110–15; Revolution, legacy of 118–19; revolutionary generation and 103, 119; socialism 108; soup kitchen and 108; taken prisoner 112; trade union activity and 115–16, 117

Montefiore, Dora 65; attacks on 13; fostering scheme and 10, 11, 12, 41, 95; kidnapping charges 11–12, 13, 95

Mooney, Joe 189, 195, 196, 199, 200

Moorhead, Lieutenant 149

Moran, D.P. 95, 146

Moran, John 185, 200

Morrissey, Aileen 194–5

Mountjoy Jail: Connolly and 7; Larkin and 8, 16; Lynn and 212–13; Molony and 107, 112; strikers and 171

Muensterberg, Hugo 74

Muldowney, Mary xvii–xviii, 185–99, 200

Mullen, Michael (Mickey) 188

Murphy, Gerry 191–2

Murphy, Mary Ellen 14

Murphy, Stephen 126, 206, 208, 228

Murphy, William Lombard 58

Murphy, William Martin xiv; Askwith Inquiry and 56; British government subsidies and 168; capitalism and 145; centenary of Dublin Lockout and 145; death of 96; dismissals and 2, 3, 4; DMP and 4; Dublin Castle and 4; Dublin Chamber of Commerce and 28; DUTC strike and 2, 167, 168; Great

Southern and Western Railway and
166; Guinness's financial aid 15; health
insurance, opposition to 164; Irish-
American perception of 74; ITGWU
members and 2, 6, 167; lampooning of
95; Larkin and 85, 95, 167; Larkinism
and 89, 145; Lockout strategy 6, 9, 167;
losses due to Lockout 168; Murphy
family's perception of 191–2; newsboys
and 53, 56; newspapers and 161; police
protection and 6; portrait commissioned
28; railway workers and 7; RIC and 4;
Shaw's criticism of 14; strike-breakers
and 2, 4; strikers, attitude to 91; unions'
demands and 24; workers, treatment
of 96; Yeats' poem denouncing 6, 170;
see also Evening Herald; Independent
Newspapers; Irish Independent; Sunday
Independent
Murphyism 166–7, 171
Myers, Kevin xiv, 102

Nation 49
National Army 138, 154
National Insurance Act (1911) 37, 164
National Library of Ireland (NLI) 212–13
National Seamen's and Firemen's Union 19
National Transport Workers' Federation
(NTWF) 8, 12, 22
National Union of Dock Labourers
(NUDL) 2; Belfast and 33, 34, 51;
Larkin and 1, 33, 34, 51
National Union of Journalists (NUJ) 189
National Union of Mine Workers (NUM)
197
National Union of Railwaymen (NUR) 21,
166
nationalism: Connolly and 131; labour
movement and 103; militant nationalism
178, 179; newsboys and 56–8
nationalists, Larkin and 86
Nationalists (Irish Party) 26, 27
Ne Temere Decree (1908) 31
Neal, Grace 11, 13
New York Civic Club Forum 73

New York Times 63, 77
newsboys xi–xii, 47–8; America and 48;
annual fundraising dinners for 49;
badge inspectors and 50–1; badges worn
by 50; Belvedere Newsboys' Club xi
58; boycott of Murphy's publications
56; census (1911) and 51; Christmas
dinner (1904) 49; conditions faced by
48–9; DMP, clashes with 53, 54, 55;
in Dublin 49–51; Dublin Lockout and
55–6; Independent newspapers, refusal
to sell 4; ITGWU and 52; Larkin and
52, 55, 56, 59; licences and 50–1; meals
and housing scheme 48; militancy
among 51–5; nationalist movement
and 56–8; newspaper distribution
and 47, 48; numbers of 49, 51; oral
histories and xi, 58–9; origins of 48–9;
perception of xi, 47, 48, 55; punishments
and 56; radicalism and 48; republican
newspapers and 57–8; strike, Derry
(1907) 51, 52; strike, Dublin (1911) xi,
47–8, 52, 53–5; victimisation of 49
Newsinger, John 52, 168
Nolan, Christy 191
Nolan, George 191
Nolan, James 190, 192
Nolan, John 5, 6
Norgrove, George 216
North Inner City Folklore Project 50–1, 59
Nugent, John Dillon (AOH) 12, 15, 42
Nugent, Laurence 150

O'Brien, Evelyn 117
O'Brien, James, Constable 110, 111
O'Brien, Joseph V. 147
O'Brien, William 14, 37, 114; arrest of
39; Connolly and 43–4; deportation
134; Joint Labour Board meeting 20;
Larkin and 198; Nineteen Thirteen - Its
Significance 198; papers at NLI 213–15;
TUC and 21, 26
O'Callaghan, John 78
Ó Callanáin, Úna 190
O'Carroll, Richard 134, 149

O'Casey, Sean ix, 124, 125; ICA and
    128, 129, 132, 149; Larkin and 209;
    Markievicz and 125, 209; *Story of the
    Irish Citizen Army, The* 124, 125, 205,
    206
O'Connell, Daniel 150
O'Connor, Bernard (Barney) 189
O'Connor, Emmet xiv, 102, 145; *Labour
    History of Ireland, A* 156
O'Connor, G.B., Major 14
O'Connor, T.P., MP 64, 94
O'Donnell, Edward T. 65
O'Donoghue, Thomas, Revd 211–12, 216
O'Donovan Rossa, Jeremiah 67, 68, 132
O'Faolain, Sean 116
O'Farrell, Elizabeth 117–18
Ó Gráda, Cormac 87
Ó hAnnagain, Donnchadh 106
O'Higgins, Kevin xvi, 152
O'Leary, Con 74, 75
O'Loughlin, F.E., Revd 90
O'Mahony, Michael S. 150
O'Mahony, Pierse, MP 13
O'Malley, Ernie 55, 57, 144, 146, 149
Oman, George 216, 230
Oman, William 136, 212, 216, 230
O'Neill, James 135, 136, 137, 138, 208, 216,
    229
oral history: *100 years later. The legacy of
    the 1913 Lockout* 186; 1913 Alternative
    Visions Oral History Group 185–7,
    198; challenging 'the condescension of
    posterity' xviii; Dublin Lockout and
    xvii–xviii; legacy of the Dublin Lockout
    185–99; newsboys and xi, 58–9; post
    memory and 186; techniques/training
    and 186–7; trade union activism,
    understanding 187–90
O'Reilly, Michael (Mick) 193, 196
Orpen, William 9, 28
O'Shea, James 54, 148, 206, 210–11, 216,
    230

Parnell, Anna 107
Parnell, Charles Stewart 67, 68

partition xi, 44, 118, 180
Partridge, William xv, 28, 135, 230; arrest
    39; death of 125, 134; ICA and 129,
    139; police brutality and 3, 5; sedition
    charges 14
Pearse, Patrick 78, 106, 109, 170; Larkin's
    methods and 86, 94; letter of surrender
    118
Perolz, Marie 112, 113, 210, 222
Philanthropic Reform Association 49–50
philanthropic societies, newsboys and 47,
    49
philanthropists: *Gaelic American*'s criticism
    of 77; *Irish World*'s criticism of 74
Phoblacht, An 154, 155
Pinkerton National Detective Agency 76
Plunkett, George Noble, Count 114, 136
Plunkett, James, *Strumpet City* 188, 197
Plunkett, Joseph 9, 106, 109
Plunkett, Josephine, Countess 11, 114
police: distrust of 148; raids on tenements
    147; riots and 147; *see also* Dublin
    Metropolitan Police (DMP); Royal Irish
    Constabulary (RIC)
political violence, role of 177
Poole, Christopher (Christy) 136, 137, 215,
    216, 230
Poor Law Inquiry (1836) 87
possessive individualism xvii, 180
post memory 186
poverty/the poor: attitudes to 170;
    attributed to 'foreign domination' 86,
    94; deserving and undeserving poor 89;
    Dublin Lockout and 145; nationalist
    politicians and 93; pawn tickets,
    number of 88, *see also* rural poor; slums;
    tenements; urban poor
Proclamation of the Irish Republic 113,
    115, 119, 179, 180; distribution,
    newsboys and 57; printing of 109
proselytising 17; fostering scheme and 41,
    42, 95; Larkin and accusations of 12
prostitution 92
Protestants: AOH attack on Sunday school
    party 36–7; Belfast and 30, 32; Home

Rule and 31; *Ne Temere Decree* and 31; strike in Larne (1913) 35
Provisional Sinn Féin 154–5

Quinn, Jim 187–8
Quirke, Michael (Mick) 150

railway workers: lockout (1911) and 7, 166, 167; refusal to join dispute 21, 166; strike in Dublin 52–3
Rand, Lucille 11, 13, 65
Rechabite Order 31–2
Redmond, John 5, 6, 36, 64, 68, 170, 176
Redmondism: neo-Redmondism 179; urban poor and 163–5
Redmondites 37–8, 63, 164
Renny-Tailyour, Colonel 15
republicans/republicanism 114, 118; in the 1980s 155; in 2013 155; *Bean na hÉireann* and 107; Inghinidhe na hÉireann 104, 105; moralistic discourse of 105; urban poor and 155
Rerum Novarum (Leo XIII) 189
revolution, Europe and 178
revolutionary decade 163; class struggle and 152, 163; legacy of Lockout 180–1
Robbins, Frank 137, 231; BMH statement 209; Easter Rising and 206, 216; ICA and 132–3, 135, 136, 137–8, 207; Larkin and 207; *Under the Starry Plough: Recollections of the Irish Citizen Army* 126, 205, 206–7
Rowe, Bridget 19
'Royal commission on Sewerage and Drainage' (1879) 87
Royal Dublin Horse Show 4
Royal Irish Constabulary (RIC): baton-charges and 3, 5, 192; Belfast strike and 42; Bloody Sunday 3, 166; citizens' injuries and 5; class divisions and 146, 153; Murphy and 4; police strike in Belfast (1907) 33; port guarded by 15; strike-breakers, protection and 14
Rudmose-Brown, T.D. 13, 170

rural Ireland: idealisation of life 151–2; social hierarchy and 146
rural poor 146; migration to urban centres 86
Russell, George (Æ) 9, 95
Russian revolution 178
Ryan, W.P. xiii, 85, 198

St Enda's School 78–9
Salmon, Eugene and Elizabeth 6
San Francisco Tribune 63
Saothar 156
Savoy Chocolates 31
Scargill, Arthur 197
sectarianism 33, 34, 44, 145
Seddon, James 8, 24, 25
sedition 14, 162; Larkin and 6, 12–13
'September 1913' (Yeats) 6, 170
Sexton, James 1
Shackleton, Richard 89
Shackleton's Mill 20, 89, 173
Shanahan, Jennie 136, 137
Shaw, George Bernard 14
Sheehy, David, MP 94
Sheehy-Skeffington, Francis 12, 15, 43, 206
Sheehy-Skeffington, Hannah 179
Sherlock, Lorcan (Dublin Lord Mayor) 2, 5, 8, 26, 28, 167
Shipping Federation 15, 16, 33, 43, 168, 174
Shovelin, Nora 188, 200
Sinn Féin 86, 104, 105, 114, 118, 138; Markievicz and 137; militant nationalism and 179; O'Casey's views on 206; social class and 56–7, 152; urban poor and 150, 151; voters, class and 155
SIPTU 187, 199, 200
Skinnider, Margaret 110, 137, 232
Sloan, Tom, MP 32
slum landlords 26, 93; Dublin Corporation and 28, 88–9; naming of 28
slums xii, xvii, 87, 93, 180; clearance, Larkin and 165; perception of 92; slum dwellers, perception of 147
Smillie, Bob 22

social class: Dáil and 152; death rates
87; history of 156; perceptions about
xvi; prejudice and xiii, 85, 96, 125;
professional class 87; revolutionary
movement and 152; social inferiority
and 133; US, class conflict and 66; *see
also* class divisions; class warfare; middle
classes; working classes
social injustice 62, 65, 66, 91
socialism 69–70; British 164; Catholic
Church and 90; denunciation of 89–90;
dismissal as un-Irish 145; Gurley Flynn
and 72; labour movement and 26, 72, 89
Socialist Party of Ireland (SPI) 26, 34, 36
Society of St Vincent de Paul 13, 17
Sodality of the Sacred Heart 15
Southern Unionists, Home Rule and 170
soviets: Molony and 114; in Munster 152,
177
Spanish Civil War 40
Story of the Irish Citizen Army, The
(O'Casey) 124, 125, 205, 206
strike-breakers (scabs): arrival from Britain
13, 15; attacks on 19–20, 28, 176;
Connolly's warnings and 14; Dublin
Port and 18, 21; farm work and 14,
18, 19; fines and 24; Jacob's and 14;
licensed revolvers and 171; magistrates,
lenient treatment by 24, 27, 171; police
guard and 18; Shipping Federation and
15; shootings and 19–20, 22, 23, 24,
27, 171; strikers and 10; *see also* 'free
labourers'
strikers: assaults by 27, 28; children's
Christmas party 25; DMP, scuffles
with 25; evictions and 196; Glasgow,
one-way tickets to 28; ICA and 128,
129; imprisonment and 24, 25; Larkin
advises return to work 27; nationalist
MPs' hostility towards 93–4; perception
of xiii 85, 94; US textile workers 72–3;
weekly income 25
strikes: Belfast (1907) 33; Cork docks strike
(1908) 1; Derry newsboys (1907) xi,
51; Dublin newsboys (1911) xi, 47–8,

52, 53; Dublin railway workers (1911)
52–3; farm workers and 154; General
Strikes (1918, 1919, 1920) 153; Irish-
Americans and 62; spread to County
Dublin 7; United States and 62, 65, 66
suffrage/suffragists xvii, 6, 73, 113, 165, 170,
180
Sunday Independent 20, 155, 161
Sunday Magazine 77
Swifte, E.G. (magistrate) 4, 5
sympathetic strikes 91; Board of Trade
statistics and 166; Connolly and 172;
Dublin Port and 174; TUC and 22, 25,
40, 172, 174
syndicalism 9, 17, 64, 85, 89, 90, 165;
Connolly's defence of 171; Larkin and
166

Talbot de Malahide, Lord 18
Technical Electrical and Engineering Union
(TEEU) 186
Tedcastle McCormick and Company 19, 28
television: business programmes and 156;
depiction of working class Dubliners
156
Temple, William (*later* Archbishop of
Canterbury) 40
tenements 86–7; class solidarity and 195;
collapse of Church Street houses 6, 15,
186; condition of 87, 88, 93; description
of 57; Dublin Housing Inquiry (1913)
186; funerals of victims 6; households
headed by charwomen 193; impact
of Lockout and 194–5; inquiry into
housing conditions 15; numbers living
in 87; photographs and 186; police
raids, destruction and 147; single-
roomed accommodation 87; tenement
dwellers, perception of ix 89; in urban
areas outside of Dublin 93
Thompson, E.P. 156
Thompson, Robert Ellis 70, 75
Thompson, William 39
Times 93
Titanic, RMS 30

Toiler 10, 27, 90, 91, 92, 133
Town Tenants Association 164
Trade Disputes Act (1906) 165
Trade Union Congress (TUC) xvii,
   3; Bloody Sunday reports and 5;
   cessation of aid 28; Co-Op bakeries
   and 8; conference 21–2; Connolly and
   171–2; Dublin Lockout debate and
   21–2; Dublin strike committee and 20;
   Dublin strike fund 26, 167; employers,
   talks and 20, 21, 24; food and fuel
   shipments 8, 9, 27; funds raised by 8;
   Hare, SS and 8, 27; ITGWU workers,
   support for 21; Larkin and 9, 16, 17,
   21; Larkin's attack on leadership 18, 40,
   168; mass rally on Sackville Street and
   6; negotiations with Dublin employers
   7; Parliamentary Committee 8, 9, 16,
   17, 20, 26; Special Delegate Conference
   (1913) 174; support for Dublin workers
   3, 7, 168, 196; support for ITGWU
   men 5, 171; sympathetic strikes and 22,
   25, 40, 172, 174
trade union movement *see* labour
   movement
trade unionists: charges and 4; DMP raids
   and 4; Irish Volunteers and 149; Swifte's
   Proclamation 4, 5
trade unions: middle-class professionals and
   xvi, 155–6; Molony and 115–16, 117
Trades Boards Act (1909) 37
Travellers 151
Traynor, Patrick 27
Treaty, Anglo-Irish 154, 180; anti-Treaty
   side 138, 153, 154, 177; Molony and
   115; pro-Treaty side 153
Triangle Shirtwaist Factory Fire 73
Truce (1921–2) 177
tuberculosis 87–8
Tully, George 206, 232
Tyrone Herald 93

Ulster Covenant (1912) xiv, 37, 101
Ulster Steamship Company 42
Ulster Volunteer Force 37

*Under the Starry Plough: Recollections of the
   Irish Citizen Army* (Robbins) 126, 205,
   206–7
Unemployed Workmen Act 50
unemployment benefit 165
unionists: Devlin and 170; Dublin Lockout
   and 170–1; Home Rule, opposition to
   17, 19, 31, 33, 37, 39; Irish-American
   perception of 73–4, 75; Larkin and 170
UNITE 199
United Building Labourers' Union 28
United Ireland 49
United Irish League of America (UILA) 63,
   67, 68, 78
United Irish League (UIL) 18, 64
United Kingdom Employers' Defence
   Union (UKEDU) 17
United States of America (USA): census
   (1910) 69; class conflict and 66;
   coverage of Lockout 63–5; Dillingham
   Commission 69, 70; immigration, 'old'
   and 'new' 69–70; immigration xii, 66,
   69–70; industrial unrest and 62, 65,
   66, 75, 76; Irish-American nationalist
   newspapers 62–3; IWW and 64, 65;
   labour movement 70, 72; Larkin and
   129, 130, 168; Paterson textile workers'
   strike 72–3, 75
United Steel Company 76
University College Dublin Archives 233
urban poor 89, 146–7, 150; contempt for
   xiii, 85; emerging nationalism and ix,
   86; Home Rule party/IPP and 150–1,
   164; Larkin and 95; perception of xiii,
   85, 96, 146–7, 150, 152; Redmondism
   and 163–5; relief fund (1905) 50; Sinn
   Féin and 150, 151; *see also* newsboys;
   slums; tenements

Valiant, The (US supply ship) 139
Varadkar, Leo xvi, 155
Victoria, Queen 104

Wales, sympathetic action and 16
Walker, William 31–2, 33, 35, 36

Walkerism 32

Walkerites 37, 37–8; Connolly and 38–9;
    ITUC&LP and 38

Walsh, John 'Miley' 195–6

Walsh, William, Archbishop of Dublin
    2; food and clothing distribution 13;
    fostering scheme, condemnation of 11,
    13, 95, 169–70; peace initiative and 12,
    167; strikers' children, exclusion of 190

Walton, G.H. 17

War of Independence xi, 44, 125, 135, 138,
    179

war industries, unions and 176

Washington Post 64

Waterford 150

Wexford Lockout (1911) 192

Whelan, Fergus 188–9

White, Sir George 39–40, 127

White, James R. (Jack), Captain 17, 23,
    39–40, 131; ICA and 40, 127–9, 137,
    207; Misfit: An Autobiography 205, 207;
    Spanish Civil War and 40

White, John xiii, 85–96, 232

Williams, J.E. 166

Williams, Robert 12, 22

Wilson, Havelock 19, 43

Wilson, John, MP 25

women: arrest/internment 112; class
    divisions among workers 148;
    Conditions of Employment Act (1935)
    and 115; earnings 193; employment in
    Dublin 31, 92; equality and 115–16;
    exclusion from republican movement
    114; ICA and 110, 116, 132, 137,
    209–10; independence from Britain
    and 180–1; Irish Volunteers and 132;
    ITGWU protest march and 12; Jacob's
    lockout and 6, 22, 173, 193; lesbian
    network 117–18; linen industry and x,
    30, 35; linen workers' strike 35; Lockout

and 192–4; militant nationalism and
    179; neo-Redmondism and 179;
    political activism and 179; prostitution
    92; Redmond's refusal to seek votes for
    6; right to vote 115; 'separation women'
    150, 151; Sinn Féin and 114; status
    of 115; street politics and 105; unions,
    role in 192–3; wages and 92; see also
    Inghinidhe na hÉireann

Women's Unionist Club 17

workers: militarism and 176–8; prison
    sentences and 14

Workers' Republic 108, 154, 207, 213

Workers' Suffrage Federation 113

Workers' Union of Ireland (WUI) 187,
    197–8

working classes 152, 181; British 156;
    casual work and 88; class solidarity
    and 195–6; class struggle and xvi, 62;
    death rate 87; emigration in the 1950s
    xvi, 155; government housing inquiry
    87; health insurance/medical benefits
    164–5; housing and 86–7; ICA and
    xv, 133; infectious diseases and 87–8;
    Irish Worker and 52; ITGWU and 89;
    Larkin and 91; skilled workers 133, 149;
    social divisions within 148, 149; street
    violence/gangs and xiv–xv, 124; TV
    depictions of 156; underemployment
    and 88; unskilled workers 31, 88, 89,
    133, 149; 'written out of history' xiii,
    198; see also newsboys; slums; tenements;
    urban poor

World War I 43, 44, 131, 134, 168, 176

World War II 163

Wright, Arnold 87

Yeates, Pádraig x, xiv, xvi, 1–29, 52, 70, 102,
    161–81, 198

Yeats, W.B., 'September 1913' 6, 170